Elementary Modern Standard Arabic

Part 2

Arabic Grammar and Vocabulary
Lessons 31–45   Appendices

edited by
Peter F. Abboud
PROFESSOR OF ARABIC, UNIVERSITY OF TEXAS, AUSTIN

Ernest N. McCarus
PROFESSOR OF ARABIC, UNIVERSITY OF MICHIGAN

CONTRIBUTORS
Peter F. Abboud
Zaki N. Abdel-Malek
Najm A. Bezirgan
Wallace M. Erwin
Mounah A. Khouri
Ernest N. McCarus
Raji M. Rammuny
George N. Saad

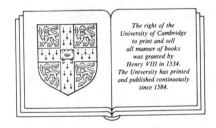

The right of the
University of Cambridge
to print and sell
all manner of books
was granted by
Henry VIII in 1534.
The University has printed
and published continuously
since 1584.

Cambridge University Press

Cambridge
New York   New Rochelle
Melbourne Sydney

Published by the Press Syndicate of the University of Cambridge
The Pitt Building, Trumpington Street, Cambridge CB2 1RP
32 East 57th Street, New York, NY 10022, USA
10 Stamford Road, Oakleigh, Melbourne 3166, Australia

First published by Department of Near Eastern Studies, University
of Michigan 1968
Revised edition 1976
First published by Cambridge University Press 1983
Reprinted 1983, 1984, 1986(twice), 1987

Printed in the United States of America

Library of Congress catalogue card number: 82-22021

British Library Cataloguing in Publication Data
Elementary modern standard Arabic.—2nd ed.
　Vol. 2
　1. Arabic language—Grammar
　I. Abboud, Peter F. II. McCarus, Ernest N.
　492'.782421 PJ6075
ISBN 0 521 27295 5 Part 1
ISBN 0 521 27296 3 Part 2

Tapes to accompany this volume can be purchased from:
Media Resources Center, Tape Duplication Services,
416 S. Fourth Street, Ann Arbor, MI 48109, USA

INTRODUCTION

Part Two is a continuation of Part One; it begins the transition to the intermediate level of Arabic. Lessons 31-40 anticipate the format of Modern Standard Arabic. Intermediate Level[1] in that the new vocabulary of each lesson is introduced in Preparatory Sentences which present the new item in a meaningful context; for the most part the Preparatory Sentences themselves constitute a connected narrative or discourse. Following the sentence the new item is given in its "citation" or dictionary form: (1) for nouns and adjectives, the nominative singular; the plural, preceded by a dash (any alternative plurals are separated by commas); and any preposition that characteristically occurs with this word in this meaning and (2) for verbs: perfect tense, third masculine singular; the imperfect stem vowel for Form I verbs; the verbal noun, preceded by a comma; and any prepositions that characteristically go with this verb in this meaning. The vocabulary items in the Preparatory Sentences are generally all found in the Basic Text of that lesson; the Additional Vocabulary, on the other hand, are not in the Basic Text but are found later in this and in succeeding lessons and must be mastered. Passive vocabulary (words necessary to a particular passage but not necessarily repeated or drilled elsewhere, and which the student is not required to master) is enclosed in brackets [   ]. In the Basic Text and other passages, passive vocabulary is underlined and translated in the margin.

Lessons 41-45 constitute a second transition; at this point the Basic Text is no longer translated into English. Since there are few grammatical items introduced in these lessons, the translation should be well within the capabilities of the student. Further, the amount of drills diminishes in favor of more reading selections with each succeeding lesson.

In addition to English-Arabic and Arabic-English glossaries, a number of appendices are included for the use of students. Appendix I gives full conjugations of representative types of verb. Appendices IV and VI list by lesson all the adjectives and verbs occurring in both parts of the course, with inactive verbs starred(*). Appendix V lists all the particles in this course subclassified by part of speech. Appendices II and III list the Arabic names of the days and months and the states of the Arab World.

---

[1]By P. Abboud, E. Abdel-Massih, S. Altoma, W. Erwin, E. McCarus and R. Rammuny, Center for Near Eastern and North African Studies, Ann Arbor, Michigan, 1971.

Abbreviations and Symbols

AP	active participle	-	a prefix or suffix must be added here
acc.	accusative		
adj.	adjective	→	is to be changed to
adv.	adverb	( )	feminine of the preceding masculine form
C	any consonant		
coll.	collective		
conj.	conjunction	[ ]	passive vocabulary
d., du., D	dual	/	alternate form
DD	identical second and third radicals	‡	new root
e.g.	for example	‡‡	one of two homophonous roots
e.o.	each other		
ex., Ex.	for example	A. obj. → E. subj.	the object of the Arabic sentence corresponds to the subject of the English sentence
f., F.	feminine; female		
F	first radical in a root		
foll.	following; followed		
G	glide		
gen.	genitive		
imperf.	imperfect	E. subj. → A. obj.	the subject of the English sentence corresponds to the object of the Arabic sentence
indic.	indicative		
juss.	jussive		
L	last radical in a root		
lit.	literally		
m., M.	masculine; male	ط ١	اَلطّالِبُ الْأَوَّلُ
M	second of three radicals in a root	ط ٢	اَلطّالِبُ الثّانِي
n	noun		
neg.	negative		
(nisba)	nisba adjective of preceding entry		
nom.	nominative		
o.s.	oneself		
obj.	object		
p., pl., P.	plural		
prep.	preposition		
pron.	pronoun		
Q.A.	questions and answers		
s., S.	singular		
S	second of four radicals		
S₁	the first student		
S₂	the second student		
s.o.	someone		
s.th.	something		
suff.	suffix		
T	third of four radicals		
T	teacher		
v	any vowel		
VN	verbal noun		
1	first person		
2	second person		
3	third person		

TABLE OF CONTENTS

الدرس الحادى والثلاثون

أ ‑ اَلْجُمَلُ التَّمْهِيدِيَّةُ

A. **Preparatory sentences**

١ ‑ لي صديق أمريكي يدرّس التاريخ المصريّ القديم في جامعة شيكاغو وهو يَزُورُ مصر كل سنة لمشاهدة آثارها .

1 I have an American friend who teaches ancient Egyptian history at the University of Chicago and he <u>visits</u> Egypt every year to see the ruins.

زارَ ‑ُ ، زِيارَةٌ

to visit

٢ ‑ في السنة اثنان وخمسون اسبوعا وفي الاسبوع سبعة أيام .

أُسْبُوعٌ ‑ أَسابِيعُ

2 There are fifty-two <u>weeks</u> in a year and seven days in a week.

week

٣ ‑ رجع أخي من فرنسا بعد الحصول على الدكتوراه ، فَاحْتَفَلَتِ العائلة برجوعه احْتِفالاً عظيماً. حضر الحَفْلَةَ كثير من الاصدقاء وأَحْضَرَ بعضهم الهَدايا الى أخي.

3 My brother returned from France after obtaining his doctorate and the family <u>had</u> a great <u>celebration</u> in honor of his return. Many of our friends attended the <u>party</u> and some of them <u>brought</u> <u>gifts</u> to my brother.

(ب) احْتَفَلَ ، احْتِفالٌ

حَفْلَةٌ ‑ حَفْلاتٌ

أَحْضَرَ ، إحْضارٌ

هَدِيَّةٌ ‑ هَدايا

VIII to celebrate

party, festive event, celebration, ceremony
IV to bring, take

gift, present

٤ ‑ احتفلنا بزَواج صديقي احتفالا كبيرا . دامَتِ الاحتفالات سبعة أيام ، وحضرها الاهل والاصدقاء.

زَواجٌ

دامَ ‑ُ ، دَوامٌ

4 We had a great **celebration** for my friend's marriage. The festivities lasted <u>seven days</u>, and they were attended by family and friends.

marriage, getting married

to last, endure

٥ ‑ قالت صحف اليوم ان اجتماع الوزراء بدأ في الساعة الثامنة من مساء أمس ، وان الوزراء انصرفوا في ساعة مُتَأَخِّرَةٍ من اللَّيْلِ.

5 Today's papers said that the ministers' meeting began at 8:00 yesterday evening, and that the ministers left at a <u>late</u> hour of the <u>night</u>.

تَأَخَّرَ ، تَأَخُّرٌ

V to become late, be delayed; to fall behind; to linger, hesitate

لَيْلٌ

nighttime, night (as opposed to day)

٦ ــ جاءَكْرِيستوفِر كولُمْبُس الى امريكا
في سنة ١٤٩٢ .

Christopher Colombus came to America in 1492.

جاءَ ﹘ ، مَجيءٌ

to come

٧ ــ ذهبت مع طلاب صفّي مساءَ أمس الى
مطعم عربيّ . وفي نفس الليلة
ذهبنا معا الى السينما لمشاهدة
فيلم "كليوباترا". خرجنا مـــن
السينما في ساعة متأخّرة ، وذهب
كلّ منّا الى بيته كي يَنامَ .

I went with the students in my class yesterday evening to an Arabic restaurant. The same night we went together to the movies to see "Cleopatra." We left the movie at a late hour, and each of us went home to sleep.

نامَ ـَ ، نَوْمٌ

to sleep, fall asleep, go to sleep, go to bed

٨ ــ ذهب المراسلون الى مؤتمر الوزراء
فاستقبلهم المشرف على المؤتمر
عند الباب ثم أَجْلَسَهُمْ وَراءَ الوزراء .

The reporters went to the ministers' conference; they were met at the door by the person in charge of the conference who then seated them behind the ministers.

أَجْلَسَ ، إِجْلاسٌ
وَراءَ

IV to ask or make s.o. sit down, seat s.o.

behind

٩ ــ صديقي موظّف كبير . وصلتني رسالة
منه قال فيها : أحبّ أن تزورني
في مكتبي . مكتبي في بناءٍ كبير
جدّا ، لذلك سأطلب من سكرتيرتي
أن تستقبلك عند الباب الخارجيّ،
وأن تَسيرَ بِكَ الى مكتبي، ثمّ أن
تَعودَ بِكَ الى الباب الخارجيّ بعد
الزيارة .

My friend is a senior official. I received a letter from him in which he said, "I would like you to visit me at my office. My office is in a very large building, therefore I will ask my secretary to meet you at the outer door, and to bring you to my office, and then to take you back to the door of the building after the visit."

سارَ ﹘ ، سَيْرٌ بِ
عادَ ﹘ ، عَوْدَةٌ بِ

to take, lead, march (s.o.)

to take s.o. back, to bring s.o. back

١٠ ـ السيارات كثيرة جدّاً في طُرُقِ بيروت ، خاصّةً وَسْطَ المدينة ، لكنّي شاهدت بعض الناس في بيروت يَسيرونَ وسط الطريق بين السيارات .

Cars are most numerous in the <u>streets</u> of Beirut, especially in the <u>middle</u> of town. Nevertheless I saw some people <u>walking</u> in the middle of the street among the cars.

طَريقٌ ـ طُرُقٌ

(m. and f.) way, road, street

وَسْطَ

middle, midst, in the middle of

سارَ ـِ ، سَيْرٌ ، مَسيرٌ

to move, get going, march, walk; go; to progress, function, run

١١ ـ في لبنان مدن كبيرة ، لكن فيه كذلك قُرًى صغيرة قَليلَةَ الشُكّانِ ومن اجمل القرى اللبنانية قرية بِشْمِزّين القريبة من بيروت .

There are big cities in Lebanon, but there are also small <u>villages</u> with <u>few inhabitants</u>. One of the most beautiful Lebanese villages is the village of Bishmizzin, which is near Beirut.

قَرْيَةٌ ـ قُرًى

village

قَليلٌ ـ قَلائِلُ ، قِلالٌ

few, small (in number), scant

ساكِنٌ ـ سُكّانٌ

inhabitant, resident, occupant; (p.) population

١٢ ـ أذهب الى مكتبي في الصباح . وعند الظهر أذهب الى مطعم قريب من مكتبي فآكل وأشرب القهوة ، ثمّ أعودُ الى مكتبي . وفي المساء أرجع الى بيتي .

I go to my office in the morning. At noon I go to a restaurant near my office and eat and have my coffee. Then I <u>return</u> to my office. In the evening I return home.

عادَ ـُ ، عَوْدَةٌ

to return, go back, come back

١٣ ـ ذهبت مع صديق لي الى مَقْهًى صغير وشربنا هناك قهوة عربية .

I went with a friend of mine to a small <u>café</u>, and there we drank Arabian coffee.

مَقْهًى ـ مَقاهٍ

café, coffeehouse

Vocabulary note: The imperative of جاءَ 'to come' (جِئْ ، جيئي , etc.) is normally replaced by تَعالَ (m.s.), تَعالَيْ (f.s.), تَعالا (d.), and تَعالَوْا (m.p.) 'come!'

عُرْسٌ في قرية اردنيّة

wedding

كنت ازور قرية اردنيّة فعلمت أنّ صديقا لي من سكّان القرية
سيتزوّج بعد أسبوع · طلب صديقي منّي أن احضر احتفالات الزواج فحضرتها
دامت الاحتفالات أسبوعا : كان الناس يجيئون كل ليلة الى بيت

dabka (a folk dance) | العَريس فَيُهَنِّئُونَ العائلة ويتحدّثون معا مدّة ، ثم يقبلون على الدَّبْكَة | **bridegroom; they congratulate singing**

والغِناء ، وفي ساعة متأخّرة من الليل يرجعون الى بيوتهم ليناموا ·

groom | وفي اليوم السابع ، وهو يوم العُرْس ، جاء الناس الى بيت العَريس | **wedding**

فتحدّثوا معا مدّة ساعة ، ثمّ أجلسوا العريس على كرسيّ وساروا به في

dabka | طرق القرية وسط الغِناء والدَّبْكَة · وعند الظهر عادوا به الى البيت | **singing**

فأستقبلهم أهله بالترحيب · قدّم الطعام بعد ذلك فأكل الناس ·

bride | وبعد الظهر أحضرت النساء العَروسَ وسرن وراءها الى بيت

bridal couple | العريس وهناك تمّ الزواج ، ثم قدّم الاصدقاء الهدايا للعَروسَيْن في

حفلة جميلة ·

B. Basic text

A Wedding in a Jordanian Village

I was visiting a Jordanian village when I learned that a friend of mine, one of the inhabitants of the village, was going to get married in a week. My friend asked me to attend the wedding festivities, and I did.

The festivities lasted a week. The people would come every night to the bridegroom's house and congratulate the family and talk together for a while. Then they would begin dancing the dabka and singing and at a late hour of the

4

night they would return to their homes to sleep.

On the seventh day, the day of the wedding, the people came to the bridegroom's house and conversed for an hour. Then they seated the groom on a
chair and marched him through the streets of the village amidst singing and
dabka. At noontime they brought him back home, and his family received them
with a warm welcome. Food was served after that, and the people ate.

And in the afternoon, the women brought the bride and walked behind her
to the groom's house, and there the marriage took place. Then the friends presented gifts to the newlyweds at a beautiful party.

C. Grammar and drills   ج ــ القواعد والتمارين

> 1. Hollow verbs: Form I
>
> 2. Indeclinable nouns and adjectives
>
> 3. Invariable nouns and adjectives
>
> 4. Causative ـِ with verbs of motion
>
> 5. Collective nouns and unit nouns
>
> 6. Verbal nouns: Summary

1. Hollow verbs: Form I.

Verbs whose middle radical is W or Y have stems with a long or short vowel
between the first and last radicals instead of a second consonant. For example,
the verb زارَ 'to visit' (root Z W R) has the perfect stem zaar- in زارَ 'he
visited', and zur- in زُرْنا 'we visited'. These are called hollow verbs. All
hollow verbs have two forms of the perfect stem and also two forms of the imperfect stem. One form has a long vowel, and this is used with suffixes beginning with a vowel, for example zaar-at زارَتْ 'she visited'; the other has a

5

short vowel, used with suffixes beginning with a consonant, for example zur-tu زُرْتُ 'I visited', or when there is no suffix, for example لَمْ أَزُرْ 'I did not visit.' There are three types of Form I hollow verbs, each with different vowel patterns. The conjugations of the three types are given below:

Type 1: Perfect stems FaaL-/FuL-

          Imperfect stems -FuuL-/-FuL-

These are verbs whose middle radical is W, illustrated below by زارَ 'to visit' (root Z W R).

زارَ – يَزورُ

	PERFECT	IMPERFECT			
		Indicative	Subjunctive	Jussive	Imperative
3 MS	زارَ	يَزورُ	يَزورَ	يَزُرْ	
FS	زارَتْ	تَزورُ	تَزورَ	تَزُرْ	
2 MS	زُرْتَ	تَزورُ	تَزورَ	تَزُرْ	زُرْ
FS	زُرْتِ	تَزورينَ	تَزوري	تَزوري	زوري
1 S	زُرْتُ	أَزورُ	أَزورَ	أَزُرْ	
3 MD	زارا	يَزورانِ	يَزورا	يَزورا	
FD	زارَتا	تَزورانِ	تَزورا	تَزورا	
2 D	زُرْتُما	تَزورانِ	تَزورا	تَزورا	زورا
3 MP	زاروا	يَزورونَ	يَزوروا	يَزوروا	
FP	زُرْنَ	يَزُرْنَ	يَزُرْنَ	يَزُرْنَ	
2 MP	زُرْتُمْ	تَزورونَ	تَزوروا	تَزوروا	زوروا
FP	زُرْتُنَّ	تَزُرْنَ	تَزُرْنَ	تَزُرْنَ	زُرْنَ
1 P	زُرْنا	نَزورُ	نَزورَ	نَزُرْ	

The active participle of all Form I hollow verbs has the regular pattern FaaʔiL, with a ʔ hamza serving as the middle radical:

6

$$\boxed{\text{زائِرٌ} \quad \text{'visiting'}}$$

The **verbal nouns** of Form I hollow verbs, like those of Form I verbs in general, are of various patterns. The verbal noun of زارَ 'to visit' is

$$\boxed{\text{زِيارَةٌ} \quad \text{'(act of) visiting'}}$$

The hollow verbs of Type 1 which have occurred thus far are the following:

Perfect	Imperfect	AP	VN	
زارَ	يَزورُ	زائِرٌ	زِيارَةٌ	'to visit'
عادَ	يَعودُ	عائِدٌ	عَوْدَةٌ	'to return'
قالَ	يَقولُ	قائِلٌ	قَوْلٌ	'to say'
كانَ	يَكونُ	كائِنٌ	كَوْنٌ	'to be'

Type 2: **Perfect stems   FaaL-/FiL-**

  Imperfect stems   -FiiL-/-FiL-

These are verbs whose middle radical is <u>Y</u>, illustrated below by سارَ 'to walk, march' (root <u>S Y R</u>).

سارَ – يَسيرُ 'to walk'

	PERFECT	IMPERFECT			
		Indicative	Subjunctive	Jussive	Imperative
3 MS	سارَ	يَسيرُ	يَسيرَ	يَسِرْ	
FS	سارَتْ	تَسيرُ	تَسيرَ	تَسِرْ	
2 MS	سِرْتَ	تَسيرُ	تَسيرَ	تَسِرْ	سِرْ
FS	سِرْتِ	تَسيرينَ	تَسيري	تَسيري	سيري

7

1 S	سِرْتُ	أَسِيرُ	أَسِيرَ	أَسِرْ	
3 MD	سَارَا	يَسِيرَانِ	يَسِيرَا	يَسِيرَا	
FD	سَارَتَا	تَسِيرَانِ	تَسِيرَا	تَسِيرَا	
2 D	سِرْتُمَا	تَسِيرَانِ	تَسِيرَا	تَسِيرَا	سِيرَا
3 MP	سَارُوا	يَسِيرُونَ	يَسِيرُوا	يَسِيرُوا	
FP	سِرْنَ	يَسِرْنَ	يَسِرْنَ	يَسِرْنَ	
2 MP	سِرْتُمْ	تَسِيرُونَ	تَسِيرُوا	تَسِيرُوا	سِيرُوا
FP	سِرْتُنَّ	تَسِرْنَ	تَسِرْنَ	تَسِرْنَ	سِرْنَ
1 P	سِرْنَا	نَسِيرُ	نَسِيرَ	نَسِرْ	

Active participle: سَائِرٌ

Verbal noun: سَيْرٌ، مَسِيرٌ

The two hollow verbs of this type which have occurred so far are:

Perfect	Imperfect	AP	VN	
سَارَ	يَسِيرُ	سَائِرٌ	سَيْرٌ	'to walk'
جَاءَ	يَجِيءُ	جَاءٍ	مَجِيءٌ	'to come'

(The AP of جَاءَ is a "defective" adjective; see C.34.3.)

Type 3: Perfect stems FaaL-/FiL-

Imperfect stems -FaaL-/-FaL-

This type includes verbs with middle radical W and verbs with middle radical Y. The conjugation is the same in both cases; it is illustrated below by نَامَ 'to sleep, go to sleep' (root N W M).

8

نامَ – يَنامُ 'to sleep'

	PERFECT	IMPERFECT			
		Indicative	Subjunctive	Jussive	Imperative
3 MS	نامَ	يَنامُ	يَنامَ	يَنَمْ	
FS	نامَتْ	تَنامُ	تَنامَ	تَنَمْ	
2 MS	نِمْتَ	تَنامُ	تَنامَ	تَنَمْ	نَمْ
FS	نِمْتِ	تَنامينَ	تَنامي	تَنامي	نامي
1 S	نِمْتُ	أَنامُ	أَنامَ	أَنَمْ	
3 MD	ناما	يَنامانِ	يَناما	يَناما	
FD	نامَتا	تَنامانِ	تَناما	تَناما	
2 D	نِمْتُما	تَنامانِ	تَناما	تَناما	ناما
3 MP	ناموا	يَنامونَ	يَناموا	يَناموا	
FP	نِمْنَ	يَنَمْنَ	يَنَمْنَ	يَنَمْنَ	
2 MP	نِمْتُمْ	تَنامونَ	تَناموا	تَناموا	ناموا
FP	نِمْتُنَّ	تَنَمْنَ	تَنَمْنَ	تَنَمْنَ	نَمْنَ
1 P	نِمْنا	نَنامُ	نَنامَ	نَنَمْ	

Active participle: نائِمٌ

Verbal noun: نَوْمٌ

The two hollow verbs of this type which have occurred so far are:

Perfect	Imperfect	AP	VN	
نامَ	يَنامُ	نائِمٌ	نَوْمٌ	'to sleep'
زالَ	يَزالُ	زائِلٌ	زَوالٌ	'to cease'

9

<u>Passive voice</u>. In the passive voice, all three types of Form I hollow verbs have exactly the same vowel patterns and the same conjugations. Only their passive participle forms differ.

Passive: <u>Perfect stems</u> FiiL-/FiL-

<u>Imperfect stems</u> -FaaL-/-FaL-

The passive conjugation is illustrated below by زيرَ 'to be visited' (imperfect يُزارُ). Note that, as always in the passive, the imperfect subject-markers have the vowel <u>u</u>, and there is no imperative.

زيرَ – يُزارُ 'to be visited'

	PERFECT	IMPERFECT		
		Indicative	Subjunctive	Jussive
3 MS	زيرَ	يُزارُ	يُزارَ	يُزَرْ
FS	زيرَتْ	تُزارُ	تُزارَ	تُزَرْ
2 MS	زِرْتَ	تُزارُ	تُزارَ	تُزَرْ
FS	زِرْتِ	تُزارينَ	تُزاري	تُزاري
1 S	زِرْتُ	أُزارُ	أُزارَ	أُزَرْ
3 MD	زيرا	يُزارانِ	يُزارا	يُزارا
FD	زيرَتا	تُزارانِ	تُزارا	تُزارا
2 D	زِرْتُما	تُزارانِ	تُزارا	تُزارا
3 MP	زيروا	يُزارونَ	يُزاروا	يُزاروا
FP	زِرْنَ	يُزَرْنَ	يُزَرْنَ	يُزَرْنَ
2 MP	زِرْتُمْ	تُزارونَ	تُزاروا	تُزاروا
FP	زِرْتُنَّ	تُزَرْنَ	تُزَرْنَ	تُزَرْنَ
1 P	زِرْنا	نُزارُ	نُزارَ	نُزَرْ

The <u>passive participles</u> of Form I hollow verbs have the pattern <u>maFuuL</u> if the middle radical is <u>W</u>; <u>maFiiL</u> if it is <u>Y</u>. These are illustrated below (the examples for Types 2 and 3 are of new verbs, since those that have occurred are all intransitive and so do not have passives):

<u>Type 1</u>

زارَ – يَزورُ   مَزورٌ 'visited'

<u>Type 2</u>

باعَ – يَبيعُ   مَبيعٌ 'sold'

<u>Type 3</u> (middle radical <u>W</u>)

خافَ – يَخافُ   مَخوفٌ 'feared'

<u>Type 3</u> (middle radical <u>Y</u>)

نالَ – يَنالُ   مَنيلٌ 'obtained'

    <u>Summary</u>. Given below is a chart summarizing the main features of the three types of Form I hollow verbs and their passives. In the "Perfect" column, the first form given for each verb is the 3 m.s., to illustrate the stem with a long vowel, and the forms in parentheses under it is the 1 s. form, illustrating the stem with a short vowel. In the "Imperfect" column the forms are respectively the 3 m.s. and (in parentheses) the 3 f.p. Note that in the passive the conjugation is the same in all types, except for the passive participles. Verbal nouns, which vary widely in their patterns, are not shown.

Note: The quadriliteral سَيْطَرَ على forms its passive like a hollow verb: سُيْطِرَ على ; example:

كَيْفَ سُيْطِرَ عَلَيْهِمْ ؟   'How did they come to be dominated?'

11

Active	Perfect	Imperfect	Active Participle
Type 1	زارَ (زُرْتُ)	يَزورُ (يَزُرْنَ)	زائِرٌ 'to visit'
Type 2	سارَ (سِرْتُ)	يَسيرُ (يَسِرْنَ)	سائِرٌ 'to walk'
Type 3	نامَ (نِمْتُ)	يَنامُ (يَنَمْنَ)	نائِمٌ 'to sleep'

Passive	Perfect	Imperfect	Passive Participle
Type 1	زيرَ (زِرْتُ)	يُزارُ (يُزَرْنَ)	مَزورٌ 'to be visited'
Type 2	بيعَ (بِعْتُ)	يُباعُ (يُبَعْنَ)	مَبيعٌ 'to be sold'
Type 3 (Middle radical W)	خيفَ (خِفْتُ)	يُخافُ (يُخَفْنَ)	مَخوفٌ 'to be feared'
Type 3 (Middle radical Y)	نيلَ (نِلْتُ)	يُنالُ (يُنَلْنَ)	مَنيلٌ 'to be obtained'

Now do Drills 1 (on tape), 2,3,4, and 5.

Drill 1. (On tape) Conjugation: Hollow verbs, perfect tense.

Drill 2. (Also on tape) Conjugation: Hollow verbs, imperfect tense.

'Will you visit Egypt or Iraq?' — أ : هل ستزور مصر أم العراق ؟

'I will visit Egypt. As for Iraq, I won't visit it this year.' — ط : سأزور مصر ، أمّا العراق فلن أزوره هذا العام .

١ - هل ستزورين السودان أم الكويت ؟

٢ - هل سنزور ليلى أم نادية اليوم ؟

٣ - هل سيزوران العريس اليوم أم غدا ؟

٤ - هل سيزرن بغداد أم البصرة ؟

12

٥ ـ هل ستزوران الجامعة أم المتحف ؟

٦ ـ هل سيزورون العريس أم الاصدقاء ؟

__Drill 3.__ (Also on tape) Conjugation: Hollow verbs, imperfect tense.

'Have you visited Egypt?'   أ : هل زرت مصر ؟

'No, I haven't, but I will   ط : لا،لم أزرها ، ولكني سأزورها قريبا .
visit it soon.'

١ ـ هل زرتم بغداد ؟   ٤ ـ هل زارتا الآثار المصرية ؟

٢ ـ هل عادوا ؟   ٥ ـ هل زاروا باريس ؟

٣ ـ هل جئن لزيارتكم ؟   ٦ ـ هل عدن من المؤتمر ؟

__Drill 4.__ Written.

Form the **active participles** from the following verbs.

زار ، سار ، نام ، عاد ، دام ، قال

__Drill 5.__ Written. Completion.

Fill in the blank with the **appropriate verbal noun:**

'I went to Iraq for a short visit.'   زرت العراق ـــــ قصيرة . ←

زرت العراق زيارة قصيرة .

١ ـ ساروا ـــــ طويلا .

٢ ـ عاد الوزير الى مصر أمس ، وبعد ـــــ ه قابل رئيس الجمهورية .

٣ ـ سيجيء قريبا ، ولكننا لا نعرف موعد ـــــ ه .

٤ ـ سوف أنام بعد ساعة ، ولكني سأقرأ هذه المقالة قبل الـــــ .

13

٥ ــ يرغب في الذهاب الى فرنسا ، ولن أقاوم ـــــــ ـه .

٦ ــ يعتقد ان شعبه أعظم الشعوب ، وهو مخلص في ـــــــ ـه .

٧ ــ تختلف مصر عن امريكا ـــــــ ـــــــ عظيما .

٨ ــ قابلت ابنته الكبيرة ـــــــ قصيرة .

2. Indeclinable nouns and adjectives

The nouns and adjectives introduced in previous lessons have been of several inflectional types, as follows:

Triptotes: Singulars and broken plurals which take nunation and three case endings. These form the great majority of nouns and adjectives, e.g. كِتابٌ

Diptotes: Singulars and broken plurals which never take nunation, and have three case endings when definite or serving as the first term of an idāfa, but otherwise only two case endings (See 13.C.4.), e.g. مَكاتِبُ

Sound feminine plurals, which take nunation and have only two case endings, e.g. مُعَلِّماتٌ

Duals and masculine sound plurals, which do not take nunation and have only two case endings, e.g. مُعَلِّمونَ ، مُعَلِّماتٌ

In this lesson there are occurrences of two other inflectional types, called indeclinable and invariable. The latter are discussed in 3 below. Indeclinable nouns and adjectives take nunation, but have no distinctions of case at all. Two examples are مَقْهًى 'coffeehouse' and قُرًى 'villages', the forms of which are as follows:

14

	Indefinite	Definite
Nom./Gen./Acc.	مَقْهًى 'a coffeehouse'	اَلْمَقْهى 'the coffeehouse'
		مَقْهى صَدِيقِي 'my friend's coffeehouse'
Nom./Gen./Acc.	قُرًى 'villages'	اَلْقُرى 'the villages'

All indeclinables end, in all three cases, in **-an** (indefinite) or **-aa** (definate). In a few words these endings are spelled with ا , for example

عَصًا 'a stick'   اَلْعَصا 'the stick'

but in most words they are spelled with ى , as in مَقْهًى above.

Indeclinables result when a word has a pattern with stem vowel **a**, and a root whose last radical is **W** or **Y**. For example, both جُمْلَةٌ 'sentence' and قَرْيَةٌ 'village' have a broken plural of the pattern FuMaL (stem vowel **a**). The root of جُمْلَةٌ is J M L, and the plural is جُمَلٌ . The root of قَرْيَةٌ , however, is Q R Y. If we place this root, as is, into the pattern FuMaL, the results would be a stem **quray-**. But such a stem cannot occur with the short vowels of case endings, for this reason: If we added the vowel case endings to such a stem, we would have **quray-u**, **quray-i**, **quray-a**, and these final sequences (-ayu, -ayi, -aya) are not possible in Arabic. There is a general phonological rule, applying to all words in the language, to the effect that the (hypothetical) sequence of **ay-** plus **any** short vowel is automatically changed to **aa**. This is illustrated by the chart below (with hypothetical forms in parentheses).

Pattern FuMaL-		
Nom. (al-qur*ay*u)		
Gen. (al-qur*ay*i)	al-quraa ٱلْـقُرَى	'the villages'
Acc. (al-qur*ay*a)		

Similarly, when nunation is involved, the sequences -ayun, -ayin, and -ayan are all changed to -an:

Nom. (qur*ay*un)		
Gen. (qur*ay*in)	quran قُرًى	'villages'
Acc. (qur*ay*an)		

Exactly the same rules apply when the final radical is W. The sequences -awu, -awi, and -awa all become -aa, and -awun, -awin, and -awan all become -an. This is illustrated by the word عَصًا 'stick', whose pattern is FaMaL (like قَلَم 'pencil') and whose root is ʕ Ṣ W :

Pattern FaMaL		
Nom. (ʔal-ʕaṣ*aw*u)		
Gen. (ʔal-ʕaṣ*aw*i)	ʔal-ʕaṣaa اَلْـعَصَا	'the stick'
Acc. (ʔal-ʕaṣ*aw*a)		
Nom. (ʕaṣ*aw*un)		
Gen. (ʕaṣ*aw*in)	ʕaṣan عَصًا	'the stick'
Acc. (ʕaṣ*aw*an)		

Indeclinables with final radical Y are always spelled with final ى alif maqṣuura), as in اَلْـقُرَى 'the villages' (but, as is always the case with this

16

letter, it becomes ا (ʔalif) if a suffix is added: قرانا 'our villages').
Indeclinables with final radical W are spelled with final ا (ʔalif) only in
words whose stems contain no consonant other than a radical, for example,
اَلْعَصا 'the stick'. In stems containing a non-radical consonant, such as
مَقْهًى 'coffeehouse' (root Q H W), the final radical W is treated as though
it were Y, and such words are therefore spelled with final ى .

Some indeclinables are singular nouns or adjectives, some are plurals;
a singular indeclinable may have a plural which is not an indeclinable, or
vice versa.

Singular indeclinables have regular dual forms in which the radical Y or
W appears as a regular consonant. In other words, when the dual endings
-aani and -ayni are added to a singular stem ending in w or y, no unpermitted
sequences result, and no changes need be made. Thus the singular عَصا 'stick'
(root ʕ S W, pattern FaMaL) has the stem ʕasaw-; this stem plus the dual
endings gives

Nom.:	عَصَوانِ	'two sticks'
Gen./Acc.:	عَصَوَيْنِ	

The singular مَقْهًى 'coffeehouse' has the root Q H W, but here, as explained
above, the final radical W is treated as though it were Y, and the stem is
thus maqhay-. The dual forms are:

Nom.:	مَقْهَيانِ	'two coffeehouses'
Gen./Acc.	مَقْهَيَيْنِ	

17

Now do Drills 6, 7 (on tape), 8.

Drill 6. Expansion.

a. 'an Iraqi student'   طالب عراقيّ   : أ

'Is this an Iraqi student?'   ؟ هل هذا طالب عراقيّ   : ١ط

'Did you see an Iraqi student?'   ؟ هل شاهدت طالبا عراقيا   : ٢ط

'Are you looking for an Iraqi   ؟ هل تبحث عن طالب عراقيّ   : ٣ط
student?'

٥ ــ طالبان سودانيّان .   ١ ــ مراسل سوريّ .

٦ ــ مقهى عربيّ .   ٢ ــ قرى لبنانية .

٧ ــ موظفات جديدات .   ٣ ــ أدباء مصريّون .

٤ ــ استاذات امريكيات .

b. 'the Iraqi student'   الطالب العراقيّ   : أ

'Is this the Iraqi student?'   ؟ هل هذا هو الطالب العراقي   : ١ط

'Did you see the Iraqi student?'   ؟ هل شاهدت الطالب العراقيّ   : ٢ط

'Are you looking for the Iraqi   ؟ هل تبحث عن الطالب العراقيّ : ٣ط
student?'

٥ ــ الطالبان الجديدان .   ١ ــ المراسل الخاصّ .

٦ ــ المقهى العربيّ .   ٢ ــ القرى اللبنانيّة .

٧ ــ الموظفات التونسيات .   ٣ ــ الادباء السوريّون .

٤ ــ الاستاذان الاجنبيّان .

Drill 7. (On tape) Transformation: Pronominal suffixes.

Drill 8. (Also on tape) Question/answer: Dual.

'How many Jordanian students are there   ؟ كم طالبا اردنيا في صفّك   : أ
in your class?'

18

'There are two Jordanian students
in my class.'

ط : في صفّي طالبان اردنيان .

١ ـ كم مقهى عربيّاً في هذه المدينة ؟   ٥ ـ في كم قرية تونسيّة سكنت ؟

٢ ـ كم مقهى عربيّاً تعرف ؟   ٦ ـ كم قرية ليبيّة زرتم ؟

٣ ـ الى كم مقهى عربيّ ذهبوا ؟   ٧ ـ كم مقهى في شارع الجمهوريّة ؟

٤ ـ كم قرية من قرى لبنان   ٨ ـ كم جملة جديدة في هـذا
أعجبك ؟   الدرس ؟

3. Invariable nouns and adjectives

In addition to indeclinables, described in 2 above, another inflectional

type is illustrated in this lesson: <u>invariable nouns and adjectives</u>. These

words have <u>no distinction of case</u>, and <u>do not take nunation</u>; they are com-

pletely invariable. All such words end in <u>-aa</u>, some spelled with ا and

others with ى . Example:

> هَدَايا 'gifts'   اَلْهَدايا 'the gifts'

Invariables include some words borrowed from foreign languages, and a

great many place-names. These are usually spelled with final ا . Examples:

> سينَما   'cinema, movies'
> أمْريكا   'America'
> فَرَنْسا   'France'
> بَريطانْيا   'Britain'

Native Arabic invariables result from patterns ending in -aa, such as <u>FuMLaa</u>, where the final _-aa_, spelled ى, is quite separate from the final radical.

This suffix ى is a marker of feminine gender; examples which have occurred

thus far are:

```
┌─────────────────────────────────────────────────────┐
│ Pattern FuMLaa:                                      │
│                                                      │
│     كُبْرى      (f. elative)   'biggest'              │
│                                                      │
│     عُلْيا      (f. elative)   'highest'              │
├─────────────────────────────────────────────────────┤
│ Pattern FaMaaLaa (a broken plural pattern):          │
│                                                      │
│     صَحارى          'deserts'                         │
│                                                      │
│     هَدايا          'gifts'                           │
└─────────────────────────────────────────────────────┘
```

These forms are spelled with final ى unless the preceding letter (the final

radical) is ي , in which case they are spelled with final ا (second ex-

ample of each pattern above).

Drill 9. (On tape) Question/answer: Invariables.

4. Causative بـ with verbs of motion.

The preposition بـ has various meanings:

(a) 'in, at, on' (place and time):

```
┌─────────────────────────────────────────────────────┐
│  الجامِعَةُ الأمْريكيَّةُ    'The American University in Cairo' │
│  بِالْقاهِرَةِ                                          │
│  بِاللَّيْلِ            'at night', 'by night'          │
└─────────────────────────────────────────────────────┘
```

(b) 'by means of, by, with' (instrument):

```
┌─────────────────────────────────────────────────────┐
│  سافَرَ بِالسَّيّارَةِ.    'He travelled by car.'        │
│                                                      │
│  كَتَبَها بِقَلَمي.       'He wrote them with my pencil.' │
└─────────────────────────────────────────────────────┘
```

It also occurs in many verb-preposition idioms such as عُرِفَ بِ , سَمَحَ بِ ,
تَأَثَّرَ بِ , and , تَقَدَّمَ بِ , أَخْبَرَ بِ , طَالَبَ بِ , فَكَّرَ بِ , رَحَّبَ بِ .

The preposition بِ can also combine with a group of verbs--generally with
the meaning of going, coming, arriving, arising, etc.--to form verb-preposition idioms. These idioms have causative meaning--to cause someone to come
or go somewhere, i.e. to bring or to take someone somewhere. In the story
of Al-Jāḥiẓ (Lesson 29) is the sentence

> ذَهَبَتْ بِهِ إِلَى الصَّائِغِ. 'She took him to the goldsmith.'

The verb ذَهَبَ alone means "to go"; as a verb-preposition idiom with بِ ,
however, it has the causative meaning "to take" and is, of course, transitive.
The following examples are with verbs from this and previous lessons.

Verb of arriving	Verb of bringing
سَارَ 'to walk, march, go'	سَارَ بِ 'to march, walk' (someone)
عَادَ 'to return, go/come back'	عَادَ بِ 'to take, bring (s.o. or s.th.) back'
ذَهَبَ 'to go'	ذَهَبَ بِ 'to take' (s.o. or s.th.)
جَاءَ 'to come'	جَاءَ بِ 'to bring'
رَجَعَ 'to return'	رَجَعَ بِ 'to take, bring back'
تَقَدَّمَ 'to advance, come forward'	تَقَدَّمَ بِ 'to come forward with, to present (s.th.)'

Since these verb-preposition idioms are transitive, they can also be made
passive: the verb is always in the third masculine singular, while the under-
goer of the action is the object of the preposition, as in

21

Active:

> جا ءوا بها . 'They brought her.'

Passive:

> جيء بها . 'She was brought.'

This passive verb is __impersonal__, in that it is invariably in the third masculine singular.

__Drill 10.__ Transformation: Active ⟶ passive.

'Her father took her to school.' ⟵ ذَهَبَ بها والدها الى المدرسة .

'She was taken to school.' ذُهِبَ بها الى المدرسة .

١ ـ جاء به صديقي الى البيت .

٢ ـ ساروا به في شوارع القرية .

٣ ـ ذهبنا به الى المصنع في الصباح .

٤ ـ احتفل أهله برجوعه .

٥ ـ حافظنا عليه كل المحافظة .

٦ ـ هذا رجل يعتمد الناس عليه .

٧ ـ سوف تجيء السكرتيرة به الى المكتب .

٨ ـ سوف يسيرون به في طرق القرية .

٩ ـ سوف اذهب به الى مكتب المدير .

5. __Collective nouns and unit nouns__

We have had two Arabic words for "night", لَيْل 'night, nighttime' and

لَيْلَةٌ 'night, a night'. There is an important difference in the meaning of the two Arabic words. The shorter one, لَيْلٌ , refers to night as a concept, night as opposed to day, for example. The one ending in ـَةٌ , on the other hand, refers to one unit of nighttime, that is, one night, or perhaps to a specific night, as in اَللَّيْلَةَ 'tonight'. There are many such pairs in Arabic. Those like لَيْلٌ are called <u>collective nouns</u> and are grammatically masculine singular. Those like لَيْلَةٌ are called <u>unit nouns</u>; they are derived from the corresponding collective by the addition of ـَةٌ , and are thus feminine singular.

Unit nouns are regularly made plural by the feminine sound plural suffix ـَاتٌ , e.g. لَيْلَاتٌ 'nights', or occasionally by a broken plural, e.g. لَيَالٍ 'nights'.

We have had one other unit noun, وَرَقَةٌ 'a piece (or sheet) of paper'. The corresponding collective noun is وَرَقٌ 'paper', paper in general as opposed to other materials. A collective noun denoting a material or substance refers to that material or substance in the mass, or to all instances of that material in the abstract; thus one says بَيْتٌ مِنْ وَرَقٍ 'a house of paper' (not, for example, of brick). The unit noun denotes one piece of that mass; it is the unit noun that is usually used with numerals, e.g. خَمْسُ وَرَقَاتٍ 'five sheets of paper'. Some collectives may also take a broken plural as well as a unit noun, e.g. أَوْرَاقٌ 'papers, kinds of paper'.

Finally, some collectives do not have a corresponding unit noun, although it itself may be made plural. Thus, زَيْتٌ 'oil' has no unit noun, but does have a plural زُيُوتٌ 'oils'. With such collectives units may be expressed by

23

phrases meaning 'a head of', 'a piece of', 'a drop of', etc., e.g. نُقْطَةُ زَيْتٍ

'a drop of oil', or فِنْجانُ زَيْتٍ 'a cup of oil.'

6. Verbal nouns: Summary

a. Form I Verbal nouns.

In Lesson 16 verbal nouns of Form I were introduced, and on pages 314-5 all patterns occurring up to that point were listed. Following are some of the Form I verbal noun patterns that have appeared since or (with examples in parentheses) will be occurring in subsequent lessons in this book.

Verbal Noun Pattern:	Examples:	
1. FaMiiL	رَحَلَ ــَ ، رَحيلٌ	'to move away'

Comment:

This pattern is often used for verbs of moving, as above, or for verbs of animal or other sounds of nature, e.g. (نَهَقَ ــَ ، نَهيقٌ 'to bray (donkey)').

m. FaMiL	ضَحِكَ ــَ ، ضَحِكٌ	'to laugh'
n. FayLuuLa(t)	دامَ ــُ ، دَوامٌ ، دَيْمومَةٌ	'to last, go on'
	سارَ ــِ ، سَيْرٌ ، سَيْرورَةٌ	'to move (on), march, go'
	صارَ ــِ ، صَيْرٌ ، صَيْرورَةٌ	'to become')

Comment:

This pattern is limited to Hollow Verbs of Form I, for the most part are intransitive, and generally have the meaning of "becoming, moving, being", etc. It often occurs along with another, more common verbal noun, as in the examples above.

o. FuMaaL   (نُهاقٌ ، ـَـ نَهَقَ)   'to bray (donkey)')

Comment:

Often used for natural sounds.

p. FiMlaan   عَرَفَ ـِـ ، مَعْرِفَةٌ ، عِرْفانٌ   'to know'

                 فَقَدَ ـِـ ، فَقْدٌ ، فِقْدانٌ   'to lose, miss s.th.)

b. <u>The masḍar mīmī</u>. The following verbal noun with a prefixed ma- has **also** occurred:

q. maFMiLa(t)   عَرَفَ ـِـ ، مَعْرِفَةٌ   'to know'

This verbal noun introduces a large number of verbal nouns which are formed with a prefixed ـَـ ma- ; it is accordingly referred to in Arabic as a مَصْدَرٌ ميميّ <u>masḍar</u> <u>mīmī</u>, a verbal noun (<u>masḍar</u>) beginning with <u>mīm</u> (the letter م). With hollow verbs pattern q has the following shape:

r. maFiiLa(t)   شاءَ ـَـ ، مَشيئَةٌ   'to wish, will'

                 سارَ ـِـ ، سَيْرٌ ، مَسيرَةٌ   'to move (on), march, go'

s. maFMiL   وَلَدَ يَلِدُ ، وِلادَةٌ ، مَوْلِدٌ   'to give birth to, bear)

With hollow verbs pattern <u>s</u> has the following shape:

t. maFiiL   جاءَ ـِـ ، مَجيءٌ   'to come'

                 سارَ ـِـ ، سَيْرٌ ، مَسيرٌ   'to move (on), march, go'

                 عاشَ ـِـ ، عَيْشَةٌ ، مَعيشَةٌ   'to live')

                 صارَ ـِـ ، مَصيرٌ   'to become')

Pattern <u>u</u> is also for hollow verbs:

u. maFaaL   قالَ ـُـ ، قَوْلٌ ، مَقالٌ   'to say'

Pattern <u>v</u>, with omission of the first radical <u>W</u>, is for assimilated verbs (see L.33.C.1)

v. MiLa(t)   (صِفَةٌ ، وَصْفٌ ، يَصِفُ وَصَفَ)   'to describe')

(وُثُوقٌ ب ، ثِقَةٌ ، يَثِقُ وَثَقَ)   'to place one's
confidence in')

(هِبَةٌ ، وَهْبٌ ، يَهَبُ وَهَبَ)   'to give')

These verbal noun patterns are not exhaustive, but they are representative of most Form I patterns and should afford you a good idea of what you
can expect to encounter. Remember the following points: (1) Many verbs
have more than one verbal noun, as illustrated in the examples above. Verbal
nouns are given in most Arabic dictionaries, although patterns like <u>n</u> above
tend to be rare if they are alternate to other verbal nouns, and so are sometimes not listed as verbal nouns in some dictionaries. (2) Some patterns are
used exclusively with certain types of root, viz. <u>n</u>, <u>r</u>, <u>t</u>, <u>u</u> and <u>v</u>. (3) Some
patterns are associated with certain meanings, such as <u>1</u> and <u>o</u> above and

g. FaMaaLa(t): abstraction   سَلامَةٌ   'safety'

i. FiMaaLa(t): office or occupation   دِرَاسَةٌ   'studying'

وِزَارَةٌ   'ministry' (office
of وَزِيرٌ)

إمَارَةٌ   'emirate')

k. FuMuuL: intransitive verb of motion; passive meaning

وُصُولٌ   'arrival'

سُرُورٌ   'being pleased'
='pleasure')

(4) Some verbs taking more than one verbal noun have verbal nouns showing
differences in meaning; illustrations:

26

All verbal nouns with the same meaning:

$$\text{سارَ ـِ ، سَيْرٌ ، سَيْرُورَةٌ ، مَسِيرٌ ، مَسِيرَةٌ}\quad \text{'to move (on), go'}$$

<u>Verbal nouns with different meanings:</u>

وَصَلَ ، وُصُولٌ 'to arrive'   (رَأَى ، رُؤْيَةٌ 'to see')

وَصَلَ ، وَصْلٌ ، صِلَةٌ 'to connect, join')   (رَأَى ، رَأْيٌ أَنَّ 'to be of the opinion that')

c. **Verbal nouns of a single occurrence.**

Verbal nouns refer to the notion of the action or state expressed by the verb. Thus شُرْبٌ 'drinking' is the act of drinking in the abstract, without reference to agent, completion, frequency of action, etc. It is possible to specify a single occurrence of an act by suffixing the feminine suffix ـَةٌ -<u>a(t)</u> to the verbal noun; if the verb is of Form I the suffix is usually added to the pattern FaML; Examples:

Verbal Noun		Noun of One Occurrence	
أَكْلٌ	'eating'	أَكْلَةٌ	'a bite'
ضَحِكٌ	'laughing'	ضَحْكَةٌ	'a laugh'
شُرْبٌ	'drinking'	شَرْبَةٌ	'a drink, sip, swallow
فِكْرٌ	'thinking')	فِكْرَةٌ	'thought, idea, concept'
إِكْرَامٌ	'honoring'	إِكْرَامَةٌ	'an act of honoring'

This noun of single occurrence can be made dual or plural in the regular way:

شَرِبَ شَرْبَتَيْنِ .   'He took two sips.'

ضَحِكَتْ ضَحَكاتٍ .   'She laughed several times.'
          ("She laughed several laughs.")

Verbal nouns, thus, are analogous to collective nouns (C.5 above) in that they refer to actions in the abstract, while a noun of unity in ـَة may be formed from them to denote a single instance of that kind of action; this noun may then also be made dual or plural if the number of acts is to be specified.

The noun of single occurrence specifies a particular act; it sometimes goes beyond that to develop a specialized kind of meaning. Thus, أَكْلَة means not only 'a bite' but also 'a meal', or even 'a tasty treat'. شَرْبَة may mean not only 'a drink, sip, swallow' but also 'a dose (of medicine); a laxative'. As is usual with such "rules" as this, this statement is made to help the student recognize and classify forms and meanings as he encounters them, and not necessarily to create new forms at will.

d. __Verbal nouns of Form II.__

In L.17,C.5 (p. 331) the Form II verbal noun pattern taFMiiL is described. There is also a secondary pattern taFMiLa(t) that occurs with a few verbs, with no difference in meaning. (As we shall see in L.37.C.1 the pattern taFMiya(t) is the regular pattern for "defective" verbs.) Example:

قَدَّمَ ، تَقْدِيمٌ ، تَقْدِمَةٌ   'to present, offer'

Words of the pattern taFMiLa(t) used as nouns may take a broken plural or a feminine sound plural:

تَقْدِمَةٌ ــ ات ، تَقَادِمُ   'present, gift'

Finally, there is a special Form II verbal noun pattern taFMaaL which has __intensive__ meaning: to do something again and again. An example is تَكْرَارٌ '(constant) repetition' from كَرَّرَ 'to repeat', which does not occur in this book. Sometimes this verbal noun pattern is used with Form I verbs, e.g. تَسْيَارٌ

28

'(constant) moving' for سارَ ـِ 'to move (on)'.

D. Comprehension passage

د ـ نُصوصٌ لِلْفَهْمِ

Read the following passage and then do Drill 11.

جُحا والنــــــاس

كنت يوما في مقهى مع صديق سعودي فقال لي :

هل تعرف قصة جُحا مع الناس ؟

قلت : لا . ما قصّته ؟

قال : في احد الايام تحدث جحا الى الناس فقال :

هل تعرفون ماذا سأقول لكم ؟

قالوا : لا . نحن لا نعرف .

ignorance قال جحا : جَهْلُكم إِذَنْ هو خير لكم . ثم انصرف . **then, in that case**

وبعد ايام عاد جحا الى الناس وقال :

هل تعرفون ماذا سأقول لكم ؟

they answered أَجابوا : نعم . نحن نعرف .

فقال جحا : معرفتكم اذن هي خير لكم . ثم انصرف .

وبعد ايام عاد اليهم وقال :

هل تعرفون ماذا سأقول لكم ؟

قال نصفهم : نعم . نحن نعرف . وقال نصفهم الآخر : لا . نحن لا نعرف .

those who do not know فضحك جحا وقال : إِذَنْ العارفون منكم يخبرون الجاهِلينَ . ثم انصرف . **then**

Drill 11. Question/answer.

1. In the foregoing anecdote, how many times did Juhā address the people?

2. Did Juhā have something to tell the people? Explain.

3. Why did the people say "Yes, we know" when they previously had said

29

"No, we don't"?

4. What answer did Juhā get when he asked his question for the third time? Why do you think he got this type of answer?

5. What situation would cause a person to relate the anecdote?

6. Do you think Juhā is a real character or a symbolic figure? Why do you think so?

E. General drills   هـ ـ التمارين العامة

Drill 12. Written أَنْ / أَنَّ -clauses.

To the main sentence, add the items in parentheses using أَنْ / أَنَّ or إِنَّ and then translate the sentence into English.

١ ـ لم اكن اعلم (الاجتماع السياسي دام ثلاث ساعات) •

٢ ـ قيل لي (بينكم ادباء عرب) •

٣ ـ يجب (يحضرون) كتبهم معهم •

٤ ـ يرغب ابني في (يسافر) الى باريس لدراسة الادب الفرنسي •

٥ ـ سوف تمنعك الحكومة من (تنشر) هذا الكتاب •

٦ ـ ساعدته على (يدرس) القواعد الصعبة •

٧ ـ اعلم (يفضّلون) العمل هنا على العمل في السودان •

٨ ـ اظهر الكاتب في مقاله (تقدمت الصناعة) في مصر تقدّما عظيما•

٩ ـ احبّ (يحترم ابني) اساتذته •

Drill 13. Written. Transformation: Active → passive.

١ ـ سوف يسألكم الاستاذ عن رأيكم في هذه المشكلة الدولية •

٢ ـ يقول المصريون ان نجيب محفوظ من اعظم كتاب القصة المعاصرين•

٣ ـ سوف يذكر الكاتب اعمال الحزب في الكتاب •

٤ - سيعيّــن الوزير رئيسا جديدا للجامعة هذا الاسبوع •

٥ - في جميع بــلاد العالم تقاوم الشعوب الحكم الاجنبي •

٦ - سوف تنشئ الحكومة عددا من المصانع الجديدة هذا العام •

٧ - ينتخب الشعب الرئيس الامريكي كل اربع سنوات •

٨ - في الشرق الاوسط يستقبل الناس الزائر بالترحيب والاكرام •

Drill 14. Written. Expansion: Relative clauses,

Rewrite the following sentences using the expressions in parentheses to modify the underlined words.

'I met a man in the director's office.(from Syria)'

قابلت رجلا في مكتب المدير •
(من سوريا) ←

'I met a man from Syria in the director's office.'

قابلت رجلا من سوريا في مكتب المدير •

١ - بعض المهندسين عرب وبعضهم آجانب • (تستخدمهم شركة أرامكو)

٢ - يتحدث الكتاب عن وضع المرأة العربية • (ترجمتهُ)

٣ - مي زيادة أديبة عربية معروفة • (أحبها جبران خليل جبران)

٤ - نازك الملائكة من الاديبات المعروفات • (تأثرت بهنّ النهضة الادبية في العالم العربي)

٥ - قاسم أمين من اهمّ المفكرين العرب • (طالبوا بأن تمنح المرأة حقوقها الاجتماعية)

٦ - قابلت استاذا فرنسيا امس • (يدرّس في جامعة القاهرة)

٧ - قرأت كتابا عن الكاتبين طهُ حُسَين وعبّاس العَقّاد • (خدما الادب العربي خدمة عظيمة)

٨ - ذكر الكاتب في مقالته أديبتين هامتين لهما مكانة عالية • (هما مي زيادة ونازك الملائكة) •

31

٩ ــ لا اعرف الرجل ٠ (في مكتب المدير)

١٠ ــ نشرت جريدة النيويورك تايمز مقالة عن النساء العربيات (يطالبن بحرية التصرف)

١١ ــ الاستاذتان العربيتان من لبنان ٠ (في جامعة جورجتاون)

Drill 15. Vocabulary.

Fill in the blanks using the words provided.

غالب ، صغير ، مستعدة ، منتشرة ، يعود ، اراسل ، انتقلت ، حافظت على ٠ عاصرت ، زمن ٠

١ ــ ــــــ ــــــ صديقا من امريكا منذ ــــــ طويل ٠

٢ ــ ــــــ ــــــ عائلتي الى بغداد منذ سنة ٠

٣ ــ هذه المجلة ــــــ في كل العالم العربي ٠

٤ ــ اذهب الى المكتبة بعد الصف في ــــــ الاحيان ثم ارجع الى البيت٠

32

أ ـ اَلْجُمَلُ التَّمْهِيدِيَّةُ

A. Preparatory sentences

الزيت العربي

Arab Oil

١ ـ مَوارِدُ الزَّيْتِ كثيرة في بعض البُلْدانِ العربية ، لكنّها قليلة في البعض الآخر .

Oil resources are plentiful in some Arab countries, but they are few in others.

مَوْرِدٌ ـ مَوارِدُ

resource

زَيْتٌ ـ زُيوتٌ

(coll.) oil, petroleum

بَلَدٌ ـ بُلْدانٌ ، بِلادٌ

(m. and f.) country

٢ ـ من الدول الغَنِيّةِ بـالزيت: الكويت والسعوديّة والعراق وليبيا ومن الدول العربيّة الفَقيرةِ فــي موارد الزيت: سوريا ولبنــان والاردن وتونس .

Among the countries rich in oil are Kuwait, Saudi Arabia, Iraq and Libya; included among the Arab states that are poor in resources are Syria, Lebanon, Jordan and Tunisia.

غَنِيٌّ ـ أَغْنِياءُ (بِ)

rich, wealthy (in)

فَقيرٌ ـ فُقَراءُ (في)

poor (in)

٣ ـ اِسْتَفادَتْ تلك الدول الغنيّةُ بـالزيت اسْتِفادةً كبـيرة من انتاج الزيت فَنَتيجةً لانتاجه تقدّم الاقتصاد في تلك الدول تقدّماً عظيما .

Those countries rich in oil have benefited greatly from the production of oil, and as a result of it the economies of those countries have advanced greatly.

اِسْتَفادَ ، اِسْتِفادةً (من ، بـ)

X to benefit (from); to utilize, use

نَتيجةٌ ـ نَتائِجُ

result, consequence

نَتيجةً لِـ

as a result of

٤ ـ كانَ لانتاج الزيت تأثير كبـير على الاقتصاد العربي .

Oil production has had great influence on Arab economies.

٥ ــ فقد حَسَّنَ الاوضاع الاقتصاديّـــة الى حد بعيد وبِسَبَبِ الزيت أصبحت في العالم العربي اليوم دول غنيّة .

It has improved economic con- ditions to a great extent, and because of oil there have come to be rich countries in the Arab world today.

حَسَّنَ ، تَحْسينٌ
سَبَبٌ ــ أَسْبابٌ
بِسَبَبِ

II to improve (s.th.)

cause, reason

because of, by reason of

٦ ــ كان انتاج الزيت في مصر قليلا لكنّه ازْدادَ في السنوات الاخيرة وسَبَّبَ ذلك تقدّما عظيما فـــي الوضع الاقتصادي .

Oil production in Egypt used to be small but it has increased in recent years, and that has brought about great advances in the economic situation.

اِزْدادَ ، اِزْديادٌ

سَبَّبَ ، تَسْبيبٌ

VIII to increase, grow larger, multiply

II to cause, bring about, produce

٧ ــ يَحْتاجُ انتاج الزيت الى خِبْرَةٍ كبيرة .

The production of oil requires great expertise.

اِحْتاجَ ، اِحْتِياجٌ الى ، لـ

[خِبْرَةٌ]

VIII to need, require

[experience; expertise]

٨ ــ أَقامَتْ شركات الزيت عددا كبيرا من المصانع في العالم العربــى ولم تكن اقامة هذه المصانـــع أمرا سهلا .

The oil companies have built a great number of factories in the Arab world, and the build- ing of these factories was not an easy matter.

أَقامَ ، إِقامَةٌ

IV to reside, dwell, stay; to construct, build, set up

٩ ــ تَمْتازُ شركة أرامكو بِأنّها اكبر شركة للزيت في الشرق الاوسط .

Aramco is distinguished by the fact that it is the largest oil company in the Middle East.

اِمْتازَ ، اِمْتِيازٌ بـ

VIII to be distinguished, characterized by

١٠ ـ تَشْتَرِكُ الحكومة السعوديّة الآن في إدارَتِها مع الشركات الامريكيّة .

The Saudi government now <u>participates</u> with the American companies <u>in managing</u> it.

اِشْتَرَكَ ، اِشْتِراكٌ في

VIII to participate, cooperate in

أدارَ ، إدارَةٌ

IV to direct, manage, administer

١١ ـ في السنوات الاخيرة اسْتَطاعَ المهندسون العرب ان يشاركوا الاجانب في الاشراف على انتاج الزيت .

In recent years, Arab engineers <u>have been able</u> to participate with the foreigners in supervising oil production.

اِسْتَطاعَ ، اِسْتِطاعَةٌ

X (with acc. object or foll. by أنْ) to be able to, can

١٢ ـ في مقابلة صحفية قال وزير سعوديّ: نُريدُ أن تكون شركة ارامكوا عربيّة .

In a press interview a Saudi minister said, "<u>We want</u> Aramco to be Arab."

أرادَ ، إرادَةٌ

IV to want, wish, desire

ب ـ النص الاساسيّ

الزيت العربي

تمتاز بلدان عربية كثيرة بأنّها غنية بموارد الزيت ، ومن تلك البلدان المَمْلَكَةُ العربيّة السعوديّة والكويت وليبيا والعراق ودولة الإماراتِ العَرَبيّةِ المُتّحِدَةِ والجزائر . وتُعتبر المَمْلَكَةُ العربيّة السعودية من أغنى دول العالم بالزيت ومن أكثرها انتاجا له .

kingdom

United Arab Emirates

ليس انتاج الزيت سهلا ، فهو يحتاج الى جهود عظيمة . وقد أقامت الشركات الاجنبيّة المصانع الحديثة في البلاد العربية لانتاجه ؛ وتدير الدول العربية اليوم عددا غير قليل من هذه المصانع ، ولكنّ بعض الدول العربية تريد السيطرة على جميع المصانع التي فيها .

35

تقدّم الاقتصاد في الدول العربية بسبب الزيت ، بل إنّ الجَزِيرَةَ
العربية تعتمد على الزيت كل الاعتماد لانها فقيرة في الموارد الاقتصاديّة
الاخرى ، ولانّها صحراويّة ومياهها قليلة . ولعلّنا نستطيع أن نقول إنّ
الجَزِيرَةَ العربيّة "هِبَةُ الزيت " كما قال هيرودتس ان مصر "هِبَةُ النيل ".

gift

كان للزيت تأثير عظيم على الحياة الاجتماعية في العالم العربي :
فقد استخدمت شركات الزيت عددا كبيرا من الموظفين وسبّب ذلك تغيّرا
في الحياة العربية بعض المناطق ؛ كذلك استفادت الحياة الاجتماعية
من ازدياد الدَّخْلِ .

income,
revenue

ونتيجة لانتاج الزيت استطاعت الدول العربية أن تؤثّر في
السياسة العالمية الى حدّ بعيد ، ولعلّ لذلك علاقةً بالمؤتمرات السياسيّة
الكثيرة التى اشتركت فيها الدول العربية أخيرًا .

وقد قدّمت الدول العربية المنتجة للزيت مساعدات اقتصادية كبيرة
للدول العربية الفقيرة ، بل إنّ بعض الدول العربية الغنية بالزيت
قدّمت مساعدات اقتصاديّة لدول اسلاميّة غير عربية ولدول غير اسلاميّة خارج
العالم العربيّ . وكان هذا سببا هامّا في تحسين العلاقات بين هذه الدول
والعالم العربيّ .

Questions   أسئلـــــة

١ ــ اذكر بعض البلدان العربية الغنية بالزيت .

٢ ــ لماذا يسمح للشركات الاجنبية بانتاج الزيت في البلدان العربية ؟
   كيف تعرف أنّ بعض الدول العربية غير سعيدة بذلك ؟

٣ ــ هل تأثير الزيت على الاقتصاد العربيّ أعظم من تأثيره على الاقتصاد
   الامريكي ؟ لماذا ؟

٤ ــ ماهي الدول التي تساعدها البلدان العربية الغنية بالزيت ؟

٥ ــ أثّر الزيت على ثلاثة أوضاع في الشرق الاوسط . ما هي تلك الاوضاع ؟

B. Basic text

Arab Oil

Many Arab countries are distinguished by the fact that they are rich in
oil resources. Among these countries are the Saudi Arabian Kingdom, Kuwait,
Libya, Iraq, the United Arab Emirates, and Algeria. The Saudi Arabian Kingdom
is considered to be one of the richest countries in the world in oil and one
of the biggest producers of oil.

It is not easy to produce oil, for it requires great efforts. Foreign
companies have set up modern factories in the Arab countries to produce oil;
the Arab states today manage not a small number of these factories, but some
Arab states wish to control all the factories found there.

The economies of the Arab states have advanced because of oil. Indeed,
the Arabian Peninsula is completely dependent on oil because it is poor in
other economic resources, and because it is desert with little water. We
can perhaps say that the Arabian Peninsula is "the Gift of Oil," just as
Herodotus said that Egypt was "The Gift of the Nile."

Oil has had great influence on the social life of the Arab World: the
oil companies have used a great number of employees, and that has affected
a change in the life of the Arabs in some areas. The increase in income has
also benefited (their) social life.

As a result of (their) oil production the Arab states have been able to
influence world politics to a great extent, and perhaps that is related to
the many political conferences that the Arab states have participated in recently.

37

The oil-producing Arab countries have offered considerable economic assistance to the poor Arab countries; indeed, some oil-rich Arab countries have presented economic aid to non-Arab Islamic nations and to non-Islamic countries outside the Arab world. This is an important reason for the improvement in relations between these countries and the Arab world.

C. **Grammar and drills**   ج – القواعد والتمارين

> 1. Hollow verbs: Derived Forms
>
> 2. Hollow roots: Phonological rules
>
> 3. Accusative of specification: Tamyīz
>
> 4. The clause introducer إِنَّ 'verily'

1. Hollow verbs: Derived Forms

In five of the derived Forms (II, III, V, VI and IX), verbs with middle radical W or Y are conjugated like strong verbs. For example, عَيَّنَ 'to appoint' (II) is exactly like دَرَّسَ 'to instruct' (II), and تَنَاوَلَ 'to take up' (VI) is conjugated exactly like تَرَاسَلَ 'to correspond with each other' (VI). This discussion, then, deals only with Forms IV, VII, VIII and X.

Derived hollow verbs follow the same rules as Form I hollow verbs; the big difference is that there is only one conjugation type for each Form. As a matter of fact, all hollow derived verbs have, in the perfect tense, long stems in aa and short stems in a. In the imperfect tense, Forms VII and VIII also have long stems in aa and short stems in a, while the long and short imperfect stems for IV and X are ii and i.

Each Form will now be taken up in turn.

38

The Form IV hollow stems are:

	Long Stem	Short Stem
Perfect Tense	?aFaaL-	?aFaL-
Imperfect Tense	-FiiL-	-FiL-

The conjugation of the two tenses will be illustrated with أَدَارَ 'to direct, manage, run' (s.th.)

أَدَارَ – يُدِيرُ 'to direct'

	PERFECT	IMPERFECT Indicative	Subjunctive	Jussive	Imperative
3 MS	أَدَارَ	يُدِيرُ	يُدِيرَ	يُدِرْ	
FS	أَدَارَتْ	تُدِيرُ	تُدِيرَ	تُدِرْ	
2 MS	أَدَرْتَ	تُدِيرُ	تُدِيرَ	تُدِرْ	أَدِرْ
FS	أَدَرْتِ	تُدِيرِينَ	تُدِيرِي	تُدِيرِي	أَدِيرِي
1 S	أَدَرْتُ	أُدِيرُ	أُدِيرَ	أُدِرْ	
3 MD	أَدَارَا	يُدِيرَانِ	يُدِيرَا	يُدِيرَا	
FD	أَدَارَتَا	تُدِيرَانِ	تُدِيرَا	تُدِيرَا	
2 D	أَدَرْتُمَا	تُدِيرَانِ	تُدِيرَا	تُدِيرَا	أَدِيرَا
3 MP	أَدَارُوا	يُدِيرُونَ	يُدِيرُوا	يُدِيرُوا	
FP	أَدَرْنَ	يُدِرْنَ	يُدِرْنَ	يُدِرْنَ	
2 MP	أَدَرْتُمْ	تُدِيرُونَ	تُدِيرُوا	تُدِيرُوا	أَدِيرُوا
FP	أَدَرْتُنَّ	تُدِرْنَ	تُدِرْنَ	تُدِرْنَ	أَدِرْنَ
1 P	أَدَرْنَا	نُدِيرُ	نُدِيرَ	نُدِرْ	

The passive voice stems are:

	Long Stem	Short Stem
Perfect	?uFiiL-	?uFiL-
Imperfect	-FaaL-	-FaL-

Examples are

أُدِيروا 'they (m.p.) were directed'	أُدِرْنَ 'they (f.p.) were directed'
يُدارونَ 'they (m.p.) are directed'	يُدَرْنَ 'they (f.p.) are directed'

	Pattern	Illustration
Active Participle	muFiiL-	مُديرٌ 'directing'
Passive Participle	muFaaL-	مُدارٌ 'directed'
Verbal Noun	?iFaaLa(t)	إدارةٌ 'direction, management'

Note the ـة on the verbal noun.

The Form IV hollow verbs that have occurred so far are:

أَقامَ ، إقامةٌ 'to erect, construct'
أَرادَ ، إرادةٌ 'to desire, wish'

b. Form VII

	Long Stem	Short Stem
Perfect Tense	-nFaaL-	-nFaL-
Imperfect Tense	-nFaaL-	-nFaL-

إِنْحَازَ – يَنْحَازُ الى 'to side with, join, be partial to'

	PERFECT	IMPERFECT			
		Indicative	Subjunctive	Jussive	Imperative
3 MS	اِنْحَازَ	يَنْحَازُ	يَنْحَازَ	يَنْحَزْ	
FS	اِنْحَازَتْ	تَنْحَازُ	تَنْحَازَ	تَنْحَزْ	
2 MS	اِنْحَزْتَ	تَنْحَازُ	تَنْحَازَ	تَنْحَزْ	اِنْحَزْ
FS	اِنْحَزْتِ	تَنْحَازِينَ	تَنْحَازِي	تَنْحَازِي	اِنْحَازِي
1 S	اِنْحَزْتُ	أَنْحَازُ	أَنْحَازَ	أَنْحَزْ	
3 MD	اِنْحَازا	يَنْحَازانِ	يَنْحَازا	يَنْحَازا	
FD	اِنْحَازَتا	تَنْحَازانِ	تَنْحَازا	تَنْحَازا	
2 D	اِنْحَزْتُما	تَنْحَازانِ	تَنْحَازا	تَنْحَازا	اِنْحَازا
3 MP	اِنْحَازوا	يَنْحَازونَ	يَنْحَازوا	يَنْحَازوا	
FP	اِنْحَزْنَ	يَنْحَزْنَ	يَنْحَزْنَ	يَنْحَزْنَ	
2 MP	اِنْحَزْتُمْ	تَنْحَازونَ	تَنْحَازوا	تَنْحَازوا	اِنْحَازوا
FP	اِنْحَزْتُنَّ	تَنْحَزْنَ	تَنْحَزْنَ	تَنْحَزْنَ	اِنْحَزْنَ
1 P	اِنْحَزْنا	نَنْحَازُ	نَنْحَازَ	نَنْحَزْ	

Active Participle	munFaaL-	مُنْحَازٌ الى	'partial to'
Verbal Noun	-nFiyaal-	اِنْحِيازٌ	'partiality'

There are no passives in Form VII.

41

c. Form VIII

	Long Stem	Short Stem
Perfect Tense	-FtaaL-	-FtaL-
Imperfect Tense	-FtaaL-	-FtaL-

اِزْدَادَ – يَزْدَادُ 'to increase, multiply, grow'

	PERFECT	IMPERFECT			
		Indicative	Subjunctive	Jussive	Imperative
3 MS	اِزْدَادَ	يَزْدَادُ	يَزْدَادَ	يَزْدَدْ	
FS	اِزْدَادَتْ	تَزْدَادُ	تَزْدَادَ	تَزْدَدْ	
2 MS	اِزْدَدْتَ	تَزْدَادُ	تَزْدَادَ	تَزْدَدْ	اِزْدَدْ
FS	اِزْدَدْتِ	تَزْدَادِينَ	تَزْدَادِي	تَزْدَادِي	اِزْدَادِي
1 S	اِزْدَدْتُ	أَزْدَادُ	أَزْدَادَ	أَزْدَدْ	
3 MD	اِزْدَادَا	يَزْدَادَانِ	يَزْدَادَا	يَزْدَادَا	
FD	اِزْدَادَتَا	تَزْدَادَانِ	تَزْدَادَا	تَزْدَادَا	
2 D	اِزْدَدْتُمَا	تَزْدَادَانِ	تَزْدَادَا	تَزْدَادَا	اِزْدَادَا
3 MP	اِزْدَادُوا	يَزْدَادُونَ	يَزْدَادُوا	يَزْدَادُوا	
FP	اِزْدَدْنَ	يَزْدَدْنَ	يَزْدَدْنَ	يَزْدَدْنَ	
2 MP	اِزْدَدْتُمْ	تَزْدَادُونَ	تَزْدَادُوا	تَزْدَادُوا	اِزْدَادُوا
FP	اِزْدَدْتُنَّ	تَزْدَدْنَ	تَزْدَدْنَ	تَزْدَدْنَ	اِزْدَدْنَ
1 P	اِزْدَدْنَا	نَزْدَادُ	نَزْدَادَ	نَزْدَدْ	

Active Participle	muFtaaL-	مُزْدَادّ 'increasing'
Verbal Noun	-FtiyaaL-	اِزْدِيَادّ 'increase'

42

The passive is rare in Form VIII.

Other hollow VIII verbs are

اِحْتاجَ الى	'to need'	(Ḥ W J)
اِمْتازَ بِ	'to be distinguished, characterized by'	(M Y Z)

d. **Form X**

	Long Stem	Short Stem
Perfect Tense	-staFaaL-	-staFaL-
Imperfect Tense	-staFiiL-	-staFiL-

اِسْتَفادَ ‒ يَسْتَفيدُ (مِن ، بِ) 'to benefit (from)'

	PERFECT	IMPERFECT			
		Indicative	Subjunctive	Jussive	Imperative
3 MS	اِسْتَفادَ	يَسْتَفيدُ	يَسْتَفيدَ	يَسْتَفِدْ	
FS	اِسْتَفادَتْ	تَسْتَفيدُ	تَسْتَفيدَ	تَسْتَفِدْ	
2 MS	اِسْتَفَدْتَ	تَسْتَفيدُ	تَسْتَفيدَ	تَسْتَفِدْ	اِسْتَفِدْ
FS	اِسْتَفَدْتِ	تَسْتَفيدينَ	تَسْتَفيدي	تَسْتَفيدي	اِسْتَفيدي
1 S	اِسْتَفَدْتُ	أَسْتَفيدُ	أَسْتَفيدَ	أَسْتَفِدْ	
3 MD	اِسْتَفادا	يَسْتَفيدانِ	يَسْتَفيدا	يَسْتَفيدا	
FD	اِسْتَفادَتا	تَسْتَفيدانِ	تَسْتَفيدا	تَسْتَفيدا	
2 D	اِسْتَفَدْتُما	تَسْتَفيدانِ	تَسْتَفيدا	تَسْتَفيدا	اِسْتَفيدا
3 MP	اِسْتَفادوا	يَسْتَفيدونَ	يَسْتَفيدوا	يَسْتَفيدوا	
FP	اِسْتَفَدْنَ	يَسْتَفِدْنَ	يَسْتَفِدْنَ	يَسْتَفِدْنَ	

2 MP	اِسْتَفِيدُوا	تَسْتَفِيدُوا	تَسْتَفِيدُوا	تَسْتَفِيدُونَ	اِسْتَفَدْتُمْ
FP	اِسْتَفِدْنَ	تَسْتَفِدْنَ	تَسْتَفِدْنَ	تَسْتَفِدْنَ	اِسْتَفَدْتُنَّ
1 P	نَسْتَفِدْ	نَسْتَفِيدَ	نَسْتَفِيدَ	نَسْتَفِيدُ	اِسْتَفَدْنا

Active Participle:	mustaFiiL- مُسْتَفِيدٌ 'benefitting'
Verbal Noun	-stiFaaLa(t)- اِسْتِفَادَةٌ 'benefit'

Note the presence of ـَةٌ on hollow Form X verbal nouns, as in the case of hollow IV verbal nouns.

The passive voice stems are:

	Long Stem	Short Stem
Perfect Tense	-stuFiiL-	-stuFiL-
Imperfect Tense	-staFaaL-	-staFaL-

Examples:

أُسْتُفِيدَ مِنْ ذلِكَ .   'That was benefited from.' =
'Benefit was derived from that.'
يُسْتَفَادُ مِنْ ذلِكَ .   'Benefit is derived from that.'

The other Form X hollow verb which has occurred so far is:

اِسْتَطَاعَ ، اِسْتِطَاعَةٌ   to be able (to)'

Note: اِسْتَطَاعَ may be followed by a verbal noun in the accusative or by an أَنْ clause, as in

الـقَوْلَ إِنَّ ...
نَسْتَطِيعُ   'We can say that...'
أَنْ نَقولَ إِنَّ ..

Summary of derived hollow verbs:

Form	Tense	Long Stem	Short Stem	Examples
IV	Perfect	?aFaaL-	?aFaL-	أَدَرْتُ أَدَارَ
	Imperfect	-FiiL-	-FiL-	يُدِرْ يُدِيرُ
VII	Perfect	-nFaaL-	-nFaL-	اِنْحَزْتَ اِنْحَازَ
	Imperfect	-nFaaL-	-nFaL-	يَنْحَزْ يَنْحازُ
VIII	Perfect	-FtaaL-	-FtaL-	اِزْدَدْتَّ اِزْدَادَ
	Imperfect	-FtaaL-	-FtaL-	يَزْدَدْ يَزْدادُ
X	Perfect	-staFaaL-	-staFaL-	اِسْتَفَدْتُ اِسْتَفَادَ
	Imperfect	-staFiiL-	-staFiL-	يَسْتَفِدْ يَسْتَفِيدُ

Now do Drills 1 (on tape), 2, 3, and 4.

<u>Drill 1.</u> (On tape) Conjugation: Hollow verbs, perfect and imperfect.

<u>Drill 2.</u> (Also on tape) Hollow verbs, jussive and subjunctive.

'We benefited greatly from the new factory.'	أ ــ استفدنا من المصنع الجديد استفادة كبيرة .
'We did not benefit greatly from the new factory.'	ط ١ ــ لم نستفد من المصنع الجديد استفادة كبيرة .
'We will never benefit greatly from the new factory.'	ط ٢ ــ لن نستفيد من المصنع الجديد استفادة كبيرة .

٤ ــ أدار المصنع خمس سنوات .   ١ ــ ازداد عدد المدارس في هذه المنطقة ازديادا كبيرا .

٥ ــ استطاعوا ان يحققوا تقدما كبيرا .   ٢ ــ احتجتُ الى سيّارة جديدة .

٦ ــ احتاجت الى كتب عربية .   ٣ ــ أقمن في مصر زمنا طويلا .

45

٧ – استطعت أن اقابل الوزير.

٨ – ازددنا احْتِراماً للمدير. in respect (See C.3 below)

Drill 3. Transformation: Verb → active participle.

T: 'Who is it who supervises the administration of this factory? Mr. Farid Ali.'

من الذي يشرف على ادارة هذا المصنع ؟

السيد فريد علي. ←

S: 'Mr. Farid Ali is the one who supervises the direction of this factory.'

السيد فريد علي هو المشرف على ادارة هذا المصنع

١ – من الذين يحتاجون الى كتب نجيب محفوظ ؟ طلابي.

٢ – من الذين يستفيدون من السياسة الجديدة ؟ العمّال.

٣ – من اللواتي يمتزن بحبهن للحرية ؟ الامريكيات.

٤ – من اللواتي يطالبن بتغيير سياسة الجامعة ؟ الاستاذات.

٥ – من الذي ترجم الكتاب ؟ فرانسيس وليم.

٦ – من الذي يدير هذا المكتب ؟ السيد سامي بَشير.

Drill 4. Written. Completion.

Fill in the blanks:

Active Participle	Passive Participle	Imperfect Passive	Imperfect Active	Perfect Passive
	مقام			
مدير				
				استفيد
محتاج	(rare)	(rare)		(rare)
			يستعيد	
		يعاد (IV)		

2. Hollow roots: Phonological rules

In this and the previous lesson you have learned the conjugation of hollow verbs in terms of long and short stems. It may be of interest to review these forms in terms of the mechanics of pronunciation--that is, phonological rules. Such rules may show that the irregularities are, in reality, regular and consistent in their own way, and so facilitate the memorization of the forms. This discussion will deal primarily with verbs and participles; it also applies to many verbal noun patterns.

The basic assumption here is that in the conjugation of a hollow verb we start off with a regular stem which is then changed for phonological considerations; compare the following verbs:

	STEM	3 MS		
Pattern	FaMvL-			
Strong verb	daras-	darasa	دَرَسَ	'he studied'
Hollow verb	zawur-	zawura ⟶ zaara	زارَ	'he visited'
Pattern	FMuL			
Strong verb	-drus-	yadrusu	يَدْرُسُ	'he studies'
Hollow verb	-zwur-	yazwuru ⟶ yazuuru	يَزورُ	'he visits'

We will present a set of rules that predict the kinds of changes illustrated in زارَ — يَزورُ and all other hollow verbs. Our point of departure is the principle that the consonants w and y, as the second radical of a root, tend to be modified by adjacent vowels in the course of conjugating the verb or the formation of participles and most verbal nouns. w and y will be referred to as glides and represented by the symbol G, and C symbolizes "any conson-

47

ant".

a. Verbs

<u>Rule H1</u>. <u>A glide between two short vowels is dropped: vGv — vv</u>. If the resultant combination is two identical vowels, then these constitute a long vowel. Illustration:

VII   in<u>h</u>awaza —▶ in<u>h</u>aaza = اِتَّحَازَ 'he took sides'

VIII   izd<u>ay</u>ada —▶ izd<u>aa</u>da = اِزدَاكَ 'it increased'

It is impossible in Arabic to have a sequence of two different vowels; if the resultant VV combination consists of two different vowels, then it must undergo rule H2. Illustration:

I   n<u>aw</u>ima —▶ n<u>ai</u>ma: go to rule H2.

I   s<u>ay</u>ira —▶ s<u>ai</u>ra: go to rule H2.

I   z<u>aw</u>ura —▶ z<u>au</u>ra: go to rule H2.

I   z<u>uw</u>ira —▶ z<u>ui</u>ra: go to rule H2.

<u>Rule H2</u>. This rule applies to either a combination of <u>two different short vowels</u>, vv, or of <u>one glide and one short vowel, Gv or vG</u>: <u>Any combination of two short vowels or of one glide plus one short vowel becomes a long vowel</u>:

$$
\left.
\begin{array}{l}
\text{vv (=different vowels)} \\
\text{vG} \\
\text{Gv}
\end{array}
\right\} \longrightarrow \text{vv (=one long vowel)}
$$

The changes take the following form:

(a) If the combination in question begins with <u>a</u>, the result is <u>aa</u>; if it begins with a short vowel other than <u>a</u>, the result is <u>ii</u>. Examples:

48

Original:			becomes:	Original:	Rule H1	Rule H2		
a	w	i	aa	nawima	→ naima	→ naama	نامَ	'he slept'
	y	u		sayira	→ saira	→ saara	سارَ	'he walked'
				zawura	→ zaura	→ zaara	زارَ	'he visited'

Original:			becomes:	Original:	Rule H1	Rule H2		
u	w	i	ii	zuwira	→ zuira	→ ziira	زِيرَ	'he was visited'
	y			buyiʕa	→ buiʕa	→ biiʕa	بيعَ	'it was sold'

This rule also applies to derived participles of Forms VII and VIII.

Example:

Form VIII, Root MYZ, 'distinguish'

muFtaMiL-	Rule H1	Rule H2		
mumtayiz	→ mumtaiz	→ mumtaaz	مُمْتازٌ	'distinguished'

(b) If the combination in question begins with a glide, that glide is assimilated to the following vowel. An exception is the combination yu which results in ii. Thus:

Original:		becomes:	Examples:			
w	a	→ aa	yanwamu → yanaamu	يَنامُ	'he sleeps'
y			?istafyada → ?istafaada	اِسْتَفادَ	'he benefited'
w	i	→ ii	yudwiru → yudiiru	يُديرُ	'he manages'
y			yasyiru → yasiiru	يَسيرُ	'he walks'
w	u	uu	yazwuru → yazuuru	يَزورُ	'he visits'
y		ii			

49

This rule also applies to **all** participles and to some noun patterns; a following long vowel acts here the same as a short vowel. Examples:

<u>Passive participles, Form I</u> (with long vowel):

maFMuuL:

mazwuur ⟶ mazuur   مَزورٌ   'visited'

mabyuuʕ ⟶ mabiiʕ   مَبِيعٌ   'sold'

<u>Active participle, Form IV</u>:

muFMiL:

mudwir ⟶ mudiir   مُدِيرٌ   'director'

<u>Passive participle, Form IV</u>:

muFMaL

mudwar ⟶ mudaar   مُدارٌ   'directed'

<u>Noun of Place</u>:

maFMaL

makwan ⟶ makaan   مَكانٌ   'place'

<u>Verbal noun, Form IV</u> (with suffixing of ـَةٌ):

ʔiFMaaL

ʔidwaar ⟶ ʔidaara(t) إِدارَةٌ   'administration'

<u>Verbal noun, Form X</u> (with suffixing of ـَةٌ):

ʔistiFMaaL

ʔistiFyaad ⟶ ʔistifaada(t) اِسْتِفادَةٌ   'benefit'

<u>Rule L1.</u> ["L" refers to long vowels.]

A long vowel in a closed syllable is shortened, except before a doubled consonant. [A "closed syllable" is one which ends in a consonant that is not followed by a vowel, such as the underlined syllables in da<u>ras</u>ta 'you studied' and dara<u>sat</u> 'she studied.']

50

Original:	becomes:	Original	Rule H2	Rule L1		
CVVCC	CVCC	?adwartu	?adaartu	?adartu	أَدَرْتُ	'I directed'
CVVC	CVC	yazwur	yazuur	yazur	لَمْ يَزُرْ	'he didn't visit'

This rule does not apply to Form I verbs in the perfect tense (see Rule H3 below).

It does not apply in doubled roots, as in هامّ 'important'.

Rule H3: For Form I verbs in the perfect tense only. The vowel of the perfect tense short stem of Form I hollow verbs is u if the imperfect tense stem vowel is u, and it is i otherwise. Thus:

Perfect Long Stem	Imperfect Stem Vowel	Perfect Short Stem	Examples		
aa	a	i	naama-yanaamu-nimtu	نِمْتُ	'I slept'
	i		saara-yasiiru-sirtu	سِرْتُ	'I walked'
	u	u	zaara-yazuuru-zurtu	زُرْتُ	'I visited'

b. Verbal nouns

Rule H4. iwaa becomes iyaa. (That is, w, which is produced in the back part of the mouth, becomes y after i, as both y and i are produced in the front part of the mouth.) (There are occasional exceptions to this rule.) Ex.

FiMaaLa(t) (Form I Verbal Noun):   Exception:

ziwaara(t) → ziyaara(t) زِيَارَةٌ 'visit'   اِحْتَوَى ، اِحْتِوَاءٌ 'to contain,
(?iḥtiwaa?) include'

c. Participles

Rule H5. For Form I participles only. The second radical w or y is replaced by ? in the active participle of Form I verbs. Examples:

51

<u>FaaMiL</u>

zaawir ——► zaa?ir   زاِئرٌ   'visiting'

saayir ——► saa?ir   ساِئرٌ   'going'

<u>d. Notes</u>

(1) None of these rules apply to doubled <u>ww</u> or <u>yy</u>, as in أَوّلُ 'first' or
نَغيّرُ 'change'.

(2) Combinations <u>aw</u> and <u>ay</u> do not change, e.g. نَوْمٌ 'sleep' and سَيّرٌ
'going'. The combinations <u>uwa</u> and <u>iya</u> are also stable.

3. <u>Accusative of specification: Tamyīz</u>

The sentence

| هُوَ أَعْظَمُ مِنَ الْجاحِظِ إِنْتاجًا . | 'He is greater than Al-Jāhiz in literary output.' |

is equal in meaning to

| إِنْتاجُهُ أَعْظَمُ مِنْ إِنْتاجِ الْجاحِظِ . | 'His output is greater than Al-Jāhiz's output.' |

Similarly, the sentence

| إِنْتاجُ السَّعوديّةِ مِنَ الزَّيْتِ أَكْثَرُ مِنْ إِنْتاجِ مُعْظَمِ الدُّوَلِ الْأُخْرى . | 'Saudi Arabia's oil production is greater than that of most other countries.' |

can be changed to

| اَلسَّعوديّةُ أَكْثَرُ مِنْ مُعْظَمِ الدُّوَلِ الْأُخْرى إِنْتاجًا لِلزَّيْتِ . | 'Saudi Arabia produces more oil than most other countries.' |

The noun إِنْتاجًا in the first and last sentences above is in the <u>accusative</u>

<u>case</u>, is <u>indefinite</u>, and has the meaning of "with respect to, in terms of,

52

in, as to". This use of the noun is called <u>accusative of specification</u>, or

<u>tamyīz</u> (Arabic تَمْيِيزٌ 'singling out, discrimation, specification'). The

tamyīz noun, or accusative of specification, can typically be construed as

the equivalent of the first term of an idāfa which is the subject or object

of a verb or, as in the examples above, as the subject of an equational

sentence. The tamyīz construction <u>must</u> be used for the comparative or super-

lative degree of derived participles (or for adjectives of color, like أَحْمَرُ

'red'), together with an elative adjective like أَكْثَرُ 'more', أَكْبَرُ 'greater',

أَقَلُّ 'less', etc. Illustrations:

أَنْتَ مُخْلِصٌ جِدًّا ، يا زُهَيْرُ ، لكِنَّ سَلْوى أَكْثَرُ مِنْكَ إِخْلاصًا .	'You are very sincere, Zuhair, but Salma is more sincere than you are' (Lit., "greater as to sincerety").
لَسْتُ مُسْتَعِدًّا كُلَّ الإِسْتِعْدادِ، لكِنِّي أَكْثَرُ مِنْكَ اسْتِعْدادًا وَجَمالٌ أَكْثَرُنا اسْتِعْدادًا .	'I am not fully prepared, but I am more prepared than you are, and Jamal is the most prepared of us all.'

Now do Drill 5.

<u>Drill 5</u>. Written. Elative with accusative of specification.

Rewrite the following sentences using the accusative of specification,

and then translate the rewritten sentences into English. <u>Ex</u>.

'Salim's respect for his professors
is greater than that of the other
students for them.'
احترام سليم لأساتذته أعظم من احترام الطلاب الآخرين لهم . ⟵

'Salim respects his professors most
of all the students.'
سليم اعظم الطلاب احتراما لاساتذته .

١ ـ انتاج السعودية للزيت أكثر من انتاج الدول العربيّة الاخرى له .

٢ ـ احتياجي اليك اعظم من احتياج الناس الآخرين اليك .

53

٣ ـ مطالبة الامريكيات بحقوقهن أعظم من مطالبة النساء الاخريات بتلك الحقوق ·

٤ ـ تقدّم امريكا في الصناعة أعظم من تقدّم الدول الاخرى ·

٥ ـ نجاح اللبنانيّين في التجارة اعظم من نجاح معظم العرب الآخرين·

4. The clause introducer اِنَّ 'verily'

The particle اِنَّ 'verily, truly, indeed' comes at the beginning of a clause or sentence. It is one of the sisters of اِنَّ 'that', which means that (a) it cannot be immediately followed by a verb and (b) the subject of its clause is in the accusative case. (If there is a declinable predicate it will be in the nominative case.) Illustrations:

اِنَّ السَّعوديَّةَ تَعْتَمِدُ على الزَّيْتِ كُلَّ الإِعْتِمادِ ·	'Indeed Saudi Arabia is totally dependent on its oil.'
اِنَّ بَعْضَ الدُّوَلِ الْعَرَبِيَّةَ غَنِيَّةٌ بِالزَّيْتِ ·	'Some Arab states are rich in oil.'

اِنَّ intensifies the truth value of the following statement; English does not have an exact equivalent, and it is often best left untranslated.

D. Comprehension passages   د ـ نصوص للفهم

Read the following passage and then do Drills 6 and 7 which are based on it.

الكويت

الكويت دولة عربية قريبة من العراق ، أكثرها صحراء ، وليس فيها أنهار ·

assembly   يحكم الكويت أميرٌ يساعده وزراء . وللكويت مَجْلِسٌ وطنيّ يُنتَخَب   prince

members   أعْضاوُهُ الخمسون كل أربعة أعوام .

نصف السكّان كويتيّون ، أما النصف الآخر فيشمل مصريّين وفِلَسْطِينِيّينَ

وأمريكيين وغيرهم . أكثر السكان مسلمون ، وهناك ايضا عدد قليل من غير

المسلمين . واللغة الرسمية في الكويت هي اللغة العربيّة ، لكنّ الكثيرين

يتكلّمون اللغة الانكليزية كذلك .

والكويت من أغنى بلدان العالم بموارد الزيت وأكثرها انتاجا له؛

income,   لذلك تقدّم اقتصادها تقدّما عظيما ، وازداد دَخْلُها ازديادا كبيرا .
revenue

wealth   استفادت الكويت من ثَرْوَتِها العظيمة ، فقد استطاعت الحكومة أن

تقيم المصانع وتنشئ المدارس وترسل الطلاب الى بعض الدول العربيّة

الاخرى والى الغرب للحصول على الشهادات الجامعية .

capital   عاصِمَةُ الكويت هي مدينة الكويت ، وهي من أحدث المدن في الشرق

الاوسط بل في العالم .

Drill 6. Written.

Fill in the blanks, using the previous text:

١ ـ المسلمون في الكويت ـــــــ ، وغير المسلمين ـــــــ ـــــــ .

٢ ـ اللغة الـ ـــــــ هي اللغة الاجنبيّة التي يتكلمها أكثر الكويتيين.

٣ ـ الكويت غنية بـ ـــــــ ـــــــ .

٤ ـ يذهب الطلاب الكويتيون الى ـــــــ للدراسة في الجامعات .

٥ ـ مدينة الكويت ـــــــ ـــــــ .

٦ ـ اللغة الرسمية في الكويت هي ـــــــ ـــــــ .

Drill 7. Written.

1. Write brief notes in English on Kuwait's

    a. geography

55

b. political system

c. use of its wealth

2. Now listen to the passage on tape; then do Drill 8, which is based on it.

<u>Drill 8</u>. Written. Question/answer on Aural Comprehension passage.

Listen to the passage recorded on tape(جَمال عَبْدُ النّاصِر); then answer

the following questions in English.

أسئلـــــة :

١ ــ ما الذي أراده جمال عبد الناصر للاقتصاد المصري ؟

٢ ــ لماذا عمل جمال عبد الناصر على أن تتقدّم الصناعة في مصر ؟

٣ ــ هل استخدم عبد الناصر مهندسين أجانب ؟ لماذا ؟

٤ ــ هل منع عبد الناصر الشركات الاجنبية من البحث عن الزيت في مصر ؟

٥ ــ هل ازداد انتاج مصر من الزيت في زمن الرئيس عبد الناصر ؟

٦ ــ لماذا يحترم المصريون عبد الناصر ؟

E. <u>General drills</u>   هـ ــ التمارين العامة

<u>Drill 9</u>. Completion. Verbal nouns.

Fill in the blanks with the appropriate verbal nouns, and then translate

the sentences.

١ ــ بحثنا الموضوع ــــــــ شاملا •

٢ ــ زارت ابنتي العراق ــــــــ قصيرة •

٣ ــ رحب اهلي بي ــــــــ عظيما •

٤ ــ قاوم العرب الحكم الاجنبيّ ــــــــ عظيمة •

٥ ــ أكرموا الزائر كل الـ ــــــــ •

٦ ــ أقام صديقي في تونس ــــــــ قصيرة •

56

٧ ـ تصرفت ــــــــ حسنا •

٨ ـ استفادت منه هذه الدول ــــــــ عظيمة •

٩ ـ تغيّر الوضع السياسيّ ــــــــ كبيرا •

١٠ ـ سوف نتعاون معكم كل الـ ــــــــ •

١١ ـ أنتم تختلفون عنا بعض الـ ــــــــ •

١٢ ـ استقبل المصريون الوزير الامريكي ــــــــ جميلا •

١٣ ـ سيطرت الشركات الاجنبية على التجارة ــــــــ كبيرة •

١٤ ـ هل ازداد انتاج الزيت ــــــــ كبيرا في الاعوام الاخيرة ؟

<u>Drill 10</u>. Transformation: Active ➔ passive (perfect, subjunctive, jussive).

'The government established many factories.'   اقامت الحكومة مصانع كثيرة'. ➔

a. 'Many factories were established.'   اقيمت مصانع كثيرة •

b. 'Not many factories were established.'   لم تقم مصانع كثيرة •

c. 'Many factories must be established.'   يجب أن تقام مصانع كثيرة •

١ ـ انتخب الناس احد المرشحين •

٢ ـ استقبلها الناس استقبالا عظيما •

٣ ـ استفادت الشركة من المهندسين الاجانب •

٤ ـ أقامت الحكومة سدّا كبيرا على النهر •

٥ ـ بذل السياسيون جهودا كبيرة لتغيير الوضع •

٦ ـ طالبنا الشعب بتغيير سياستنا •

<u>Drill 11</u>. Transformation: Singular ➔ plural.

Fill in the blanks:

English	Plural	Singular
		منطقة
	صور	
		لهجة
		اسبوع
	مسافات	
		رأي
		قصة
	بيوت	
month		
		أسلوب
	قرى	
		مجلّة

English	Plural	Singular
		وجه
		سبب
	جيران	
		أخ
		ليلة
	رجال	
		حلّ
	فنون	
engineer		
		قلب
	عمّال	
gift		

Drill 12. Written. Composition.

Write brief notes on the subject " أمريكا ", using the following outline as a guide:

٦ ــ الاقتصاد .   ١ ــ الدول القريبة من أمريكا .

٧ ــ الحكومة .   ٢ ــ الولايات الامريكية .

٨ ــ العلاقات الخارجية .   ٣ ــ الأنهار .

٩ ــ الجامعات والطلاب الأجانب .   ٤ ــ السكان .

٥ ــ اللغة .

Drill 13. Written. Vocabulary.

Fill in the blanks with the most appropriate word from among the words in the following list:

58

تراسل ، يتابعون، نجاح، انتخاب ، صغير ، ثورة ، المحافظة ، قال ،
عِلْم ، البلاد ، تتوفر ، يظهر ، حكما ، مقالة ، زهاب ، مجتمع ، خاص ،
العالي، شرء فم ، حاجة ، علّمني .

١ ــ يجب ان تتوفر للمرأة كل حقوقها لخير ـــــــ .

٢ ــ يقول قائد ـــــــ : اننا سنقاوم لبناء ـــــــ جديد .

٣ ــ لها اهتمام ـــــــ بـ ـــــــ ابنها في الامتحانات .

٤ ــ ـــــــ رجل كبير ـــــــ استفدت منها كل حياتي .

٥ ــ هل ـــــــ دراستهم الجامعية في مشيغان ؟

٦ ــ زهبنا الى ذلك المكان ـــــــ ومن هناك شاهدنا جمال المدينة .

٧ ــ ـــــــ الحبيبان لمدة سنة ثم انقطعت الرسائل بينهما .

٨ ــ ـــــــ الحزب الوطني اهتماما كبيرا بـ ـــــــ على حقوق الشعب .

٩ ــ لسنا بـ ـــــــ الى مراسلين جدد .

59

الدرس الثالث و الثلاثون

أ ـ اَلْجُمَلُ التَّمْهِيدِيَّةُ

A. __Preparatory sentences__

حديث مع مساعد مندوب ,الجزائر

__A Conversation with the Assistant__
__of the Algerian Delegate__

١ ـ الطالب : اَلسَّلامُ عَلَيْكُمْ .

1 Hello. ("Peace be with you.")

٢ ـ السيد لطفي : وَعَلَيْكُمُ السَّلامُ .

2 Hello. ("And with you be peace.")

٣ ـ الطالب : هل حَضْرَتُكَ موظف فـي مُنَظَّمَةِ الأُمَمِ الْمُتَّحِدَةِ ؟

3 Are you an official in the __United__
__Nations Organization?__

مُنَظَّمَةٌ ـ اتٌ

organization

أُمَّةٌ ـ أُمَمٌ

nation, people

اِتَّحَدَ ، اِتِّحادٌ (بـ)

VIII to unite, be united; to federate (with)

الأُمَمُ الْمُتَّحِدَةُ

The United Nations

٤ ـ السيد لطفي : أنا مساعد لِمَنْدوبِ الجزائر .

4 I am an assistant to the Algerian
__delegate.__

مَنْدوبٌ ـ ونَ

delegate, representative,
deputy

٥ ـ ط : كيف تختلف منظمة الامـــم المتحدة عن الجامِعَـــةِ العربية ؟

5 How does the United Nations differ
from the __Arab League?__

٦ ـ ل : المحافَظة على السلام مـن أهم أُهْدافِ كِلْتا المنظّمتين لكنَّ المنظمة الأولـــــى عالمية والمنظمة الثانية تقدّم خدماتها للـــدول العربية فقط .

6 The preservation of peace is one of
the most important __objectives__ of
__both__ organizations, but the first
one is world-wide and the second
organization offers its services
to only the Arab states.

هَدَفٌ ـ أَهْدافٌ

target; aim, object, objective,
intention, goal

كِلا ، كِلَيْ (كِلْتا ، كِلْتَيْ)

both (see C. 3)

60

٧ — ط : هل للأمم المتحدة نَشاطٌ
يَتَّصِلُ بالصناعة ؟

Does the UN have any <u>activities</u>
which are <u>connected with</u> industry?

نَشاطٌ ــ ات

energy, activity, action

اِتَّصَلَ ، اِتِّصالٌ (بـ)

VIII to be connected with,
bear on, have to do with; to
get in touch with, contact (s.o.)

٨ — ل : نعم وهي أيضا تقــدِّم
للإنسان خدمات ثَقافِيّةٌ
واجتماعِيّة .

Yes. It also offers <u>cultural</u> and
social services to <u>mankind</u>.

إنْسانٌ

man, human being, person

ثَقافَةٌ ــ ات

culture, refinement

٩ — ط : نستطيع إذَنْ أن نَصِفَ الامم
المتحدة بأنّها أكثر من
منظمة سياسية ؟

<u>Therefore</u> we can <u>describe</u> the UN
as more than a political organization?

إذاً ، إذَنْ

then, therefore, in that case

وَصَفَ يَصِفُ ، وَصْفٌ (بِأنَّهُ)

to describe, depict s.th. (as being)

١٠ — ل : هذا مِمّا لا شَكَّ فيه .

That is <u>something that</u> there is
no <u>doubt</u> about.

مِمّا = مِن + ما

a thing which, something which

شَكٌّ ــ شُكوكٌ (في ، بـ)
لا شَكَّ (في)

doubt (about), suspicion (over)

there is no doubt (about); no
doubt (about)

١١ — ط : هل تدير الدول الكبــرى
منظمة الامم المتحدة ؟

Do the big nations run the United
Nations?

١٢ — ل : لا. للمنظمة سكرتير عامٌّ
وللْجَمْعِيّةِ العامَّةِ رئيس
وهما أهم الموظفين ،لكن
الدول الكبرى لا تعيّنهما
بل ينتخبهما الأعْضاءُ.

No. The organization has a secre-
tary <u>general</u>, and the <u>General Assem-
bly</u> has a president, and they are
the two most important officials.
However, they are not appointed by
the big powers but are elected by
the <u>members</u>.

عامٌّ

general

[الجَمْعِيّةُ العامّةُ]

[The General Assembly]

عُضْوٌ ــ أعْضاءٌ

member

١٣ ـ ط : هل تتعاون الجامعة العربية مع الامم المتحدة ؟	Does the Arab League cooperate with the United Nations?

١٤ ـ ل : الجامعة العربية تعمل على حل مشكلات الـــدول العربية ومن هــــذه المشكلات ما يتّصل بـالاوضاع العالمية . يجب اذن ان تتعاون المنظّمتان .	The Arab League works for the resolution of the problems of the Arab states, and some of their problems involve world conditions. It is necessary, then, for the two organizations to cooperate with each other.

١٥ ـ ط : يقال إنّ منظّمة الامم المتّحدة لم تنجح في حلّ مشكلات العرب وإنّ العرب لذلك لا يَضَعونَ ثِقَتَهُمْ فيها .	It is said that the United Nations has not been successful in solving the Arabs' problems and that the Arabs therefore do not **place** their **confidence** in the UN.

وَضَعَ يَضَعُ، وَضْعٌ	to put, place, lay; to compose, draft (a document)
وَثِقَ يَثِقُ ، ثِقَةٌ (ب)	to trust, have confidence (in)

١٦ ـ ل : لا اعتقد أن هذا صحيح . لقد حقّقت الامم المتّحدة كثيـــرا من اهدافها ، لذلك نَجِـــدُ العرب كغيرهم من الشعـوب يضعون ثقتهم فيها . ألا تعلـم ان للدول العربية مندوبين في المنظمة ؟	I don't believe that that is **right**. The UN has realized many of its objectives. We thus **find** that the Arabs, like other peoples, do place their trust in it. Don't you know that the Arab states have delegates at the organization?

صَحيحٌ ـ صِحاحٌ	right, true, correct
وَجَدَ يَجِدُ، وُجودٌ	to find

١٧ ـ ط : هل هناك منظمات احـــرى كالجامعة العربية ؟	Are there other organizations like the Arab League?

١٨ ـ ل : هناك ـ كما تعلم ـ حِلْفُ ناتو وحِلْفُ وارْسو . وقد أُسِّسا بعد الحَرْبِ العالميّة الثانية وفي كليهما عدد من الدول الصغرى والكبرى .	There is - as you know - the NATO **Pact** and the Warsaw Alliance. They were **founded** after the second World **War**, and there are several large and small nations in both of them.

[حِلْفٌ ـ أَحْلافٌ]   [pact, alliance]

أَسَّسَ ، تَأْسيسٌ   II to found, establish

حَرْبٌ ـ حُروبٌ   (f.) war

كِلْتَيْ   (d. and gen.) both

١٩ ـ ط : شكرًا يا أستاذ لطفي •   Thank you, Mr. Lutfi.

٢٠ ـ ل : عفوًا • مع السلامة •   You're welcome. Goodbye.

مفردات اضافية   Additional vocabulary

وَقَعَ يَقَعُ ، وُقوعٌ   to be located

Vocabulary note

حَضَرَةٌ ـ حَضَراتٌ 'presence' is used with a pronoun suffix as a
respectful form of address: "your excellence, your eminence". The singular
form is used with singular pronoun suffixes, e.g. حَضَرَتُكِ or حَضَرَتُكَ ,
and the plural is used with plural suffixes, e.g. حَضَراتُكُمْ . The usual
translation in English is "you".

ب ـ النص الاساسي

منظّمة الامم المتّحدة

احتمعت بعد الحرب العالميّة الثانية بعض الدول الكبرى وعدد
من الدول الصغرى في مدينة سان فرانسيسكو واتّفقت على تأسيس منظّمة
الامم المتّحدة ، ووضعت ميثاقًا لها •

charter

general   للمنظّمة سكرتير عامّ ، وللدول الاعضاء مندوبون فيها •

من أهداف هذه المنظمة المحافظة على السلام العالميّ وحقوق
الانسان ، ولذلك نجد أنّ معظم شعوب العالم تضع ثقتها الكبيرة فيها
وتصفها بأنّها من أهم المنظّمات السياسية •

ونشاط منظّمة الامم المتحدة لا يتّصل بالسياسة فقط ، فأنّ لها

branches   فُروعًا تقدّم للعالم خدمات ثقافيّة وتربويّة واجتماعية • ومن أهمّ تلك

الفروع منظّمة اليونِسْكو التي تعمل على تقدّم الثقافة والعلوم ،

ومنظّمة العمل الدولية التي تقدّم المساعدات الاقتصاديّة للدول الصغرى

ولكلتا المنظمتين مُمَثّلونَ في العالم العربيّ .

representatives

ومِمّا لا شكَّ فيه أنَّ المنظّمة نجحت في حلّ كثير من المشكـــلات

الدوليّة ، وصحيح أيضا أنّها لم تحقّق جميع اهدافها لأنّ بعض الدول لا

تتعاون معها كلّ التعاون .

B. Basic text

The United Nations Organization

After World War II some of the great powers and a number of small nations
met in San Francisco and agreed to establish the United Nations Organization
and drew up a charter for it.

The organization has a secretary-general, and member nations have delegates
to it.

One of the goals of this organization is the preservation of world peace
and of human rights; and therefore we find that most of the peoples of the
world place great trust in it and describe it as one of the most important
political organizations.

The activities of the UN do not have to do with politics alone, for it
has branches that offer the world cultural, educational and social services.
One of the most important of those branches is UNESCO, which works for the advancement of culture and the sciences, and the World Labor Organization which
offers economic aid to the small countries. Both organizations have representatives in the Arab world.

One thing about which there is no doubt is that the UN has been successful
in solving many international problems. It is also true that it has not been
able to realize all its goals because some nations do not fully cooperate with
it.

> 1. Assimilated verbs
>
> 2. Noun-noun apposition
>
> 3. The لا of absolute negation
>
> 4. The noun كِلا 'both'

1. Assimilated verbs

Verbs whose first radical is <u>W</u>, e.g. وَصَفَ 'to describe' (root <u>WṢF</u>), share three distinctive features: (a) the <u>W</u> is dropped in the imperfect of Form I verbs; (b) the <u>W</u> is assimilated to <u>t</u> in Form VIII; and (c) <u>W</u> is assimilated to a preceding <u>i</u>; i.e., <u>iw</u> becomes <u>ii</u> in Forms IV and X. In all other cases, assimilated roots behave like strong roots. These three changes will now be explained in detail, using the following verbs as illustrations:

وَصَفَ	(root WṢF)	'to describe'
وَصَلَ	(WṢL)	'to arrive'
وَجَدَ	(WJD)	'to find'
وَجَبَ	(WJB)	'to be necessary'
وَقَعَ	(WQʕ)	'to be located'
وَثِقَ	(WθQ)	'to trust'
وَعَدَ	(WʕD)	'to promise'

(a) <u>Form I assimilated verbs</u>. The perfect tense is conjugated like any other verb we have encountered; e.g., the third person perfect is given below of وَصَفَ

3 MS	وَصَفَ	3 MD	وَصَفا	3 MP	وَصَفوا
FS	وَصَفَتْ	FD	وَصَفَتا	FP	وَصَفْنَ

In the imperfect, however, the <u>W</u> is dropped. The conjugation of the imperfect of وَصَفَ 'to describe' is given below:

	Indicative	Subjunctive	Jussive	Imperative
3 MS	يَصِفُ	يَصِفَ	يَصِفْ	
FS	تَصِفُ	تَصِفَ	تَصِفْ	
2 MS	تَصِفُ	تَصِفَ	تَصِفْ	صِفْ
FS	تَصِفِينَ	تَصِفِي	تَصِفِي	صِفِي
1 S	أَصِفُ	أَصِفَ	أَصِفْ	
3 MD	يَصِفانِ	يَصِفا	يَصِفا	
FD	تَصِفانِ	تَصِفا	تَصِفا	
2 D	تَصِفانِ	تَصِفا	تَصِفا	صِفا
3 MP	يَصِفونَ	يَصِفوا	يَصِفوا	
FP	يَصِفْنَ	يَصِفْنَ	يَصِفْنَ	
2 MP	تَصِفونَ	تَصِفوا	تَصِفوا	صِفوا
FP	تَصِفْنَ	تَصِفْنَ	تَصِفْنَ	صِفْنَ
1 P	نَصِفُ	نَصِفَ	نَصِفْ	

The principal parts of our illustrative Form I assimilated verbs are:

	Perfect	Imperfect	Active Participle	Verbal Noun
to describe	وَصَفَ	يَصِفُ	واصِفٌ	وَصْفٌ
to arrive	وَصَلَ	يَصِلُ	واصِلٌ	وُصولٌ
to find	وَجَدَ	يَجِدُ	واجِدٌ	وُجودٌ
to be necessary	وَجَبَ	يَجِبُ	واجِبٌ	وُجوبٌ
to be located	وَقَعَ	يَقَعُ	واقِعٌ	وُقوعٌ
to draw up	وَضَعَ	يَضَعُ	واضِعٌ	وَضْعٌ
to trust	وَثِقَ	يَثِقُ	واثِقٌ	ثِقَةٌ
to promise	وَعَدَ	يَعِدُ	واعِدٌ	وَعْدٌ

66

You will note that there are certain regularities of form with these verbs:

(1) In the perfect tense the stem vowel is usually <u>a</u>, and the imperfect stem vowel is <u>i</u>. (The exceptions تَقَعُ and يَضَعُ can be explained as a matter of assimilating the <u>i</u> to <u>a</u> before a pharyngeal or "back" consonant.)

(2) The active participle and verbal nouns are regular in form. With some verbs, however, the verbal noun may lose the <u>W</u>. For example, وَصَلَ in the meaning of "to connect, join, link" has the verbal nouns وَصْلٌ and صِلَةٌ, which mean "connecting, joining", and also "juncture, connection, link," وَصَفَ in addition to وَصْفٌ has the noun صِفَةٌ, 'quality, property, attribute' and also 'adjective'.

(3) وَصَلَ 'to arrive' and وَصْلٌ ، وَصَلَ 'to connect, link' also illustrate a general pattern: that the transitive verb takes the verbal noun pattern FaML while the intransitive verbal noun pattern is FuMuuL. (وُجودٌ for وَجَدَ 'to find' means both "finding" and "being found; existence".)

(4) The verb وَقَعَ in the meaning 'to be situated, be located' occurs in the third person masculine and feminine imperfect only. The verb وَجَبَ 'to be necessary' occurs only in the third masculine singular, (and usually in the imperfect), and takes only an أَنْ- clause or verbal noun as subject.

(5) Assimilated verbs are perfectly regular in the passive conjugation, being spelled like any strong verb. The passive imperfect, third masculine singular, accordingly, is written يُولَدُ 'he is born.' The point to be made here is that the combination <u>uw</u> is pronounced <u>uu</u>; يولَدُ, then, is pronounced <u>yuuladu</u>. It also applies to all assimilated verbs, imperfect active and passive, in Form IV. This is a general pronunciation-spelling rule, and applies to all words in the language.

(b) In Form VIII the radical <u>W</u> is assimilated to the reflexive <u>t</u> throughout all stems of the verb and verbal noun. Thus, <u>?iwtaṣala</u> → <u>?ittaṣala</u>:

67

Principal Parts: Form VIII

	Perfect	Root	Imperfect	Verbal Noun	Active Participle
to get in contact with	اِتَّصَلَ ب	WṢL	يَتَّصِلُ	اِتِّصال	مُتَّصِل
to agree on	اِتَّفَقَ على	WFQ	يَتَّفِقُ	اِتِّفاق	مُتَّفِق
to unite	اِتَّحَدَ	WḤD	يَتَّحِدُ	اِتِّحاد	مُتَّحِد

It is this feature that gives initial W verbs the name "assimilated".

(c) Assimilation of W to i, Forms IV and X. There is a general rule which applies to MSA as a whole to the effect that when w follows i in the same syllable it is changed to i: that is, iw becomes ii. Thus the verbal nouns of Form IV and X assimilated verbs take the following shapes:

Form	Verb	Verbal Noun	
		underlying shape	occurring shape
IV	أَوْجَدَ 'to create'	(?iwjaad) →	إيجاد 'creation' ?iijaad
X	اِسْتَوْطَنَ 'to settle down'	(?istiwṭaan) →	اِسْتيطان 'settling down' ?istiiṭaan

Now do Drills 1 (on tape), 2, 3 and 4.

<u>Drill 1</u>. (On tape) Conjugation: Assimilated verbs.

<u>Drill 2</u>. (Also on tape) Transformation: Perfect ⟶ imperfect with سَ.

'The minister arrived today.' وصل الوزير اليوم • ⟵

'The minister will arrive today.' سيصل الوزير اليوم •

١ ــ وصفوا في كتابهم مكانة العامل •   ٥ ــ وضعنا الهدية على الطاولة •

٢ ــ النساء وصلن الى المسرح •   ٦ ــ والداه وصلا اليوم •

٣ ــ وثقت الدول الصغرى في المنظمة •   ٧ ــ هل وصلتما بعد بداية المحاضرة ؟

٤ ــ وصف لنا حفر القناة الجديدة •   ٨ ــ وجدت المقالة التي تحدثت اليكم عنها •

Drill 3. (Also on tape) Transformation: Perfect ⟶ jussive with لم .

'The big powers have agreed to
cooperate in industry.'

اتفقت الدول الكبرى على التعاون
في الصناعة . ⟵

'The big powers have not agreed
to cooperate in industry.'

لم تتفق الدول الكبرى على التعاون
في الصناعة .

٥ ـ وصلن قبل بداية الاجتماع .

١ ـ اتصل نشاط المنظمة بالتجارة
الدولية .

٦ ـ ولدتا في مدينة البصرة .

٢ ـ وجدنا الكتاب بالمكتبة .

٧ ـ وضعت الكتاب على طاولة
الاستاذ .

٣ ـ اتحدت الدول الثلاث .

٤ ـ هل وصفت مكانة المرأة ؟

Drill 4. Written. Dictionary drill and completion; translate the perfect.

Imperfect Active	Verbal Noun	Passive Participle	Active Participle	Perfect Active
	استيثاق			
يتّجه				
			موجب	
			واصف	
يثق				
		متّفق		
				وعد
	موجود			
			واضع	
		متّبع		
			والد	وعد

2. Noun-noun apposition

In the Basic text, the phrase اَلدُّوَلُ الأَعْضاءُ 'the member nations' is

a phrase consisting of two nouns, with the second noun <u>in apposition to</u> the

first. In such phrases both nouns refer to the same entity: here "the nations" are "members" and "the members" are "nations". Nouns in apposition agree in case and definiteness.

Apposition is frequently found in phrases consisting of a title and a name, for example

اَلْأُسْتَاذُ كَرِيمٌ	'Professor Karim'
اَلرَّئِيسُ جَمَال عَبْد النَّاصِر	'President Gamal Abd Al-Nasir'

Now do Drill 5.

<u>Drill 5</u>. Written. Combination.

Combine the following pairs of sentences to produce an appositive construction. <u>Ex.</u>

'The famous writer described the political situation in his article.'

وصف الكاتب المشهور الوضع السياسيّ في مقاله .

'The famous writer is Ahmad Karim'

الكاتب المشهور هو احمد كريم .

'The famous writer Ahmad Karim described the political situation in his article.'

وصف الكاتب المشهور احمد كريم الوضع السياسيّ في مقاله .

١ ـ قابلت صديقه امس . صديقه مدير البنك الوطنيّ .

٢ ـ تتعاون الدول مع منظمة الامم المتحدة . الدول اعضاء في المنظمة .

٣ ـ تحدّثت صديقاتك محي عن الامر . صديقاتك طالبات .

٤ ـ تكلّمت مع ابنها . ابنها طبيب .

٥ ـ كتب رسالة الى حبيبته . حبيبته هي نانسي .

٦ ـ رجع ابني من فرنسا امس . ابني الذي رجع هو بشير .

٧ ـ كتب الاديب الكبير كتبا كثيرة . الاديب الكبير هو طه حسين .

٨ ـ اجتمع رئيس الجمهورية بالوزراء . رئيس الجمهورية هو انور جمال .

٩ ـ تحدّثت مع السيد حسين بشير . السيد حسين بشير مساعد المدير .

3. لا of absolute negation

In the sentence

> لا شَكَّ في ذٰلِكَ .   'There is no doubt about that.'

the negative لا is followed immediately by a noun in the <u>accusative case</u>, <u>without the definite article</u>, and <u>without nunation</u>. This لا is called the لا of absolute <u>negation</u> and may be translated as "there is no...(at all), there is not a...," etc. In some instances "there is" is omitted, as for example in لا شَكَّ 'no doubt.' Other examples:

> لا سَلامَ في الْعالَمِ الْيَوْمِ .   'There is no peace in the world today.'
>
> لا أَحَدَ في هٰذِهِ الطّائِرَةِ .   'There is no one on this airplane.'
>
> لا شَيْءَ .   'There is nothing.' or 'Nothing.'

If the noun negated by لا is modified by a following adjective, that adjective may be inflected in any of three ways:

(1) -<u>un</u> (nominative with nunation), since the noun <u>functions as the subject</u> of an equational sentence and is indefinite:

> لا فِكَرَ جَديدةٌ فــي مَقالَتِهِ .   'There are no new ideas in his article.'

or, (2) -<u>an</u> (accusative with nunation), to agree in <u>case</u> with the actual case of the modified noun: لا فِكَرَ جَديدةً 'There are no new ideas'.

or, (3) -<u>a</u> (accusative without nunation), to agree in case and definiteness with the modified noun: لا فِكَرَ جَديدةَ 'there are no new ideas'.

Now do Drill 6.

<u>Drill 6</u>. Negation with لا and translation

'There is no one in the office.'

أ : ليس في المكتب أحدٌ . ←

ط : لا أَحَدَ في المكتب .

71

٦ - ليس في صديق يفضّل نفسه عليك خير .

١ - ليس له عمل .

٧ - ليس هناك حقوق بدون واجبات .

٢ - ليس لنا رأي في هذا الموضوع .

٨ - ليس هناك شيء يعجبها .

٣ - ليس لمشكلتها حلّ .

٩ - ليس هناك نجاح بدون عمل .

٤ - ليس لي علم بالأمر .

٥ - ليس له أهل ولا اصدقاء .

4. The noun كِلا 'both'

The noun كِلا fem. كِلْتا 'both' is used only with a following dual noun in the genitive or with a dual pronoun suffix; it is singular in number. كِلا has the following forms:

	Masculine	Feminine
Nominative	كِلا	كِلْتا
Gen./Acc.	كِلَيْ	كِلْتَيْ

a. **With pronouns.** If __كِلا__ receives the pronoun suffix it must be inflected for case:

وُلِدَ كِلاهُما في دِمَشْقَ .	'They were both born in Damascus.'
ضَحِكَتْ كِلْتاهُما .	'They both laughed.'
هَلْ ذَكَروا كِلْتَيْهِما ؟	'Did they mention both of them?'
نَثِقُ بِكِلَيْهِما .	'We trust both of them.'

b. **With nouns.** Used before nouns, __كِلا__ is not declined:

كِلا الرَّجُلَيْنِ يَتَّفِقُ عَلى ذلِكَ .	'Both men are agreed on that.'
رَأَيْتُ كِلا الرَّجُلَيْنِ وكِلْتا الْمَرْأَتَيْنِ هُناكَ .	'I saw both men and both women there.'
أَشْرَفوا عَلى بِناءِكِلا السَّدَّيْنِ .	'They supervised the building of both dams.'

72

Alternatively, كِلا plus a pronoun suffix may be used in apposition to a dual

noun:

رَأَيْتُ الرَّجُلَيْنِ كِلَيْهِما .	'I saw both men.'
أَكْمَلْنا الْجُمْلَتَيْنِ كِلْتَيْهِما .	'We finished both sentences.'

D. **Comprehension passage**   نُصوصٌ لِلْفَهَمِ — د

Read the following passage and then do Drill 7, which is based on it.

Dag Hammarskjold   داغ همرشولــــــد

they lived   يعتبر داغ همرشولد من أعظم الرجال الذين عاشوا في هذا القرن

realm   ومن أكثرهم نشاطا في مَيْدانِ السياسة الدولية والسلام العالميّ .

Sweden   ولد في بداية القرن في السُّويد لعائلة معروفة ، واثناء الحرب

العالمية الأولى أصح والده رئيسا للوزارة . حصل على الدكتوراه فـي

الاقتصاد السياسيّ من جامعة ستكهولم عندما كان في الخامسة والعشريـن

من عمره ، ثم عمل في وزارة الخارجية . ولما كان في السابعة والاربعين

من عمره أرسلته حكومته الى الامم المتحدة فانتخب سكرتيرا عامّا للمنظمة

بـعد عام واحد .

بـذل داغ همرشولد جهده كله كي يصل الى حلّ لمشكلات الشعوب ،

فاحترمته الدول ـ الكبرى منها والصغرى ـ ووضعت ثقتها فيه . وسـوف

يتحدث التاريخ عن جهود همرشولد لخدمة السلام عندما كان سكرتيرا عامّا

للأمم المتحدة ، وسوف يذكر خاصة ان همرشولد سافر الى الكونغو لحلّ

soldiers   مشكلة الحَرْبِ الأَهْلِيَّةِ هناك وأرسل جُنودَ الأمم المتحدة الى منطقة الشرق   civil war

nation-   الاوسط للمحافظة على السلام بـعد أن أمَّمَ الرئيس عبد الناصر شركة قناة

lized

he died   السويس،وقدسَقَطَتْ طائرة همرشولد اثناء عودته من الكونغو فَماتَ فـى

fell, crashed

lost   السادسة والخمسين من عمره ، وبـذلك فَقَدَ العالم سياسيا مخلصا وانسانا

soldier   كبير القلب وجُنْدِيًّا من أعظم جنود السلام .

73

Drill 7. Written. Question/answer.

Read the comprehension passage and then answer the following questions.

١ – هل كان داغ همرشولد أمريكيا أم أوربيا ؟

٢ – ماذا تعرف عن عائلة همرشولد ؟

٣ – ما هي أعلى شهادة جامعية حصل عليها همر شولد ؟

٤ – هل عمل همر شولد سياسيا قبل أن يعمل في الامم المتحدة ؟

٥ – على أي وظيفة حصل همر شولد في منظمة الامم المتحدة ؟

٦ – لماذا احترمت الدول همر شولد ؟

٧ – هل قدّم همر شولد خدمات للسلام فى الشرق الاوسط ؟

٨ – متى مات همر شولد ؟

E. **General drills**   هـ – التمارين العامة

Drill 8. Written.

Paraphrase each of the following sentences in as many ways as you can, without introducing much change in meaning. **Ex.**

خرج فريد ضاحكا

خرج فريد يضحك

كان فريد يضحك عندما خرج ← خرج فريد وهو يضحك

كان فريد يضحك وهو خارج

كان فريد يضحك عند خروجه

١ – كان غنيا عندما ترك مصر .

٢ – كان فقيرا عندما جاء الى هذه البلاد .

٣ – كان يضحك أثناء تحدّثه الى الطلاب .

٤ – كان رئيس الجمهورية فى فرنسا عندما اجتمع الكونغرس .

٥ – كنت طالبا فى جامعة ولاية يوطا عندما صادقته .

<u>Drill 9.</u> (Also on tape) Perfect ⟶ negative perfect ⟶ imperfect.

'Did your friend return from ⟵ (غدا) ؟ هل عاد صديقك من بيروت ؟ – أ
Beirut?'(tomorrow)

'No he didn't. He might
return tomorrow.' ط – لا، لم يعد. لعلّه يعود غدا .

١ – هل نشر مقالك ؟ غدا

٢ – هل وصل الوزير الى نيويورك ؟ مساء اليوم

٣ – هل كتب الاستاذ كتابا عن القومية العربية ؟ السنة القادمة

٤ – هل درّس الاستاذ لين في جامعة القاهرة ؟ العام القادم

٥ – هل شاهدوا الآثار ؟ الاسبوع القادم

٦ – هل طالبن بمقابلة رئيس الجامعة ؟ غدا

٧ – هل أكملت كتابة المقالة ؟ هذا الاسبوع

٨ – هل اقامت الحكومة المصانع الجديدة ؟ هذا العام

٩ – هل تقدّمت وداد بطلب لمقابلة وزير الخارجية ؟ غدا

١٠ – هل تغيّر الوضع الاقتصادي ؟ قريبا

١١ – هل تعاونت الدولتان في تطوّر الصناعة؟في بداية العام القادم

١٢ – هل انعقد المؤتمر ؟ الاسبوع القادم

١٣ – هل انتقل الموظف الى أسوان ؟ بعد أسبوعين

١٤ – هل ازداد عدد المدارس في هذه المنطقة ؟ قريبا

١٥ – هل قابلتم رئيس الجامعة بشأن هذا الامر ؟ بعد مدة قصيرة

١٦ – هل تمكن من الحصول على وظيفة ؟ ولا شك

<u>Drill 10.</u> Written. Translation.

Translate the following sentences into Arabic.

1. Ṭāhā Ḥusayn was one of the greatest contemporary literary figures.

75

2. I have a friend who worked in many positions, including teaching in secondary schools.

3. There are big cities in Egypt, but there are also small villages. Egyptian villages are among the poorest in the Middle East.

4. The Egyptian museum is distinguished by the fact that it is the largest in the Arab World, and the fact that its ruins are among the most ancient.

5. My son drew a picture of me in which I have a large head, two small eyes, two long ears and one hand. When my husband returned from work, he looked at the picture and recognized (knew) me.

6. The foreign minister and his friend were found guilty (were sentenced) in the Middle East oil matter. The people were convinced by this that the rights of each man are equal to the rights of his brother.

<u>Drill 11</u>. Vocabulary.

Rewrite the sentences below substituting for the underlined words synonyms from the following list; make all necessary changes:

خرجت ، بناء ، انصرفت ، أخذت ، يؤسس ، يجلس ، بيت

١ ــ يريد السياسيّ ان <u>ينشئ</u> حزبا جديدا .

٢ ــ <u>ذهبت</u> الوالدة بابنها الصغير الى الطبيب .

٣ ــ <u>دار</u> كريم مفتوحة في كل وقت لكل غريب محتاج .

76

أ ـ الجُمَلُ التَّمهيديَّة

A. <u>Preparatory sentences</u>

كتاب عن الاغاني العربية الحديثة

<u>A Book about Modern Arabic Songs</u>

١ ـ أَلَّفَ باحِثٌ غربي معروف كتاباً عن الأغاني العربية الحديثة تمّ طَبْعُهُ في لندن .

1 A well-known western <u>researcher</u> has <u>written</u> a book about modern Arabic <u>songs</u> which was <u>printed</u> in London.

أَلَّفَ ـ تَأْليفٌ   II to compose, write

باحِثٌ ـ ون   researcher

أُغْنِيَةٌ ـ ات ، أغانٍ   song

طَبَعَ ـَ ، طَبْعٌ   to print

تمّ ـِ   to be completed; to take place

٢ ـ يُعَدّ هذا الكتاب اليوم من أهمّ المَصادِرِ الاجنبيّة لدراسة الاغنية الحديثة وَيَوَدّ كثير من الناس ان يحصلوا عليه .

2 This book <u>is considered</u> today one of the most important foreign <u>sources</u> for the study of modern song, and many people <u>wish</u> to obtain it.

عَدَّ ـُ ، عَدّ   to count, compute; (with two acc.) to consider (s.th.) to be (s.th.)

مَصْدَرٌ ـ مَصادِرُ   origin; source

وَدَّ ـَ ، وُدّ   to wish, want, desire

٣ ـ يقول المؤلّف إن الاغاني العربية الحديثة تُصَوِّرُ الحياة الاجتماعية والادبية في العالم العربي الى حدّ بعيد .

3 The author says that to a great extent modern Arabic songs <u>depict</u> social and literary life in the Arabic world.

صَوَّرَ ، تَصْويرٌ   II to paint, draw; to picture, depict, portray

٤ ـ يعتبر المؤلّف امّ كُلثوم وفَيْروز ومُحَمَّد عَبْد الوَهّاب وفَريد الأَطْرَش من اشهر المُغَنّينَ العرب الذين عاشوا في هذا القرن وَوَهَبوا حياتهم للفنّ .

4 The author considers Umm Kulthoum, Fairouz, Muhammad Abd Al-Wahhab and Farid Al-Atrash among the most famous Arab <u>singers</u> who have <u>lived</u> in this century and who have <u>dedicated</u> their lives to art.

مُغَنٍّ ـ مُغَنّونَ (مُغَنِّيَةٌ ـ ات) singer, vocalist

عاشَ ـُ ، عَيْشَةٌ ، مَعيشٌ to live, be alive

وَهَبَ يَهَبُ ، هِبَةٌ ، وَهْبٌ to give, grant, present (s.o.) (s.th.), endow (s.o.) (with s.th.)

٥ ـ يَقول المؤلّف فى نِهاية الكتاب : 5. The author says at the end of the book:

نِهايَةٌ ـ ات end, termination

أ ـ إنّ مكانة أمّ كُلثوم كانت اعلى من مكانة أيِّ مغنّية اخرى ، وانّ مدرسة للغناءِ ماتَت بِمَوْتِ أمّ كُلثوم . a. that the position of Umm Kulthoum is greater than that of any other singer, and that a school of singing died with the death of 'Umm Kulthoum.

أيّ (in a question) which? what?; (in a statement) any, any...at all; (with negative) not any; no

مات ـُ ، مَوْتٌ to die

ب ـ انّ اغنية " زوروني كُلّ سَنَة مَرَّةً " من اجمل الاغاني التى تغنّيها فَيْروز . b. that " زوروني كُلّ سَنَة مَرَّةً " ["Visit me once every year"] is one of Fairouz's most beautiful songs.

مَرَّةٌ ـ ات one time; once

ج ـ انّ كثيرا من شُعَراءِ العَرب المعاصرين ألّفوا اغاني لمحمّد عبد الوهّاب . c. that many of the contemporary Arab poets have composed songs for Muhammad Abd Al-Wahhab.

شاعِرٌ ـ شُعَراءُ poet

د ـ انّ الاغاني المصرية انتشرت فى الدول العربية كلّها ، ممّا يَدُلُّ دَلالَةً واضِحَةً على تقدّم الاغنية المصرية الحديثة . d. that Egyptian songs have spread over all Arab countries, a thing which clearly indicates the advanced state of modern Egyptian song.

78

دَلَّ ــُـ دَلالَةً (على)	to show, point (to), indicate, give evidence (of)
وَضَحَ يَضَحُ ، وُضوحٌ	to be, become clear; to come to light

هـ ــ انّ بعض هذه الاغاني العربية يؤلَّف بالفصحى وبعضها الآخر يؤلَّف بالعامية .	e. that some of these Arabic songs are composed in the literary language and some in the colloquial.

المفردات الإضافيّة	Additional vocabulary

٦ ــ لا تزال الشعوب العربية تطالب بالوَحْدَةِ . ولا أشكُّ في أنّها سَتَحُلُّ معظم مشاكلها قريبًا .	The Arab people are still demanding __unity__. And I do not __doubt__ that they __will__ soon __solve__ most of their problems.

وَحْدَةٌ ــ ات	unity, union, unit
شَكَّ ــُـ ، شَكٌّ (في ، بـ)	to doubt, suspect, question
حَلَّ ــُـ ، حَلٌّ	to solve, resolve; to disband, dissolve, break up

ب ــ النص الاساسي

ابو الفرج الاصبهاني

ابو الفرج الاصبهاني من اشهر الادباء العرب . ولد فى اصبهان فى نهاية القرن التاسع الميلاديّ . عاش اكثر حياته فى بغداد ودرس هناك الادب والشعر والتاريخ . ثمّ اتّصل بِسَيْفِ الدَوْلَةِ الحَمْدانِي أَميــــرِ [Prince] حَلَبَ الذي استقبله بكلّ ترحيب واكرام . مات ابو الفرج فى بغداد فى [Aleppo] النصف الثانى من القرن العاشر وقد وهب حياته للبحث والتأليف .

الّف ابو الفرج كتبا كثيرة لكنّ اشهرها هو " الاغاني " الذي يُعَدّ من اهمّ ما ألّف فى القرن العاشر وهو مصدر اساسيّ يودّ الباحثون فى تاريخ الادب العربى ان يحصلوا عليه . تمّ تأليف الكتاب فى خمسين عاما ، وقد جمع المؤلَّف فيه اخبار المغنيين والادباء والشعراء القدماء منهم والمعاصرين له . ولكتاب " الاغاني " اهمّيّة كبرى لانه يصوّر حياة العرب الاجتماعية والادبيّة فى العَصْرِ الجاهِليّ [Pre-Islamic era] حتى نهاية القرن التاسع

79

Būlāq   طبع كتاب الاغاني لاوّل مرّة في بولاق بمصر في النصف الثاني

volume   من القرن التاسع عشر ، وهو عشرون جُزْءًا كلّها جميلة اللغة سهلـة

الاسلوب ۰

B. **Basic text**

Abū Al-Faraj Al-Iṣbahānī

Abū Al-Faraj Al-Isbahānī is one of the most famous of Arab men of letters.
He was born in Isfahan at the end of the ninth century A.D. He lived most of
his life in Baghdad and studied there literature, poetry, and history. Then he
came in contact with Sayf Al-Dawla Al-Ḥamdānī, Prince of Aleppo, who received
him with the warmest of welcomes and honor. Abū Al-Faraj died in Baghdad in
the second half of the tenth century, having dedicated his life to research and
writing.

Abū Al-Faraj wrote many books, but the most famous of them is Kitāb al-Aghānī,
("The Book of Songs") which is considered one of the most important things composed in the tenth century; it is a basic source, one that researchers in the
history of Arabic literature desire to acquire. The composition of the book was
completed in fifty years; the author collected in it information about singers,
writers and poets both ancient and contemporary to him. Kitāb al-Aghānī is a
book of major importance because it depicts the social and literary life of the
Arabs from the Pre-Islamic era to the end of the ninth century, and because it
gives clear evidence of the development of literary styles. In his book the
author cites from ancient Arabic poetry things which have not been mentioned
by any other writer.

Kitāb al-Aghānī was printed for the first time in Būlāq in Egypt in the second half of the nineteenth century; it is in twenty volumes, all of them

beautiful in language and easy in style.

C. <u>Grammar and drills</u>   ج - القواعد والتمارين

1. Doubled verbs: Form I

2. Doubled roots: Phonological rules

3. Defective nouns and adjectives

4. Verbs with two accusatives: Summary

5. Optional وَ 'and' in adjective strings

1. <u>Doubled verbs: Form I</u>

In a number of Arabic verbs the second and third radicals are identical.

For example, the verb يَدُلّ 'he points' has the root <u>DLL</u>, with the second

and third radicals <u>L</u>; this kind of root is symbolized by FDD ("First, Doubled,

Doubled"). Verbs with double roots are called <u>doubled verbs</u>.

Doubled verbs have two stems, a regular one if the inflectional suffix

begins with a consonant (as in يَدْلُلْنَ 'they (f.p.) point', <u>ya-dlul-na</u>, just

like يَدْرُسْنَ 'they (f.p.) study', <u>ya-drus-na)</u>, and a <u>doubled</u> one if the suffix

begins with a vowel (as in يَدُلّ 'he points', <u>ya-dull-u</u>). A doubled stem is

one where the second and third radicals are not separated by a vowel. The stems

for the two tenses of Form I verbs are illustrated below:

	Pattern	Example	
Perfect tense:			
Regular stem	FaDvD-	دَلَلْتُ	'I pointed'
Doubled stem	FaDD-	دَلَّ	'he pointed'
Imperfect tense:			
Regular stem	-FDvD-	يَدْلُلْنَ	'they (f.p.) point'
Doubled stem	-FvDD-	يَدُلّ	'he points'

As stated above, the <u>regular stem occurs before suffixes beginning with a consonant</u> (t- or n-), and the <u>doubled stem occurs before vowels</u> (-a, -aa, -u, -uu). If there is no inflectional suffix (indicated in the writing system with <u>sukuun</u> °), as in the jussive or imperative, there is a choice between using the regular stem or, usually, substituting the corresponding subjunctive form (without the تَ prefix in the imperative, of course). Both of these are given in the chart below, which illustrates the full conjugation of the doubled verb دَلَّ 'to point, indicate'.

	PERFECT	IMPERFECT			
		Indicative	Subjunctive	Jussive	Imperative
3 MS	دَلَّ	يَدُلُّ	يَدُلَّ	يَدْلُلْ / يَدُلَّ	
FS	دَلَّتْ	تَدُلُّ	تَدُلَّ	تَدْلُلْ / تَدُلَّ	
2 MS	دَلَلْتَ	تَدُلُّ	تَدُلَّ	تَدْلُلْ / تَدُلَّ	أُدْلُلْ / دُلَّ
FS	دَلَلْتِ	تَدُلِّينَ	تَدُلِّي	تَدُلِّي	دُلِّي
1 S	دَلَلْتُ	أَدُلُّ	أَدُلَّ	أَدْلُلْ / أَدُلَّ	
3 MD	دَلَّا	يَدُلَّانِ	يَدُلَّا	يَدُلَّا	
FD	دَلَّتَا	تَدُلَّانِ	تَدُلَّا	تَدُلَّا	
2 D	دَلَلْتُمَا	تَدُلَّانِ	تَدُلَّا	تَدُلَّا	دُلَّا
3 MP	دَلُّوا	يَدُلُّونَ	يَدُلُّوا	يَدُلُّوا	
FP	دَلَلْنَ	يَدْلُلْنَ	يَدْلُلْنَ	يَدْلُلْنَ	
2 MP	دَلَلْتُمْ	تَدُلُّونَ	تَدُلُّوا	تَدُلُّوا	دُلُّوا
FP	دَلَلْتُنَّ	تَدْلُلْنَ	تَدْلُلْنَ	تَدْلُلْنَ	أُدْلُلْنَ
1 P	دَلَلْنَا	نَدُلُّ	نَدُلَّ	نَدْلُلْ / نَدُلَّ	

Active Participle: دَالّ   'pointing, indicating'

Passive Participle: مَدْلُول   'indicated'

Verbal Noun: دَلَالَة   'indicating, indication'

The passive participles of doubled verbs are regular; the active participle

pattern for all Form I verbs, however, is FaaDD (<u>the i has been lost because</u>
<u>the inflectional suffix</u> begins with a vowel).

As with all Form I verbs, there is a great variety of verbal noun patterns,
some verbs having more than one. All verbal noun patterns of doubled verbs, however, are regular in that they do not take any special shape because they are
based on doubled roots. (Note, for example, the noun عَدَد 'number' which has
the regular stem ʕadad- even though a vowel follows.) In the Arabic writing
system two contiguous identical consonants are, of course, written as one letter
with <u>shadda</u>, so that the verbal noun pattern FaDD, which is exactly parallel to
FaML, is written with two consonant letters, like عَدّ 'counting' which is parallel
to فَتْح 'opening; conquest'.

Now do Drill 1.

The verb دَلّ has the stem vowel <u>a</u> in the perfect (as seen in the 1.s. دَلَلْتُ
'I pointed', stem dalal-) and the stem vowel <u>u</u> in the imperfect. This is true
of most Form I doubled verbs, and most of these are also transitive. There are
two other types, both of which are illustrated in this lesson. One is تَمّ
'to be completed', which has <u>a</u> in the perfect and <u>i</u> in the imperfect; most such
verbs are intransitive. The patterns for the regular and doubled stems of this
type of verb are

	Pattern	Example
Perfect: Regular stem	FaDaD-	تَمَمْنَ 'they (f.p.) were completed')
Doubled stem	FaDD-	تَمّ 'it was completed'
Imperfect: Regular stem	-FDiD-	يَتْمِمْنَ 'they (f.p.) will be completed')
Doubled stem	-FiDD-	يَتِمّ 'it will be completed'

(The verb تَمَّ itself occurs only in the third person masculine singular or feminine singular. The feminine plural, which is possible in poetry in case of personification, is given above for purposes of illustration.)

The final type has <u>i</u> in the perfect and <u>a</u> in the imperfect, like وَدَّ 'to wish, want; to love, like,' and ظَلَّ 'to continue, keep doing s.th'. The patterns for this type are

	Pattern	Example	
Perfect tense: Regular stem	FaDiD-	وَدِدْتُ	'I wished'
Doubled stem	FaDD-	وَدَّ	'he wished'
Imperfect tense: Regular stem	-FDaD-	يَوْدَدْنَ	'they (f.p.) wish'
Doubled stem	-FaDD-	يَوَدُّ	'he wishes'

The three types of stem-vowel patterns are compared below:

Perfect	Imperfect	Example	
a	u	دَلَّ — يَدُلُّ	'to point'
a	i	تَمَّ — يَتِمُّ	'to be completed'
i	a	وَدَّ — يَوَدُّ	'to wish'
		(وَدِدْتُ	'I wished')

Now do Drill 2.

Passive voice of doubled verbs.

Doubled verbs likewise have two stems in the passive voice. The stems are the same as for the active voice, the only difference being the use of the passive vowel patterns <u>u</u> - <u>i</u> (perfect passive) and <u>u</u> - <u>a</u> (imperfect passive) instead of the various active patterns.

84

The stems are:

Passive Voice	Pattern	Example	
Perfect tense:			
Regular stem	FuDiD-	عُدِدْتُ	'I was considered'
Doubled stem	FuDD-	عُدَّ	'he was considered'
Imperfect tense:			
Regular stem	-FDaD-	يُعْدَدْنَ	'they (f.p.) are considered'
Doubled stem	-FaDD-	يُعَدَّ	'he is considered'

Except for the difference in vowel pattern, passive doubled verbs are conjugated just like active ones. (There is, of course, no passive imperative.)

The following chart summarizes the principal parts of the Form I doubled verbs that we have had so far including حَلَّ ـُ 'to solve' and شَكَّ ـُ في 'to doubt, suspect' whose verbal nouns we have had:

	حَلَّ	شَكَّ	دَلَّ	عَدَّ	تَمَّ	ظَلَّ	وَدَّ
Perfect 3MS tense 1 S	حَلَّ / حَلَلْتُ	شَكَّ / شَكَكْتُ	دَلَّ / دَلَلْتُ	عَدَّ / عَدَدْتُ	تَمَّ / —	ظَلَّ / ظَلِلْتُ	وَدَّ / وَدِدْتُ
Imperfect tense 3 MS 3 FP	يَحُلُّ / يَحْلُلْنَ	يَشُكُّ / يَشْكُكْنَ	يَدُلُّ / يَدْلُلْنَ	يَعُدُّ / يَعْدُدْنَ	يَتِمُّ / —	يَظَلُّ / يَظْلَلْنَ	يَوَدُّ / يَوْدَدْنَ
Act. part.	حَالٌّ	شَاكٌّ	دَالٌّ	عَادٌّ	تَامٌّ	ظَالٌّ	وَادٌّ
Pass. part.	مَحْلُولٌ	مَشْكُوكٌ فِيهِ	مَدْلُولٌ	مَعْدُودٌ	—	—	—
Verbal noun	حَلٌّ	شَكٌّ	دَلَالَةٌ	عَدٌّ	تَمَامٌ	ظَلٌّ ، ظُلُولٌ	وُدٌّ

When doubled verbs are introduced in future vocabularies the perfect stem vowel is to be understood to be a unless the 1 S perfect form is given, e.g.

وَدَّ (وَدِدْتُ) ـَ ، وُدٌّ   to wish, want

As a general rule, the perfect stem vowel is <u>i</u> when the imperfect stem vowel is <u>a</u>.

Now do Drill 3.

<u>Drill 1</u>. (On tape) Conjugation: FaDaD.

<u>Drill 2</u>. (On tape) Conjugation: FaDiD.

<u>Drill 3</u>. Written.

Rewrite the verb in parenthesis in the passive, making all necessary changes.

١ ــ (عدّ) الكويت من أغنى الدول العربية بالزيت ٠

٢ ــ في مصر أديبات (عدّ) من أشهر الأديبات العربيّات ٠

٣ ــ لم (عدّ) هذا الكتاب هامّا عندما نشر ، لكنّه (عدّ) الآن من أهم الكتب ٠

٤ ــ لم (حلّ) المشكلة الى الآن ، لعلّها (حلّ) قريبا ٠

٥ ــ لن (حلّ) مشكلاتنا بدون التعاون التام ٠

2. Doubled roots: Phonological rules

This note is provided as supplementary to the basic information given in note 1 above; it provides an explanation of the changes peculiar to doubled roots in terms of pronunciation, or phonological rules. As usual, F means "first radical"; M means "second radical"; L, "third radical"; D, "either of two identical radicals"; C, "any consonant"; and v, "any vowel".

This discussion deals exclusively with verbs and adjectives; it does not involve nouns in general.

The basic assumption is that <u>there is a tendency for two identical con-sonants separated by a short vowel to cluster together</u>; thus DvD ⟶ DD. We must also bear in mind the fact that <u>a sequence of three consonants in a row</u> (e.g. <u>ddn</u>) <u>is impossible in Arabic</u>. The following rules must be applied in the order given; that is, Rule D2 applies only when the condition for Rule D1 is not satisfied; and Rule D3 applies when the conditions for Rule D1 and Rule D2 do not apply.

<u>Rule D1</u>. If the second D is not followed by a vowel, there is <u>no change</u>. (Period . signifies end of word.)

86

Formula	DvDC DvD. } → no change		
Examples	ᶜadadtu	عَدَدْتُ	'I counted'
	wadidtu	وَدِدْتُ	'I wished'
	yaᶜdudna	يَعْدُدْنَ	'they (f.p.) count'
	yawdadna	يَوْدَدْنَ	'they (f.p.) wish'
	yaᶜdud.	لَمْ يَعْدُدْ (لَمْ يَعُدَّ)	'he did not count'
	yawdad.	لَمْ يَوْدَدْ (لَمْ يَوَدَّ)	'he did not wish'

There is likewise no change if one of the D's is itself doubled, as in

Form II and V verbs (قَرَّرَ II 'to decide', or تَعَدَّدَ V 'to be numerous').

Rule D2. If the first D is immediately preceded by a consonant, that D switches

places with the following vowel.

Formula	CDvDv	→	CvDDv	
Examples	yaᶜ<u>d</u>udu	→	yaᶜ<u>u</u>ddu	يَعُدُّ 'he counts'
	yaw<u>d</u>adu	→	yaw<u>a</u>ddu	يَوَدُّ 'he wishes'
	?aj<u>d</u>adu	→	?aj<u>a</u>ddu	أَجَدُّ 'newer'
	?aᶜ<u>z</u>izaa?u	→	?aᶜ<u>i</u>zzaa?u	أَعِزَّاءُ 'dear' (p.)
	?aṭ<u>b</u>ibaa?u	→	?aṭ<u>i</u>bbaa?u	أَطِبَّاءُ 'doctors'

Notes: (1) أَجَدُّ exemplifies the elative pattern for doubled roots:

Strong root	?aFMaLu (elative)
Doubled root	?aFDaDu → ?aFaDDu (elative)

(2) أَعِزَّاءُ exemplifies the ?aFMiLaa?u broken plural pattern for

doubled roots (see L. 13, C. 3, pattern 12):

Strong root	FaMiil → ?aFMiLaa?
Doubled root	FaDiiD → ?aFDiDaa? → ?aFiDDaa?u

87

<u>Rule D3</u>. <u>A short vowel between the two identical consonants is dropped.</u>

Formula	vDvDv	→	vDDv		
Examples	^cadada	→	^cadda	عَدَّ	'he counted'
	wadida	→	wadda	وَدَّ	'he wished'
	labuba	→	labba	لَبَّ	'he became intelligent'
	taamimun	→	taammun	تامٌّ	'complete'

Summary chart of changes:

vDvDv → vDDv	عَدَّ	'he counted'
CDvDv → CvDDv	يَعُدُّ	'he counts'
	أَجَدُّ	'newer'

3. <u>Defective nouns and adjectives</u>

Inflectional types of nouns and adjectives include triptotes, diptotes, duals, sound plurals, indeclinables and invariables; these have all been described. The last of the inflectional types is a group known as <u>defective</u> nouns and adjectives. These words take nunation, but have only two case endings (nominative and genitive being the same). There are both singular and plural defectives; the latter do not take nunation in the accusative indefinite. The forms of the singular noun مُغَنٍّ 'singer' and the plural noun أَغانٍ 'songs' are shown below as examples:

		Indefinite			Definite
<u>Singular</u>	Nom./Gen.	مُغَنٍّ	'singer'		اَلْمُغَنِّي
	Acc.	مُغَنِّيًا			اَلْمُغَنِّيَ
<u>Plural</u>	Nom./Gen.	أَغانٍ	'songs'		اَلْأَغاني
	Acc.	أَغانِيَ			اَلْأَغانِيَ

88

Note the following points:

(1) The nominative and genitive case forms are always identical, ending in ٍ -in when indefinite and ي ii when definite.

(2) The accusative forms are all quite regular; that is, they are exactly like non-defective words of the same pattern, with Y serving as the last radi- cal. For example, the accusative مُغَنِّيًا (root G N Y is exactly like the accusative مُدَرِّسًا 'teacher' (root D R S), as the diagram below shows:

| mu | d | a | rr | i | s | an |
| mu | ġ | a | nn | i | y | an |

(3) The plural accusative indefinite forms also are regular in not tak- ing nunation since plural defectives all have diptote patterns. Thus the accu- sative indefinite أَغَانِيَ 'songs' is exactly like the accusative indefinite of the diptote أَجَانِبَ 'foreigners', which has the same pattern:

| ?a | j | aa | n | i | b | a |
| ?a | ġ | aa | n | i | y | a |

It is the nominative/genitive indefinite forms of plural defectives which are irregular, since they take nunation even though they have diptote patterns.

Defectives result when a root with last radical W or Y is combined with a pattern which has stem vowel i . To show how this works, let us consider two roots combined with the pattern FaaMiL. (This is the pattern for ordinal numbers, among other things.) The root X M S (a strong root, with no W or Y), combined with this pattern, gives the stem xaamis- خَامِس 'fifth', and regu- lar case endings and nunation can be added to this stem with no problem. The root θ N Y however, combined with the same pattern, gives the stem θaaniy- 'second'. If we added the regular case endings and nunation to this stem the following forms would result:

89

	Indefinite	Definite
Nom.	(θaan<u>iyun</u>)	(ʔaθθaan<u>iyu</u>)
Gen.	(θaan<u>iyin</u>)	(ʔaθθaan<u>iyi</u>)
Acc.	θaaniyan	ʔaθθaaniya

The forms in parentheses are not possible Arabic words, as they contain sequences (underlined above) which are not permitted by the phonological structure of the language. Such sequences are automatically changed as follows:

-iyun ⎫ → -in	-iyu ⎫ → -ii
-iyin ⎭	-iyi ⎭

Thus both θaan<u>iyun</u> (nominative) and θaan<u>iyin</u> (genitive) become θaanin ثانٍ , and both ʔaθθaan<u>iyu</u> and ʔaθθaan<u>iyi</u> become ʔaθθaanii اَلثَّانِي • The sequences <u>-iyan</u> and <u>-iya</u>, which occur in the accusative, are permitted, and the accusative forms therefore remain unchanged. Following is a list of the defective nouns and adjectives which have occurred so far:

Singulars		Plurals	
ثانٍ	'second'	أَغانٍ	'songs'
عالٍ	'high'	كَراسٍ	'chairs'
جاءٍ	'coming'	لَيالٍ	'nights'
مُغَنٍّ	'singer'		
مُساوٍ	'equal'		

The <u>feminine</u> forms corresponding to masculine defectives are regular. This is so because when the feminine suffix ة —_ -a(t)- is added to a stem ending in -iy-, the resulting sequence -iya(t)- is a permissible one: thus the feminine stem of عالٍ (stem ʕaaliy-) is ʕaaliya(t)- عالِيَة , and endings may be added to this as to any feminine stem ending in ة . Contrast the

90

masculine and feminine forms of عالٍ 'high' below:

Indefinite		
	Masculine	Feminine
Nom.	عالٍ	عالِيَةٌ
Gen.		عالِيَةٍ
Acc.	عالِيًا	عالِيَةً
Definite		
Nom.	العالي	العالِيَةُ
Gen.		العالِيَةِ
Acc.	العالِيَ	العالِيَةَ

The masculine <u>dual</u> forms are also regular, for the same reasons. (The feminine duals are formed regularly from the feminine singular.)

	Masculine	Feminine
Nom.	عالِيانِ	عالِيَتانِ
Gen./Acc.	عالِيَيْنِ	عالِيَتَيْنِ

The <u>masculine sound plural</u> forms, however, are again the result of regular phonological changes. To illustrate, let us take the (singular) stem <u>muġanniy-</u> 'singer', and add to it the masculine sound plural endings:

Nom.	(muġann<u>iyuu</u>na)
Gen./Acc.	(muġann<u>iyii</u>na)

These forms are not possible, as they contain the unpermitted sequences <u>-iyuu-</u> and <u>-iyii-</u>. Such sequences are automatically changed, as follows:

-iyuu-	⟶	-uu-
-iyii-	⟶	-ii-

91

Thus the actual sound plural forms are:

Nom.	muġannuuna	مُغَنّونَ
Gen./Acc.	muġanniina	مُغَنّينَ

The feminine sound plurals are formed regularly from the feminine singular:

Nom.	مُغَنِّياتٌ
Gen./Acc.	مُغَنِّياتٍ

Now do Drills 4 and 5.

Note that the citation form of defective nouns and adjectives is the nominative singular indefinite, e.g. مُغَنٍّ 'singer', عالٍ 'high'.

<u>Drill 4</u>. Written. Definite ━► indefinite.

Make the underlined expressions indefinite; then vocalize them.

١ ــ تزوّجت صديقتي <u>المغنّي اللبناني</u> .

٢ ــ تحدّثت ايضا الى <u>الطالب الثاني</u> .

٣ ــ المتحف الوطنيّ هو <u>البناء العالي</u> .

٤ ــ سمعت <u>الاغاني الجديدة</u> التي تغنّيها فيّروز .

٥ ــ قرأت كتابا عن <u>المغنّي اللبناني</u> الذي رحل الى مصر .

٦ ــ ألّفت كتابا عنوانه " <u>الليالي الثلاث</u> " .

٧ ــ استمعنا لمحاضرة عن <u>السدّ المساوي</u> في اهميته لسدّ أسوان .

<u>Drill 5</u>. Written.

Rewrite the words in parentheses in their correct form.

١ ــ من ال (مغنّ) الذي حضر الحفلة ؟

٢ ــ كان في الحفلة (مغنّ) كثيرون .

٣ ــ صديقي أمريكيّ ، لكنه يعرف شيئا عن ال (أغان) العربية .

٤ ــ ترك ابي بيروت بعد ثلاث (ليلة) حاملا هدايا كثيرة في يده .

٥ ـ قرأت المقالة الأولى أمس ، وسأقرأ المقالة (ثان) اليوم •

٦ ـ أقامت مصر سدًّا (عال) ، وهو قريب من أسوان •

٧ ـ سمعت(أغان) أمريكيّة كثيرة ، وقد أعجبني بعضها •

٨ ـ لعلّ الـ (مغنّ) اللبنانية فَيْروز أشهر الـ (مغنّ) العربيّات، ولعلّ الـ (مغنّ) المصريّ عَبْدُ الوَهّاب أشهر الـ (مغنّ) العرب •

٩ ـ نساء أمريكا (مساو) للرجال في الحقوق ، لكنّ النساء في بعض الدول لسن (مساو) للرجال •

١٠ ـ عَبْدُ الحَليم حافِظ وفَريد الأَطْرَش (مغنّ) مشهوران •

١١ ـ كانت أُمّ كُلْثوم وأَسْمَهان (مغنّ) من أشهر (مغنّ) اللواتـــي عرفهنّ العالم العربيّ •

١٢ ـ اعجبتني (أغنية) نانسي سيناترا !

١٣ ـ هذه المقالة هامّة جدًّا ، وهاتان (مساو) لها في الاهمية •

4. Verbs with two accusatives: Summary

Verbs that take two accusatives are of three types: (1) verbs of giving, after which the first accusative is the recipient (indirect object) and the second accusative is the thing given (direct object), e.g.

مَنَحوا الطُّلّابَ حَقَّ الانْتِخابِ •	'They granted students the right to vote.'

(2) verbs of considering where the referent of the first accusative is considered to be equivalent to what is designated by the second accusative, e.g.

اعْتَبَروا وليدا قائِدًا عَظيمًا •	'They considered Walid a great leader.'

and (3) verbs of transforming, where the referent of the first accusative is caused to become what is designated by the second accusative, as in

انْتَخَبوا كَريمًا رَئيسًا •	'They elected Karim president.'

A few comments will be given about each of these types. The term "accusative" will apply here to nouns, pronouns and adjectives; in type (2) the second accusative may be a prepositional phrase, e.g.

اِعْتَبَرُوهُ مِنْ أَعْظَمِ الْأُدَبَاءِ .	'They considered him one of the greatest writers.'

(1) <u>Verbs of giving</u>. In addition to مَنَحَ 'to grant' there are various verbs meaning "to give", such as وَهَبَ – يَهَبُ 'to give, donate'. وَهَبَ differs from مَنَحَ in that a variation from the two-accusative construction is often encountered; in addition to the sentence

وَهَبَ بِلَادَهُ حَيَاتَهُ .	'He gave his country his life.'

one can also say

وَهَبَ حَيَاتَهُ لِبِلَادِهِ .	'He gave his life for ("to") his country.'

Another example:

وَهَبُوا الْمُرَاسِلَ سَيَّارَةً .	'They gave the reporter a car.'
وَهَبُوا سَيَّارَةً لِلْمُرَاسِلِ .	'They gave a car to the reporter.'

Verbs that, like وَهَبَ , can take either two accusatives or an accusative object and a prepositional phrase with لِ will be identified in the vocabularies by the notation "(هِ or لِ)".

(2) <u>Verbs of considering</u> include verbs such as:

اِعْتَبَرَ	'to consider' (s.o.) (s.th.)
عَدَّ	'to consider' (s.o.) (s.th.)
رَأَى	'to regard, consider' (s.o.) as (s.th.)
وَجَدَ	'to find' (s.o.) (to be) (s.th.)
عَرَفَ	'to know' (s.o.) as (s.th.)

(Notice that اِعْتَقَدَ is not a verb of considering.) In the sentence

نَعْتَبِرُها أَكْثَرَ الطُّلابِ وَالطّالِباتِ إِخْلاصًا .	'We consider her the sincerest of all the students.'

the two accusatives are equivalent to

هِيَ أَكْثَرُ الطُّلابِ وَالطّالِباتِ إِخْلاصًا .	'She is the sincerest of all the students.'

That is to day that after <u>verbs of considering</u> the two accusatives stand in a relationship to each other of subject and predicate in an equational sentence.

(3) <u>Verbs of transforming</u> include

عَيَّنَ	'to appoint' (s.o.) (s.th.)
جَعَلَ	'to make' (s.o.) (s.th.)
اِنْتَخَبَ	'to elect' (s.o.) (s.th.)

These verbs cause something (the first accusative) to change to something different (the second accusative), as in

اِنْتَخَبوا كَريمًا رَئيسًا .	'They elected Karim president.'

This sentence is equivalent to

أَصْبَحَ كَريمٌ رَئيسًا نَتيجةً لِاَنْتِخابِهِمْ .	'Karim became president as a result of their election.'

<u>Passive of verbs with two accusatives</u>. Any of the constructions above can be made passive by (a) omitting the subject of the active verb, as usual; (b) making the first accusative the subject of the passive verb. The second accusative (or prepositional phrase in its place) remains unchanged. Illustrations:

95

(1) Verbs of giving:

Active: وَهَبَتْ أَوْلادَها مِئَةَ رِيالٍ .	'She gave her children a hundred rials.'
Passive: وُهِبَ أَوْلادُها مِئَةَ رِيالٍ .	'Her children were given a hundred rials.'

Active: وَهَبَتْ مِئَةَ رِيالٍ لِأَوْلادِها .	'She gave a hundred rials to her children.'
Passive: وُهِبَتْ مِئَةُ رِيالٍ لِأَوْلادِها .	'A hundred rials were given to her children.'

(2) Verbs of considering:

Active: عَدَدْنا الْمَلِكَ فَيْصَل مِنْ أَعْظَمِ الْقُوّادِ الْعَرَبِ .	'We considered King Faisal one of the greatest Arab leaders.'
Passive: عُدَّ الْمَلِكُ فَيْصَل مِنْ أَعْظَمِ الْقُوّادِ الْعَرَبِ .	'King Faisal was considered one of the greatest Arab leaders.'

(3) Verbs of transforming:

Active: عَيَّنوهُ وَزيرًا أَمْسِ .	'They appointed him minister yesterday.'
Passive: عُيِّنَ وَزيرًا أَمْسِ .	'He was appointed minister yesterday.'

Now do Drills 6 and 7.

Drill 6. Written. Verbs with two accusatives.

1. Paraphrase the following sentences by changing the underlined verb and making any other necessary changes. Ex.

96

'Some people consider Arabic to be one of the most beautiful of languages.'

يعتبر بعض الناس اللغة العربية من أجمل اللغات . ←

'Some people believe that Arabic is one of the most beautiful of languages.'

يعتقد بعض الناس أنّ اللغة العربية من أجمل اللغات .

١ ــ تعتبر منظمة الامم المتحدة من أهم المنظمات العالمية .

٢ ــ يُعَدُّ أبو الْفَرَج الْإِصْبهاني من أعظم الأدباء العرب الذين عاشوا فى القرن التاسع .

٣ ــ منحت مصر نساءها حق العمل .

٤ ــ اعتبر جامعة هارفارد من أعظم الجامعات الأمريكيّة .

٥ ــ اعتقد ان الحصول على الدكتوراه من هذه الجامعة مشكلة .

٦ ــ عينها المدير مساعدة له .

٧ ــ اصبح رئيسا للجمهوريّة نتيجة للانتخابات الأخيرة .

Drill 7. Written.

From the verbs in parentheses choose the most appropriate one to fill in the blank in each of the following sentences:

١ ــ هل ـــ موريتانيا دولة عربية ؟   (تمنـــح، تقع ، تعدّ)

٢ ــ أحبّته و ـــ قلبها .   (عينته ، تزوجته ، وهبته)

٣ ــ ـــ الشعب رئيسا جديدا للجمهورية .   (انتخب ، عيّن ، منح)

٤ ــ ـــ الوزير رئيسا للجامعة .   (انتخب ، عيّن ، وهب)

٥ ــ ـــ أنّ قناة السويس أهم من قناة بناما .(أعتقد، أعدّ، أنتخب)

٦ ــ لا ـــ هذا المؤلّف من المؤلّفين المشهورين.(نعتبر، نعتقد، نمنح)

5. Optional وَ 'and' in adjective strings

In English, when two or more adjectives precede a noun, they are not normally connected by "and", for example "a long, hard lesson". When the series of adjectives is in the predicate position, however, "and" is required:

97

"The lesson is long and hard." In Arabic, وَ 'and' is normally not used between adjectives in a noun-adjective phrase, and may also be omitted in a series of predicate adjectives:

اَلدَّرْسُ الطَّويلُ الصَّعْبُ   'the long, hard lesson'

اَلدَّرْسُ طَويلٌ صَعْبٌ .   'The lesson is long (and) hard.'

These comments also apply to adjective iḍāfas, e.g.

عِشْرونَ جُزْءًا كُلُّها جَميلَةُ اللُّغَةِ   '...twenty volumes, all of which
سَهْلَةُ الأُسْلــوبِ .   are beautiful of language (and)
easy of style.'

Modifiers of nouns may be adjectives or adjectival iḍāfas, as illustrated above. They may also be phrases, e.g. رَجُلٌ مِنْ مِصْرَ 'a man from Egypt', or clauses, e.g. اَلرَّجُلُ الذي قابَلْتُــهُ 'the man whom I met'. A string of phrases or a string of clauses are usually joined by وَ :

رَجُلٌ بِدونِ خِبْرَةٍ وَبِدونِ شَهاداتٍ   'a man without experience and without degrees'

رَجُلٌ أُحِبُّهُ وَأَحْتَرِمُهُ   'a man whom I like and respect'

If combinations of types of modifiers occur, the normal order of occurrence is (1) adjectives, (2) adjectival iḍāfas, (3) prepositional phrases, and (4) clauses. The conjunction وَ is not then used to link them:

السَّيِّدُ فَريد رَجُلٌ مَعْروفٌ حَسَنُ الأَخْلاقِ   'Mr. Farid is a well-known man of
مِنْ مِصْرَ يَعْمَلُ في مُنَظَّمَةِ الأُمَمِ الْمُتَّحِدَةِ .   excellent character from Egypt
who works at the United Nations.'

Now do Drill 8.

Drill 8. Deletion of وَ .

Read the following sentences deleting the conjunction وَ which joins the

98

modifiers in each of the following sentences. Translate each sentence.

١ ـ " الحياة " جريدة سياسية ويوميّة .

٢ ـ روكفلر رجل غنيّ ومعروف .

٣ ـ مصر دولة عربية واسلامية .

٤ ـ منظمة الامم المتحدة منظمة سياسيّة ودولية .

٥ ـ أكثر دروس هذا الكتاب صعبة وغير واضحة .

٦ ـ قابلت هنا رجلا قصيرا وقبيح الوجه .

٧ ـ " الاهرام " جريدة هامة ومعروفة .

٨ ـ أنت صديق عزيز ومخلص .

٩ ـ بعض الجرائد العربية صعبة اللغة وقبيحة الاسلوب .

١٠ ـ رجع سعيدا وضاحكا .

D. **Comprehension passage**

ﺩ ـ نصوص للفهم

Read the following passage and then do Drill 9, which is based on it.

الوحـــدة العربيّة

كان الرئيس جمال عبد الناصر من الذين عملوا على تحقيـــــق الوحدة العربية . وقد عمل ايضا على تقدّم العلاقات مع الدول الاسلاميـــة والأَفْريقيّةِ غير العربية .   African

وفي بداية النصف الثاني من هذا القرن اتحدت دولتان عربيتان هما مصر وسوريا واصبحتا تعرفان باسم " الجمهورية العربية المتحدة " وقد كان جمال عبد الناصر القائد الذي حقق الوحدة .

رحب الناس في سوريا ومصر بالوحدة كل الترحيب ، واحتفلوا بـها والّف عنها شعر كثير وغَنّى هذا الشعر أشهر المغنين العرب . لكـــنّ   sang الوحدة لم تدم سوى ثلاث سنوات . ولا يزال كثير من العرب حتى اليـــوم يعتقدون أنّ الوحدة العربية هى الفكرة التي تجمعهم معا . وهم يعتبرون

one of the forms of الجامِعَةَ الْعَرَبَيَّةَ صورَةٌ مِنْ صُوَرِ الوحدة . The Arab League

وفي السنوات الاخيرة اصبحت موريتانيا والصومال عضوين فـــي Somalia Mauritania

الجامعة العربية . وقد ساعد ذلك على تَوْطيدِ العلاقات مع الدول الافريقية consol-idating

عامّةٌ .

Drill 9. Written. True/false. صَوابٌ أَمْ خَطأٌ

In the light of the foregoing passage, indicate which of the following

statements are true and which are false.

١ ـ عمل جمال عبد الناصر على تقدّم العلاقات بين العرب فقط .

٢ ـ كان لبنان عضوا في " الجمهورية العربية المتحدة " .

٣ ـ تم الاتحاد بين مصر وسوريا في زمن جمال عبد الناصر .

٤ ـ الصومال عضو في الجامعة العربية .

٥ ـ موريتانيا ليست بلدا افريقيا .

٦ ـ قاوم المصريون الاتحاد مع سوريا .

٧ ـ ليس في العالم العربي منظمة تجمع العرب معا .

٨ ـ لا يعتبر العرب الوحدة امرا هاما .

E. General drills هـ ـ التمارين العامة

Drill 10. Written. Completion.

In column (a) give the verbal noun, in (b) its pattern and in (c) another

verbal noun of the same pattern.

	(c)		(b)	(a)
Ex.	قَبُول 'acceptance'		FuMuuL	وصول	وصل

عقد

نام

فكّر

راسل

احضر

تطلّب

تناول

استطاع

ازداد

انصرف

حضر

Drill 11. Written. Sentence formation.

Form a sentence in which the items in parentheses modify the preceding

noun. Do not change the form of the noun.

١ ـ الرئيس (وهب حياته) .

٢ ـ المؤلفتان (كتبتا عن حقوق المرأة) .

٣ ـ رجلان (جاءا الى أمريكا) .

٤ ـ أدباء (أسلوبهم جميل) .

٥ ـ الاستاذات (من العالم العربيّ) .

٦ ـ القواد (قاوموا الحكم) .

٧ ـ طيبة (تحدثت في أحد كتبها) .

٨ ـ المرأة (تطالب بحقوقها) .

٩ ـ دول (تمتاز بجمالها) .

<u>Drill 12.</u> Written. Passive —→ active.

Change the sentences to the active, using the most appropriate agent from

the following list. Indicate where more than one agent can be used and which ones.

الاستاذ ، رئيس الوزراء، فَيْروز ، المساعد ، زوجتي ، الوزراء، الحقوق ،
المستشرقون ، رئيس الجمهورية ، الجامعة ، التجارة ، الحكومة ،المغنون
الناس، الصناعة ، المقاومون ، ابني .

١ – ذهب به الى مكتب المدير .

٢ – يُحترم الرجل الذي يقدم خدمات للوطن .

٣ – تُرجمت بعض كتب الجاحِظ الى اللغات الأوربية .

٤ – سوف يؤجّل اجتماع الوزراء الى الاسبوع القادم .

٥ – سوف يُخرّج عدد كبير من الاطبّاء هذا العام .

٦ – مُنع المقاومون لرئيس الجمهوريّة من ترك البلاد .

٧ – سيسأل عنه قريبا .

<u>Drill 13.</u> Translation.

أ – رجع اخي من لندن بعد أن درس الأدب الانكليزي هناك أربعة أعوام .
وقد احتفل برجوعه احتفالا كبيرا حضره الاهل وعدد كبير من الاصدقاء ..

ب – كانت ليبيا الى زمن قريب من الدول العربية الفقيرة ، أمّا اليوم
فهي من اغنى دول الشرق الاوسط لان انتاجها من الزيت ازداد ازديادا
كبيرا .

ج – يعتبر المسلمون اسلوب القرآن اجمل اساليب الكتابة العربية ،
ويعتبرون اساليب الكتّاب المعاصرين اقلّ جمالا ، اما اللهجات
العامية فاكثر العرب يفضلون ألّا تستخدم في كتابة الادب .

د – سمعت في نشرة الاخبار ان منظمة التحرير الوطني اصدرت تقريرايربط- liberation

102

فيه بين تحسين الوضع الاقتصادى وبداية مقاومة الحكومة ، فاخرج
الرئيس قائد المنظمة من البلد .

ه ‍ - هناك روابط هامة بين اعضاء العائلة العربية .

و ‍ - اخذ الطلاب يتعلّمون المفردات الجديدة التي جاءت في الدرس .

Lesson Thirty-five

أ ـ اَلْجُمَلُ التَّمْهيديَّةُ

A. Preparatory Sentences

دراســــة

A Study

عن الاماكن المقدسة

of Holy Places

١ ـ أَعَدَّ صديق لي ـ وهو استاذ الدراسات الاسلاميّة في جامعة دمشق ـ دراسة طويلة عن الاماكن المُقَدَّسَةِ في الشرق الاوسط .

A friend of mine, who is Professor of Islamic Studies at the University of Damascus, has **prepared** a lengthy study of the **holy** places in the Middle East.

أَعَدَّ ، إعْدادٌ

IV to prepare, make s.th. ready

مُقَدَّسٌ ـ ون

holy, sacred

٢ ـ إسْتَمَرَّ اعداد هذه الدراسة ثلاثة اعوام وقد بحث المؤلّف موضوعه بحثا حَسَناً شاملا .

The preparation of the study **lasted** three years; the author had researched his subject **well** and thoroughly.

إسْتَمَرَّ ، إسْتِمْرارٌ

X to last; to continue, persist, keep on

حَسَنٌ ـ حِسانٌ

good, fine, excellent, beautiful

٣ ـ إهْتَمَّتْ جامعة الرياض بالدراسة ونشرتها في العام الماضي .

The University of Riyad **took an interest in** the study and published it **last** year.

إهْتَمَّ ، إهْتِمامٌ (ب)

VIII to take an interest (in) show concern (over)

ماضٍ ـ ماضونَ

past, bygone; last (time)

٤ ـ قال الكاتب في دراسته : الشرق الاوسط مَهْدُ الأديانِ الثلاثة : المَسيحيّةُ واليَهوديّةُ والإسلامُ .

The author says in his study, "The Middle East is the **cradle** of the three **religions**: Christianity, Judaism, and Islam.

[مَهْدٌ ـ مُهودٌ]

[cradle, bed]

دينٌ ـ أَديانٌ

religion

المَسيحيّةُ

Christianity

اليَهوديّةُ

Judaism

الإسْلامُ

Islam

٥ ― القُدْسُ مدينة مقدّسة عند كـلّ
هذه الاديان.ففيها الامـاكـن
المقدّسة التـاليَةُ ؛ ـ
المَسْجِدُ الأَقْصى وَقُبّةُ الصّخَـرةِ
وكَنيسةِ القِيامَةِ وحائِطُ المَبْكى.

Jerusalem is a holy city for all
these religions. For in it are the
following holy places: the Al-Aksa
Mosque, the Dome of the Rock, the
Church of the Holy Sepulchre ("the
Church of the Resurrection") and
the Wailing Wall.

القُدْسُ — Jerusalem

تالٍ — following, subsequent, next

[المَسْجِدُ الأَقْصى] — [Al-Aksa Mosque]

[قُبّةُ الصّخَرَةِ] — [The Dome of the Rock]

[كَنيسةُ القِيامَةِ] — [The Church of the Holy Sepulchre]

[حائِطُ المَبْكى] — [The Wailing Wall]

٦ ― يزورالقدسالمسلمون و المَسيحيّونَ
و اليَهودُ من جميع بـلـدان العالم.
يزور المَسيحيّون ايضا بَيْتَ لَحْمَ
ويزور المسلمون مكّةَو المَدينةَ.

Muslims, Christians, and Jews from
all countries of the world visit
Jerusalem. The Christians also
visit Bethlehem, and the Muslims
visit Mecca and Medina.

مَسيحيٌّ ― ون — Christian

يَهوديٌّ ― يَهودٌ — Jew, Jewish

[بَيْتَ لَحْمٌ] — [Bethlehem]

[مَكّةٌ] — [Mecca]

[المَدينةُ] — [Medina]

٧ ― ذكر صديقي في دراسته انّ في
مكّة الآن بـعض الفَنادقِالحديثة.

My friend mentions in his study
that there are now some modern
hotels in Mecca.

فُنْدُقٌ ― فَنادِقُ — hotel

٨ ― وَعَدَني صديقي مُنْذُ ثلاثة اسابيع
يـأنْ يرسل اليّ نُسْخَةً من الدراسة.
وقد ارسلـها هذا الاسبوع فشكَرْتُهُ
كل الشكر .

My friend promised me three weeks
ago to send me a copy of the study.
He sent it this week, and I thanked
him heartily.

وَعَدَ يَعِدُ، وَعْدٌ (بـ) — to promise s.o. (s.th.)

مُنْذُ — since; ago; since the time that

105

نَسْخَةٌ ـ نُسَخٌ

copy

شَكَرَ ـُـ ، شُكْرٌ (على)

to thank s.o., be thankful, grateful (for)

المفردات الاضافية

Additional vocabulary

٩ ـ مَرَرْنا بِمدنٍ كثيرةٍ عندما كنا في الشرق الاوسط في الشهر الماضي.

We **went through** many cities when we were in the Middle East last month.

مَرَّ ـُـ ، مُرورٌ (بـ)

to pass by, go by, go through

ب ـ النص الاساسيّ

زيــــارة للقـــــدس

عندما كنت طالباً في جامعة هارفارد درست الشيء الكثير عن تاريخ الشرق الاوسط وعن آثاره الدينية . كان اساتذتي يقولون انّ الشرق الاوسط

cradle

مَهْدُ الاديان الثلاثة : اليهودية والمسيحية والاسلام ؛ وكانوا كذلك يقولون

specialis

من واجب كل مُتَخَصِّصٍ في الدراسات العربية والاسلامية ان يزور الشرق الاوسط، خاصة الاماكن المقدسة .

وفي العام الماضي سافرت الى القدس لزيارة الاماكن المقدّسة من اسلامية ومسيحية ويهودية . وفي المطار استقبلني صديق اعرفه منذ ايام الدراسة . اخذني صديقي بسيارته الى الفندق وبعد الغَداءِ سألته عـن

lunch

اهم الآثار الدينية التي يجب ان ازورها ، فذكر لي عددا منها ووعدني ان يذهب معي لزيارتها . وفي المساء اعدت زوجة صديقي لنا الطعام ، فأكلنا وشربنا القهوة العربية .

في صباح اليوم التالي زرنا المسجد الاقصى وقبة الصخرة وكنيسة

القيامة ، ومررنا بحائط المَبّكى . وفي اليوم الثالث زرنا الاماكــــن المقدسة في بَيْتَ لَحَمَ . خلال زيارتي هذه ، التي استمرت اربـعة ايام ، اكرمني صديـقي كل الاكرام واهتم بي اهتماما حسنا ، فشكرته على ذلك ثم سافرت لـزيارة بـعض المدن الاخرى في الشرق الاوسط .

B. <u>Basic text</u>

<u>A Visit to Jerusalem</u>

When I was a student at Harvard University, I studied a great deal about
the history of the Middle East and about its religious monuments. My
professors used to say that the Middle East was the cradle of the three
religions--Judaism, Christianity and Islam. They would likewise say, "It is
necessary for every specialist in Arabic and Islamic studies to visit the
Middle East, especially the holy places."

Last year I traveled to Jerusalem to visit the holy places--Islamic,
Christian and Jewish. At the airport I was met by a friend whom I had known
since school days. My friend took me in his car to the hotel; after lunch
I asked him about the most important religious monuments that I should visit.
He mentioned a number of them to me and promised to go with me to visit them.
That evening my friend's wife prepared some food for us, and we ate and drank
Arabic coffee.

The next morning we visited the Al-Aksa Mosque, the Dome of the Rock, and
the Church of the Holy Sepulchre, and we passed by the Wailing Wall. On the
third day we visited the holy places in Bethlehem. During this visit of mine,
which lasted four days, my friend showed me great hospitality and looked after
me in every way. I thanked him for that and then left to visit some other
cities in the Middle East.

> 1. Doubled verbs: Derived Forms
>
> 2. Demonstrative modifying first term of idāfas
>
> 3. مُنْذُ 'since, ago'

1. Doubled verbs: Derived Forms

Verbs with double roots occur not only in Form I (34.C.1) but also in the derived Forms. In Forms II and V, verbs with double roots are exactly like strong verbs, for example, حَقَّقَ 'to realize' and تَحَقَّقَ 'to be realized'. In Forms III and VI, verbs with double roots are rare, and will not be dealt with here. In the derived Forms, as in Form I, verbs with double roots have regular stems (used with consonant suffixes) and doubled stems (used with vowel suffixes) in each of the tenses, but are simpler than Form I in having only one vowel pattern each. In all the Forms discussed below the perfect stem vowel is _a_ and the imperfect stem vowel is _i_. These derived Forms are described individually below. Active conjugations are given in full. Passive conjugations, where they exist, are like the active in each Form, differing only in the vowel patterns.

Form IV

Perfect tense	Pattern	Examples	
Regular stem	?aFDaD-	أَعْدَدْتُ	'I prepared'
Doubled stem	?aFaDD-	أَعَدَّ	'he prepared'
Imperfect tense			
Regular stem	-FDiD-	يُعْدِدْنَ	'they (f.p.) prepare'
Doubled stem	-FiDD-	يُعِدُّ	'he prepares'

108

The full active conjugation of the verb أَعَدَّ 'to prepare' (root ʕ D D) is given below. Note that, as in Form I doubled verbs, there are optional variations for those forms of the jussive and imperative which normally have no suffix (are written with <u>sukuun</u>); the doubled stem is the more common variant.

أَعَدَّ – يُعِدُّ 'to prepare'

Form IV	PERFECT	IMPERFECT			
		Indicative	Subjunctive	Jussive	Imperative
3 MS	أَعَدَّ	يُعِدُّ	يُعِدَّ	يُعْدِدْ/ يُعِدَّ	
FS	أَعَدَّتْ	تُعِدُّ	تُعِدَّ	تُعْدِدْ/ تُعِدَّ	
2 MS	أَعْدَدْتَ	تُعِدُّ	تُعِدَّ	تُعْدِدْ/ تُعِدَّ	أَعْدِدْ/ أَعِدَّ
FS	أَعْدَدْتِ	تُعِدِّينَ	تُعِدِّي	تُعِدِّي	أَعِدِّي
1 S	أَعْدَدْتُ	أُعِدُّ	أُعِدَّ	أُعْدِدْ/ أُعِدَّ	
3 MD	أَعَدَّا	يُعِدَّانِ	يُعِدَّا	يُعِدَّا	
FD	أَعَدَّتَا	تُعِدَّانِ	تُعِدَّا	تُعِدَّا	
2 D	أَعْدَدْتُما	تُعِدَّانِ	تُعِدَّا	تُعِدَّا	أَعِدَّا
3 MP	أَعَدُّوا	يُعِدُّونَ	يُعِدُّوا	يُعِدُّوا	
FP	أَعْدَدْنَ	يُعْدِدْنَ	يُعْدِدْنَ	يُعْدِدْنَ	
2 MP	أَعْدَدْتُمْ	تُعِدُّونَ	تُعِدُّوا	تُعِدُّوا	أَعِدُّوا
FP	أَعْدَدْتُنَّ	تُعْدِدْنَ	تُعْدِدْنَ	تُعْدِدْنَ	أَعْدِدْنَ
1 P	أَعْدَدْنا	نُعِدُّ	نُعِدَّ	نُعْدِدْ/ نُعِدَّ	

Active participle: muFiDD مُعِدٌّ 'having prepared'

Verbal noun: ?iFDaaD إِعْدادٌ 'preparation'

The <u>passive</u> stem patterns are as follows:

	Pattern	Examples	
PERFECT Regular stem	?uFDiD-	أُعْدِدْتُ	'I was prepared (made ready)'
Doubled stem	?uFiDD-	أُعِدَّ	'it was prepared'
IMPERFECT Regular stem	-FDaD-	يُعْدَدْنَ	'they (f.p.) are prepared'
Doubled stem	-FaDD-	يُعَدُّ	'it is prepared'

Passive participle: muFaDD مُعَدّ 'prepared, made ready'

Form VII doubled verbs.

The patterns for the two tenses are illustrated with اِنْضَمَّ إلى 'to join, unite, join forces with':

	Pattern	Examples	
PERFECT Regular stem	-nFaDaD-	اِنْضَمَمْتُ	'I joined'
Doubled stem	-nFaDD-	اِنْضَمَّ	'he joined'
IMPERFECT Regular stem	-nFaDiD-	يَنْضَمِمْنَ	'they (f.p.) join'
Doubled stem	-nFaDD-	يَنْضَمُّ	'he joins'

The full conjugation is illustrated below:

اِنْضَمَّ – يَنْضَمُّ الى 'to join'

Form VII	PERFECT	IMPERFECT			
		Indicative	Subj.	Jussive	Imperative
3 MS	اِنْضَمَّ	يَنْضَمُّ	يَنْضَمَّ	يَنْضَمِمْ / يَنْضَمَّ	
FS	اِنْضَمَّتْ	تَنْضَمُّ	تَنْضَمَّ	تَنْضَمِمْ / تَنْضَمَّ	
2 MS	اِنْضَمَمْتَ	تَنْضَمُّ	تَنْضَمَّ	تَنْضَمِمْ / تَنْضَمَّ	اِنْضَمِمْ / اِنْضَمَّ
FS	اِنْضَمَمْتِ	تَنْضَمِّين	تَنْضَمِّي	تَنْضَمِّي	اِنْضَمِّي
1 S	اِنْضَمَمْتُ	انْضَمُّ	انْضَمَّ	أَنْضَمِمْ / أَنْضَمَّ	

3 MD	إِنْضَمَّا	يَنْضَمَّان	يَنْضَمَّا	يَنْضَمُّوا
FD	إِنْضَمَّتا	تَنْضَمَّان	تَنْضَمَّا	تَنْضَمَّا
2 D	إِنْضَمَمْتُما	تَنْضَمَّان	تَنْضَمَّا	تَنْضَمَّا	انضما
3 MP	إِنْضَمُّوا	يَنْضَمُّونَ	يَنْضَمُّوا	يَنْضَمُّوا
FP	إِنْضَمَمْنَ	يَنْضَمَمْنَ	يَنْضَمَمْنَ	يَنْضَمَمْنَ
2 MP	إِنْضَمَمْتُمْ	تَنْضَمُّونَ	تَنْضَمُّوا	تَنْضَمُّوا	انضموا
FP	إِنْضَمَمْتُنَّ	تَنْضَمَمْنَ	تَنْضَمَمْنَ	تَنْضَمَمْنَ	انضممن
1 P	إِنْضَمَمْنا	نَنْضَمُّ	نَنْضَمَّ	نَنْضَمَّ / نَنْضَمُّ

Active participle: munFaDD مُنْضَمّ 'having joined'

Verbal noun: -nFiDaaD- إِنْضِمام 'joining'

There are no passives in Form VII.

In Forms VII, VIII and IX the imperfect stem vowel <u>i</u> occurs <u>only in the feminine plural forms</u>; the vowel most often seen in imperfect stems in these verbs, accordingly, is <u>a</u>.

<u>Form VIII doubled verbs</u> will be exemplified by اِهْتَمَّ بِ 'to be concerned over, take interest in':

	Pattern	Examples
PERFECT		
Regular stem	-FtaDaD-	اِهْتَمَمْتُ 'I showed interest'
Doubled stem	-FtaDD-	اِهْتَمَّ 'he showed interest'
IMPERFECT		
Regular stem	-FtaDiD-	يَهْتَمِمْنَ 'they (f.p.) show interest'
Doubled stem	-FtaDD-	يَهْتَمُّ 'he takes interest'

The full active conjugation follows:

111

$$\text{اِهْتَمَّ} - \text{يَهْتَمُّ}$$ 'to take an interest in'

Form VIII	PERFECT	IMPERFECT			
		Indicative	Subj.	Jussive	Imperative
3 MS	اِهْتَمَّ	يَهْتَمُّ	يَهْتَمَّ	يَهْتَمِمْ / يَهْتَمَّ	
FS	اِهْتَمَّتْ	تَهْتَمُّ	تَهْتَمَّ	تَهْتَمِمْ / تَهْتَمَّ	
2 MS	اِهْتَمَمْتَ	تَهْتَمُّ	تَهْتَمَّ	تَهْتَمِمْ / تَهْتَمَّ	اِهْتَمِمْ / اِهْتَمَّ
FS	اِهْتَمَمْتِ	تَهْتَمِّينَ	تَهْتَمِّي	تَهْتَمِّي	اِهْتَمِّي
1 S	اِهْتَمَمْتُ	أَهْتَمُّ	أَهْتَمَّ	أَهْتَمِمْ / أَهْتَمَّ	
3 MD	اِهْتَمَّا	يَهْتَمَّانِ	يَهْتَمَّا	يَهْتَمَّا	
FD	اِهْتَمَّتَا	تَهْتَمَّانِ	تَهْتَمَّا	تَهْتَمَّا	
2 D	اِهْتَمَمْتُمَا	تَهْتَمَّانِ	تَهْتَمَّا	تَهْتَمَّا	اِهْتَمَّا
3 MP	اِهْتَمُّوا	يَهْتَمُّونَ	يَهْتَمُّوا	يَهْتَمُّوا	
FP	اِهْتَمَمْنَ	يَهْتَمِمْنَ	يَهْتَمِمْنَ	يَهْتَمِمْنَ	
2 MP	اِهْتَمَمْتُمْ	تَهْتَمُّونَ	تَهْتَمُّوا	تَهْتَمُّوا	اِهْتَمُّوا
FP	اِهْتَمَمْتُنَّ	تَهْتَمِمْنَ	تَهْتَمِمْنَ	تَهْتَمِمْنَ	اِهْتَمِمْنَ
1 P	اِهْتَمَمْنَا	نَهْتَمُّ	نَهْتَمَّ	نَهْتَمِمْ / نَهْتَمَّ	

Active participle: muFtaDD مُهْتَمٌّ بِـ 'showing interest in'

Verbal noun: -FtiDaaD- اِهْتِمامٌ 'interest'

The passive patterns are exemplified by اِحْتَلَّ 'to occupy' since اِهْتَمَّ - does not occur in the passive:

	Pattern	Examples
PERFECT		
Regular stem	-FtuDiD-	أُحْتُلِلْنا 'we were occupied'
Doubled stem	-FtuDD-	أُحْتُلَّ 'it was occupied'
IMPERFECT		
Regular stem	-FtaDaD-	يُحْتَلَلْنَ 'they (f.p.) are occupied'
Doubled stem	-FtaDD-	يُحْتَلُّ 'it is occupied'

Passive participle: -muFtaDD- مُحْتَلّ 'occupied'

Form IX verbs are based on strong roots, e.g. اِحْمَرَّ 'to turn red', root
H̱ M̱ Ṟ. The final radical is doubled, however, and all IX verbs are conjugated exactly like doubled verbs.

	Pattern	Example	
PERFECT			
Regular stem	-FMaLaL-	اِحْمَرَرْتُ	'I turned red'
Doubled stem	-FMaLL-	اِحْمَرَّ	'he turned red'
IMPERFECT			
Regular stem	-FMaLiL-	يَحْمَرِرْنَ	'they (f.p.) turn red'
Doubled stem	-FMaLL-	يَحْمَرُّ	'he turns red'

Form IX verbs, which mean 'to become (color) _or_ (defect)', are relatively
rare in Modern Standard Arabic; no IX verb occurs in this text. Merely for
the sake of completeness, however, the full conjugation of Form IX verbs is
illustrated here.

The full conjugation follows:

اِحْمَرَّ ـ يَحْمَرُّ 'to turn red'

Form IX	PERFECT	IMPERFECT			
		Indicative	Subj.	Jussive	Imperative
3 MS	اِحْمَرَّ	يَحْمَرُّ	يَحْمَرَّ	يَحْمَرِرْ / يَحْمَرَّ	
FS	اِحْمَرَّتْ	تَحْمَرُّ	تَحْمَرَّ	تَحْمَرِرْ / تَحْمَرَّ	
2 MS	اِحْمَرَرْتَ	تَحْمَرُّ	تَحْمَرَّ	تَحْمَرِرْ / تَحْمَرَّ	اِحْمَرِرْ / اِحْمَرَّ
FS	اِحْمَرَرْتِ	تَحْمَرِّينَ	تَحْمَرِّي	تَحْمَرِّي	اِحْمَرِّي
1 S	اِحْمَرَرْتُ	أَحْمَرُّ	أَحْمَرَّ	أَحْمَرِرْ / أَحْمَرَّ	

3 MD	اِحْمَرّا	يَحْمَرّانِ	يَحْمَرّا	يَحْمَرّا	
FD	اِحْمَرّتا	تَحْمَرّانِ	تَحْمَرّا	تَحْمَرّا	
2 D	اِحْمَرَرْتُما	تَحْمَرّانِ	تَحْمَرّا	تَحْمَرّا	اِحْمَرّا
3 MP	اِحْمَرّوا	يَحْمَرّونَ	يَحْمَرّوا	يَحْمَرّوا	
FP	اِحْمَرَرْنَ	يَحْمَرِرْنَ	يَحْمَرِرْنَ	يَحْمَرِرْنَ	
2 MP	اِحْمَرَرْتُمْ	تَحْمَرّونَ	تَحْمَرّوا	تَحْمَرّوا	اِحْمَرّوا
FP	اِحْمَرَرْتُنَّ	تَحْمَرِرْنَ	تَحْمَرِرْنَ	تَحْمَرِرْنَ	اِحْمَرِرْنَ
1 P	اِحْمَرَرْنا	نَحْمَرّ	نَحْمَرّ	نَحْمَرِرّ / نَحْمَرّ	

Active participle: muFMaLL-   مُحْمَرّ   'having turned red'

Verbal noun: -FMiLaaL-   اِحْمِرارٌ 'redness'

There is no passive for Form IX.

Form X doubled verbs will be exemplified by   اِسْتَمَرَّ 'to last, endure;
to continue, keep on.'

	Pattern	Example	
PERFECT			
Regular stem	-staFDaD-	اِسْتَمْرَرْتُ	'I continued'
Doubled stem	-staFaDD-	اِسْتَمَرَّ	'he continued'
IMPERFECT			
Regular stem	-staFDiD-	يَسْتَمْرِرْنَ	'they (f.p.) continue'
Doubled stem	-staFiDD-	يَسْتَمِرُّ	'he continues'

The full conjugation follows:

اِسْتَمَرَّ ـ يَسْتَمِرُّ 'to continue'

Form X	PERFECT	IMPERFECT			
		Indic.	Subj.	Jussive	Imperative
3 MS	اِسْتَمَرَّ	يَسْتَمِرُّ	يَسْتَمِرَّ	يَسْتَمْرِرْ / يَسْتَمِرَّ	
FS	اِسْتَمَرَّتْ	تَسْتَمِرُّ	تَسْتَمِرَّ	تَسْتَمْرِرْ / تَسْتَمِرَّ	
2 MS	اِسْتَمْرَرْتَ	تَسْتَمِرُّ	تَسْتَمِرَّ	تَسْتَمْرِرْ / تَسْتَمِرَّ	اِسْتَمْرِرْ / اِسْتَمِرَّ
FS	اِسْتَمْرَرْتِ	تَسْتَمِرِّينَ	تَسْتَمِرِّي	تَسْتَمِرِّي	اِسْتَمِرِّي
1 S	اِسْتَمْرَرْتُ	أَسْتَمِرُّ	أَسْتَمِرَّ	أَسْتَمْرِرْ / أَسْتَمِرَّ	
3 MD	اِسْتَمَرَّا	يَسْتَمِرَّانِ	يَسْتَمِرَّا	يَسْتَمِرَّا	
FD	اِسْتَمَرَّتَا	تَسْتَمِرَّانِ	تَسْتَمِرَّا	تَسْتَمِرَّا	
2 D	اِسْتَمْرَرْتُما	تَسْتَمِرَّانِ	تَسْتَمِرَّا	تَسْتَمِرَّا	اِسْتَمِرَّا
3 MP	اِسْتَمَرُّوا	يَسْتَمِرُّونَ	يَسْتَمِرُّوا	يَسْتَمِرُّوا	
FP	اِسْتَمْرَرْنَ	يَسْتَمْرِرْنَ	يَسْتَمْرِرْنَ	يَسْتَمْرِرْنَ	
2 MP	اِسْتَمْرَرْتُمْ	تَسْتَمِرُّونَ	تَسْتَمِرُّوا	تَسْتَمِرُّوا	اِسْتَمِرُّوا
FP	اِسْتَمْرَرْتُنَّ	تَسْتَمْرِرْنَ	تَسْتَمْرِرْنَ	تَسْتَمْرِرْنَ	اِسْتَمْرِرْنَ
1 P	اِسْتَمْرَرْنا	نَسْتَمِرُّ	نَسْتَمِرَّ	نَسْتَمْرِرْ / نَسْتَمِرَّ	

Active participle: mustaFiDD- مُسْتَمِرّ 'continuing'

Verbal noun: -stiFDaaD اِسْتِمْرارٌ 'continuing' (noun)

Passive stem patterns are illustrated with اِسْتَرَدَّ 'to demand back, reclaim'

	Pattern	Examples	
PERFECT			
Regular stem	-stuFDiD-	أُسْتُرْدِدْتُ	'I was brought back'
Doubled stem	-stuFiDD-	أُسْتُرِدَّ	'he was brought back'
IMPERFECT			
Regular stem	-staFDaD-	يُسْتَرَدُّ	'he is reclaimed'
Doubled stem	-staFaDD-	يُسْتَرْدَدْنَ	'they (f.p.) are reclaimed'

Passive participle: mustaFaDD- مُسْتَرَدّ 'reclaimed'

Now do Drills 1 (on tape), 2 and 3.

<u>Drill 1</u>. (On tape) Conjugation.

<u>Drill 2</u>. Conjugation.

Give the correct form of the verb and vocalize it. <u>Ex.</u>

اعدّ + أنا ⟵ أَعْدَدْتُ

اهتمّ + أنتم ⟵ _____   يمرّ + أنتما ⟵ _____

أحبّه + أنتِ ⟵ _____   يستمرّ + نحن ⟵ _____

شكّ + هم ⟵ _____   يدلّ + أنا ⟵ _____

اهتمّ + نحن ⟵ _____   استمرّ + أنتَ ⟵ _____

أعدّ + هي ⟵ _____   استعدّ + نحن ⟵ _____

<u>Drill 3</u>. Written.

Fill in the blanks in the following chart; X means "not applicable".

Perfect	Imperfect	Active Participle	Passive Participle	Verbal Noun
			مُعَدّ	
			X	اِهْتِمام
		مُنْضَمّ	X	
اِحْمَرَّ			X	
		وادّ	X	
عَدّ				
	يَسْتَرِدّ			
أَحَبّ				
		X	مُحْتَلّ	
				دَلالَة
اِسْتَمَرّ			X	

116

2. Demonstrative modifying first term of idāfas

We have seen demonstrative phrases as second term of an idāfa, as in

مُحاضَراتُ هٰذا الأُسْتاذِ	'this professor's lectures'
مُعْظَمُ هٰذِهِ الجُمَلِ	'most of these sentences'

(The demonstrative phrases are underlined.)

If the demonstrative modifies the <u>first term</u> of the idāfa, however, it must follow the entire idāfa; it agrees with the first noun, as usual, in number, gender and case. For example:

مُحاضَراتُ الأُسْتاذِ هٰذِهِ	'these lectures of the professor's'
كِتابي هٰذا	'this book of mine'
زِيارَتي تِلْكَ	'that visit of mine'

(The demonstrative phrases are underlined.)
Now do Drill 4.

<u>Drill 4</u>. Written. Translation.

1. I do not like these goals of theirs.

2. This book of hers is great.

3. Did these friends of his come to the meeting?

4. These two articles of Professor Smith's are now published.

5. Where is that daughter of yours?

3. مُنْذُ 'since, ago'

مُنْذُ 'since' is both a preposition and a conjunction. As a preposition it may be translated "since, from; for; ago", as in

وَعَدَني بِذٰلِكَ مُنْذُ سَنَةٍ .	'He promised me that a year ago.'
يَعْمَلُ مُتَرْجِمًا في مُنَظَّمَةِ الأُمَمِ المُتَّحِدَةِ مُنْذُ ثَلاثَةِ أَسابيعَ فَقَطْ.	'He has been working as a translator at the United Nations for only three weeks.'

117

أَعْرِفُهُ مُنْذُ إِنْشاءِ الْمَجَلَّةِ .   'I have known him since the founding of
the magazine.'

مُنْذُ الْآنَ   'from now on'

The second and third sentences deserve further note. In these two sentences the Arabic verb is in the imperfect tense; these sentences literally read "He is working as a translator...for only three weeks." and "I know him since the founding of the magazine." Arabic regularly uses the imperfect tense in this way as the equivalent of English present perfect verbs in expressions like "have been (doing)."

In a past time context the Arabic imperfect with مُنْذُ is translated with a past perfect expression, e.g.

كُنْتُ أَعْرِفُهُ مُنْذُ سَنَةٍ .   'I had known him for a year.'

As a conjunction مُنْذُ means "since, from the time that," as in

أَعْرِفُهُ مُنْذُ كُنْتُ طالِبًا في
الْجامِعَةِ .   'I have known him since I was a
student at the university.'

مُنْذُ زُرْنا الْقُدْسَ   'from the time that we visited
Jerusalem'

D. **Comprehension passages**   د - نصوص للفهم

(1) Read the following passage and then do Drill 5.

The Holy Bible   ترجمات الكِتابِ الْمُقَدَّس

الكِتابُ الْمُقَدَّس كِتابٌ دِينيّ أثّر على حياة عدد كبير من الناس في

بلدان العالم كلها المسيحية منها وغير المسيحيّة .

118

وقد اهتمّ رجال الدين منذ زمن بعيد بترجمة الكتاب المقدّس .

ففي بداية النصف الثاني من القرن الخامس عشر كان عدد الترجمات
ثلاثا وثلاثين ، وفي بداية القرن التاسع عشر كان عددها احدى وسبعين .

أما اليوم فان اللغات التي ترجم اليها الكتاب المقدس تَزيدُ علـــى ــــــ exceed
مئتين وخمسين .

كان جان ويكلف (John Wycliffe)   أوّل من اعدّ ترجمـــة
انكليزية للكتاب المقدّس كلّه ، واستمرّت الجهود في الأعوام التاليـــة
لتحسين الترجمة الانكليزيّة ، خاصة بعد ان انتشرت المعرفة باللغات
الأَصْليّةِ . وفى بداية القرن السابع عشر نشرت ترجمة انكليزيّة جديـــدة   original
أعدها اربعة وخمسون مترجما تحت اشراف الْمَلِكِ الانكليزيّ جيمز الأوّل ، وقد   king
عرفت هذه الترجمة عند الانكليز "بالترجمة الرسمية " ، ولا يزال الكثيرون
يعتبرونها احسن الترجمات القديمة ، بل ان البعض يعتبرونها احسن من
الترجمات التى نشرت في القرن العشرين .

أمّا الترجمات العربيّة الحديثة فقد بدأت فى القرن التاسع عشر،
ومن الذين اشتركوا فيها ثلاثة رجال مشهورون وهـم   : ناصيف اليازجي
وابنه إبْراهيمُ ، وبُطْرُسُ الْبُسْتانيّ . وقد استخدمت العربيّة الفصحى فـى
اكثر الترجمات لانها اللغة الْمُشْتَرَكَةُ بين العرب ، لكنّ أَجْزاءً من الكتاب   ctions   common
المقدّس نشرت اخيرا بـاللهجات العاميّة .

Drill 5. Written. Completion.

Fill in the blanks with the appropriate words (or expressions).

119

١ – تأثّر بالكتاب المقدّس ـــــــ ـــــــ في ـــــــ البلدان .

٢ – بدأت ترجمة الكتاب المقدّس منذ ـــــــ ـــــــ .

٣ – أوّل من ترجم الكتاب المقدّس الى الانكليزيّة ـــــــ . وكان الهدف
من الترجمات التالية ـــــــ ـــــــ .

٤ – أعدّ " الترجمة الرسميّة " ـــــــ .

٥ – لا يزال الكثيرون يعتبرون " الترجمة الرسميّة " ـــــــ ـــــــ .

٦ – استخدمت ـــــــ ـــــــ في أكثر الترجمات العربية .

(2) Listen to the passage on tape and then do Drill 6, which is based on it.

<u>Drill 6</u>. Written. Question/answer.

١ – من هو صلاح الدين الايّوبي ؟

٢ – لماذا أرسل الأوربيّون <u>جُنودَهم</u> الى البلاد العربيّة في زمـــــــن soldiers
صلاح الدين ؟

٣ – هل تعاون جميع العرب مع صلاح الدين في مقاومة الأوربيين ؟

٤ – ماذا كانت <u>نَتيجةَ</u> الحرب بين صلاح الدين والأوربيين ؟ result

٥ – ما رأى الأوربيين اليوم في صلاح الدين ؟

٦ – هل تعرف بأي اسم عرفت الحروب بين صلاح الدين والأوربيين ؟

هـ – <u>التمارين العامّة</u>   E. <u>General drills</u>

<u>Drill 7</u>. Matching: Iḍāfa.

Match the noun or noun phrase in (a) with one from column (b) so as to

obtain the most appropriate iḍāfa.

b	a
الوجه	١ ــ رئيس
الصف	٢ ــ جميلة
المكانة	٣ ــ مدينة
النيل	٤ ــ كتاب
مديرة المدرسة	٥ ــ مشكلة
" الاغانى "	٦ ــ باب
الدروس	٧ ــ عالي
الجمهورية	٨ ــ أسهل
الشرق الاوسط	٩ ــ نهر
بيروت	١٠ــ سكرتيرة

Drill 8. Nominalization.

    Change the verbal noun phrases to clauses. Ex.

'He wants to obtain a university   ⟵   يريد الحصول على شهادة جامعيّة .
     degree.'

                                يريد ان يحصل على شهادة جامعيّة .

١ ــ سافرت الى الولايات المتحدة للتدريس في جامعة مشيغان .

٢ ــ يريد رئيس الجامعة تعيين استاذين جديدين .

٣ ــ أودّ الحصول على شهادة جامعيّة فى العلوم السياسيّة .

٤ ــ ذهبن امس بعد الظهر الى السينما لمشاهدة فلم اجنبى .

٥ ــ اجتمع عدد من قادة البلاد السياسيّين لتأسيس حزب جديد .

٦ ــ يجب عليك احترام الوالديك .

٧ ــ ذهبوا الى الشرق الاوسط لزيارة الاماكن المقدّسة .

٨ ــ يجب عليكم التعاون الى ابعد حدّ .

٩ ــ بذلوا جهودا عظيمة لتحسين الاوضاع الاقتصادية في البلاد .

١٠ ــ تمكنّا من الوصول الى حلّ لمشكلتهما .

Drill 9. Written. Translation.

1. They believe that he is from the Sudan.

2. I know that she will succeed in her exams.

3. We must elect the best candidate.

4. They have made great efforts to solve this problem.

5. He applied for a job at the University of Kuwait.

6. Many of the most famous political thinkers meet in this old coffeehouse at night.

7. The boy walked through the streets of the city, searching for his little sister.

8. They (f. d.) requested me to bring my notes.

9. I was late and hadn't eaten, and I wished for sleep.

Drill 10. Written. Perfect ←→ imperfect and translation.

Change the verb from the perfect to the imperfect or vice-versa; write it in the column under "verb", and then give a good translation of it. Ex.

Translation	Verb	Sentence
"they prefer"	يفضّلون على	فضّلوا الطعام الفرنسيّ على الطعام الامريكيّ .

١ ــ استطعنا حضور المؤتمر .

٢ ــ يعملن في مكتب رئيس الجامعة .

٣ ــ يتّبع في كتبه اسلوبا يختلف عن اسلوب معاصريه .

٤ ــ وداد ومريم سكنتا في مدينة سان فرانسيسكو .

٥ ــ تغيّرت الاوضاع الاجتماعيّة في هذه البلاد تغيّرا كثيرا .

٦ ــ ماذا فعلت في نهاية الاسبوع ؟

٧ ــ تضع الدول العربيّة ثقتها بالأمم المتحدة .

٨ ــ أين طبعت هذه الكتب ؟

٩ ــ استفاد الاقتصاد العربي من الزيت استفادة كبيرة .

١٠ ـ قدّما لبلادهما خدمات كبيرة .

١١ ـ يؤلّف ذلك الكاتب كتبا ومقالات كثيرة .

١٢ ـ اقيمت مصانع كثيرة في مصر .

١٣ ـ هل يسمح لها بالذهاب ؟

١٤ ـ استطاع أولئك الوزراء ان يحضروا المؤتمر .

١٥ ـ نريد ان نزور لبنان قريبا .

Drill 11. Written.

Fill in the blanks with one of the words listed below.

(مرّة ، قرية ، نمت ، شكّ ، المقدّسة ، نهضة ، عاش ، اللهجات ، أغنية ،
حلّ ، تسير ـ ، الماضي ، فندق ، نهاية ، تصوّر ، اجلس ، القرآن ،
واضح ، افقر ، مات ، خلال ، تعود ـ)

١ ـ ـــــ ـــــ كتبها الحياة الاجتماعية في مصر .

٢ ـ لا ـــــ ان فيروز من اشهر المغنيّات في العالم العربيّ .

٣ ـ تختلف ـــــ العربيّة من بلد الى بلد .

٤ ـ موريتانيا من ـــــ ـــــ الدول العربيّة .   Mauritania

٥ ـ في الاسبوع ـــــ ذهبت لزيارة صديق لي في ـــــ لبنانية .

٦ ـ لم يستطيعوا الوصول الى ـــــ لمشكلتهم .

٧ ـ تطورت الفصحى والعامية تطورا كبيرا ـــــ تاريخهما الطويل .

٨ ـ من المدن ـــــ في العالم العربيّ مَكّةُ والقُدْسُ .   Mecca

٩ ـ ـــــ ـــــ معظم حياته في واشنطن ، لكنّه ـــــ ـــــ في شيكاغو .

١٠ ـ زرت باريس أكثر من ـــــ ـــــ .

١١ ـ ـــــ ـــــ في ـــــ هيلتون ليلة واحدة فقط .

١٢ ـ انصرفوا قبل ـــــ ـــــ الاجتماع .

١٣ ـ ـــــ ـــــ بنا القصة الى زمن قديم .

123

Drill 12. Written. Vocabulary.

Fill in the blanks with the most appropriate word from among the words in the following list:

(تراسل ، يتابع ، نجاح ، انتخاب ، صغير ، الثورة ، المحافظة ، قال ، علّم ، البلاد ، تتوفر ، يظهر ، حكماء ، مقالة ، ذهاب ، مجتمع ، خاص ، عال ، شرّ ، فم ، حاجة .

١ – يجب ان تتوفر للمرأة كل حقوقها لخير ــــــ .
            (country)

٢ – يقول قائد ــــــ : اننا سنقاوم لبناء ــــــ جديد .

٣ – لها اهتمام بــ ــــــ ابنها فى الامتحانات .

٤ – ــــــ رجل كبير ــــــ استفدت منها كل حياتى .
        (taught me)

٥ – هل ــــــ دراستهم الجامعيّة فى مشيغان ؟

٦ – ذهبنا الى مكان ــــــ ومن هناك شاهدنا جمال المدينة .

٧ – ــــــ الحبيبان لمدة سنة ثم انقطعت الرسائل بينهما .

٨ – ــــــ الحزب الوطني اهتماما كبيرا بــ ــــــ على حقوق الشعب .

٩ – لسنا بــ ــــــ الى مراسلين جدد .

Drill 13. Aural comprehension.

Listen to the passage on tape; then write an English summary of it.

أ ـ الجمل التمهيديّة   **A. Preparatory sentences**

زيارة الى سولت ليك سيتي   <u>A Visit to Salt Lake City</u>

١ ـ لي صديق من المَمْلَكَةِ الاردنيّة وهي دولة عربية يحكمهـا مَلِكٌ معروف .

I have a friend from the <u>Kingdom</u> of Jordan, an Arab country ruled by a well-known <u>king</u>.

مَمْلَكَةٌ ـ مَمالِكُ   kingdom, monarchy

مَلِكٌ ـ مُلوكٌ (مَلَكِيٌّ)   king (nisba: royal, royalist)

٢ ـ صديقي من مدينة صغيرة تقع قُرْبَ البَحْرِ الأَحْمَرِ .

My friend is from a small town which is situated <u>near</u> the <u>Red Sea</u>.

قُرْبَ   near, in the vicinity of

بَحْرٌ ـ بِحارٌ   sea

أَحْمَرُ ـ حُمْرٌ   red

البَحْرُ الأَحْمَرُ   the Red Sea

٣ ـ يدرس صديقي الآن في جامعـة يوطا ، وهي جامعة كانت فـي بِدايَةِ أَمْرِها صغيرة ، لكنّها الآن جامعة كبيرة .

My friend is now studying at the University of Utah. It is a university that was small <u>at first</u>, but is now a large university.

في بِدايَةِ الأَمْرِ   in the beginning, at first

٤ ـ دَعاني صديقي لزيارته فـي مدينة سولت ليك سيتي عاصِمَةِ يوطا وَلَقِيَني عند وصولــي بالترحيب والاكرام .

My friend <u>invited</u> me to visit him in Salt Lake City, the <u>capital</u> of Utah, and on my arrival he <u>met</u> me with a warm welcome and kind hospitality.

دَعا ـُ ، دَعْوَةٌ، دُعاءٌ (لِ ، الى)   to call, call upon; to invite (to)

عاصِمَةٌ ـ عَواصِمُ   capital, capital city

لَقِيَ ـَ ، لِقاءٌ   to encounter, meet; to find

سولت ليك سيتي مدينة جميلة في شَمالِ يوطا تُحيطُ بِها الجبالُ .	٥	Salt Lake City is a beautiful city in the <u>north</u> of Utah, <u>surrounded</u> by <u>mountains</u>.

شَمالٌ — north

أحاطَ ، إحاطةٌ بِ — IV to surround

جَبَلٌ — جِبالٌ — mountain

بُنِيَ قَصْرُ حاكِمِ يوطا على احد هذه الجبال .	٦	The <u>mansion</u> of the <u>Governor</u> of Utah <u>was built</u> on one of those mountains.

بَنَى ــ بِناءٌ — to build; construct

قَصْرٌ ــ قُصورٌ — castle, palace (here: mansion)

حاكِمٌ ــ حُكّامٌ — governor; ruler

يَرى بعض الناس أن سولت ليك سيتي أهمية دينية خاصّة ويُحكى انّ فيها آثارا للهنود الامريكيّين ترجع الى عَهدٍ بعيد .	٧	Some people <u>believe</u> that Salt Salt City has special religious importance; <u>it is said</u> that there are in it relics of American <u>Indians</u> which go back to a far-off <u>era</u>.

رَأى يَرى ، رَأيٌ (أَنّ) — to opine, be of the opinion (that)

حكى ــ ، حُكِيَ ، حِكايةٌ — to tell, relate

[هُنْديٌّ ــ هُنودٌ] — [Indian]

عَهدٌ ــ عُهودٌ — age, era, time

في سولت ليك سيتي سَتَرى آثارا لها اهمية عند بعض رجال الدين.	٨	You will see in Salt Lake City relics of importance in the view of some men of religion.

رَأى يَرى ، رُؤْيَةٌ — to see

بَقيتُ في سولت ليك سيتي خمسة ايام رجعت بعدها الى نيويورك.	٩	I <u>stayed</u> in Salt Lake City for five days, after which I returned to New York.

بَقِيَ ــَ ، بَقاءٌ — to remain, stay; (with foll. imperfect) to go on, continue

126

١٠ ــ اللَّوْنُ الاحمر مـن ألوان العَلَمِ الامريكي .

The <u>color</u> red is one of the colors of the American <u>flag</u>.

لَوْنٌ ــ أَلْوانٌ

color

عَلَمٌ ــ أَعْلامٌ

flag, banner

ب ــ النص الاساسي

ثلاث مدن اثرية عربية

دعانـي صديـق اردنـي لزيـارة بـعض الامـاكن الاثريّة فـى الشرق الاوسط ، فذهبـت بـعد نهـاية العـام الـدراسي المـاضي . لقيت مــــن صديقـي عند وصولـي كل ترحيب واكرام ، وبـقيت معه مـدّة شهر زرت خلالـها ثلاث مدن اثريّة هي البَـتْـراءُ وتَـدْمُـرُ وجَرَشُ .

البَـتْراءُ

Petra

في القرن الخامس قَبْلَ المِيلادِ بـنى الأَنْبـاطُ عاصمتـهم البـتراء فى مكان قريب من البـحر الاحمر تحيط بـه الجبـال العـالية . يرى الزائـر في هذه المدينة عددا من هَيـاكِلِ الأنبـاط وقصورهم . كانت مَمْلكةُ الأنبـاط تشمل دمشق وأَجْزاءٌ من فِلَسْطينَ ، كمـا كانت تشمل بـعض المناطق الواقعة على البـحر الاحمر . ويرى البـعض ان الانبـاط عرب كانوا في بـداية امرهم بـدوًا ، وانـهم كانـوا يتكلّمون العـربـية ويستخدمون اللغة الأَرامِيَّةَ في الكتابـة .

the Nabateans — B.C.

temples — parts — Aramaic

127

تقع تَدْمُرُ في الصحراء السورية قرب دمشق ، ويحكى أنّ الـذي

jinn, demons بناها هو الملك سُلَيْمانُ بْنُ داود بمساعدة الجِنّ • وقد كانـــت

للمدينة اهمِّية تجارية كبيرة • وفي الربع الثالث من القرن الثالث

Zenobia الميلادي حكمتها ملكة مشهورة بجمالها هي زَنّوبِيا التي تُعرف عنـــد

العرب باسم " زَيْنَبُ " •

Romans وقد سيطر الرومان على تَدْمُرَ في عهد الملكة زَنّوبِيا ، وفـي

الربع الثاني من القرن السابع الميلادي فتحها القائد العربـــــي

خالِدُ بْنُ الوَليد •

جَرَشُ Jerash

تقع جَرَشُ في الاردنّ الى الشمال من عَمّانَ عاصمة المملكة الاردنية

Hellenic وقد بُنيت في العهد الهِلِّينيّ وكانت من المدن الفِلَسْطينية المذكورة

The Bible في الكتاب المقدس • وفي جَرَشَ اليوم آثار رومانية جميلة كثيرة •

B. __Basic text__

Three Ancient Arab Cities

A Jordanian friend invited me to visit some of the archeological sites
in the Middle East, and I went after the end of the past academic year. Upon
my arrival, I encountered on the part of my friend every (kind of) welcome
and hospitality, and I stayed with him for a period of a month, during which
I visited three ancient cities: Petra, Palmyra, and Jerash.

__Petra__

In the fifth century B.C. the Nabateans built their capital, Petra, in

128

a place near the Red Sea surrounded by high mountains. In this city the visitor sees a number of the Nabateans' temples and palaces.

The Nabateans' kingdom included Damascus and parts of Palestine, as well as some areas lying on the Red Sea. Some are of the opinion that the Nabateans were Arabs who had been bedouins at first, and that they spoke Arabic, but used the Aramaic language in writing.

Palmyra

Palmyra is located in the Syrian Desert near Damascus, and it is said that the one who built it was King Sulaymān Ibn Daʼūd (King Solomon) with the help of jinns. The city had great commercial importance. In the third quarter of the third century A.D. it was ruled by a queen famous for her beauty, Zenobia , who is known among the Arabs by the name of "Zaynab."

The Romans gained control over Palmyra in the time of Queen Zenobia, and in the second quarter of the seventh century A.D. the Arab general Khālid Ibn al-Walīd conquered it.

Jerash

Jerash is situated in Jordan, to the north of Amman, the **capital of** the Kingdom of Jordan. It was built in the Hellenic era, and it was one of the **P**alestinian cities mentioned in the Bible. In Jerash today there are many beautiful Roman ruins.

C. <u>Grammar and drills</u>   ج — القواعد والتمارين

> 1. Defective verbs: Form I
> 2. The verb رَأى 'to see'
> 3. Adjectives of color

1. Defective verbs: Form I

Verbs whose last radical is W or Y constitute a group known as defective
verbs. These verbs, which occur in all the ten Forms except IX, have some
forms which are quite regular. For example, the perfect tense stem of دَعا
'to invite' (root D ʕ W) is دَعَوْ- daʕaw- . This stem is used with suffixes
beginning with a consonant and with the dual suffix -aa, and works exactly
like any Form I strong verb of the pattern FaMaL-:

| katab-naa | كَتَبْنا | 'we wrote' |
| daʕaw-naa | دَعَوْنا | 'we invited' |

In other forms of a defective verb, however, the stem cannot be so
neatly separated from the suffixes. In these forms, the ending of the stem
fuses with the beginning of the suffixes, as a result of automatic phonological changes, in such a way as to make it difficult to say where the stem ends
and the suffix begins. For example, if we take the regular stem daʕaw- as a
base, and add to it the 3 m.s. suffix -a, the resultant form is daʕawa.
This form is not possible, however, as it contains an unpermitted sequence
-awa. Such a sequence is always automatically changed to -aa; thus daʕawa
becomes daʕaa, and that is the actual 3 m.s. form دَعا 'he invited.' Fusions of this sort are what distinguish defective verbs from others; they
occur only with some (not all) suffixes beginning with a vowel. In the following paragraphs Form I defective verbs are described in detail: those of
the derived Forms will be taken up in Lesson 37.

Form I defective verbs fall into three types, with different vowel patterns.

(1) <u>Type 1</u>. Perfect stem: <u>FaMaw-</u>

Imperfect stem: <u>-FMuw-</u>

These are verbs whose final radical is <u>W</u>, for example; دَعا (imperfect يَدْعو) 'to invite' (root <u>D</u> <u>ʕ</u> <u>W</u>). The active conjugation of this verb is given below:

'to invite' دَعا – يَدْعو

	PERFECT	IMPERFECT			
		Indicative	Subjunctive	Jussive	Imperative
3 MS	دَعا	يَدْعو	يَدْعُوَ	يَدْعُ	
FS	دَعَتْ	تَدْعو	تَدْعُوَ	تَدْعُ	
2 MS	دَعَوْتَ	تَدْعو	تَدْعُوَ	تَدْعُ	أُدْعُ
FS	دَعَوْتِ	تَدْعِينَ	تَدْعِي	تَدْعِي	أُدْعِي
1 S	دَعَوْتُ	أَدْعو	أَدْعُوَ	أَدْعُ	
3 MD	دَعَوا	يَدْعُوانِ	يَدْعُوا	يَدْعُوا	
FD	دَعَتا	تَدْعُوانِ	تَدْعُوا	تَدْعُوا	
2 D	دَعَوْتُما	تَدْعُوانِ	تَدْعُوا	تَدْعُوا	أُدْعُوا
3 MP	دَعَوْا	يَدْعونَ	يَدْعوا	يَدْعوا	
FP	دَعَوْنَ	يَدْعونَ	يَدْعونَ	يَدْعونَ	
2 MP	دَعَوْتُمْ	تَدْعونَ	تَدْعوا	تَدْعوا	أُدْعوا
FD	دَعَوْتُنَّ	تَدْعونَ	تَدْعونَ	تَدْعونَ	أُدْعونَ
1 P	دَعَوْنا	نَدْعو	نَدْعُوَ	نَدْعُ	

<u>Active participle</u>: <u>FaaMiy-</u>

131

	Singular	Plural	
Masculine	داعٍ	داعونَ	'inviting, calling'
Feminine	داعِيَةٌ	داعِياتٌ	

Verbal nouns: <u>FuMaa?</u>

دُعاءٌ ، دَعْوَةٌ   'invitation, call'

The following points may be made about these forms:

(1) The perfect stem of this verb is دَعَوْ- <u>daʕaw-</u>. All the forms consisting of this stem plus a suffix beginning with a consonant, or the suffix <u>-aa</u>, are quite regular. The other forms result from fusions of the final <u>-aw</u> of the stem with suffixes beginning with a vowel other than <u>-aa</u>, for example:

(daʕawa) ⟶ daʕ<u>aa</u>	دَعا	'he invited'
(daʕawat) ⟶ daʕ<u>at</u>	دَعَتْ	'she invited'
(daʕawuu ⟶ daʕ<u>aw</u>	دَعَوْا	'they (m.p.) invited'

(In the 3 M.S. perfect, the final <u>-aa</u> in دَعا is spelled with ا <u>alif</u>. This is true only of Form I defective verbs of Type 1, with final radical <u>W</u>. In all other defective verbs it is spelled with ى <u>alif maqsuura</u>.)

(2) The imperfect stem is دْعُوْ- -dʕuw-. All the forms consisting of this stem plus either a suffix beginning with a consonant, or one of the suffixes <u>-aa</u>, <u>-aani</u>, or <u>-a</u>, are quite regular. The other forms result from fusions of the final <u>-uw-</u> of the stem with suffixes beginning with vowels other than <u>-aa</u> or <u>-a</u>, for example:

(yadʕuwu) ⟶ yadʕ<u>uu</u>	يَدْعو	'he invites'
(yadʕuw-uuna ⟶ yadʕ<u>uuna</u>	يَدْعونَ	'they (m.p.) invite'
(tadʕuw-iina) ⟶ tadʕ<u>iina</u>	تَدْعينَ	'you (f.s.) invite'

132

(Note: The 3 m.p. and 3 f.p. forms are identical, but this identity comes about through different processes:)

3 m.p.	(yadʕuw-uuna)	→ yadʕuuna	يَدْعونَ
f.p.	(yadʕuw-na)	→ yadʕuuna	يَدْعونَ

The uu in the m.p. form is the result of the fusion of the final -uw of the stem and the -uu- of the suffix. The uu in the f.p. form is the final -uw of the stem (which before a consonant is pronounced uu, and written uu in the trancription.) The same applies also to the 2 m.p. and 2 f.p. forms.

(3) In those jussive and imperative forms which (in strong verbs) have no suffix, the final w of the stem is dropped, leaving only the short vowel u:

(lam yadʕuw-)	→ lam yadʕu	لَمْ يَدْعُ	'he did not invite'
(ʔudʕuw-)	→ ʔudʕu	اُدْعُ	'invite!'

(4) The active participle stem pattern for all defective form I verbs is FaaMiy-; thus these active participles (in their m.s. form) are all defective adjectives (see 34.C.2). The final consonant of the stem is always y, even for verbs with last radical W.

(5) As always with Form I, there are various verbal noun patterns for defective verbs. If the pattern has a vowel aa before the last radical, as in the example above, a final radical W or Y is always replaced by hamza:

(duʕaaw	→ duʕaaʔ	دُعاءٌ	'invitation'

Another Type 1 verb is تَلا 'to follow' whose active participle تالٍ 'following' was introduced in Lesson 35. Its verbal noun is تُلُوّ .

Now do Drill 1. (On tape)

    (2) <u>Type 2</u>. Perfect stem: <u>FaMay-</u>

                       Imperfect stem: <u>-FMiy-</u>

These are verbs whose final radical is <u>Y</u>, for example بَنَى (imperfect يَبْنِي)

'to build' (root <u>B N Y</u>). The active conjugation of this verb is given below.

بَنَى – يَبْنِي 'to build'

	PERFECT	IMPERFECT			
		Indicative	Subjunctive	Jussive	Imperative
3 MS	بَنَى	يَبْنِي	يَبْنِيَ	يَبْنِ	
FS	بَنَتْ	تَبْنِي	تَبْنِيَ	تَبْنِ	
2 MS	بَنَيْتَ	تَبْنِي	تَبْنِيَ	تَبْنِ	اِبْنِ
FS	بَنَيْتِ	تَبْنِينَ	تَبْنِيَ	تَبْنِي	اِبْنِي
1 S	بَنَيْتُ	أَبْنِي	أَبْنِيَ	أَبْنِ	
3 MD	بَنَيا	يَبْنِيانِ	يَبْنِيا	يَبْنِيا	
FD	بَنَتا	تَبْنِيانِ	تَبْنِيا	تَبْنِيا	
2 D	بَنَيْتُما	تَبْنِيانِ	تَبْنِيا	تَبْنِيا	اِبْنِيا
3 MP	بَنَوْا	يَبْنُونَ	يَبْنُوا	يَبْنُوا	
FP	بَنَيْنَ	يَبْنَيْنَ	يَبْنَيْنَ	يَبْنَيْنَ	
2 MP	بَنَيْتُم	تَبْنُونَ	تَبْنُوا	تَبْنُوا	اِبْنُوا
FP	بَنَيْتُنَّ	تَبْنَيْنَ	تَبْنَيْنَ	تَبْنَيْنَ	اِبْنِينَ
1 P	بَنَيْنا	نَبْنِي	نَبْنِيَ	نَبْنِ	

Active participle: <u>FaaMiy-</u>

	Singular	Plural	
Masculine	بَانٍ	بَانُونَ	'building, constructing'
Feminine	بَانِيَةٌ	بَانِيَاتٌ	

Verbal noun: <u>FiMaa?</u>

بِنَاءٌ   'building, construction'

Note the following points:

(1) The perfect stem of this verb is بَنَيَ <u>banay-</u>. The forms with suffixes beginning with a consonant or <u>-aa</u> are regular. The other forms result from fusions of the final <u>-aw</u> of the stem with vowel suffixes other than <u>-aa</u>, for example:

(ban<u>ay</u>-a) → banaa	بَنَى	'he built'
(ban<u>ay</u>-at) → banat	بَنَتْ	'she built'
(ban<u>ay</u>-uu) → banaw	بَنَوْا	'they (m.p.) built'

(Note that the final <u>-aa</u> of بَنَى is spelled with ى . This is true of all defective verbs except those of Form I with final radical <u>W</u>.)

(2) The imperfect stem is -بْنِيَ- <u>-bniy-</u>. The forms with suffixes beginning with a consonant, or the suffixes <u>-a</u>, <u>-aa</u>, <u>-aani</u>, are regular. The other forms result from fusions of the final <u>-iy-</u> of the stem with vowels other than <u>-a</u> or <u>-aa</u>, for example:

(yabn<u>iyu</u>) → yabnii	يَبْنِي	'he builds'
(tabn<u>iy</u>-iina) → tabniina	تَبْنِينَ	'you (f.s.) build'
(yabn<u>iyuu</u>na) → yabnuuna	يَبْنُونَ	'they (m.p.) build'

(3) In those jussive and imperative forms which (in strong verbs) have
no suffix, the final y of the stem is dropped, leaving only the short vowel
i:

(lam yabn<u>iy</u>) ⟶	lam yabni	لَمْ يَبْنِ	'he did not build'
(?ibn<u>iy</u>) ⟶	?ibni	اِبْنِ	'build!'

(4) The m.s. form of the active participle (pattern <u>FaaMiy-</u>) is a defective adjective بانٍ.

(5) The verbal noun pattern for this particular verb is <u>FiMaa?</u>. If
the pattern has a vowel <u>aa</u> before the last radical, as this one does, a final
<u>W</u> or <u>Y</u> is always replaced by <u>hamza</u>:

(binaa<u>y</u>) ⟶	binaa?	بِنَاءٌ	'building'

Now do Drill 2. (On tape)

(3) <u>Type 3</u>   Perfect stem: <u>FaMiy-</u>
                  Imperfect stem: <u>-FMay-</u>

This type includes both verbs with final radical <u>W</u> and verbs with final
radical <u>Y</u>, but the conjugation is exactly the same in either case:
<u>all</u> verbs of this type have stems ending in y. As an example we shall use
the verb لَقِيَ (imperfect يَلْقَى) 'to find, meet.' The root of this verb is
<u>L Q Y</u>, but the verb forms would be the same even if the root were <u>L Q W</u>.

لَقِيَ – يَلْقى 'to find, meet'

	PERFECT	IMPERFECT			
		Indicative	Subjunctive	Jussive	Imperative
3 MS	لَقِيَ	يَلْقى	يَلْقى	يَلْقَ	
FS	لَقِيَتْ	تَلْقى	تَلْقى	تَلْقَ	
2 MS	لَقِيتَ	تَلْقى	تَلْقى	تَلْقَ	اِلْقَ
FS	لَقِيتِ	تَلْقَيْنَ	تَلْقَيْ	تَلْقَيْ	اِلْقَيْ
1 S	لَقِيتُ	أَلْقى	أَلْقى	أَلْقَ	
3 MD	لَقِيا	يَلْقَيانِ	يَلْقَيا	يَلْقَيا	
FD	لَقِيَتا	تَلْقَيانِ	تَلْقَيا	تَلْقَيا	
2 D	لَقِيتُما	تَلْقَيانِ	تَلْقَيا	تَلْقَيا	اِلْقَيا
3 MP	لَقُوا	يَلْقَوْنَ	يَلْقَوا	يَلْقَوا	
FP	لَقِينَ	يَلْقَيْنَ	يَلْقَيْنَ	يَلْقَيْنَ	
2 MP	لَقِيتُمْ	تَلْقَوْنَ	تَلْقَوا	تَلْقَوا	اِلْقَوا
FP	لَقِيتُنَّ	تَلْقَيْنَ	تَلْقَيْنَ	تَلْقَيْنَ	اِلْقَيْنَ
1 P	لَقِينا	نَلْقى	نَلْقى	نَلْقَ	

Active participle: <u>FaaMiy-</u>

	Singular	Plural	
Masculine	لاقٍ	لاقونَ	'meeting'
Feminine	لاقِيَةٌ	لاقِياتٌ	

Verbal noun: <u>FiMaa?-</u>

لِقاءٌ '(act of) meeting'

Note the following points:

(1) The perfect stem of this verb is <u>laqiy-</u>. All the perfect forms except the 3 m.p. لَقو‍ا are regular, for example:

laqiy-a	لَقِيَ	'he met'
laqiy-tu = laqiitu	لَقيتُ	'I met'

The 3 m.p. form is the result of the fusion of the final <u>-iy</u> of the stem with the <u>-uu</u> of the suffix:

(laqiy-uu) ➝ laquu	لَقوا	'they (m.p.) met'

(2) The imperfect stem is <u>-lqay-</u>. The forms with this stem and suffixes beginning with a consonant or the suffixes <u>-aa</u> or <u>-aani</u> are regular. The other forms result from fusions of the final <u>-ay-</u> of the stem with vowels other than <u>-aa</u>, for example:

(yalqay-u)	➝ yalqaa	يَلْقى	'he meets'
(talqay-iina)	➝ talqayna	تَلْقَيْنَ	'you (f.s.) meet'
(yalqay-uuna)	➝ yalqawna	يَلْقون	'they (m.p.) meet'
(yalqay-a)	➝ yalqaa	يَلْقى	'he meets' (subj.)

(3) In those jussive and imperative forms which (in strong verbs) have no suffixes, the final <u>y</u> of the stem is dropped, leaving only the short vowel <u>a</u>:

(lam yalqay)	➝ lam yalqa	لَمْ يَلْقَ	'he did not stay'
(?ilqay)	➝ ?ilqa	اِلْقَ	'meet!'

(4) The m.s. form of the active participle (pattern FaaMiy-) is a defective adjective لاقٍ .

(5) The verbal noun pattern of this verb is <u>FiMaa?-</u>.   If the pattern
has a vowel <u>aa</u> before the last radical, as this one does, a final <u>W</u> or <u>Y</u> is
always replaced by <u>hamza</u>:

(liqaay)	liqaa?	لِقاءٌ	'meeting'

Now do Drill 3. (On tape)

(4) <u>Passive</u>.   Perfect stem: <u>FuMiy-</u>
           Imperfect stem: <u>-FMay-</u>

The passive conjugation is the same for all three types of Form I defective verbs, for example:

	ACTIVE		PASSIVE		
	<u>Perf.</u>	<u>Imperf.</u>	<u>Perf.</u>	<u>Imperf.</u>	
<u>Type 1</u>	دَعا	يَدْعو	دُعِيَ	يُدْعى	'to invite'
<u>Type 2</u>	بَنى	يَبْني	بُنِيَ	يُبْنى	'to build'
<u>Type 3</u>	لَقِيَ	يَلْقى	لُقِيَ	يُلْقى	'to meet'

The passive forms have endings exactly like those of Type 3. The full conjugation of لُقِيَ 'to be met' is given below as an illustration.

	PERFECT	IMPERFECT		
		Indicative	Subjunctive	Jussive
3 MS	لُقِيَ	يُلْقى	يُلْقى	يُلْقَ
FS	لُقِيَتْ	تُلْقى	تُلْقى	تُلْقَ
2 MS	لُقِيتَ	تُلْقى	تُلْقى	تُلْقَ

FS	لَقِيتِ	تُلْقَيْنَ	تُلْقَيْ	تُلْقَيْ
1 S	لُقِيتُ	أُلْقى	أُلْقى	أُلْقَ
3 MD	لُقِيَا	يُلْقَيَانِ	يُلْقَيَا	يُلْقَيَا
FD	لُقِيَتَا	تُلْقَيَانِ	تُلْقَيَا	تُلْقَيَا
2 D	لُقِيتُما	تُلْقَيَانِ	تُلْقَيَا	تُلْقَيَا
3 MP	لُقوا	يُلْقَوْنَ	يُلْقَوْا	يُلْقَوْا
FP	لُقِينَ	يُلْقَيْنَ	يُلْقَيْنَ	يُلْقَيْنَ
2 MP	لُقِيتُمْ	تُلْقَوْنَ	تُلْقَوْا	تُلْقَوْا
FP	لُقِيتُنَّ	تُلْقَيْنَ	تُلْقَيْنَ	تُلْقَيْنَ
1 S	لُقينا	نُلْقى	نُلْقى	نُلْقَ

Now do Drill 4. (On tape)

The passive participle patterns are the same for Types 2 and 3, different for Type 1:

Type 1:	maFMuww	مَدْعُوّ	'invited'
Type 2:	maFMiyy	مَبْنِيّ	'built'
Type 3:	maFMiyy	مَلْقِيّ	'met'

Now do Drills 5, 6, 7, 8 and 9.

Drill 1. (On tape) Conjugation: FaMaw.

Drill 2. (On tape) Conjugation: FaMay.

Drill 3. (On tape) Conjugation: FaMiy.

Drill 4. (On tape) Conjugation: Passive of Defectives I.

Drill 5. (Also on tape) Substitution.

أ : زار مصر هذا الصيف . نحن   a. 'He visited Egypt this summer. (We)'

ط : زرنا مصر هذا الصيف .   'We visited Egypt this summer.'

١ ــ دعا عددا من الطلاب الى المؤتمر . أنا

٢ ــ بقي في سوريا أسبوعا . هم

٣ ــ دعا الاستاذ الزائر الى الاجتماع . هي

٤ ــ لقي أخاه قرب مكتبي . هما

٥ ــ هل بقي في السينما حتّى ساعة متأخّرة من الليل ؟ أنتما

٦ ــ هل بنيتَ بيتا جديدا ، أنتِ

أ : سيزور العراق هذه السنة (نحن)'   b. 'He will visit Iraq this year. (We)'
'We will visit Iraq this year.'

ط : سنزور العراق هذه السنة .

١ ــ سيدعو بعض المراسلين الى المؤتمر . (انا)

٢ ــ لعله يبقى في تونس عاما . (أنتنّ)

٣ ــ سوف يلقاني قرب المدرسة . (هما)

٤ ــ هل سيبقى في لبنان زمنا طويلا ؟ (أنتما)

٥ ــ كم طالبة دعا الى حفلة الزواج ؟ (أنتِ)

٦ ــ سيبنى عددا من الفنادق في هذه المنطقة . (هم)

Drill 6.   Imperative and negative imperative.

أ : ادع المدير . المساعد   'Call the director. The assistant.'

ط : ادع المدير ، ولكن لا تدع   'Call the director, but do not
المساعد .   call the assistant.'

١ ــ القى صديقتك . والدتها   ٤ ــ القين مندوب الطلاب . المراسل

٢ ــ ادعوا الطلاب . الاساتذة   ٥ ــ ابقين معه . معها

٣ ــ ادع السكرتيرة . أختها   ٦ ــ ادعوا الطبيب . المهندس

141

Drill 7. Written. Transformation: Perfect ⟶ jussive and subjunctive.

'Have you visited your friend?' (soon)   هل زرت صديقك ؟ قريبا

'I haven't visited him until now   لم أزره حتّى الآن ، ولكنّي أريد

but I want to visit him soon.'   ان ازوره قريبا .

١ ـ هل دعوتم مريم الى الحفلة ؟ اليوم

٢ ـ هل لقيت المراسل الأجنبيّ ؟ غدا

٣ ـ هل دعوا وداد الى حفلة الزواج ؟ هذا الاسبوع

٤ ـ هل لقين المدير ؟ بعد يومين

٥ ـ هل بنوا المدرسة الجديدة ؟ هذه السنة

٦ ـ هل دعت الطلاب الى الحفلة ؟ اليوم

Drill 8. Written. Transformation: Verbal noun ⟶ verb.

Give the verb which corresponds to each of the underlined words; then

translate the sentences:

١ ـ وصلتني دعوة لحضورحفلة زواج .

٢ ـ قابلته بعد مضيّ سنة على رجوعه من فرنسا .

٣ ـ لن نتمكّن من البقاء طويلا في هذه المدينة .

٤ ـ أحبها منذ اللقاءالأوّل .

٥ ـ لم اسمع هذا الكلام قبل اليوم .

٦ ـ البنتاجون بناءكبير جدّا .

Drill 9. Written. Transformation. Perfect: Active ⟶ passive.

a.   'We invited the friends to the party.' دعونا الاصدقاء الى الحفلة : أ

   'They were invited to the party. دعوا الى الحفلة . هم اذن : ط

   They are guests, then.'   مدعوّون .

١ ـ دعوت المراسلة الى الاجتماع . ٢ ـ حكى الناس القصتين .

٣ ــ دعت جاراتها الى بيتها .   ٥ ــ بنوا مدرسة على الجبل .

٤ ــ بنينا البيتين قرب الجبل .   ٦ ــ دعونا الاستاذات الى المؤتمر .

b. Rewrite the passive sentences in the imperfect.

2. **The verb** رَأَى **'to see'**

The verb رَأَى (imperfect يَرى) 'to see' is a defective verb with root

R ? Y. It has two irregular features: First, the middle radical **?** is lost

in the imperfect. Second, the perfect tense is conjugated like the perfect

of بَنَى 'to build' (see Type 2 verbs in C.1 above), while the imperfect tense

is conjugated like the imperfect of رَقِيَ (see Type 3 verbs in C.1 above).

The full conjugation follows:

	PERFECT	IMPERFECT			
		Indicative	Subjunctive	Jussive	Imperative
3 MS	رَأَى	يَرى	يَرى	يَرَ	
FS	رَأَتْ	ترى	ترى	تَرَ	
2 MS	رَأَيْتَ	ترى	ترى	تَرَ	رَ
FS	رَأَيْتِ	تَرَيْنَ	تَرَيْ	تَرَيْ	رَيْ
1 S	رَأَيْتُ	أَرى	أَرى	أَرَ	
3 MD	رَأَيا	يَرَيانِ	يَرَيا	يَرَيا	
FD	رَأَتا	تَرَيانِ	تَرَيا	تَرَيا	
2 D	رَأَيْتُما	تَرَيانِ	تَرَيا	تَرَيا	رَيا
3 MP	رَأَوْا	يَرَوْنَ	يَرَوْا	يَرَوْا	
FP	رَأَيْنَ	يَرَيْنَ	يَرَيْنَ	يَرَيْنَ	

143

2 MP	رَأَيْتُمْ	تَرَوْنَ	تَرَوْا	تَرَوْا	رَوْا
FP	رَأَيْتُنَّ	تَرَيْنَ	تَرَيْنَ	تَرَيْنَ	رَيْنَ
1 P	رَأَيْنا	نَرى	نَرى	نَرَ	

(The imperative forms of this verb are rarely used.)

Active participle: FaaMiy-

	Singular	Plural
Masculine	رَاءٍ	رَاءُونَ
Feminine	رَائِيَةٌ	رَائِياتٌ

Verbal noun: FuMLa(t)   FaML

رُؤْيَةٌ 'seeing'   رَأْيٌ 'view, opinion'

In the passive also, the middle radical **?** **is lost in the imperfect.**

Otherwise the passive is conjugated like that of any Form I defective verb

(see Passive in C.1 above). Examples:

رُئِيَ	'he was seen'	يُرى	'he is seen'
رُئِيتُ	'I was seen'	أُرى	'I am seen'
رُوُوا	'they (m.p.) were seen'	يُرَوْنَ	'they (m.p.) are seen'

The passive participle is مَرْئِيٌّ 'seen'.

Now do Drill 10.

Drill 10. (On tape) Conjugation: رأى

3. Adjectives of color

Adjectives of color have a special set of patterns in Arabic, exemplified

below by أَحْمَرُ 'red'.

	Pattern	Example: 'red'
masc. sing.	?aFMaL^2	أَحْمَرُ
fem. sing.	FaMLaa?^{2}	حَمْرَاءُ
m./f. plur.	FuML	حُمْرٌ

(The symbol ^{2} denotes a diptote pattern.)

The duals for masculine and feminine are ?aFMaLaani and FaMLaawaani res-
pectively, e.g. أَحْمَرَانِ and حَمْرَاوَانِ . The common colors are:

	?aFMaL^2 (m.s.)	FamLaa?^{2} (f.s.)	FuML (p.)
'red'	أَحْمَرُ	حَمْرَاءُ	حُمْرٌ
'white'	أَبْيَضُ	بَيْضَاءُ	بِيضٌ
'black'	أَسْوَدُ	سَوْدَاءُ	سُودٌ
'green'	أَخْضَرُ	خَضْرَاءُ	خُضْرٌ
'yellow'	أَصْفَرُ	صَفْرَاءُ	صُفْرٌ
'blue'	أَزْرَقُ	زَرْقَاءُ	زُرْقٌ
'brown-skinned, tawny	أَسْمَرُ	سَمْرَاءُ	سُمْرٌ
'blond, fair	أَشْقَرُ	شَقْرَاءُ	شُقْرٌ

The adjective أَسْمَرُ refers only to skin color (brown, tawny), while أَشْقَرُ

refers to a person's hair (blond, fair-haired) or skin (fair-complexioned).

These two adjectives commonly take the feminine plural form FaMLaawaat, i.e.

شَقْرَاوَاتٌ and سَمْرَاوَاتٌ . The plural of أَبْيَضُ 'white' ?abyadu should be buyd

according to the formula FuML; the form that actually occurs is بِيضٌ biid,

showing the change uy ➞ ii parallel to the change ui ➞ ii of Rule H2,

L.32.C.2 (p. 49). Corresponding to adjectives of color are nouns of color,

145

mostly of the pattern FuMla(t):

حُمْرَةٌ 'redness' زُرْقَةٌ 'blueness'

خُضْرَةٌ 'greenness' سُمْرَةٌ 'brownness'

صُفْرَةٌ 'yellowness' شُقْرَةٌ 'blondness'

The pattern FaMaaL is used for nouns with hollow roots: بَيَاضٌ 'white-ness' and سَوَادٌ 'blackness'.

A third pattern, FaMaL, also occurs, as with شَقَرٌ 'blondness', زَرَقٌ 'blue-ness'.

Nouns of color are used in expressing degree of comparison in color; this is achieved through use of أَكْثَرُ 'more' or أَشَدُّ 'more intense' plus the noun of color as an accusative of specification:

أَشَدُّ سَوَادًا 'blacker' أَقَلُّ سَوَادًا 'less black'

أَشَدُّ بَيَاضًا 'whiter' أَقَلُّ بَيَاضًا 'less white'

أَكْثَرُ حُمْرَةً 'redder' أَقَلُّ حُمْرَةً 'less red'

Form IX verbs are derived from adjectives of color of the pattern ?aFMaL[2], e.g. اِسْوَدَّ 'to turn black' and اِزْرَقَّ 'to turn blue'.

Other color adjectives are derived from nouns by the nisba suffix, e.g. بُرْتُقَالِيٌّ 'orange' (color) from بُرْتُقَالٌ 'orange' (fruit) and بُنِّيٌّ 'brown' (referring to objects) from بُنٌّ 'coffee beans, coffee'.

Drill 11. Substitution.

'Red is one of the colors of the American flag.'
(Green-Kuwaiti)

أ : اللون الاحمر من ألوان العلم الامريكيّ . ___ أخضر ، كويتيّ .

'Green is one of the colors of the Kuwaiti flag.'

ط : اللون الاخضر من الوان العلم الكويتيّ .

146

١ ـ أسود، أردنيّ .   ٦ ـ أخضر، أردنيّ .

٢ ـ أبيض، مصريّ .   ٧ ـ أسود، مصريّ .

٣ ـ أحمر، مصريّ .   ٨ ـ أزرق، امريكيّ .

٤ ـ أحمر، أردنيّ .   ٩ ـ أحمر، كويتيّ .

٥ ـ أبيض، امريكيّ .   ١٠ ـ بنّى ، قطريّ .

Drill 12.   Substitution.

'This pencil is red and this paper   أ : هذا القلم أحمر اللون ، وهذه
is red too.'   (white)   الورقة حمراء اللون أيضا . أبيض

'This pencil is white and this paper ط : هذا القلم أبيض اللون ، وهذه
is white too.'   الورقة بيضاء اللون ايضا .

أسود ، أحمر ، أخضر ، أصفر ، أزرق ، بنّيّ

Drill 13.   Rewrite the word in parenthesis in its correct form and then

vocalize it fully.

١ ـ فى امريكا ناس يعرفون بالهنود الامريكيين ، وهم اقلّ عددا مـــــن
الـ (أبيض) والمعروف ايضا ان الـ (أسود) فى امريكا اقلّ من الـ(أبيض) .

٢ ـ يعرف سكّان بعض الدول بالـ (أصفر) .

٣ ـ من سكّان العالم من يعرفون بالـ (أبيض) ، ومن يعرفون بالـ (أسود)
ومن يعرفون بالـ (أصفر) ، ولكن ليس منهم من يعرفون بالـ (أزرق) او
الـ (أخضر) .

٤ ـ كان في المؤتمر نساء (أسود) كما كان فيه نساء (أبيض) .

٥ ـ في المدرسة استاذان (أسود) وأستاذتان (أسود) .

147

٦ـ الامريكيّون أكثر (أبيض) من العرب •

٧ـ هؤلاء أكثر (أسود) من أولئك •

٨ـ ماء البحر أكثر (أزرق) من ماء النهر •

D. <u>Comprehension passage</u>   د ـ <u>نصوص للفهم</u>

Read the following passage and then do Drill 14 which is based on it.

مذكرات زائر امريكـــــــــيّ

thesis;   ارنست كمبل طالب في جامعة كورنيل ، وهو الآن يعدّ <u>رسالَةً</u> عن الوضع
treatise
السياسيّ في الشرق الاوسط •

زار كمبل عددا من الدول العربيّة في العام الماضي ، وكتب أثناء

We present, submit to you   زيارته مذكّرات <u>نَعْرِضُ عَلَيْكَ</u> بعضها :

September   ٣ <u>أَيْلولَ</u> (سِـتَمْبِر) سنة ١٩٧٥•

وصلت الى بيروت ، عاصمة لبنان ، منذ يومين ، وسكنت في فندق صغير؛
لكنّ صديقي اللبنانيّ بَشير شاهين طلب مِنّي أن انتقل الى بيته وان ابقى

generous I leave   هناك حتى <u>ارحل عن</u> لبنان • الشعب اللبنانيّ <u>كَريمٌ</u> : لقد لقيت من عائلة
صديقي كل الترحيب والاكرام • لعلّ احدهم يذهب الى امريكا فأكرمه •

السيّارات هنا كثيرة جدًّا : سيّارات ليس لها عدد تذهب وتجيء فـي

camels   شوارع العاصمة • أين <u>الجِمالُ</u> التي قيل لي اني سأراها في البلاد العربيّة ؟!

٥ <u>أَيْلولَ</u> (سبتمبر) سنة ١٩٧٥•

لقد زرت أكثر الدول الأوربيّة فلم ار أجمل من لبنان : مدنه جميلة ،
وقراه جميلة ، وجباله جميلة ، وكلّ شيء فيه جميل • والشعب اللبنانيّ يعلم
ذلك كلّ العلم ، وهو لذلك يحبّ لبنان كلّ الحبّ •

٦ سِـتَمْبِر سنة ١٩٧٥•

148

قلت امس ان الشعب اللبنانيّ كَريمٌ ، واقول اليوم انه ايضا شعب t[rous] تجارة . ولعلّ السبب في ذلك انّ لبنان في وسط العالم ، وانّه يقع على البَحْرِ الأَبْيَضِ الْمُتَوَسِّطِ ، وان موارده قليلة . ولكن اذا اردت ان تجد The Mediterranean [ars], markets من الناس اكراما فلا تذهب الى الأَسْواقِ .

١٥ أَيْلُول (سِبْتَمْبَر) سنة ١٩٧٥ .

تابعت سفري ووصلت الى عمّان،عاصمة المملكة الاردنيّة ، مساء امس؛ وانا الآن اسكن في فندق على مسافة قصيرة من قصر الملك . كل الذين قابلتهم في الفندق يعرفون اللغة الانكليزيّة .

الحياة في عمان كالحياة في غيرها من المدن العربيّة ؛ عمل كثير، ونشاط ليس له نهاية ، وزوّار يذهبون وغيرهم يجيئون . لكنّ عمّان تختلف عن بيروت . فيم تختلف ؟ لست متأكّدا ! وكيف استطيع ان أتأكّد بعد بقائي هنا يوما واحدا ؟ احتاج الى وقت اطول .

٢٧ تِشْرين الأوّل (أُكْتوبر) سنة ١٩٧٥ . [ober]

منذ ثلاثة ايام وصلت الى بور سعيد بعد زيارة قصيرة لِقُبْرُصَ . ومن [us] قُبْرُصَ ذهبت في سَفينةٍ مصرية صغيرة الى السويس ، ثم جئت بالاوتوبيس الى ship القاهرة .

بور سعيد مدينة مصريّة كبيرة تقع على البحر الابيض المتوسّط ، اما السويس فهي مدينة مصرية تقع على البحر الاحمر قرب سيناءَ . والقناة [i] التي تربط بور سعيد بالسويس هي قناة السويس . في تلك القناة سارت سَفينَتُنا . هذه اذن هي القناة التي تتحدّث عنها صحف الغرب والتي اثرت في حياة مصر تأثيرا عظيما ! كنت انظر في مياهها فأرى الف صورة وصورة واقرأ الف قصة وقصة واسمع الف حكمة وحكمة : كنت ارى صورا لحياة مصر واقرأ قصصًا من تاريخها .

١٠ كانون الاول (ديسمبر) سنة ١٩٧٥ . [mber]

١٠ كانون الاول (ديسمبر) سنة ١٩٧٥

انا الآن في مدينة تونس، وبعد اسبوع اعود الى الولايات المتحدة •

مما لا شك فيه ان تونس دولة عربية وان شعبها عربي ، لكن الحياة هنا تختلف عن الحياة في الدول العربية الاخرى • الحياة فى مدينة تونس اقرب الى الحياة في اوربا • أيكون ذلك لانّ الفرنسيين اثروا على الشعب التونسي تاثيرا كبيرا ، ام لان العاصمة التونسية قريبة من اوربا ، ام لان عددا كبيرا من السياسيين والاساتذة التونسيين قد تعلموا في اوربا ام لان مدينة تونس تستقبل كلّ عام عددا غير قليل من الزوار الاوربيين ، ام لهذه الاسباب كلها ولاسباب اخرى لا اعرفها ؟

Drill 14. Written.

١ ــ من هو ارنست كمبل ؟

٢ ــ اذكر بعض المدن العربية التي زارها كمبل فى العام الماضي •

٣ ــ اين سكن كمبل اثناء زيارته للبنان ؟

٤ ــ ما رأي كمبل في لبنان ؟ وما رأيه في الشعب اللبناني ؟

٥ ــ ما عاصمة الاردن ؟

٦ ــ صف الحياة التي رآها كمبل في الاردن ؟

٧ ــ هل ذهب كمبل من بور سعيد الى السويس بالطائرة ؟

٨ ــ اكان كمبل يعرف شيئا عن حياة مصر وتاريخها قبل زيارته للشرق الاوسط ؟ كيف علمت ذلك ؟

٩ ــ كيف تختلف الحياة في تونس عن الحياة في الدول العربية الاخرى؟

١٠ ــ هل يزور تونس كل عام اوربيون كثيرون ؟

١١ ــ ترجم الى الانكليزية مذكرة ٥ ايلول (سبتمبر).

E. **General drills**

Drill 15. Written. Completion: Cognate accusative

'He became interested in the subject.'

اهتمّ بالموضوع

'He became greatly interested in the
subject.'

اهتمّ بالموضوع اهتماما عظيما .

'He became fully interested in the
subject.'

اهتمّ بالموضوع كلّ الاهتمام .

'He became somewhat interested in the
subject.'

اهتمّ بالموضوع بعض الاهتمام

٧ ـ أحبّته ...   ١ ـ لقى صديقه ....

٨ ـ نجحت الثورة ...   ٢ ـ أشكّ فى قوله ...

٩ ـ يختلف الفن العربى عن الفن   ٣ ـ احتفلوا برجوعى ...
الغربىّ ...   ٤ ـ تغيّر الوضع الاقتصادىّ ...

١٠ ـ يعتمدون علينا ...   ٥ ـ انتشرت الصناعة فى مصر...

١١ ـ استقبل الوزير ...   ٦ ـ وصف الكاتب حياة الشعب
الليبىّ .

Drill 16. Written. Sentence formation.

Use each of the following words in a meaningful sentence:

سبّب ـ توفّر ـ أنشأ ـ تراسل ـ مجلّة ـ نسخة ـ نشاط ـ ثقافة ـ تصرّف ـ
وَعَدَ

أ ـ الجمل التمهيدية

العائلة الامريكية

A. **Preparatory sentences**

The American Family

١ ـ سَعْدٌ: صباح الخير يا بيتر.

Good morning, Peter.

٢ ـ بيتر: صباح النور.

Good morning.

٣ ـ سَعْدٌ: اريد أن اسألك عن بعض الامور التي تتصل بالعائلة الامريكية.

I wish to ask you about some matters that have to do with the American family.

٤ ـ بيتر: حسنا. ماهي اسئلتك؟

Fine. What are your questions?

٥ ـ س: سمعت ان للأمِّ الامريكية مكانة مساوية لمكانة الاب.

I have heard that the American <u>mother</u> has a position equal to that of the father.

أُمٌّ ـ أُمَّهاتٌ

mother

٦ ـ ب: الرأي السائِدُ هو ان مكانتها مساوية لمكانة الاب، لكنّ وظيفتها في العائلة مختلفة عن وظيفته. فهي التي تَقومُ بتربية الاولاد مثلا.

The <u>prevalent</u> view is that her status is equal to that of the father, but her function in the family is different from his, for she is the one who <u>carries out</u> the rearing of the children, for example.

سادَ ـ ُ ، سِيادَةٌ
قامَ ـ ُ ، قِيامٌ ب

to prevail, reign; master, rule

to undertake, concern o.s. with, practice

٧ ـ س: هل مكانة المرأة مساوية لمكانة الرجل في كلّ العائلات الامريكية؟

Is the woman's position equal to the man's in all American families?

٨ ـ ب: في عدد كبير من العائلات. وعلى الرَّغْمِ من ذلك فمكانتها اقل من مكانته في بعض العائلات الفقيرة.

In a large number of them, but <u>in spite of</u> that her prestige is less than his in some poor families. Most Americans still consider

واكثر الامريكيّين ما زالوا يعتبرون الرجل مَسْؤولًا عَنِ العائلة .

the man to be <u>responsible for</u> the family.

عَلى الرُّغْمِ مِن .. فَ

in spite of

مَسْؤُولٌ – ون (عن)

responsible (for); an official

٩ – س : القانونُ الامريكي يمنح المرأة نفس حقوق الرجل ، أليس كذلك؟

American <u>law</u> grants women the same rights as men, doesn't it?

قانونٌ – قَوانينٌ

law; code; regulation

١٠ – ب : المرأة اليوم تطالب مطالبة قَوِيَّةً بمثل هذا القانون .

Women today are <u>strongly</u> demanding such a law.

قَوِيٌّ – أَقْوِياءٌ

strong, powerful

١١ – س : اهذا هو القانون الذي يُسمَّى " قانون الحقوق المدنية "؟

Is this the law that <u>is called</u> the "Civil Rights" law?

سَمَّى ، تَسْمِيَةٌ

II to name, call

[الحُقوقُ المَدَنِيَّةُ]

[Civil Rights]

١٢ – ب : لا . هو الذي يُدْعى " قانون التساوي في الحقوق " .

No, it is the one that <u>is called</u> the "Equal Rights Law."

دَعا ـ ، دُعاءٌ (ب)

to call, name (s.o.) (s.th.)

[التَّساوي في الحُقوقِ]

[Equal Rights]

١٣ – س : في أيّ عمر يَسْتَقِلّ الاولاد؟

At what age do the children <u>become independent</u>?

اِسْتَقَلَّ ، اِسْتِقْلالٌ

X to be , become independent

١٤ – ب : اكثرهم يستقلّون قبل العشرين من عمرهم .

Most of them are on their own by the age of twenty.

153

١٥ ــ س : يقال ان العائلة الامريكية لا تربطها بأقارب روابط قوية .

It is said that the American fam-ily is not bound by strong ties to its <u>relatives</u>.

قَرِيبٌ ــ أَقَارِبُ ، أَقْرِبَاءُ

relative, relation

١٦ ــ ب : احيانا . فالامريكي قَـدْ يقيم في ولاية ويقيم اقاربه في ولاية اخرى بعيدة. وليس من عادات الاقارب ان يَتَبَادَلُوا الزيارات او يستقبلوا الضُيوفَ بِدونِ تحديد المواعيد .

Sometimes. The American <u>might</u> reside in one state while his relatives reside in another one far away. And it is not the rela-tives' <u>custom</u> to <u>exchange</u> visits or have <u>guests without</u> setting the dates.

قَدْ

(before imperfect) perhaps, maybe; sometimes

عَادَةٌ ــ اتٌ

custom, habit

تَبَادَلَ ، تَبَادُلٌ

VI to exchange

ضَيْفٌ ــ ضُيُوفٌ

guest

بِدونِ = دونَ

without

١٧ ــ س : شكرا . أنستطيع أن نتابع بحث هذا الموضوع غدا ؟

Thanks. Can we continue the dis-cussion of this subject tomorrow?

١٨ ــ ب : إذا أحببت .

<u>If</u> you like.

إذا

if; when; whenever

المفردات الاضافية

Additional vocabulary

١٩ ــ لماذا يَقولونَ لِأحمد "ابو اسعد؟"

Why do they <u>call</u> Ahmad "Abu As'ad"?

قال ــُ قَوْلٌ لِـ

to call s.o. s.th.

٢٠ ــ غَنّى عن رجل فقير ليس عنده دولار.

He <u>sang</u> about a poor man who did not have a <u>dollar</u>.

غَنّى ، غِناءٌ
دولار ــ ات

II to sing
dollar

٢١ ــ إنْ

if, if it should be that

٢٢ ــ لَوْ .. لَـ

if, if it were that

154

العائـــلة العربيـــة

العائلة العربية هي الوحدة الاساسية في بناء المجتمــع

العربـــــيّ .

varies...
according to
the various

تَخْتَلِفُ العائلة العربية بـاخْتِلاف البلدان والاديان والوضع

الاجتماعيّ ، فالعائلة فى ليبيا مثلا تختلف عن العائلة فى مصر ،

والعائلة في المملكة العربية السعودية تختلف عنها فى لبنان.كذلك

تختلف العائلة المسلمة عن العائلة المسيحيّة او العائلة اليـهوديّة .

وتختلف العائلة الغنيّة عن العائلة الفقيرة .

characteris-
tics

وعلى الرغم من هذه الاختلافات فان هناك <u>صِفات</u> تمتاز بـها

العائلة العربية .

generosity

فالعائلة العربية معروفة بـال<u>كَرَم</u> ، فهي تظهر للضيـــف

الترحيب وتقدّم له الطعام . وكثير من العائلات العربية تطلب من الزائر

ان يشاركها طعامها حتى اذا لم يكن مدعوّا . ولذلك كلّه تأثير علـى

sons and
daughters

<u>البَنِينَ والبَنات</u> ، فالعربيّ يعتبر الآكل معه ضيفا حتى اذا كانا فـي

مطعم .

والعربي يحترم جيرانه ويساعدهم عندما يحتاجون الـــى

المساعدة ، والعرب يقولون : <u>إنَّ النَبِيَّ قَدْ أَوْصى بِسابِعِ جارٍ</u> .

الاب رأس العائلة العربية ، وهو المسؤول عنها اقتصاديا

واجتماعيا . يحترمه اعضاء العائلة الى ابعد الحدود ، ويقدّم هـو

لاعضاء عائلته كل خدمة يستطيع تقديمها . والامّ سيّدة البيت ومديرتـه :

تقوم بـتربية اولادها ويقدّم لـها زوجها واولادها اعظم الاحترام .والعرب

يقولون : <u>الجَنَّةُ تَحْتَ أَقْدامِ الأُمَّهاتِ</u> .

يقوم الاب والامّ بتربية اولادهما <u>ويُوَفِّران</u> لهم كل حاجاتهم   they provide

<u>الى</u> ان يستقلّوا في حياتهم ، وعند ذلك يقوم كل ابن بتقديم المساعدة   until

لوالديه .

ومن العادات العربية ان يدعى الوالدان باسم ابنهما الاكبر ، فيقال

للوالد " ابو أسعد " وتسمّى الوالدة " أمّ اسعد " اذا كان اسم ابنهما

الاكبر " اسعد " .

من أهمّ <u>صفات</u> العائلة العربية ان هناك رابطة قوية بين اعضائها .   characteristics

ولا تشمل تلك الرابطة الوالدين واولادهما فقط ، بل تشمل ايضا <u>الأعمامُ</u>   paternal
uncles

<u>والأخْوَالَ</u> وغيرهم من الاقارب . والتعاون لا يكون بين اعضاء العائلة   maternal
uncles

الواحدة فقط ، بل يكون ايضا بين عائلات الاقارب . ومن السائد بين

العرب ان يتبادل الاقارب الزيارات في <u>الأعْيَا</u>د ، بل وبدون <u>مُناسَبَة</u> .   holidays;
occasions

ويقيم الابن او الابنة في بيت الوالدين الى يوم الزواج ، وقد يقيم

الابن في بيت والديه بعد زواجه . ومن المعروف ان ابناء العائلة

يستطيعون ان يتزوّجوا من بنات اعمامهم واخوالهم .

B. **Basic text**

The Arab Family

The Arab family is the basic unit in the structure of Arab society.

The Arab family varies according to country, religion and social condition;

the family in Libya, for example, is different from the family in Egypt, and

the family in the Kingdom of Saudi Arabia is different from that of Lebanon.

The Muslim family likewise is different from the Christian or the Jewish fam-

ily, and the rich family is different from the poor one.

156

In spite of these differences there are characteristics by which the Arab family is distinguished:

The Arab family is famous for its hospitality; it shows the guest a warm welcome and offers him food. Many Arab families ask the guest to share their food with them, even if he has not been invited. All of this has its influence on the children, for the Arab considers anyone eating with him as his guest, even if they are in a restaurant.

The Arab respects his neighbors and helps them when they need help. Arabs say "The Prophet has entrusted (to us) the seventh neighbor" (that is, we are responsible not for our next-door neighbor alone, but for all our neighbors up to seven and more.)

The father is the head of the Arab family, and he is responsible for it economically and socially. He is respected by the members of his family to the greatest extent, and he presents to the members of his family every service that he can. The mother is the lady of the house and its manager--she undertakes the upbringing of her children and her husband and her children accord her the greatest of respect. The Arabs say, "Paradise lies at the feet of the mothers."

The father and mother undertake the upbringing of their children and provide for all their needs until they begin to lead independent lives. At that point each son undertakes to offer assistance to his parents.

One of the Arabs' customs is for the parents to be called by the name of their oldest son. The father is called "Abū As'ad" and the mother is called "Umm As'ad" if their oldest son's name is As'ad.

One of the most important traits of the Arab family is that there is a strong bond between its members. Nor does that bond include the parents and their children alone, it also includes the paternal and maternal uncles and other relatives. And there is cooperation not only among the members of a single family but also between the relatives' families. A prevalant (custom) among the Arabs is for relatives to exchange visits on holidays, and even when it is not a special occasion.

The son or the daughter lives in the parents' house until their wedding day, and the son might reside in his parents' house after getting married. And it is a well-known fact that the sons in a family can marry their first cousins.

C. <u>Grammar and drills</u>   ج – ا لـقـوا عـد و الـتـمـا ريـن

---

1. Defective verbs: Derived Forms

2. قَدْ 'perhaps' with the imperfect

3. Existential sentences, "there is, there are...": Summary

4. Conditional sentences

5. Declinable prepositions

---

1. <u>Defective verbs: Derived Forms</u>

There are defective verbs in all the derived Forms (except for Form IX verbs all of which are conjugated like doubled verbs). Some defective verbs have <u>W</u> as their last radical and some <u>Y</u>, but both <u>W</u> and <u>Y</u> show up as <u>y</u> in derived verbs, and are all conjugated the same way within each Form:

158

(1) In the perfect tense, all derived defective verbs have stems ending in -ay and thus are conjugated like the perfect tense of بَنَى 'to build' (see Type 2 verbs in 36.C.1).

(2) In the imperfect tense, all have stems ending in -iy and are conjugated like the imperfect tense of بَنَى (imperfect يَبْنِي), except Forms V and VI, which have imperfect stems ending in -ay and thus are conjugated like the imperfect of لَقِيَ (imperfect يَلْقَى) (see Type 3 verbs in 36.C.1).

(3) In the passive, all have perfect stems ending in -iy and imperfect stems ending in -ay, and are conjugated like the passive of all Form I verbs (see Passive in 36.C.1).

(4) The active participle stems all end in -iy; therefore the masculine singular forms of these participles are defective adjectives (see 34.C.2).

(5) The passive participles all have stems ending in -ay; therefore their masculine singular forms are all indeclinables (see 31.C.2). Each of the derived Forms is discussed below.

Form II

STEM PATTERNS

	Perfect	Imperfect	Participle
Active	FaMMay-	-FaMMiy-	muFaMMiy-
Passive	FuMMiy-	-FaMMay-	muFaMMay-
Verbal noun: taFMiya(t)-			

Form II defective verbs are conjugated throughout like بَنَى 'to build'. Note that the verbal noun of these verbs is a feminine noun ending in ـَة. As an illustration, the following charts give all the forms of the verb سَمَّى

159

'to name, call (someone) (something)'. (Note: this verb is derived from the noun اِسْم 'name', whose root has only two radicals: S M. Since every verb must have at least three radicals, a Y is added, making the root of the verb S M Y.)

ACTIVE

	PERFECT (Stem: sammay-)	IMPERFECT (Stem: -sammiy-)			
		Indicative	Subjunctive	Jussive	Imperative
3 MS	سَمَّى	يُسَمِّي	يُسَمِّيَ	يُسَمِّ	
FS	سَمَّتْ	تُسَمِّي	تُسَمِّيَ	تُسَمِّ	
2 MS	سَمَّيْتَ	تُسَمِّي	تُسَمِّيَ	تُسَمِّ	سَمِّ
FS	سَمَّيْتِ	تُسَمِّينَ	تُسَمِّي	تُسَمِّي	سَمِّي
1 S	سَمَّيْتُ	أُسَمِّي	أُسَمِّيَ	أُسَمِّ	
3 MD	سَمَّيَا	يُسَمِّيَانِ	يُسَمِّيَا		
FD	سَمَّتَا	تُسَمِّيَانِ	تُسَمِّيَا		
2 D	سَمَّيْتُمَا	تُسَمِّيَانِ	تُسَمِّيَا		سَمِّيَا
3 MP	سَمَّوْا	يُسَمُّونَ	يُسَمُّوا		
FP	سَمَّيْنَ		يُسَمِّينَ		
2 MP	سَمَّيْتُمْ	تُسَمُّونَ	تُسَمُّوا		سَمُّوا
FP	سَمَّيْتُنَّ		تُسَمِّينَ		سَمِّينَ
1 P	سَمَّيْنَا	نُسَمِّي	نُسَمِّيَ	نُسَمِّ	

Active participle (Stem: _musammiy-_)		
	Singular	Plural
Masc.	مُسَمٍّ	مُسَمّونَ
Fem.	مُسَمِّيَةٌ	مُسَمِّيَاتٌ

Verbal noun (Stem: _tasmiya(t)-_)
تَسْمِيَةٌ

This pattern--taFMiLa(t)--is sometimes used with non-weak verbs as well, in addition to the regular pattern taFMiiL, e.g. قَدَّمَ 'to introduce' has both تَقْدِيمٌ and تَقْدِمَةٌ .

PASSIVE

	PERFECT (Stem: _summiy-_)	IMPERFECT (Stem: _-sammay-_)		
		Indicative	Subjunctive	Jussive
3 MS	سُمِّيَ	يُسَمّى	يُسَمّى	يُسَمَّ
FS	سُمِّيَتْ	تُسَمّى	تُسَمّى	تُسَمَّ
2 MS	سُمِّيتَ	تُسَمّى	تُسَمّى	تُسَمَّ
FS	سُمِّيتِ	تُسَمَّيْنَ	تُسَمَّيْ	
1 S	سُمِّيتُ	أُسَمّى	أُسَمّى	أُسَمَّ
3 MD	سُمِّيَا	يُسَمَّيَانِ	يُسَمَّيَا	
FD	سُمِّيَتَا	تُسَمَّيَانِ	تُسَمَّيَا	
2 D	سُمِّيتُمَا	تُسَمَّيَانِ	تُسَمَّيَا	

161

3 MP	سُمُّوا	يُسَمَّوْنَ	يُسَمَّوْا
FP	سُمِّينَ	يُسَمَّيْنَ	
2 MP	سُمِّيتُم	تُسَمَّوْنَ	تُسَمَّوْا
FP	سُمِّيتُنَّ	تُسَمَّيْنَ	
1 P	سُمِّينَا	نُسَمَّى	نُسَمَّيْ · نُسَمَّ

Passive participle (Stem: musammay-)	
	Singular	Plural
Masc.	مُسَمَّى	مُسَمَّوْنَ
Fem.	مُسَمَّاةٌ	مُسَمَّيَاتٌ

Form III

STEM PATTERNS

	Perfect	Imperfect	Participle
Active	FaaMay-	-FaaMiy-	muFaaMiy-
Passive	FuuMiy-	-FaaMay-	muFaaMay-
Verbal noun: muFaaMaa(t)-			

Form III defective verbs are conjugated throughout like بَنَى 'to build'. As examples, some forms of the verb نَادَى 'to call to, summon' are given below. Here, and in the illustrations for other derived verbs below, the two forms given as examples in each tense illustrate

(1) the regular stem with a suffix and (2) the stem fused with a suffix, not necessarily in that order.

ACTIVE

Perfect (Stem: naaday-)		Imperfect (Stem: -naadiy-)	
3 MS	نـادى	3 MS	يُنـادي
1 S	نـادَيْتُ	3 MD	يُنـادِيـانِ

Active participle (Stem: munaadiy-)		
	Singular	Plural
Masc.	مُنـادٍ	مُنـادونَ
Fem.	مُنـادِيَةٌ	مُنـادِيـاتٌ

PASSIVE

Perfect (Stem: nuudiy-)		Imperfect (Stem: -naaday-)	
3 MS	نُودِيَ	3 MS	يُنـادى
1 S	نُودِيتُ	3 FP	يُنـادَيْنَ

Passive participle (Stem: munaaday-)		
	Singular	Plural
Masc.	مُنـادًى	مُنـادَونَ
Fem.	مُنـاداةٌ	مُنـادَيـاتٌ

Verbal noun (Stem: munaadaa(t)-)
مُناداةٌ

163

Form IV

STEM PATTERNS

	Perfect	Imperfect	Participle
Active	?aFMay-	-FMiy-	muFMiy-
Passive	?uFMiy-	-FMay-	muFMay-
Verbal noun: ?iFMaa?-			

Form IV defective verbs are conjugated throughout like بَنى 'to build'. Note that the verbal nouns of these verbs all end in ٔ hamza, which always replaces a final radical __W__ or __Y__ after __aa__. The examples below are forms of the verb أَعْطى 'to give'.

ACTIVE

Perfect (Stem: __?aʕṭay-__)		Imperfect (Stem: __-ʕṭiy-__)	
3 MS	أَعْطى	3 MS	يَعْطي
1 S	أَعْطَيْتُ	3 FP	يَعْطينَ

Active participle (Stem: __muʕṭiy-__)	
	Singular	Plural
Masc.	مُعْطٍ	مُعْطونَ
Fem.	مُعْطِيَةٌ	مُعْطِياتٌ

We have had the active participle مساوٍ; you are now responsible for the III defective verb from which it is derived, ساوى 'to be equivalent, equal to s.th.'

PASSIVE

	Perfect (Stem: ?uˁṭiy-)		Imperfect (Stem: -ˁṭay-)
3 MS	أُعْطِيَ	3 MS	يـعْطى
3 MP	أُعْطوا	3 FP	يـعْطيَنَ

Passive participle (Stem: muˁṭay-)		
	Singular	Plural
Masc.	مُعْطىً	مُعْطَوْنَ
Fem.	مُعْطاةٌ	مُعْطياتٌ

Verbal noun (Stem: ?iˁtaa?-)
إعْطاءٌ

Form V

STEM PATTERNS

	Perfect	Imperfect	Participle
Active	taFaMMay-	-taFaMMay-	mutaFaMMiy-
Passive	tuFuMMiy-	-taFaMMay-	mutaFaMMay-
Verbal noun: taFaMMiy-			

Form V defective verbs are conjugated like بَنى 'to build' except in the active imperfect, which is like لَقِيَ (imperfect يَلْـقى) 'to find'. Shown below as illustrations are the full active conjugation of تَمَنّى 'to desire,

165

wish for', and examples of the passive. Note that the verbal noun of these
verbs is a defective noun (see 34.C.2).

ACTIVE

	PERFECT (Stem: tamannay-)	IMPERFECT (Stem: -tamannay-)			
		Indicative	Subjunctive	Jussive	Imperative
3 MS	تَمَنَّى	يَتَمَنَّى	يَتَمَنَّى	يَتَمَنَّ	
FS	تَمَنَّتْ	تَتَمَنَّى	تَتَمَنَّى	تَتَمَنَّ	
2 MS	تَمَنَّيْتَ	تَتَمَنَّى	تَتَمَنَّى	تَتَمَنَّ	تَمَنَّ
FS	تَمَنَّيْتِ	تَتَمَنَّيْنَ	تَتَمَنَّى		تَمَنَّيْ
1 S	تَمَنَّيْتُ	أَتَمَنَّى	أَتَمَنَّى	أَتَمَنَّ	
3 MD	تَمَنَّيَا	يَتَمَنَّيَانِ	يَتَمَنَّيَا		
FD	تَمَنَّتَا	تَتَمَنَّيَانِ	تَتَمَنَّيَا		
2 D	تَمَنَّيْتُمَا	تَتَمَنَّيَانِ	تَتَمَنَّيَا		تَمَنَّيَا
3 MP	تَمَنَّوْا	يَتَمَنَّوْنَ	يَتَمَنَّوْا		
FP	تَمَنَّيْنَ	يَتَمَنَّيْنَ			
2 MP	تَمَنَّيْتُمْ	تَتَمَنَّوْنَ	تَتَمَنَّوْا		تَمَنَّوْا
FP	تَمَنَّيْتُنَّ	تَتَمَنَّيْنَ			تَمَنَّيْنَ
1 P	تَمَنَّيْنَا	نَتَمَنَّى	نَتَمَنَّى	نَتَمَنَّ	

Active participle (Stem: _mutamanniy-_)	
	Singular	Plural
Masc.	مُتَمَنٍّ	مُتَمَنُّونَ
Fem.	مُتَمَنِّيَةٌ	مُتَمَنِّيَاتٌ

PASSIVE

Perfect (Stem: _tumunniy-_)		Imperfect (Stem: _-tamannay-_)	
3 MS	تُمُنِّيَ	3 MS	يُتَمَنَّى
3 MP	تُمُنُّوا	3 FP	يُتَمَنَّيْنَ

Passive participle (Stem: _mutamannay-_)	
	Singular	Plural
Masc.	مُتَمَنًّى	مُتَمَنَّوْنَ
Fem.	مُتَمَنَّاةٌ	مُتَمَنَّيَاتٌ

Verbal noun (Stem: _tamanniy-_)
تَمَنٍّ

Form VI

STEM PATTERNS

	Perfect	Imperfect	Participle
Active	taFaaMay-	-taFaaMay-	mutaFaaMiy-
Passive	tuFuuMiy-	-taFaaMay-	mutaFaaMay-
Verbal noun: taFaaMiy-			

Form VI defective verbs are conjugated like بَنَى 'to build' except in the active imperfect, which is like لَقِيَ (imperfect يَلْقَى) 'to find'. (The passive is rare in these verbs.) The examples below are forms of the verb تَلاقى 'to meet, get together'. Note that the verbal noun of these verbs is a defective noun (see 34.C.2).

ACTIVE

Perfect (Stem: talaaqay-)		Imperfect (Stem: -talaaqay-)	
3 MS	تَلاقى	3 MS	يَتَلاقى
1 P	تَلاقَيْنا	3 FP	يَتَلاقَيْنَ

Active participle (Stem: mutalaaqiy-)	
Singular	Plural
Masc.	مُتَلاقٍ	مُتَلاقونَ
Fem.	مُتَلاقِيَةٌ	مُتَلاقِياتٌ

168

Verbal noun
(Stem: _talaaqiy-_)
تَـلاقٍ

Form VII

STEM PATTERNS

	Perfect	Imperfect	Participle
Active	-nFaMay-	-nFaMiy-	munFaMiy-
Verbal noun: -nFiMaa?-			

Form VII defective verbs are conjugated like بَـنى 'to build'. They have no passive. The examples below are forms of the verb اِنْـقَضى 'to cease, come to an end'. Note that the verbal nouns of these verbs end in �‍ﺀ hamza.

ACTIVE

Perfect		Imperfect	
(Stem: -nqaḍay-)		(Stem: -nqaḍiy-)	
3 MS	اِنْـقَضى	3 MS	يَنْـقَضي
3 MD	اِنْـقَضَيَا	3 MD	يَنْـقَضِيَان

Active participle	
(Stem: _munqaḍiy-_)	
	Singular	Plural
Masc.	مُنْـقَضٍ	مُنْـقَضونَ
Fem.	مُنْـقَضِيَة	مُنْـقَضِيَات

169

Verbal noun
(Stem: -nqiᵈaa?-)
اِنْقِضاءٌ

Form VIII

STEM PATTERNS

	Perfect	Imperfect	Participle
Active	-FtaMay-	-FtaMiy-	muFtaMiy-
Passive	-FtuMiy-	-FtaMay-	muFtaMay-
Verbal noun: -FtiMaa?-			

Form VIII defective verbs are conjugated throughout like بَنى 'to build'.

The examples below are forms of the verb اِشْتَرى 'to buy'.

ACTIVE

Perfect (Stem: -štaray-)		Imperfect (Stem: -štariy-)	
3 MS	اِشْتَرى	3 MS	يَشْتَري
1 S	اِشْتَرَيْتُ	3 MD	يَشْتَريانِ

Active participle (Stem: muštariy-)	
	Singular	Plural
Masc.	مُشْتَرٍ	مُشْتَرونَ
Fem.	مُشْتَرِيَةٌ	مُشْتَرِياتٌ

170

Verbal noun
(Stem: -štiraa?-)
اِشْتِراءٌ

(Note: This particular verbal noun is rare; the Form I verbal noun شِراءٌ

is normally used instead. An example of a common Form VIII verbal noun

is اِنْتِهاءٌ 'end', from اِنْتَهى 'to come to an end'.)

Form X

STEM PATTERNS

	Perfect	Imperfect	Participle
Active	-staFMay-	-staFMiy-	mustaFMiy-
Passive	-stuFMiy-	-staFMay-	mustaFMay-
Verbal noun: -stiFMaa?-			

Form X defective verbs are conjugated throughout like بَنى 'to build'.

The examples below are forms of the verb اِسْتَثْنى 'to except'. Note that

the verbal nouns of these verbs end in ء hamza.

ACTIVE

Perfect		Imperfect	
(Stem: -staθnay-)		(Stem: -staθniy-)	
3 MS	اِسْتَثْنى	3 MS	يَسْتَثْني
1 S	اِسْتَثْنَيْتُ	3 MD	يَسْتَثْنِيانِ

Active participle	
(Stem: <u>mustaθniy-</u>)	
Singular	Plural
Masc. مُسْتَثْنٍ	مُسْتَثْنُونَ
Fem. مُسْتَثْنِيَةٌ	مُسْتَثْنِيَاتٌ

PASSIVE

Perfect	Imperfect
(Stem: -stuθniy-)	(Stem: -staθnay-)
3 MS أُسْتُثْنِيَ	3 MS يُسْتَثْنَى
3 MD أُسْتُثْنُوا	3 FP يُسْتَثْنَيْنَ

Passive participle	
(Stem: <u>mustaθnay-</u>)	
Singular	Plural
Masc. مُسْتَثْنًى	مُسْتَثْنَوْنَ
Fem. مُسْتَثْنَاةٌ	مُسْتَثْنَيَاتٌ

Verbal noun
(Stem: -stiθnaa?-)
اِسْتِثْنَاءٌ

Now do Drills 1 (on tape) and 2.

<u>Drill 1</u>. (On tape) Conjugation. Derived defective verbs.

<u>Drill 2</u>. Written. Completion.

Perfect	Imperfect	Active Participle	Passive Participle	Verbal Noun
		د اع		
				احا طة
حكى				
				بنا ء
	تسمي			
			منادى	
اعطى				
تمنّى				
استثنى				
		مساو	XXX	

2. قَدْ 'perhaps' with the imperfect

We have seen قَدْ used in various ways with perfect tense (see L.24. C.2).

قَدْ is also used with a following imperfect indicative verb in the meaning 'perhaps, maybe; sometimes'; the imperfect verb after قَدْ is negated with لا.

Examples:

قَدْ يَعْتَقِدُ الأَبُ شيْئًا وَيَعْتَقِدُ الإِبْنُ شيْئًا آخَرَ.	'The father might believe one thing and the son something else.'
وَقَدْ يَسْكُنُ الإِبْنُ مَعَ أَهْلِهِ.	'And the son sometimes lives with his family.'
لِأَنَّ وَالِدَتَهُ قَدْ لا تَسْمَحُ بِذَهابِهِ.	'Because his mother might not let him go.'

Now do Drill 3.

173

Translation: Use of قد .

١ ‍ـ قد ازوركم غدا وقد نذهب معا للمسرح •

٢ ‍ـ كنت قد اشتركت في المؤتمر الاخير •

٣ ‍ـ قد لا يتم الاتفاق بين وزيري خارجية البلدين •

٤ ‍ـ سأكون قد اكملت الدراسة عندما تصلين الى الولايات المتحدة •

٥ ‍ـ قد يكون احسن طالب في صفّه •

٦ ‍ـ قد يكون من الصحيح ان خير البلد معتمد على الحزب القومي •

٧ ‍ـ قد يكون هذا العامل الذي يعمل في حفر الآثار اكثر علما بها من

المشرف عليه •

٨ ‍ـ قد يكون هذا الرجل قبيح الوجه ولكنه ايضا كبير القلب •

3. Existential sentences, "there is, there are...": Summary.

a. Indefinite subject

In Arabic the <u>existence of a thing</u> is usually expressed by the following

type of equational sentence:

في الشَّرْقِ الأَوْسَطِ عَدَدٌ مِنَ الدُّوَلِ الْغَنِيَّةِ بِالزَّيْتِ •   'In the Middle East there are a number
of oil-rich states.'

Such sentences are characterized by an <u>indefinite subject</u> (here... عَدَدٌ مِنْ)

<u>preceded by its predicate</u> (10.C.3). The predicate must be an adverbial expres-

sion. In this example the predicate is a prepositional phrase (في الشَّرْقِ

الأَوْسَطِ), but the adverb هُنَاكَ 'there is, there are' is often used as the pre-

dicate in an existential sentence (see 17.C.1); for example:

هُنَاكَ عَدَدٌ كَبِيرٌ مِنَ الدُّوَلِ الْغَنِيَّةِ بِالزَّيْتِ وَفَقِيرَةٍ فِي الْمَوَارِدِ الأُخْرَى ؛   'There are a great number of states rich
in oil and poor in other resources.'

These sentences are usually negated with لَيْسَ , e.g.

لَيْسَ فِي الشَّرْقِ الأَوْسَطِ دُوَلٌ غَنِيَّةٌ
بِمِثْلِ هَذِهِ الْمَوَارِدِ.

'There are no states in the Middle East rich in resources such as these.'

Another way of negating existential sentences is with لا of absolute negation (see 33.C.2.):

لا دُوَلَ فَقِيرَةٌ فِي الشَّرْقِ الأَوْسَطِ.

'There are no poor countries in the Middle East.'

---

b. Definite subject

If the subject of an existential sentence is definite, then the following type of sentence is used: the definite subject, the appropriate form of يَكُونُ 'there is, there are' and the predicate. يَكُونُ is negated by لا . Examples:

وَالتَّعَاوُنُ لا يَكُونُ بَيْنَ أَعْضَاءِ الْعَائِلَةِ الْوَاحِدَةِ فَقَطْ، بَلْ يَكُونُ أَيْضًا بَيْنَ عَائِلاتِ الأَقَارِبِ.

'There is cooperation not only between members of a single family, but also between the relatives' families.'

الْمُدِيرُ يَكُونُ فِي مَكْتَبِهِ بَعْدَ السَّاعَةِ الثَّامِنَةِ كُلَّ يَوْمٍ.

'The director is (to be found) in his office every day after eight o'clock.'

In the second example يَكُونُ provides the idea of a general truth, something that can be counted on to be valid on any number of occasions.

Now do Drill 4 (on tape).

Drill 4. (On tape) Translation.

4. Conditional sentences

Arabic has three conditional particles translatable into English by "if": إِنْ , إِذَا and لَوْ . There are, however, important differences in their meanings: لَوْ 'if it were that, if' is used for a condition contrary to fact--an

175

unrealizable or untrue condition, for example, as in "if I were king". إِنْ

and اِذَا are used for possible conditions, as in "if he comes (I'll tell him)"

or "if he has been here (I'll find out)." اِنْ is a straight hypothesis--"if,

if it is the case that..., if it should be that..."-- while اِذَا 'if' <u>implies</u>

some degree of probability and sometimes implies "when, whenever."

Another important feature of Arabic conditional sentences is that the con-

ditional particles are always followed by a perfect tense verb, (or, if nega-

tive, لَمْ plus jussive) regardless of whether past, present or future time is

involved. (There is one exception to this, which will be noted below under

(2) إِنْ .) Study the following three <u>condition clauses</u> (that is, clauses begin-

ning with لَوْ, إِنْ or اِذَا):

لَوْ ذَهَبَ   'if he had gone'   (i.e., he did not go)

إِنْ ذَهَبَ   'if he goes'   (i.e., he might go)

اِذَا ذَهَبَ   'if he goes'   (i.e., he might well go)

These sentences indicate that both English and Arabic distinguish clearly

between unrealizable conditions (the first illustration above) and possible

conditions (the second two). They differ remarkably, however, in <u>how</u> they

make this distinction. <u>English expresses it through the verb but uses only

one "if" particle</u>--"<u>if</u> he had gone" versus "<u>if</u> he goes." <u>Arabic</u>, on the other

hand, <u>keeps the verb constant--only the perfect tense is used here--but changes

the "if" particle to indicate the difference.</u>

The condition clause is normally followed by a <u>result clause</u> which states

the consequences of that condition. The verb of the Arabic result clause typ-

ically is in the perfect tense, like the verb of the condition clause, but

176

other forms often occur as well. The following set of sentences illustrates typical Arabic conditional sentences, and can profitably be memorized as models of this construction:

إِنْ ذَهَبْتُ قَابَلْتُهُ .	'If I go I will meet him.'
إِذَا ذَهَبْتُ قَابَلْتُهُ .	'If (when) I go I will meet him.'
لَوْ ذَهَبْتُ لَقَابَلْتُهُ .	'If I had gone I would have met him.'

Note that the result clauses as well as the condition clauses all have perfect tense verbs; it is the difference in particle that corresponds to the difference in tense of the English verbs. Further, the result clause after لَوْ is automatically introduced by لَ, which is not to be translated into English.

There are variations possible in the structure of the conditional sentence; these will now be dealt with separately for each conditional particle.

(1) لَوْ -clauses. لَوْ deals with a condition that was not or is not true ("contrary to fact"); the result is translated in English with a conditional perfect verb ("would have gone") for past time or a simple conditional ("would go") for present or future time. Notice that the last example below refers to future time.

لَوْ دَرَسَ لَنَجَحَ .	'If he had studied he would have succeeded.'
لَوْ أَحَبَّها لَتَزَوَّجَها .	'If he had fallen in love with her he would have married her.'
لَوْ طَلَبْتَ مِنّي ذَلِكَ قَبْلَ الْيَوْم لَسَاعَدْتُكَ مُسَاعَدَةً كَبِيرَةً .	'If you had asked that of me before today I would have helped you greatly.'
لَوْ سَمَحَ لِي الْوَقْتُ لَزُرْتُ أُوروبّا .	'If time had permitted I would have visited Europe.'
لَوْ كَانَ مَعِي أَلْفُ دولار لَتَزَوَّجْتُها غَدًا .	'If I had a thousand dollars I would marry her tomorrow.'

The condition clause is negated with لَمْ and the jussive, while the result clause is negated with ما plus the perfect:

> لَوْ لَمْ يَكُنْ أُسْتاذًا لَما ساعَدْنا .   'If he had not been a professor he would not have helped us.'
>
> لَوْ كُنْتُ مَكانَكَ لَما فَعَلْتُ ذٰلِكَ .   'If I were you I would not do that.'

The last sentence could also be translated, depending on the context, "If I had been you I would not have done that."

(2) إِنْ -clauses. إِنْ introduces a purely hypothetical condition, with no implication of degree of probability of fulfillment or non-fulfillment. It can sometimes be translated with "should" - "if he should come," "if it should be so." Illustration:

> إِنْ دَرَسَ نَجَحَ .   'If he studies (if he should study) he will succeed.'

There are two important variations possible after إِنْ 'if': (a) the verbs of the condition and result clauses may be jussive rather than perfect, with no change in meaning:

> إِنْ يَدْرُسْ يَنْجَحْ .   'If he studies he will succeed.'
>
> إِنْ يَتْرُكْ دِمَشْقَ في الصَّباحِ يَكُنْ هُنا في المَساءِ .   'If he leaves Damascus in the morning he will be here in the evening.'

If the verb in the condition clause is jussive, the verb in the result clause must also be jussive.

(b) The other substitute has the _imperative_ verb in the condition clause (إِنْ is not expressed) and the _jussive_ in the result clause:

> أُدْرُسْ تَنْجَحْ .   'Study and you will succeed.'

178

<u>If the condition verb is imperative, the result verb must be jussive.</u>

If the verb in the condition clause is in the perfect tense, then the verb in the result clause can be any tense or mood besides the perfect, as required by the sense of the sentence; <u>if the result clause verb is not in the perfect</u> <u>tense, the result clause must be introduced by an untranslated</u> فَ . Illustrations:

إِنْ لَمْ يَذْهَبْ فَلَنْ أُقَابِلَهُ .	'If he does not go I will not meet him.'
إِنْ كَانَ أُسْتَاذًا مُخْلِصًا فَسَوْفَ يُسَاعِدُنَا .	'If he is a sincere professor he will help us.'
إِنِ احْتَرَمَكَ النَّاسُ فَاحْتَرِمْهُمْ وَإِنْ لَمْ يَحْتَرِمُوكَ فَلَا تَحْتَرِمْهُمْ .	'If people respect you, respect them; and if they do not, don't respect them.'
إِنْ لَمْ يَحْضُرْ فَسَنُؤَجِّلُ الاِجْتِمَاعَ .	'If he does not come, we will postpone the meeting.'
إِنْ كَانَ أُسْتَاذًا فَلَيْسَ غَنِيًّا .	'If he is a professor then he is not rich.'

(3) إِذَا -clauses. إِذَا like إِنْ means 'if', but also often contains a note of expectancy; it sometimes can be translated as 'when', especially when repeated action is involved. The condition verb is negated by لَمْ plus jussive, while the result verb may be negated in any appropriate way; again, if the verb in the result clause is not perfect tense, the result clause must be introduced by فَ . Illustrations:

إِذَا دَرَسَ نَجَحَ .	'If he studies he will succeed.'
إِذَا تَرَكَ دِمَشْقَ فِي الصَّبَاحِ كَانَ هُنَا قَبْلَ الْمَسَاءِ .	'If he leaves Damascus in the morning he will be here before evening.'
إِذَا كُنْتَ مُخْلِصًا فَسَاعِدْنَا .	'If you are sincere help us.'
إِذَا أَرَدْتَ أَنْ تُطَاعَ فَاطْلُبْ مَا يُسْتَطَاعُ .	'If you want to be obeyed request what is possible.' ('to obey' = أَطَاعَ)

179

The jussive and the imperative cannot be substituted for the perfect tense after إِذَا , as they can after إِنْ .

Note: The condition particle must be followed by a perfect tense verb. If an equational sentence, which has no verb, is to be put into a condition clause, an appropriate form of the perfect tense of كَانَ must be inserted after the condition particle. Illustration:

Equational sentence:

| مَكَانَةُ الْمَرْأَةِ مُسَاوِيَةٌ لِمَكَانَةِ الرَّجُلِ. | 'Women's status is equal to men's.' |

Condition clause:

| إِذَا كَانَتْ مَكَانَةُ الْمَرْأَةِ مُسَاوِيَةً لِمَكَانَةِ الرَّجُلِ ... | 'If women's status is equal to men's...' |

Occasionally an imperfect tense verb occurs in the same way after كَانَ, as for example:

| إِذَا كُنْتَ تُحِبُّ حُضُورَهَا ... | 'If you want to attend it...' |

Postposed conditions. Very often, in both English and Arabic, a condition clause may be used independently of any result clause, as in

| اُحْضُرْ إِلَى بَيْتِنَا غَدًا ، إِذَا أَرَدْتَ | 'Come to our house tomorrow, if you wish.' |

Or the order of the condition and result clauses may be reversed, as in

| سَأُقَابِلُ رَئِيسَ الْجَامِعَةِ إِذَا زُرْتُ بَيْرُوتَ. | 'I will meet the president of the university if I visit Beirut.' |

In such a case the rules applying to result clauses do not hold: the form of the verb will depend on the meaning intended, and فَ will be omitted. Additional illustrations:

| سَيُعَيَّنُ الْأُسْتَاذُ فَرِيدٌ وَزِيرًا إِذَا رَغِبَ فِي ذَلِكَ. | 'Mr. Farid will be appointed minister, if he so desires.' |

180

سَوْفَ أَبْحَثُ مَعَهُ ذَلِكَ الْمَوْضُوعَ إِنْ كَانَ يَرْغَبُ فِي بَحْثِهِ .	'I will discuss that subject with him if he so desires.'

In addition, the independent or postposed condition clause may be modified by expressions such as حَتَّى 'even', إِلَّا 'except' and وَ 'even' (before إِنْ or لَوْ):

يَعْتَبِرُ الْآكِلَ مَعَهُ ضَيْفًا حَتَّى إِذَا كَانَا فِي مَطْعَمٍ .	'He considers the person eating with him as a guest even if they are in a restaurant.'
تَطْلُبُ مِنَ الزَّائِرِ أَنْ يُشَارِكَهَا طَعَامَهَا حَتَّى إِذَا لَمْ يَكُنْ مَدْعُوًّا .	'It (the family) asks the visitor to partake of its food even if he has not been invited.'
لَنْ يُسْمَحَ لَكَ بِالذَّهَابِ إِلَّا إِذَا أَكْمَلْتَ عَمَلَكَ .	'You will not be permitted to go unless you finish your work.'
لَنْ أَسْتَقْبِلَهُ وَلَوْ كَانَ مَلِكًا .	'I would not receive him even if he were a king.'

Finally, it must be noted that Arabic has no word equivalent to English "would". The conditional "would", as found in the last sentence above, implies contrary-to-fact condition, or a more remote possibility than that indicated by "will". Another situation where English supplies the conditional "would" is illustrated in the following sentences:

هَلْ تُحِبُّ الْكُتُبَ ؟	'Do you like books?'
هَلْ تُحِبُّ أَحَدَ هَذِهِ الْكُتُبِ ؟	'Would you like one of these books?'

If we consider first the English equivalents, we see that English uses the simple present tense for generalizations (the first sentence above), but uses the conditional "would" to extend an invitation (the second sentence). Arabic, on the other hand, uses the same verb form for both purposes, but uses the definite article on the noun الْكُتُبَ to make a generalization or

181

abstraction ("books in general") as opposed to an indefinite noun ("some books", or "one of these books"). These two meanings blend in the following sentence:

	'Do you like going to the movies with us? (generalization)
هَلْ تُحِبُّ الذَّهابَ إلى السِّينَما مَعَنا؟	'Would you like to go to the movies with us? (invitation)

The student must learn to distinguish these meanings in Arabic according to the forms and contexts, and supply the conditional "would" as appropriate. (For "would" with past habitual meaning see 11.C.4.)

Now do Drill 5.

<u>Drill 5</u>. Written. Translation: Conditional sentences.

١ ــ لو كان صديقك لساعدك •

٢ ــ لو بذل جهودا كبيرة في الدراسة لحصل على شهادته منذ عامين •

٣ ــ لو كنت رئيسا للجمهورية لحسّنت الاوضاع الاقتصادية في مدة قصيرة •

٤ ــ ان تذهب لزيارة قصر الجمهوريّة اذهب معك •

٥ ــ ان زرتموني اكرمتكم •

٦ ــ اكرم والديك تنجح في اعمالك •

٧ ــ ان لم يقم بواجبه فلن احترمه •

٨ ــ اذا تم بناء المدارس الجديدة في نهاية هذا العام فسوف يستفاد منها استفادة كبيرة •

٩ ــ لو اقيمت المصانع في البلاد لتقدّمت الاوضاع الاقتصادية •

١٠ ــ سنزور عائلتك اذا ذهبنا الى بيروت في الاسبوع القادم •

5. Declinable prepositions

Compare the following:

دونَ كَلامٍ	'without speaking'
بِدونِ كَلامٍ	'without speaking'

In the second example the preposition دونَ 'without' is itself the object of the preposition بِ 'in; with'. دونَ represents a class of prepositions that end in -a except when they are objects of other prepositions and then end in -i. These prepositions are like nouns, which are in the accusative case when used adverbially but are in the genitive case as object of prepositions. Other noun-like prepositions are

قُرْبَ ، خِلالَ ، مِثْلَ ، بَيْنَ ، وَراءَ ، عِنْدَ ، قَبْلَ ، أُمامَ ، بَعْدَ

Prepositions spelled with one or two letters or ending in a long vowel are invariable:

حَتّى ، سِوى ، عَلى ، إلى ، عَنْ ، مَعَ ، في ، مِنْ ، كَ ، بِ ، لِ

D. Comprehension passage

نصوص للفهم د_

Read the following passage then do Drill 6, which is based on it.

الجمهورية العربية اليمنية

there arose — قامَ في اليمن قديما عدد من الممالك منها سَبَأ • والكتاب المُقَدَّس

eba; the
Bible
يذكر ان ملكة سَبَأ زارت الملك سُلَيْمانْ بْنْ دَأود • وقد ساد الديـــن

الاسلامي اليمن في القرن السابع الميلادي •

The Ottoman
Empire
سيطرت الدَوْلَةُ الْعُثْمانِيَّةُ على اليمن في عام ١٥١٧ ، لكن اليمـــن

استقلت في عام ١٩١٨ •

ولما اصبح جمال عبد الناصر رئيسا لجمهورية مصر ، انتشرت فكـــرة الوحدة بين العرب ، فاتحدت مصر وسوريا ودعيتا " الجمهورية العربية

المتحدة ." وبعد وقت قصير تم اتحاد بين اليمن والجمهورية العربيـــــة

المتحدة . لكن الوحدة بين مصر وسوريا كانت تختلف عن الاتحاد بيـــــن

اليمن والجمهورية العربية المتحدة ، فقد اصبحت مصر وسوريا دولة واحدة

soldiers تحكمها حكومة واحدة ، وتبادلتا الجُنودَ والاساتذة والموظفين والمسؤولين

الحكوميّين ، اما حكومة اليمن فقد بقيت مستقلة على الرغم من التعاون

الذي ساد بين حكومة اليمن وشعبها وبين حكومة الجمهورية العربيـــــة

seceded المتحدة وشعبها . لكنّ الاتحاد لم يدم طويلا ، فقد انْفَصَلَتْ سوريا فـــــي

nullifi سنة ١٩٦١ وأُلْغِيَ عبد الناصر الاتحاد مع اليمن في السنة نفسها .
annulle

وفي عام ١٩٦٢ قام عَبْدُ اللّهِ السّلال بثورة على الحكم الملكيّ ، واقام

حكومة جمهوريّة ، فاصبحت اليمن تسمى " الجمهورية العربية اليمنية " .

لكن الملكيين قاوموا الحكومة الجديدة ، فسبب ذلك حربا بين أَبْنـــــاء the
ordinar
was الشّعبِ اليمنيّ . وقد دامت هذه الحرب سبع سنوات . وفي عام ١٩٦٩ ثُبِّتَتْ people
establish-
ed الحكومة الجمهوريّة .

واليمن دولة فقيرة ، بل لعلها من افقر الدول العربية ، فصناعاتـها

قليلة ، والزيت غير متوفر فيها ، لكنها في السنوات الاخيرة بدأت تحصل

على مساعدات كبيرة من الدول العربية الغنية بالزيت . وقد يتقدم الوضع

الاقتصادي في اليمن اذا استمرت هذه المساعدات .

Ta'izz عاصمة الجمهورية العربية اليمنية هي صَنْعاءُ، وتَعِزُّ من اكبر مدنها . San'ā

Drill 6. Written.

Summarize the above passage in English using the following outline as a guide:

1. Yemen from ancient times until 1918.

2. Relationship with United Arab Republic.

3. Events leading to the establishment of a republican system in Yemen.

4. The economic situation in Yemen.

5. Major cities in Yemen.

E. Underline Underline General drills   هـ ــ التمارين العامّة

Drill 7. Transformation. Statement ⟶ negative.

   Give the negative of the following sentences.

١ ــ عملت الدولة على تحسين الاوضاع الاقتصادية في البلاد .

٢ ــ اذهب الى مكتبة الجامعة غدا .

٣ ــ بني سد جديد على النهر .

٤ ــ الآنسة وداد في العراق .

٥ ــ تختلف هذه اللهجة عن تلك اللهجة اختلافا كبيرا .

٦ ــ ستتحد الدولتان قريبا .

٧ ــ هذا المؤلف معروف في العالم العربي .

٨ ــ سوف اقابل مدير المصنع بعد اسبوع .

٩ ــ انتم احباء مخلصون .

١٠ ــ هذان البلدان عضوان في منظمة الامم المتحدة .

Drill 8. Recognition: Topic-comment sentences.

   In the following sentences identify the Topic-comment sentences by writing TC in the margin; then underline the topicalized noun phrase and the pronoun that refers to it. Ex.

'The Arab family is linked to its relatives by strong ties.'
         العائلة العربية تربطها بالاقارب

روابط قوية .

185

١ – يكرم العرب الضيوف ويقدمون لهم الطعام •

٢ – السد العالي تم بناؤه في زمن الرئيس جمال عبد الناصر •

٣ – استقلت معظم الدول العربية في النصف الثاني من هذا القرن •

٤ – مدير الشركة شاهدته امس في حفلة رسمية •

٥ – مندوب الجزائر اجتمع به وزير الخارجية •

٦ – لا شك ان الكويت من الدول الغنية بالزيت •

٧ – والدك شاهدته امس في مكتبة الجامعة •

٨ – الام جاءها خبر نجاح ابنتها في الامتحانات •

٩ – يضع اساتذة وطلاب الجامعة ثقتهم الكبيرة برئيس الجامعة •

١٠ – ابو احمد شاهدت فلما جديدا معه •

Drill 9. Conjugation.

Give the correct form of the verb and vocalize it. Ex.

سافَرْتُ ← انا + سافـر

Imperfect	Perfect
دعا ــ هم	اعدّ ــ انا
بني ــ هي	رجا ــ انتم
سمي ــ انتم	بنى ــ هم
لقي ــ هم	بقي ــ انت
استفاد ــ انتما	دعي ــ انتما
استعدّ ــ نحن	سمي ــ هي
وقع ــ هي	احاط ــ نحن

Drill 10. Substitution.

Substitute the word(s) in parenthesis for the underlined word(s)

the following sentences, making any necessary changes.

186

١ – البتراء هي المدينة التي تحيط بها الجبال العالية . (البتراء وجرش)

٢ – هذا هو الرجل الذي اصبح غنيا في مدة قصيرة . (نساء)

٣ – مي زيادة اديبة قدّمت خدمات كثيرة لمجتمعها . (الاديبة)

٤ – هذا هو المراسل الذي صادقته عندما كان يعمل في جريدة الحياة
البيروتية . (المراسلون)

٥ – مصر دولة تعرف بآثارها التاريخية القديمة . (مصر وسوريا ولبنان)

٦ – نانسي بنت تحب الطعام العربي . (البنت)

Christl

٧ – فلسطين هي البلد الذي عاش فيه السّيِّدُ المَسِيحُ . (البلاد)

٨ – السيد نَجيب فَرَح استاذ يدرس الادب العربي في جامعتنا . (سامية فريد)

٩ – خرج كلاهما من قصر الحَمْراءِ (Alhambra) ولا شك انهما متأثران بما
رأيا هناك . (كلتاهما)

Drill 11. Recognition: Active participle.

Underline the active participle in the following sentences and then
translate the sentences into English.

١ – اننا نعتبركم من باذلي اعظم الجهود للمحافظة على السلام .

٢ – وصل وزير الخارجية المصرية الى واشنطن حاملا معه رسالة من
الرئيس المصري الى الرئيس الامريكي .

٣ – نحن شاكرون لكم اهتمامكم بنا .

٤ – نحن على علاقة حسنة بساكني هذا البناء .

٥ – هو ذاهب لزيارة اهله في العراق في الشهر القادم .

٦ – هما متفقان على حل المشكلة بينهما لكنهما لا يزالان مختلفين على
التَّفاصيلِ .

details

٧ ــ تحدث رئيس الجامعة قائلا ان اوضاع الجامعة عامة بحاجة الــــى التغيير ٠

٨ ــ الّف نجيب محفوظ كتبا كثيرة مصورا فيها الحياة الاجتماعية في مصر ٠

٩ ــ لم تكن بعض الدول الافريقية مشتركة في المؤتمر الذي عقد اخيرا في الرباط ٠

Drill 12. Translation.

1. There are only three kingdoms in the Arab world today.

2. My brother's car is yellow; as for my car it is blue.

3. I will visit my father and mother next week.

4. The Arab honors the guest and offers him the best food he has.

5. Nancy and her husband invited us to a very beautiful party.

6. The Hilton is one of the most famous hotels in Egypt.

7. The city is surrounded by high mountains.

8. Paris is the capital of France and Nice (نيس) is one of its most important cities.

9. The king went out from his desert palace, approaching the high, green mountains of Yemen.

Drill 13. Written. Verb ⟶ verbal noun.

Replace the verbs in parentheses by the corresponding verbal nouns making any necessary changes.

١ ‒ ساعدت جهود الامم المتحدة على (حسّن) الاوضاع السياسية في العالم .

٢ ‒ قرأت كتابا عن ال (غنّى) العربي المعاصر .

٣ ‒ ليس ال (بحث) عن عمل سهلا .

٤ ‒ في العالم عدد كبير من الناس لا يعرفون ال (قرأ) و ال (كتب) .

٥ ‒ حكم عمر بن الخطاب المسلمين بعد (مات) أبي بَكرٍ .

٦ ‒ سأزور لبنان قبل (زار) مصر .

٧ ‒ في كتب نجيب محفوظ (وصف) للمجتمع المصري .

٨ ‒ يذهب الى مصر كل صيف لـ (شاهد) آثارها القديمة .

٩ ‒ يجب (أرسل) الكتب اليوم .

١٠ ‒ تريد المملكة العربية السعودية (أقام) عدد من المصانع الحديثة .

١١ ‒ ليس (تعلّم) اللغة العربية صعبا .

١٢ ‒ اتفقت الدول العربية على ال (تعاون) .

١٣ ‒ لن يعود الاستاذ الى بيته قبل (انصرف) الطلاب .

١٤ ‒ تريد فرنسا ال (اشترك) في المؤتمر الدولي القادم .

١٥ ‒ يسبّب (ازداد) عدد السكان مشكلات كبيرة .

١٦ ‒ لا اشكّ في (اهتمّ) الشعب الامريكي بهذا الموضوع .

١٧ ‒ يقاوم العرب (استخدم) اللهجات العامّية في كتابة الادب .

١٨ ‒ نريد ال (استفاد) من معرفتك .

١٩ ‒ أشرف على (ترجم) الكتاب أستاذ جامعي .

Drill 14. Written. Transformation. Perfect ⟷ imperfect with سَ .

189

١ ــ انشأوا مدارس كثيرة في القرى .

٢ ــ أسس حزبان جديدان في البلاد .

٣ ــ تمكّنت من الحصول على وظيفة في وزارة التربية .

٤ ــ تبادلا الآراء بحرّية تامّة .

٥ ــ وهبها سيارة كبيرة وهدايا كثيرة اخرى .

٦ ــ لقينا منهم كل ترحيب .

٧ ــ بقي في لبنان مدّة غير قصيرة من الزمن .

٨ ــ عاش هذا الانسان الفقير حياته كلها في قرية صغيرة ومات في تلك القرية .

٩ ــ اصبحت الدولة التي استقلّت حديثا عضوا في الامم المتحدة .

١٠ ــ سمّي اخي ابا عمر .

١١ ــ ادار المهندسون العرب مصانع الزيت التي في بلادهم .

أ – الجمل التمهيدية

A. **Preparatory sentences**

تونس

Tunisia

١ – تونس دولة عربيّة يَحُدُّها من الشمال والشرق البَحْرُ الأَبْيَضُ المُتَوَسِّط ومن الجَنوب ليبيا ومن الغرب الجزائر .

Tunisia is an Arab country <u>bounded</u> on the north and east by the <u>Medi-terranean Sea</u>, on the <u>south</u> by Libya, and on the west by Algeria.

حَدَّ – يَـ ، حَدُّ

to delineate; to set bounds to, limit, restrict

جَنوبٌ

south

[البَحْرُ الأَبْيَضُ المُتَوَسِّطُ]

[The Mediterranean Sea]

٢ – المنطقة الجنوبية من تونس صحراء واسِعَةٌ .

The southern region of Tunisia is a <u>wide</u> desert.

واسِعٌ – ون

wide, spacious; extensive

٣ – عاشت تونس تَحْتَ الحكم الفرنسيّ منذ أواخِر القرن التاسع عشر ولكن الشعب التونسى كافَحَ للحصول على استقلاله .

Tunisia lived <u>under</u> French rule from the <u>latter part of</u> the nineteenth century, but the Tunisian people <u>fought</u> to obtain their independence.

تَحْتَ

under, underneath; below, beneath

آخِرٌ – ون – أُواخِرُ

last, final; (foll. by noun of time) the latter part of, the end of; latter

كافَحَ – مُكافَحَةٌ – كِفاحٌ

III to struggle, fight, combat

مُكافِحٌ – ون

fighter, combatant

٤ – نِظامُ الحكم القائِمُ في تونس جمهوري .

The <u>system</u> of government <u>existing</u> in Tunisia is republican.

نِظامٌ – أَنْظِمَةٌ ، نُظُمٌ

system, order

قائِمٌ – ون

standing; existing

٥ – وليس فيها الا حزب سياسي واحد هو الحزب الحاكم . يَدْعو هذا

There is only one political party there, the ruling party. This party <u>calls for</u> close cooperation with the

الحزب الى التعاون مع الغرب تعاونا كبيرا، كما يدعو الى التعاون مع الدول العربية .

West; it also calls for cooperation with the Arab countries.

دَعا ـُ ، دُعاءٌ الى

to call for, advocate, urge

٦ ـ في السنوات الاخيرة ظَهَرَتْ مُحاوَلَةٌ لِتَوْحيدِ تونس وليبيا لكن هـذه المحاولة لم تنجح .

In recent years there was ("appeared") an attempt to unify Tunisia and Libya, but this attempt did not succeed.

ظَهَرَ ـَ ، ظُهورٌ

to appear, emerge

حاوَلَ ، مُحاوَلَةٌ

III to attempt, try

مُحاوَلَةٌ ـ ات

attempt, effort

وَحَّدَ ، تَوْحيدٌ

II to unify, unite

٧ ـ تحاول تونس ان تتبع سياسة عَدَمِ الانْحِيازِ وهذا مَعْناهُ انها ليست منحازة الى الشرق او الغرب .

Tunisia tries to follow a policy of non-alignment; that means she is not aligned with either East or West.

عَدَمٌ

(with foll. genitive) non-, un-, in-, dis-; (see note C.2)

انْحازَ ، انْحِيازٌ الى

VII to side with, be partial to, aligned with

عَدَمُ الانْحِيازِ

non-alignment

مَعْنًى ـ مَعانٍ

meaning, sense

٨ ـ تونس مَرْكَزٌ تجاري هام في العالم العربي .

Tunisia is an important commercial center in the Arab world.

مَرْكَزٌ ـ مَراكِزُ

center, headquarters, main office

مَرْكَزِيٌّ

central (nisba of مَرْكَزٌ)

٩ ـ في تونس زيت يستخدم اكثره مَحَلِّيًّا .

In Tunisia there is oil, most of which is used locally.

مَحَلٌّ ـ ات ، مَحالٌّ

place, location

مَحَلِّيٌّ ـ ون

local (nisba of مَحَلٌّ)

تقدّمت تونس في السنوات الاخيرة
تقدّما كبيرا في مُخْتَلِفِ الْمَيادينِ
السياسيّة والاجتماعيّة والاقتصاديّة .

Tunisia has made great advances in
the last several years in the __various__
political, social and economic __fields__.

مُخْتَلِفٌ

(with foll. gen.) various

مَيْدانٌ ـ مَيادينٌ

realm, field; arena; sphere of
activity; city square

ب ـ النص الاساسي

انظمــــــــة

الحكم والاحزاب في العالم العربي

من انظمة الحكم المتّبعة في العالم العربي المعاصر النظام
الملكي القائم في المغرب والاردن والسعوديّة ، والنظام الجمهـــــوريّ
القائم في مصر والعراق وسوريا ولبنان واليمن الشمالي واليمــــن
الجنوبي ودولة الإماراتِ العربية المتحدة والسودان والجزائر وتونس _emirates_
وليبيا وموريتانيا والصومالُ . وهناك نظامان آخران هما الإمارَةُ في _Mauritania / Somalia_
الكويت والبَحْرَيْنِ وقَطَرَ ، والسُّلْطَنَةُ في عُمانَ . _sultanate; Oman / Bahrain; Qatar_
وهذه الدول كلّها اعضاء في منظّمة اسمها الجامِعَةُ الْعَرَبِيَّـــــــةُ . _Arab League_
أُسِّست الجامِعَةُ العربية بعد الحرب العالمية الثانية ومركزها فـي
القاهرة . للجامعة العربية سكرتير عامٌّ ، ولكل من الدول الاعضــاء
مندوبون فيها . تحاول الجامعة العربية تَشْجيعَ التعاون بين العرب في _to encourage_
الميادين السياسية والاجتماعية والاقتصادية ، والدِفاعَ عن حــــقو ق _to defend_
العرب .

عاش العرب تحت الحكم العُثْمانِيِّ اربعة قرون ، وفي اواخر القرن _Ottoman_
التاسع عشر اخذت الشعوب العربية تكافح للحصول على استقلالها ، فبدأت

الاحزاب السياسية تظهر في العالم العربي ، ولكنّها لم تنتشر انتشارا
واسعا الا بعد الحرب العالميّة الاولى . ولكلّ من هذه الاحزاب اليوم
اهداف خاصّة ولكنّ اكثرها يعمل على تقدّم العالم العربي وتوحيده،
ويدعو الى سياسة عدم الانحياز ، بكلّ معنى الكلمة ، أيْ ألّا تكون *that is to say*
الدول العربية منحازة الى الشرق او الغرب .

من الاحزاب الموجودة في العالم العربي : حزب البَعْثِ والحزب *Baath ("resurrection")*
الشُيوعيُّ ، والاحزاب الاشتِراكِيَّةُ المختلفة . كما انّ هناك احزابًا *Communist* *socialist*
محليّة هامّة في مختلف بلدان العالم العربي .

أسـئـلـة

١ ـ ما هو نظام الحكم المتّبع في المغرب ؟

٢ ـ ما نظام الحكم في ليبيا ؟

٣ ـ اين يُتّبع نظام الامارة ؟

٤ ـ ماهي الدولة التي يسود فيها نظام السَلْطَنة ؟

٥ ـ ما نظام الحكم في دولة الامارات العربية المتحدة ؟

٦ ـ هل جميع الدول العربية اعضاء في الجامعة العربية ؟

٧ ـ متى أُسّست الجامعة العربية ؟ أين مركزها ؟

٨ ـ علامَ تعمل الجامعة العربية ؟

٩ ـ هل كلَّ الدول الاسلاميّة اعضاء في الجامعة العربية ؟

١٠ ـ هل كلَّ المسلمون عرب ؟ وهل كلَّ العرب مسلمون ؟

١١ ـ هل لبنان دولة عربية ؟ هل هو دولة اسلامية ؟

١٢ ـ متى بدأت الشعوب العربية تكافح للحصول على استقلالها ؟

١٣ ـ متى بدأت الاحزاب تنتشر في العالم العربي انتشارا واسعا ؟

١٤ ـ علامَ يعمل معظم هذه الاحزاب ؟

B. **Basic text**

The Systems of Government and the Parties
of the Arab World

Among the systems of government prevailing ("followed") in the contemporary Arab world are monarchies, found in Morocco, Jordan, and Saudi Arabia;
republics, found in Egypt, Iraq, Syria, Lebanon, North Yemen, South Yemen,
the United Arab Emirates; the Sudan, Algeria, Tunisia, Libya, Mauritania,
and Somalia. There are two other systems: the emirate, in Kuwait, Bahrain,
and Qatar; and the sultanate, in Oman.

All of these states are members of an organization called the Arab
League. The Arab League was founded after the Second World War, and its headquarters are in Cairo. The Arab League has a secretary-general, and each mem-
ber-state has delegates there. The Arab League endeavors to foster cooperation among the Arabs in the political, sociological, and economic spheres, and
to defend the rights of Arabs.

The Arabs lived under Ottoman rule for four centuries. Towards the end
of the nineteenth century the Arab peoples began to struggle to obtain their
independence, and political parties began to appear in the Arab world, although
they did not become widespread until after the First World War. Each of these
parties today has its own particular goals, but most of them work for the advancement and unification of the Arab world, and advocate a policy of non-
alignment in every sense of the word, that is, that the Arab states not be
aligned with either the East or the West.

Among the parties found in the Arab world are the Ba'ath Party, the

Communist Party, and the various socialist parties. There are also important

local parties in the various countries of the Arab world.

C. <u>Grammar and drills</u>   ج – القواعد والتمارين

> 1. إلّا plus negative: 'only'
>
> 2. Negation of nouns and adjectives: عَدَم

1. <u>إلّا plus negative: 'only'</u>

Compare the following two sentences:

> في تونِسَ حِزْبٌ سِياسِيٌّ واحِدٌ •   'In Tunisia there is one political
>   party.'
>
> لَيْسَ في تونِسَ إلّا حِزْبٌ سِياسِيٌّ واحِدٌ •   'There is only one political party
>   in Tunisia.'

The second sentence reads literally "There is not except one political party

in Tunisia." The particle إلّا 'except' is sometimes best translated as

"except" or "but" after a negative, but usually it, together with the negative,

is best translated as "only". It is more or less synonymous with فَقَط ,

and is equally common. Notice that a noun after إلّا has the same case as

it does in the sentence without negative plus إلّا . Additional examples:

> زُرْنا أقارِبَنا •   'We visited our relatives.'
>
> لَمْ نَزُرْ إلّا أقارِبَنا •   'We visited only our relatives.' or
>   'We did not visit anybody except
>   our relatives.

> اِنْتَشَرَتِ الأحْزابُ السِّياسِيَّةُ اِنْتِشارًا   'Political parties became widespread
> واسِعًا بَعْدَ الحَرْبِ العالَمِيَّةِ الأولى•   after World War II.'
>
> لَمْ تَنْتَشِرِ الأحْزابُ السِّياسِيَّةُ إلّا بَعْدَ   'Political parties became widespread
> الحَرْبِ العالَمِيَّةِ الأولى •   only after World War II.' or 'Poli-
>   tical parties did not become wide-
>   spread until after World War II.'

Now do Drills 1 and 2.

<u>Drill 1.</u> Substitution.

Replace غَيْرَ with إلّا in the following sentences making all necessary changes in case. <u>Ex.</u>
'I visited only France.'

لم أزر غير فرنسا .   ←

'I visited only France.'

لم أزر الّا فرنسا .

١ ــ لن أنام غير ساعة .

٢ ــ لم يطالبـن بـغير حرية الـتصرّف.

٣ ــ لم يؤلّف غير كتاب واحد .

٤ ــ لم يجدوا في المكتب غير كتاب واحد .

٥ ــ لن ندعوا الى الحفلة غير أساتذة اللغة العربيّة .

٦ ــ ليس في هذه المنطقة غير مدرسة واحدة .

٧ ــ لا يدرس غير اللغة العربيّة .

٨ ــ لا يعجبني غير أسلوب طه حُسَيْن .

<u>Drill 2.</u> (Also on tape) Negation and use of الّا .

'There is only one reporter at
the conference.'

في المؤتمر مراسل واحد فقط .   ←
ليس في المؤتمر الا مراسل واحد .

١ ــ يوجد الزيت في الجنوب فقط .

٢ ــ اتّحدت دولتان فقط .

٣ ــ دعا الى الوحدة فقط .

٤ ــ تقدّمت البلاد في الميدان السياسيّ فقط .

٥ ــ تحدّث في كتابه عن الاقتصاد المحلّي فقط .

٦ ــ كافحوا الفرنسيّين فقط .

٧ ــ يريدون النظام الجمهوريّ فقط .

٨ ــ وصف المنطقة الشمالية فقط .

٩ ــ زرت بريطانيا فقط .

197

2. Negation of nouns and adjectives: عَدَمٌ

The negative لا is used to negate nouns in absolute terms (see 33. C. 2),
e.g. لا أَحَدَ فِي الْمَطْعَمِ 'There is no one in the restaurant.' The noun
غَيْرٌ also is used to negate nouns as well as adjectives and participles
(see 22. C. 3), e.g. اَلْعَرَبُ وَغَيْرُ الْعَرَبِ 'Arabs and non-Arabs', غَيْرُ سَهْلٍ
'not easy', غَيْرُ مَعْرُوفٍ 'unknown'. There is a third way to negate nouns --
specifically, verbal nouns: the noun عَدَمٌ 'non-existence' is used with a
following verbal noun, forming with it an iḍāfa construction, and is translated
'no', 'non-', 'lack of...', etc. Examples:

Positive		Negative	
اَلإِنْحِيازُ	'taking the side of'	عَدَمُ الإِنْحِيازِ	'non-alignment'
اَلْوُجُودُ	'existence'	عَدَمُ الْوُجُودِ	'non-existence'
اَلنَّوْمُ	'sleep'	عَدَمُ النَّوْمِ	'lack of sleep'

Now do Drill 3.

Drill 3. Written. Negative words.

Fill in the blanks with غَيْرٌ , عَدَمٌ , or لا ; Translate.

١ ـ هذا الرجل ـــــ مسلم •

٢ ـ ـــــ مسلم بينهم •

٣ ـ لن تحقّق الأحزاب أهدافها لأنها ـــــ متعاونة •

٤ ـ السبب في ـــــ نجاحهم هو ـــــ ـــــ تعاونهم •

٥ ـ أما زال في العالم دول ـــــ مستقلّة ؟

٦ ـ أنت ـــــ ـــــ مهتمّ بالأمر ، ولن تستفيد من ـــــ ـــــ اهتمامك •

٧ ـ ـــــ ـــــ نجاح لمن لا يتعاونون •

٨ ـ اتحادهم ـــــ مستطاع في هذا الوقت •

٩ ـ ـــــ ـــــ رأي له في هذا الموضوع •

١٠ ـ أكثر سكان الشرق الأوسط عرب ، لكنّ بعضهم من ـــــ العرب •

١١ ـ ـــــ ـــــ عمل له •

١٢ ـ اختلفت الحكومتان لأسباب ـــــ واضحة •

198

D. Comprehension passages   د ــ نصوص للفهم

(1) Read the following passage and then do Drill 4, which is based on it.

رســـــالة

مدينة الجزائر في ٢٥ آب (أَغُسْطُس) ١٩٧٥ August

عزيزتي فرجينيا :

تسأليـني في رسالتك عن رأي العرب في الغرب والغربيّين ،وتقولين
انّ لك أصدقاء زاروا الشرق الأوسط فقابـلوا ناسا لا يحبّون الأجانب .

أودّ أن تعلمي أوّلاً أنّ العرب ، ككلّ الناس ، منهم المُتَطَرِّفونَ ومنهم -trests

المُعْتَدِلونَ ، ولكنّ المعتدلين أكثر جدّا من المتطرّفين .   moderates

وأحبّ أن تعلمي بعد ذلك أنّ دولتين غربيّتين هما بريطانيا وفرنسا
سيطرتا على الشرق الأوسط من أوائل هذا القرن حتّى عهد قريب ، فكافـح
العرب للحصول على استقلالهم كفاحا طويلا . ولقد حاولت الحكومات والشعوب
العربيّة بعد الاستقلال أن تصادق الغرب وتتعاون معه ، وممّا لا شك فيه أنّ
هذه الجهود نجحت في كثير من الأحيان ، لكنّها لم تكن ناجحة في كلّ حين.
ليس غريبا اذن أن تكون الثقة بالغرب قويّة عند بعض العرب ، وألّا تكون
قويّة عند البعض الآخر .

يجب أن تعلمي كذلك أنّ العرب في مختلف البلدان ليسوا على رأيٍ   f one pinion
واحِدٍ : فبـين العرب من يدعون الى التعاون مع الغرب في كلّ الميـاديـــن،
وبـينهم من يدعون الى مقاومة بعض الدول الغربيّة ، وبـينهم من يدعون الى
عدم الانحياز .

وهناك أمر تعرفينه كل المعرفة هو أنّ الاختلاف السياسيّ لا يدلّ فـي
كلّ الأحيان على البُغْض . فالعربيّ قد يحترم الغربيّ بل قد يحبّه على الرغم   hatred
من اختلافهما في الآراء السياسيّة . ألعلّك لم تسمعي عن دولة عربيّة ترسل
طلّابها للدراسة في دولة غربيّة على الرغم من اختلاف الحكومتين سياسيّا ؟

199

أم لعلّك لم تسمعي أنّ العرب يستقبلون الزائر الغربيّ بالترحيب والاكرام

غير متأثّرين بسياسة بلاده ؟

ليس غريبا أن يكون الأصدقاء الذين ذكرتهم قد قابلوا في الشرق

الأوسط ناسا لا يحبّون الأجانب ، ولكنّي أعتقد أنهم قابلوا أيضا أُناسـاً _{*people*}

يرحّبون بالضيف ويكرمونه . فَلْتَزوري الشرق الأوسط اذا كان سؤالك يدلّ على _{*so visit**}

رغبة في زيارته ، وَلْتَعْلَمي أنّك ستجدين منّي ومن غيري كلّ ترحيب وكل _{*and you
will see**}

اكرام .

المخلصة
وداد

* Note these uses of the jussive with the second person.

<u>Drill 4</u>. Written. Summarize briefly, in outline form, first in English and then in Arabic, the main points brought out in Widad's letter in reporting the argument that the Arabs do not like foreigners.

(2) Listen to the passage on tape and then do Drill 5, which is based on it. (Note: the word أَجْدادٌ means "ancestors".)

<u>Drill 5</u>. (On tape) Written. Aural comprehension passage.

١ – كم سنة حكم واشنطن أمريكا ؟

٢ – اذكر عملا من الأعمال الهامّة التي قام بها واشنطن عندما كان

رئيسا للولايات المتحدة . ما الذي ساعده على تحقيق أهدافه ؟

٣ – لأيّ سبب اختلف هاملتون وجفرسون ؟

٤ – ماذا كان رأي واشنطن في الحرب بين بريطانيا وفرنسا ؟

E. <u>General drills</u>   هـ – التمارين العامة

<u>Drill 6</u>. Expansion: Singular ⟶ noun of quantity plus plural.

Insert the nouns below as indicated before the underlined item making all necessary changes. <u>Ex</u>.

200

أ   :   حضر المندوب المؤتمر • بعض • ←

'The delegate attended the
conference. Some.'

ط   :   حضر بعض المندوبين المؤتمر •

'Some delegates attended the
conference.'

١ –   زرت قريبي هذا الاسبوع • بعض •

٢ –   بني فندق حديث في العاصمة • بعض •

٣ –   درست المشكلة دراسة شاملة • كلّ •

٤ –   أعجبتني الصورة • أكثر •

٥ –   تحدّث المدير الى العامل • جميع •

٦ –   يرى المهندس أنّ حفر القناة لن يكون سهلا • أكثر •

٧ –   قابلت أديبا مصريّا معروفا أثناء زيارتي للقاهرة • بعض •

٨ –   يعتقد المفكّر أنّ حرّية التصرّف من أهم حقوق الانسان • كل •

٩ –   حضر الوزير المؤتمر • أكثر •

__Drill 7__.   Transformation: كل / جميع + noun → noun + جميع / كل •

قرأت جميع الكتب • → قرأت الكتب جميعها •

'I read all of the books.'

١ –   نحترم جميع الروابط الاجتماعيّة •

٢ –   تقدّمت ليبيا في كلّ الميادين •

٣ –   ذكر الأستاذ في محاضرته جميع أنظمة الحكم •

٤ –   للبنان علاقات حسنة بكل الدول العربيّة •

٥ –   زار الوزير جميع بلاد الشرق الأوسط •

٦ –   حضر جميع الوزراء اجتماع أمس •

٧ –   سوف تؤثّر السياسة الجديدة على كلّ المناهج التعليميّة •

٨ –   حقّقت الثورة جميع أهدافها •

٩ –   سيجتمع جميع الشعراء مساء غد ليبحثوا نهضة الشعر في الادب العربيّ •

Drill 8.   Ḥāls.

'He was happy when he returned.' ⟵ كان سعيدا حين رجع ٠   :   أ

'He returned happy.'   ⟵   ٠ رجع وهو سعيد   :   ط

:   رجع سعيدا ٠

١ ـ كان مسلما عندما مات ٠

٢ ـ كان فقيرا حين جاء الى هذه البلاد ٠

٣ ـ كان يضحك أثناء تكلّمه ٠

٤ ـ كان يغنّى أغنية جميلة أثناء سيره ٠

٥ ـ كان صغيرا عندما أحبّها ٠

٦ ـ كان يفكّر أثناء خروجه من الاجتماع ٠

Drill 9.   Written: Active ⟶ passive.

'They met the visitors warmly.'   ⟵   ٠ قابلوا الزائرات بالترحيب والاكرام   :

'The visitors were met warmly.'   :   قوبلت الزائرات بالترحيب والاكرام ٠

١ ـ منعوا الباحث من استخدام هذه المصادر الهامّة ٠

٢ ـ دعت مريم استاذ اللغة العربيّة الى الحفلة ٠

٣ ـ سمّى الشعب المدينة باسم القائد ٠

٤ ـ بنت الحكومة مدارس كثيرة هذا العام ٠

٥ ـ أعدّت زوجتي الطعام ٠

٦ ـ يعدّ العرب طه حُسَيْن والعَقّاد وأَحْمَد أمين من أعظم أدباء القــــرن العشرين ٠

٧ ـ احتفلنا برجوع فريد من باريس احتفالا عظيما ٠

٨ ـ ترجم المستشرقون كثيرا من الكتب العربيّة الى اللغات الأوربيّة ٠

٩ ـ أخرجنا المراسلين من الاجتماع ٠

١٠ ــ أجّل المدير الاجتماع •

١١ ــ انتخب الشعب رئيسا جديدا للجمهوريّة •

١٢ ــ تستخدم بعض الدول الطائرات في الحرب أحيانا •

١٣ ــ علمنا أنّ رئيس الجمهوريّة سيزور مصر •

Drill 10. Numerals.

Supply the appropriate ordinal numeral in each of the following sentences:

١ ــ درست النصّ (٥) هذا الصباح • في النصّ عشرون جملة أكثرها سهلة ،
لكنّ بعضها صعبة كالجملة الـ (١٤) •

٢ ــ ما هي الكلمة الـ (١) في هذه الجملة ؟ وما هي الكلمة الـ (٢)؟

٣ ــ الشهادة الجامعيّة الـ (٣) هي الدكتوراه •

٤ ــ سوف أترك المكتب في الساعة الـ (١٠) والدقيقة الـ (٤٥) •

٥ ــ في هذا الكتاب مقالات كثيرة أهمها الـ (٢٨) •

٦ ــ هذا هو اليوم الـ (٢٦٧) من السنة •

٧ ــ ولد مُصْطَفى كامِلٌ في السنة الميلادية الـ (١٨٧٤) ، أما مُصْطَفى
لُطْفي الْمَنْفَلُوطي فولد في العام الميلادى الـ (١٨٧٦) •

٨ ــ بيتي هو البيت الـ (٢٠) في شارع الجمهوريّة •

٩ ــ رحل المسلمون عن مكّة الى المدينة في السنة الـ (٦٢٢) •

number, issue ١٠ ــ وصلنا الْعَدَدُ الـ (٢) من هذه المجلّة ثم انقطعت •

Drill 11. Question formation.

Make questions for each of the following sentences, based on the underlined portion of the sentence.

١ ــ عاصمة العراق هي بغداد •

٢ ــ أعلى جبل في العالم هو جبل افرست •

٣ ــ فتحت مصر في عهد عُمَرِ بْنِ الخَطّاب •

203

٤ ـ أكلت طعاما عربيّا .

٥ ـ تحيط الجبال بمدينة سولت ليك سيتي .

٦ ـ لون الكتاب أحمر .

٧ ـ النيل الأزرق في السودان .

٨ ـ استفاد الاقتصاد العربيّ من الزيت .

٩ ـ سافر الى فرنسا لدراسة الادب الفرنسي .

١٠ ـ تمّ الاتفاق على حفر قناة .

١١ ـ عاد بالطائرة .

١٢ ـ أحضر هذه الكتب من مصر .

١٣ ـ رأيت المراسل الأمريكيّ في مكتب الوزير .

١٤ ـ احتاجت الى الكتاب الذي عندي .

١٥ ـ وصلنا ثلاثون كتابا من كتب الجاحِظ .

١٦ ـ تتطلّب هذه الكتب دراسة طويلة .

Drill 12. Written. Translation.

The Sudan is south of Egypt. It used to be ruled by the British; later it united with Egypt for a short time, then became independent. The current system of government in the Sudan is similar to that in Egypt: this means that the Sudan is a republic.

Khartoum is the capital of the Sudan; it is a modern city whose population is largely Muslim. The University of Khartoum is one of the largest in the Middle East outside Egypt and Lebanon.

The government of the Sudan is now trying to improve the economic situation, to achieve progress in various other areas, and to solve a number of local problems.

الجمل التمهيديّة ا ـ	A. <u>Preparatory sentences</u>

مذكّرات طالب جديد

Diary of a New Student

١ ـ تركت الكويت منذ أسبوعيـــن .
وصلت الى مدينة شيكاغو مساء
الخامس من أَغُسْطُس وسكنت فــى
المدينة الجامعيّة .

I left Kuwait two weeks ago. I arrived in Chicago the evening of <u>August</u> fifth, and I resided in the university city.

أَغُسْطُس

August (in the Levant and Iraq, آب)

٢ ـ كان أوّل ما فعلته أن ارسلت
رسالة الى والديّ أخبرتهمــا
فيها بـعُنْواني الجديد .

The first thing I did was to send a letter to my parents, in which I informed them of my new <u>address</u>.

عُنْوانٌ ـ عَناوينُ

title; address

٣ ـ أَرْجو أن يصلني الرَدُّ قريبـا
لأنّي مشتاق جدّاً اليهما .

I <u>hope</u> I get an <u>answer</u> soon, because I miss them very much.

رَجا ـُ ، رَجاةٌ (أَنْ)

to hope; to wish; to request (that)

رَدَّ ـُ ، رَدٌّ (على)
رَدٌّ ـ رُدودٌ (عَلى)

to return, send back; to answer (s.o.)

answer, reply (to s.o.)

٤ ـ أثناءالاسبوع الاوّل قمـــت
بـالأعمال التالية .:

During the first week I engaged in the following activities:

٥ ـ قابلت رئيس قِسْمِ اللغـــة
الأنكليزيّة .

I met the chairman of the English <u>Department</u>.

قِسْمٌ ـ أَقْسامٌ

division, part, section; department

٦ ـ ذهبت الى مَكْتَبَةٍ قريبة مـن

I went to a <u>bookstore</u> near the univer-

205

الجامعة . لم أجد هناك قاموسَ " وبستر " الانكليزيّ الذي كنت ابحث عنه .	sity. I did not find there Webster's English **dictionary**, which I had been **looking for**.
مُكْتَبَةٌ ــ ات	library; bookstore
قاموسٌ ــ قَواميسُ	dictionary

٧ ــ ذهبت الى فَرْعٍ من فُروعِ المكتبة فوجدت طَبْعَةً قديمة منه وهي طبعة جَيّدَةٌ .

7 — I went to one of the **branches** of the bookstore and found an old **edition** of it; it was a **good** edition.

فَرْعٌ ــ فُروعٌ	branch
طَبْعَةٌ ــ ات	printing; edition
جَيّدٌ ــ جِيادٌ	good, excellent

٨ ــ قدّمت شيكًا بالثَّمَن لكنّ الشيكَ رُفِضَ .

8 — I presented a **check** **for** the **cost** (of the book) but the check was **refused**.

شيكٌ ــ ات	check
بـ	for the price of, for
ثَمَنٌ ــ أَثْمانٌ	price, cost
رَفَضَ ــُ ، رَفْضٌ	to refuse, reject

٩ ــ قرأت عددًا من الصحف التي تَصْدُرُ في هذه المدينة . لا شكّ انّ الصحف هنا تختلف كلّ الاختلاف عن صحفنا في الكويت .

9 — I read several of the newspapers which are **published** in this city. There's no doubt that the newspapers here are totally different from our newspapers in Kuwait.

صَدَرَ ــُ ، صُدورٌ	to come out, appear, be published

١٠ ــ قابلت عددا من الطلاب السوريين والمصريين، أمّا الطلاب الكويتيون فلم اقابل احدا منهم حتى الان .

10 — I met a number of Syrian and Egyptian students. As for the Kuwaiti students, I haven't met one of them so far.

١١ ــ سيبدأ العام الدراسيّ غـدا.
ارجو الّا تكون الدراسـة
هنا صعبـة . <u>وفَوْقَ ذٰلِـكَ</u>
كله ارجو ان احصل علـى
الشهادة في اقصر مدة .

The academic year begins tomorrow. I hope studying here won't be hard. <u>Above all</u>, I hope I get the degree in the shortest time (possible).

فَوْقَ

above, over, over and above

فَوْقَ ذٰلِكَ

moreover, furthermore

ب ــ <u>النص الاساسي</u>

رســــــالـــــــة

٢٣ آب (اغسطس) سنة ١٩٧٥

حضرة السيّد مدير المكتبة التجارية

<u>تَحِيَّةً</u> واحتراما <u>وَبَعْدُ</u> :

greetings

...ow then

علمت من <u>قائِمَةِ</u> مكتبتكم بصدور طبعة جديدة لقاموس <u>المُنْجِدُ</u> .
بحثت عن هذه الطبعة الجديدة التي سمعت انها جيّدة جدّا في المكتبات
الامريكيّة فعرفت انني لن اتمكّن من الحصول على نسخة منها هنا .
لذلك ارجو ان ترسلوا اليّ نسخة مع <u>القائِمَةِ</u> الاخيرة باسماء الكتب
الجديدة التي اصدرتموها .

تجدون مع رسالتي هذه شيكا بثمن الكتاب .

ولكم شكري واحترامي .

list, catalogue

المخلص
وليم جونــــون
وليم جونســـون

العنوان : ٥٦٤ شارع لنكولن
واشنطن ـ العاصمة
الولايات المتحدة الامريكية

207

الرد

٣١ آب سنة ١٩٧٥

حضرة السيد وليم جونسون :

وصلتنا امس رسالتك التى تطلب فيها ان نرسل اليك نسخة مـــــن قاموس المنجد مع قائمة بكتبنا الجديدة .

ستجد القائمة المطلوبة مع هذه الرسالة . اما المُنْجِد فلــــن

cover — نستطيع ارساله اليك الآن لأنّ الشيك لا يُؤدِّي ثمنه . لقد ازدادت اثمـــان الكتب اللبنانية اثناء الشهر الماضي كما ازدادت اثمان الكتــب الامريكيّة والاوربيّة ، وأُضيفَ الى ثمن المنجد ثلاثة دولارات . وفـــوق

was added / mailing expenses — ذلك شيكك لا يؤدي تَكاليفَ الْبَريد وهي دولار . نرجو ان ترسل شيكـا بالدولارات الاربعة وسوف نرسل اليك نسخة من المنجد عند وصول الشيك الينا .

we regret — يُؤْسِفُنا انك لم تستطع الحصول على نسخة من المنجد الجديد في امريكا . مكتبتنا كما تعلم من اكبر المكتبات اللبنانية ، ولنا فروع كثيرة خارج لبنان ، لكنّ الطبعة الاخيرة من المنجد لن تصل الى تلـــك الفروع قبل نهاية الشهر القادم .

تستطيع ان تطلب من مكتبتنا كلّ ما تريده من الكتب التي ننشرها ، فنحن لا نرفض الطلبات التي تصلنا من خارج لبنان .

لا شكّ ان وصول كتبنا اليك سيحتاج الى شيءٍ من الوقت ولكنّ اثماننا اقل من اثمان الفروع الاجنبية .

ولكم شكرنا واحترامنا .

المخلص

انيس خـــــوري

انيس خـــوري

مدير قسم الكتب العربية بالمكتبة التجارية

١ ــ ما القاموس الذي اراد السيّد وليم جونسون الحصول عليه ؟

٢ ــ هل اراد السيّد وليم جونسون الحصول على طبعة قديمة ام اراد الحصول على طبعة حديثة لهذا القاموس ؟

٣ ــ اين بحث السيّد وليم جونسون عن هذه الطبعة ؟

٤ ــ لمن ارسل السيّد وليم جونسون رسالته ؟

٥ ــ ماذا طلب في تلك الرسالة ؟

٦ ــ ماذا ارسل السيّد وليم جونسون مع رسالته ؟

٧ ــ اين كان السيّد وليم جونسون يسكن ؟ فى اي شارع ؟

٨ ــ من هو السيّد انيس خوري ؟

٩ ــ ماذا ارسل السيّد انيس خوري الى السيّد وليم جونسون ؟

١٠ ــ لماذا لم يرسل السيّد انيس خوري القاموس الى السيّد وليم جونسون ؟

١١ ــ ماذا تعرف عن المكتبة التجارية ؟

١٢ ــ ماذا يقول السيّد انيس خوري عن اثمان المكتبة التجارية ؟

B. __Basic text__

__A Letter__

August 23, 1975

Manager,
The Commercial Bookstore

Dear Sir:

I have learned from your bookstore's catalogue of the publication of a new edition of the dictionary __Al-Munjid__. I have searched for this new edition, which I have heard is a very good one, in American bookstores and have learned that I will not be able to acquire a copy of it here. Therefore I request that

you send me a copy with the latest list of new book titles that you have pub-

lished.

You will find enclosed ("with this letter of mine") a check for the price

of the book.

With my thanks and respects,

Sincerely yours,

William Johnson

William Johnson

Address:

564 Lincoln Street
Washington, D.C.
The United States of America

*   *   *   *   *

Response

31 August 1975

Dear Mr. William Johnson:

We received yesterday your letter in which you requested us to send you

a copy of the dictionary Al-Munjid together with a list of our new books.

You will find the requested catalogue enclosed in this letter. As for

Al-Munjid we will not be able to send it to you now because your check does

not cover its price. The prices of Lebanese books have increased within the

past month as have American and European book prices; three dollars has been

added to the price of Al-Munjid. Moreover, your check does not cover mailing

expenses, which come to one dollar. We hope that you will send us a check for

the four dollars, and we will send you a copy of Al-Munjid on receipt of the

check.

We are sorry that you could not obtain a copy of the new Al-Munjid in

America. Our bookstore is, as you know, one of the biggest Lebanese bookstores,

and we have many branches outside of Lebanon; the latest edition of Al-Munjid, however, will not reach those branches before the end of next month.

You can request from our bookstore any of the books we publish that you want. We do not refuse requests coming to us from abroad.

There is no doubt that it takes a bit of time for our books to reach you, but our prices are less than those of the foreign branches.

With our thanks and respects,

> Sincerely,
>
> S/Anis Khouri
> Anis Khouri
> Manager of the Arabic Books Section
> The Commercial Bookstore

C. Grammar and drills هـ ــ التمارين العامة

---

1. Definiteness in nouns: Summary

2. The مِنْ ... ما construction

3. أَنْ -clauses as statements of fact

4. Clauses as second term of an iḍāfa

---

1. Definiteness in nouns: Summary

If بِنْتُ المَلِكِ means "the king's daughter" or "the daughter of the king" (both nouns are definite) and بِنْتُ مَلِكٍ means "a king's daughter" or "a daughter of a king" or, depending on the context, "the daughter of a king" (both nouns indefinite), then how does one say in Arabic "a daughter of the king" (one noun indefinite and the second definite)? There are two ways:

بِنْتٌ لِلْمَلِكِ	'a daughter of the king's', 'a daughter of the king'
بِنْتٌ مِنْ بَناتِ المَلِكِ	'one of the king's daughters', 'a daughter of the king'

لِ in the first example means "belonging to", "of". Another example from the

211

Preparatory sentences of this lesson is فَرْعٌ مِنْ فُرُوعِ الْمَكْتَبَةِ 'one of the branches of the bookstore' or 'one of the bookstore's branches'. This construction contains a singular noun, the preposition مِنْ , the first noun repeated in the plural, and then a second noun that forms an idafa with the plural noun. If the second noun is omitted, then the plural noun takes the definite article and the resulting construction means "a, a certain ...":

كَانَ لِمَلِكٍ مِنَ الْمُلُوكِ بِنْتٌ جَمِيلَةٌ.	'A certain king had a beautiful daughter.'
يَوْمًا مِنَ الْأَيَّامِ.	'a certain day, one day, once'

This construction is often used at the beginning of narratives, when the topic is being introduced; thus يَوْمًا مِنَ الْأَيَّامِ may also be translated "once upon a time'. It is accordingly different from the idafa construction containing the pronoun أَحَدُ 'one' and a definite noun which has already been mentioned, such as

قَامَ أَحَدُ الْمَنْدُوبِينَ وَقَالَ...	'One of the delegates arose and said ...'

Now do Drill 1.

Drill 1. Transformation-translation.

a. 'He is the university professor.'   ←   •   هو استاذ الجامعة •

'He is a university professor.'   ←   •   هو استاذ جامعة •

'He is one of the university professors.'   ←   •   هو استاذ من اساتذة الجامعة •

'He is one of the professors.'   هو استاذ من الاساتذة •

٤ ــ تبادلت هديّة الزواج •		١ ــ هو مدير البنك •
٥ ــ وصل ليلة الحفلة •		٢ ــ هذا شبّاك المتحف •
٦ ــ اقاموا في قصر الملك •		٣ ــ هذه طائرة الشركة •

b. 'This is the Yemeni dialect.'   ← • هذه هي اللهجة اليمنيّة •

'This is a Yemeni dialect.'   ← • هذه لهجة يمنيّة •

'This is one of the Yemeni dialects.'   • هذه لهجة من اللهجات اليمنيّة •

١ ـ جبل عرفات هو الجبل العالي • ٤ ـ تحدّث عن الدين غير الاسلاميّ•

٢ ـ مطار لندن هو المطار الكبير • ٥ ـ كان هذا هو الامتحان السهل •

٣ ـ هذا هو الشارع الرئيسيّ •

2. The   مَا ... مِنْ   construction

Note the underlined phrase in the following sentence:

سَنُرْسِلُ إِلَيْكَ مَا نَشَرْنَا مِنْ كُتُبٍ في الشَّهْرَيْنِ الأَخِيرَيْنِ •   'We shall send you the books we have published in the last two months.'

The   مَا   at the beginning of this phrase is the indefinite relative   مَا   (see 30. C. 4), and the phrase might be translated literally as "that which we have published of books", or "what we have published by way of books". The smoothest translation, however, is usually one with a relative clause: "the books (which) we have published". Additional examples:

أَخْبِرْني بِمَا لَكَ مِنْ آراءٍ في هذا المَوْضوعِ •   'Inform me of the views you have on this subject.'
تَسْتَطيعُ أَنْ تَطْلُبَ كُلَّ مَا تُريدُهُ مِنَ الكُتُبِ الّتي نَنْشُرُها •   'You may order any of the books we publish that you want.'

مَنْ   'whoever, anyone who' may also be followed by   مِنْ   in the meaning of "by way of", as in

قُلْ لي مَنْ حَضَرَ المُؤْتَمَرَ مِنْ مُهَنْدِسينَ ؟   'Tell me what engineers attended the conference.'

Now do Drill 2.

<u>Drill 2.</u> Written. Transformation using مـا...مِنْ.

'We will send you the books
 we have published.'

سنرسل اليك الكتب التي نشرناها • ←

سنرسل اليك ما نشرناه من كتب •

١ ـ اهتمّ الرئيس بآراء التي قدّموها له •

٢ ـ اطلب الكتب التي تريدها •

٣ ـ هذه هي المقالات التي قرأتها •

٤ ـ لا اعرف شيئا عن المواضيع التي بحثت في هذا المؤتمر •

٥ ـ أعجبتنا جدّا الاماكن المقدّسة التي زرناها في القدس •

٦ ـ صف لنا الآثار التي في لبنان ؟

٧ ـ ليست كل الأشياء التي احضرتها هامة •

3. أَنْ -clauses as statements of fact.

We have learned that clauses beginning with أَنَّ 'that, the fact that'
are statements of <u>fact</u>--events or states that have been realized or that the
speaker states will be realized--while those after أَنْ are <u>possible events</u>--no
indication is given as to whether or not they will take place (see L.22, C.1.
pp. 428-430). The two meanings are contrasted below.

| أَعْرِفُ أَنَّكَ بَذَلْتَ جُهُودًا كَبِيرَةً وَأَنَّكَ سَتَنْجَحُ في مَنْهَجِكَ الْجَدِيدِ. | 'I know that you have worked very hard and that you will succeed in your new program.' |
| يَجِبُ أَنْ تُحاوِلَ أَكْثَرَ. | 'You must try harder.' |

أَنْ is regularly followed by a subjunctive verb, while أَنَّ never is.
We have now seen two instances, however, where أَنْ is followed by a <u>perfect</u>
<u>tense</u> verb; in these cases the أَنْ -clause has the meaning of statement of fact.

One of these cases is after the preposition بَعْدَ 'after' (see p. 431);
بَعْدَ أَنْ plus the verb may be translated in the following ways, depending on the

context:

214

بَعْدَ أَنْ أَعَدَّ الْأَسْئِلَةَ.	'after he prepared the questions' 'after he had prepared the questions' 'after preparing the questions' 'after having prepared the questions' 'having prepared the questions.'

The second instance of the use of أَنْ with the perfect tense occurs in

Preparatory Sentence 2 of this lesson:

كَانَ أَوَّلُ مَا فَعَلْتُهُ أَنْ أَرْسَلْتُ رِسَالَةً الى والِدَيَّ.	'The first thing I did was to send a letter to my parents.'

In this construction the أَنْ-clause serves as the predicate of an equa-

tional sentence, and again denotes a completed event. This construction is

practiced below in Drill 4.

4. <u>Clauses as second term of an iḍāfa</u>

The following expressions

أَجْمَلُ مَدِينَةٍ	'the prettiest city'
أَجْمَلُ مَا وَجَدْنَا	'the prettiest that we found'

are two instances of iḍāfa constructions; both contain an elative adjective

as the first term, while the second term of the first example is a noun and

the second term of the other is a clause introduced by the indefinite relative

pronoun مَا 'that which, what'. This illustrates the fact that clauses func-

tion like nouns, including the function of serving as second term of an iḍāfa.

The construction consisting of elative plus مَا or مَنْ plus clause is trans-

lated as "the _____est that _____." Additional examples:

هٰذا أَصْعَبُ مَا قَرَأْتُهُ.	'This is the hardest (one) that I have read.'
كَانَ أَوَّلُ مَا فَعَلْتُهُ أَنْ أَرْسَلْتُ رِسَالَةً إِلى أَهْلِي.	'The first thing that I did was to send a letter to my folks.'

215

أَوَّلُ مَنْ دَعا إِلى ذَلِكَ مُحَمَّدٌ عَلِي .   'The first one to advocate that was Muhammad Ali.'

عَلى أَتَمِّ ما يَكونُ   'in the most perfect manner conceivable'

Another instance where a clause serves as second term of an iḍāfa is after a noun of time, as in

حينَ دَرَسْتُ مَعَهُ فِي الْجامِعَةِ   'when I studied with him in the university'

This iḍāfa consists of the noun حينٌ 'time' and the clause دَرَسْتُ مَعَهُ في 'I studied with him at the university.' The noun حينٌ الْجامِعَةِ does not have nunation because it is the first term of the iḍāfa, and is accusative as an adverbial expression (see 23. C. 4). After nouns of time a clause may serve as the second term as is, without any subordinating particle. This sentence literally means, then, "at the time I studied with him in the university." Further illustrations:

يَوْمَ وُلِدَتْ   '(on) the day that she was born'

وَقْتَ كانَ مُدَرِّسًا   'when he was a teacher'

ساعَةَ دَخَلَ   'the moment he came in'

Such clauses after nouns of time may be changed to their corresponding verbal nouns, e.g.

يَوْمَ وِلادَتِها   'the day of her birth'

وَقْتَ كَوْنِهِ مُدَرِّسًا   'the time he was a teacher'

ساعَةَ دُخولِهِ   'the moment of his entrance'

Now do Drills 3 and 4.

Drill 3. Nominalization.

Change the clause following the noun of time to a verbal noun phrase. Ex.

'the day she was born'   يوم ولدت ← يوم ولادتها

'when he arrived'   عندما وصل ← عند وصوله

٧ ــ عندما اتّصل بنا   ١ ــ ساعة خرجا

٨ ــ وقت بنى هذا المتحف   ٢ ــ عندما رجعوا

٩ ــ ليلة انعقد الاجتماع   ٣ ــ وقت أقمن في القدس

١٠ ــ يوم مرّوا بنا   ٤ ــ حين وصلت

١١ ــ وقت أنتجوا الزيت   ٥ ــ يوم سافرت الى امريكا

١٢ ــ حين تطوّر الاقتصاد   ٦ ــ ليلة اجتمعت بك

Drill 4. Completion with مَنْ / ما .

Fill in the first blank with ما or مَن and the second blank with
the appropriate form of the suffix pronoun. Ex.

كان أوّل ــ فعلت ــ أن ارسلت
رسالة الى اهلى . ←

'The first thing I did was to send   كان أوّل ما فعلته أن ارسلت
a letter to my family.'   رسالة الى اهلى .

١ ــ كان آخر ــ قمنا بــ ــ من أعمال أن زرنا جريدة "الاخبار" القاهريّة .

٢ ــ هل تعرف ــ قابلت ــ في الحفلة أمس .

٣ ــ أريد ــ تريد ــ من اشياء .

٤ ــ أخبرنى بــ ــ درست مع ــ في جامعة هارفارد .

٥ ــ وطلن ــ نريد الاتصال بــ ــ .

٦ ــ أخبرنى بــ ــ فعلت ــ في العراق .

٧ ــ هل هناك ــ تحبّ ــ مريم ؟

٨ ــ أعجبني ـــــ كنتم تبحثون ـــــ هذا الصباح .

٩ ــ نازِكُ المَلائِكة هي أوّل ـــــ قرأتُ شعرا من تأليف ـــــــ .

١٠ ــ هذا ـــــ اريدك ان تعرف ـــــ .

D. Comprehension passage — د ـــ نصوص للفهم

Read the following passage and then do Drill 5, which is based on it.

رسالـــــــــة

٥ آب (اغسطس) سنة ١٩٧٥.

السيّد مدير قسم اللغة الانكليزيّة
جامعة الكويت

greetings   تَحيّةً واحتراماً .

علمتُ من الاستاذ جيم ريتشاردز ، الذي عاد الى أمريكا هـذا الاسبوع بعد زيارة قصيرة للكويت ، أنّكم محتاجون الى أستاذ لتدريـس اللغة الانكليزيّة والأدب الأمريكيّ المعاصر .

أنا طالب مصريّ أدرس الآن فى قسم اللغة الأنكليزيّة بجامعـة مشيغان ، وهى كما تعلمون من أكبر الجامعات الأمريكيّة وأشهرها . حصلت من هذه الجامعة على الماجستير في اللغة الانكليزيّة والأدب الأمريكـيّ وأكملت فيها جميع الدروس المطلوبة للدكتوراه فى الأدب الامريكيّ المعاصر.

dissertation   أمّا رِسالةُ الدكتوراه فقد أكملت معظمها ، وأرجو ان أحصل علـى الشهادة فى نهاية هذا العام الدراسى . الدكتور جيم ريتشاردز هو الاستاذ المشرف على الرسالة ، وتستطيعون أن تسألوه عنّى اذا احببتم .

شملت دراستى الجامعيّة دروسا كثيرة منها ما يتصل بعلم اللغـة

218

ومنها ما يتصل بالاساليب الحديثة المتبعة فى تدريس الانكليزيّة كلغة
اجنبيّة .

وقد شملت دراستى للادب عددا كبيرا من أدباء أمريكا المعاصرين ،
وستجدون هذا كله فى الشهادات الجامعيّة المُرْفَقَةِ بهذه الرسالة .   attached to

وقد عملت منذ حصولى على الماجستير مساعدا للاستاذ رتشاردز فى
تدريس اللغة الانكليزيّة كلغة أجنبيّة ، وكان بعض طلابى كويتيّين . كذلك
درّست الأدب ألأمريكىّ المعاصر فى جامعة مشيغان خلال الصيف الماضى .

سوف أكون فى انتظار ردّكم . وأرجو لكم وللجامعة الكويت كل نجـاح
أثناء العام الدراسىّ القادم .

المخلــــص

على فكري

الرد

٢٥ آب ١٩٧٥ .

حضرة السيّد على فكري المحترم :
أما بَعْدُ ،   now then
وصلتنا أمس رسالتك ، ويُؤْسِفُنا أنّنا لن نستطيع الاستفادة مــن   regret
خدماتك لأنّ أستاذا أمريكيّا من جورجيا حصل على الوظيفة التى ذكرتها .

نرجو لكم كلّ نجاح .

المخلص

محمود حكيـــــم

مدير قسم اللغة الانكليزيّة

جامعة الكويت

219

Drill 5. Written.

    a. List in outline form, first in English then in Arabic, all the quali-
fications for the job that Ali Fikri gives in his letter.

    b.   هل رفض طلب علي فكري ؟ لماذا ؟

E. __General drills.__   هـ ــ التمارين العامة

Drill 6. Combination: Use of the comparative.

               ← (طويل)   نهر النيل ــ نهر الامازون

'The Nile is longer than the Amazon.'   نهر النيل اطول من نهر الامازون .

                    (عزيز) .   ١ ــ الولد ــ الصديق

                    (جميل) .   ٢ ــ وداد ــ انا

               (مشهور) .   ٣ ــ طه حسين ــ شوقي ضيف

                 (فقير) .   ٤ ــ انا ــ انت

                (واضح) .   ٥ ــ محاضراتك ــ محاضراته

                (جديد) .   ٦ ــ سيارتك ــ سيارتى

                (قويّ) .   ٧ ــ أنت ــ هو

                (قبيح) .   ٨ ــ هنّ ــ هى

Drill 7. Combination: Use of the superlative.

         ← (طويل) .   نهر النيل ــ نهر في العالم

'The Nile is the longest river in the world.'   نهر النيل اطول نهر في العالم .

      (مشهور) .   ١ ــ الجامعة الامريكية ــ جامعة في لبنان .

      (جميلة) .   ٢ ــ هي ــ بنت في تونس .

      (قديم) .   ٣ ــ هذا القصر ــ قصر في فرنسا .

      (كبير) .   ٤ ــ نيويورك ــ مدينة في الولايات المتحدة .

٥ ــ احمد ــ طالب في الصف (طويل) .

٦ ــ كان ــ قائد فى العالم العربى (عظيم) .

٧ ــ هو ــ رجل في الحكومة اليوم (قوىّ) .

٨ ــ هى ــ بنت في صفّنا (قصير) .

Drill 8. (Also on tape) Verb ⟶ verbal noun.

عرف	سأل	عمل	ذهب	طبع
سمّى	عيّن	زار	دعا	وصف
انحاز	تبادل	تأكّد	أقام	ساعد
استفاد	استخدم	اهتمّ	امتاز	فضّل

Drill 9. Written. Dictionary drill.

Look up the following words in the dictionary. Ex.

	Meaning	Root	Ex.
	capacity	وعب	استيعاب
ولاء	استئصال		امانة
ابتزّ	عذوبة		مفيد
ابتاع	استنكر		انقلاب
انتحار	استمال		مؤسسة
مصابيح	خيانة		سعادة

Drill 10. Written. Translation.

1. The foreign minister of France paid an official visit to Lebanon.

2. The conference which lasted for six days was attended by twenty delegates.

3. The Arabs consider those singers among the most famous Arab singers who have lived in this century.

4. My wife is from a small village near the Red Sea.

5. I stayed in Cairo for five days, after which I returned to Damascus.

6. It is known that the Qur'an is written in classical Arabic.

7. They promised us to behave better next time.

8. He especially wants to know the Yemeni culture well.

أ - الجمل التمهيدية

A. <u>Preparatory sentences</u>

الحرّية والواجب

Freedom and Responsibility

١ - لي صديق يمنيّ اسمه احمد فَقَدَ
والديه وهو في الثامنة مـن
عمره فقام بتربيته زوج اخت
له اسمه السيّد فريد ٠

1 - I have a Yemeni friend named Ahmad
who <u>lost</u> his parents when he was
eight, and a brother-in-law of his,
Mr. Farid, undertook his education.

فَقَدَ ــ ، فَقْدٌ، فُقْدانٌ

to lose, be deprived of, miss

٢ - اهتمّ به السيّد فريد واعتبره
ابنا له وَفَتَحَ امامه ابـواب
العلم ٠

فَتَحَ ــَ ، فَتْحٌ

2 - Mr. Farid took care of him, and considered him a son (of his), and <u>open-
ed</u> the doors of knowledge before him.

to open; to conquer

٣ - أنْهى احمد دراسته الثانوية
في اليمن فارسله السيّـد
فريد الى مصر ليدرس فـى
كلّيّة الآداب بجامعة القاهرة ٠

3 - Ahmad <u>completed</u> his secondary education in Yemen, and then Mr. Farid
sent him to Egypt to study in the
<u>School of Arts</u> at Cairo University.

أنْهى ، إنْهاءٌ
كلّيّة ــ ات
كلّيّةُ الآدابِ

IV to complete, finish
college; school (of a university)
School of Arts, College of Arts and
Humanities

٤ - درس احمد في كلّيّة الآداب ،
وكان من اساتذته رجل فرنسيٌّ
معروف ساعده على فَهْمِ الادب
الفرنسيّ والثقافة الفرنسية
فهما عميقًا ٠

فَهِمَ ــَ ، فَهْمٌ
عميقٌ

4 - Ahmad studied in the School of Arts,
and among his professors was a well-
known Frenchman who helped him achieve
a <u>deep</u> understanding of French literature and French culture.

to understand, comprehend
deep, profound

<table>
<tr>
<td dir="rtl">٥ ـ وكان الاستاذ يقول دائماً لطالبه : يجب ان تذهب الى فرنسا وتحصل على الدكتوراه في الادب الفرنسي ثم تَنْفَعُ طلاب بلادك بما تتعلمـــه هناك .</td>
<td>5 — The professor <u>always</u> used to say to his student: You must go to France and get a doctorate in French literature, and then <u>benefit</u> the students of your country with what you learn there.</td>
</tr>
<tr>
<td dir="rtl">دائماً
نَفَعَ ـَ ، نَفْعٌ</td>
<td>always
to be of use to, benefit</td>
</tr>
<tr>
<td dir="rtl">٦ ـ أظهر صديقي رغبة في السفر الى فرنسا لدراسة الادب الفرنسي وساعده استاذه على تحقيق رغبته .</td>
<td>6 — My friend expressed a desire to travel to France to study French literature, and his professor helped him to realize his wishes.</td>
</tr>
<tr>
<td dir="rtl">٧ ـ قبل السفر كتب احمد الى زوج اخته يخبره بالامـــر فأُدْهَشَ ذلك زوج اخته .</td>
<td>7 — Before the trip Ahmad wrote to his brother-in-law to inform him of the matter, and this <u>surprised</u> his brother-in-law.</td>
</tr>
<tr>
<td dir="rtl">أَدْهَشَ ، إِدْهاشٌ</td>
<td>IV to surprise, astonish, amaze</td>
</tr>
<tr>
<td dir="rtl">٨ ـ كتب زوج اخته اليه يقول : انا الآن في الستين من عمري وقد اصبحت في حاجة الى مساعدتك .</td>
<td>8 — His brother-in-law wrote to him saying: "I am now sixty years old, and I have come to need your help."</td>
</tr>
<tr>
<td dir="rtl">٩ ـ قرّر احمد على الرغم من ذلك ان يسافر الى فرنسا .</td>
<td>9 — Ahmad decided, in spite of that, to travel to France.</td>
</tr>
<tr>
<td dir="rtl">١٠ ـ حصل احمد على الدكتوراه مـن جامعة السربون بعد ان كتب رسالةً بعنوان "شِعْرُ لامارْتين"</td>
<td>10 — Ahmad obtained the doctorate from the Sorbonne after writing a <u>dissertation</u> entitled "The Poetry of Lamartine".</td>
</tr>
<tr>
<td dir="rtl">رِسالةٌ ـ رَسائِلُ</td>
<td>letter; thesis, dissertation</td>
</tr>
</table>

١١ - اثناء دراسته هناك قابل فَتَاةً
فرنسيّة أحبّها وتزوّجها .

During his study there he met a
French <u>girl</u> that he fell in love
with and married.

فَتَاةٌ - فَتَيَاتٌ

girl, young woman

١٢ - أصبح أحمد بعد اكماله الدراسة
الجامعيّة مدرّسا في جامعة
فرنسيّة وكتب كتبا عميقة البحث
علميّة الاسلوب .

After completing his university
studies, Ahmad became a teacher
in a French university and wrote
books characterized by thorough
research and scholarly style.

١٣ - وما زال <u>يَتَرَقّى</u> حتى <u>صار</u> استاذا .

He continued to <u>advance</u> until he
<u>became</u> a professor.

تَرَقّى ، تَرَقٍّ

V to advance in rank, be promoted, rise

صارَ ـِ ، صَيْرٌ ، صَيْرورَةٌ

to become, come to (be)

١٤ - في بداية هذا الاسبوع وصلت
أحمد رسالة تقول ان زوج اخته
قد مات . جاء أحمد يسألني :
" أكنت <u>عَلى حقٍّ</u> فيما فعلت ؟ "

At the beginning of this week Ahmad
received a letter saying that his
brother-in-law had died. Ahmad
came and asked me, "Was I <u>right</u> in
what I did?"

(انا) على حَقٍّ

(I am) right

١٥ - لقد <u>أغْضَبْتُهُ</u> حين فضّلت حياتي
<u>ومُسْتَقْبَلي</u> على حياته ومستقبله .
العلّي <u>أسأتُ اليه</u> بذلك ؟

I <u>made him angry</u> when I chose my
life and my <u>future</u> over his. Did
I perhaps <u>harm</u> him by (doing) that?

أغْضَبَ ، إغْضابٌ

IV to anger s.o.

مُسْتَقْبَلٌ

future (n.)

أساءَ ، إساءَةٌ الى

IV to hurt, harm, act meanly
toward

١٦ - ألا يستطيع الانسان ان يهتم بحياته
ومستقبله ، ويظهر في الوقت
نفسه <u>التَّقْديرَ</u> لأهله ؟

"Can one not take an active interest
in one's own life and future, and at
the same time show <u>appreciation</u> for
one's family?"

قَدَّرَ ، تَقْديرٌ

II to appreciate, esteem; to
assess, evaluate

طــه حُسَـيْـــن

كان طهَ حسين من اشهر ادباء العرب فى القرن العشرين واعظمهم
انتاجا . وُلد فى قرية صغيرة بمصر عام ١٨٨٩ ، وفقد بَصَرُهُ حين كـان
في الثالثة من عمره . تعلّم القرآن في القرية ، ودرس فى الازهر ، ثم
تابع دراسته فى الجامعة المصرية (التى تعرف اليوم بجامعة القاهرة)
علـــى كبار الاساتذة ومن بينهم المستشرقون نالينو وجُويدي وليتْمان.
وفى عام ١٩١٤ حصل على شهادة الدكتوراه برسالته عن أبي العَـــلاء
المَعَرّي .

بعد ان انهى طه حسين دراسته فى مصر ، أرسل الى فرنسا ،
فدرس فى جامعة مونْبِلْيِيه ، ثم انتقل منها الى السوربون وهناك درس
الادب الكِلاسيكي ، وتأثّر بالادب الفرنسي والثقافة الاوربية وحصل على
شهادة الدكتوراه برسالته عن ابْنِ خَلْدون . وفي باريس قابل الفتاة
التى صارت له زوجة ولعينيه بَصَراً .

وعند رجوعه الى مصر صار استاذا للادب العربى فى كلّيّة الاداب
بالجامعة المصرية ، ثم عَميداً لهذه الكلّيّة ، ثم رئيسا لجامعة
الاسكندريَة ، وما زال يترقى حتى صار وزيرا للتربية والتعليم فـى
عام ١٩٥٠ ، ففتح ابواب المدارس لأبْنِاءِ الشَّعْبِ المصري كلّه ، واهتمّ
بتعليم الفتيات اهتماما عظيما . وقد سمّاه معاصروه عَميداً لـلادب
العربي تقديرا له ولخدماته في الميادين الادبية والثقافية .

كان لانتاجه الكبير تأثير عظيم على النهضة الادبية فـى
العالم العربي ، وساعد ذلك الانتاج مساعدة كبيرة على تقدّم الثقافة
العربية . ومن اهمّ كتبه " الأيّام " و " في الشعْر الجاهليّ "، ومستقبل
الثقافة في مصر " .

sight

under

classical

sight

dean

ordinary
people

pre-
Islamic

يتحدّث طه حسين فى كتاب " الايّام " عن حياته ودراسته فى القرية وفي الازهر قبل سفره الى باريس • وقد ترجم الكتاب الى لغات اجنبيّة كثيرة منها الانكليزيّة والفرنسيّة، ويعتبر من أَرْوَعِ الكتب الادبيّة الحديثة •

most mag-
nificent

اما كتابه " في الشعر الجاهِلِيّ " فقد كتب بأسلوب علميّ لم يكن سائدا فى مصر الحديثة قبل ذلك• أدهش الكتاب بعض الادباء، وأعجب آخرين لكنّه أغضب المُحافِظينَ الذين عدّوه اساءة الى الدين• وكان أولئك conser-
vatives المحافظون دائما يبذلون الجهود الكبيرة لمقاومة الكتاب •

و" مستقبل الثقافة فى مصر " من اهمّ كتب طه حسين، نشر بعد ان حصلت مصر على استقلالها فى عام ١٩٣٦، وفيه يقول طه حسين: انّ ثقافة أوربا هى أعظم ما وصل اليه الانسان، ويجب على المصريّين فى عهدهم الجديد ان ينقلوا هذه الثقافة الى بلادهم وينفعوا بها ابناءهم • وأظهر الكاتب فهما عميقا للمشكلات المتّصلة بنظام التعليم فى مصر، قال: يجب primary ان يكون التعليم الابْتِدائِيُّ حقّا لكل مصريّ، وان تستقلّ الجامعات اقتصاديّا وعلميّا • وأكثر رجال التربية والتعليم اليوم يعتقدون ان طه حسين كان على حقّ فى هذه الآراء •

مات طه حسين فى عام ١٩٧٣ وهو فى الرابعة والثمانين من عمره ففقد العالم العربىّ بموته أديبا كبيرا ومفكّرا من أعظم المفكّرين •

أسئلة

١ – أين تعلّم طه حسين القرآن ؟

٢ – متى درس طه حسين فى ألازهر ؟ ماذا تعتقد أنه درس هناك ؟ لماذا تعتقد ذلك ؟

٣ – ألا تزال جامعة القاهرة موجودة في مصر ؟

٤ – حصل طه حسين على الدكتوراه من مصر، ثمّ ذهب الى فرنسا للحصول على الدكتوراه من هناك • علام يدل ذلك ؟

٥ – فى كم جامعة فرنسيّة درس طه حسين ؟

٦ – هل تزوّج طه حسين فرنسيّة أم مصريّة ؟

٧ – ماذا درّس طه حسين بعد رجوعه من فرنسا ؟ لماذا اذن كانت رسالة
الدكتوراه التى كتبها فى فرنسا عن موضوع تاريخيّ ؟

٨ – لأىّ جامعة صار طه حسين رئيسا ؟

٩ – هل استفادت الفتيات عندما أصبح طه حسين وزيرا للتربية والتعليم ؟
لماذا ؟

١٠ – هل كان طه حسين يهتمّ بالسياسة ؟ كيف علمت ذلك ؟

١١ – ما الحياة التى وصفها طه حسين فى كتاب " الايّام " : حياته فى
مصر أم حياته فى باريس ؟

١٢ – ما بعض اللغات التى ترجم اليها كتاب " الايّام " ؟

١٣ – لماذا قاوم بعض الناس كتاب " فى الشعر الجاهلىّ " ؟

١٤ – عمّ تحدّث طه حسين فى كتابه " مستقبل الثقافة فى مصر " ؟

B. Basic text

Taha Hussein

Taha Hussein was one of the most famous Arab writers of the twentieth century, and one of the most prolific. He was born in a small village in Egypt
in 1889, and he lost his sight when he was three years old. He learned the
Qur'an in the village, and studied at Al-Azhar. Then he continued his studies
at the Egyptian University (which is known today as Cairo University) under
the leading professors, among them the orientalists Nallino, Guidi, and Littman.
In 1914 he obtained the doctor's degree with his dissertation on Abū al-'Alā'
al-Ma'arrī.

After Taha Hussein had completed his studies in Egypt, he was sent to France and studied at the University of Montpelier. Then he transferred from there to the Sorbonne, and there he studied classical literature. He was influenced by French literature and European culture, and he obtained the doctorate with his dissertation on Ibn Khaldūn. In Paris he met the girl who became a wife for him and sight for his eyes.

On his return to Egypt he became a professor of Arabic literature in the School of Arts at the Egyptian University, then dean of that School, then president of the University of Alexandria; and he continued to advance until he became Minister of Education in 1950. He opened the doors of the schools to the ordinary people of Egypt and he took great interest in the education of girls. His contemporaries called him the "Dean of Arabic Literature" in appreciation of him and of his services in the literary and cultural fields.

His extensive works had great influence on the literary movement in the Arab world and helped greatly in the advancement of Arab culture. Among the most important of his books are Al-Ayyām ("The Days"), Fī al-Shiᶜr Al- Jāhilī ("On Pre-Islamic Literature") and Mustaqbal Al-Thaqāfa fī Miṣr ("The Future of Culture in Egypt").

In Al-Ayyām Taha Hussein talks about his life and studies in the village and at Al-Azhar before his trip to Paris. The book has been translated into many foreign languages including English and French, and is considered one of the most magnificent of modern literary works.

As for his book Fī Al-Shiᶜr Al-Jāhilī, it was written in a scholarly style not previously common in modern Egypt. The book surprised some literary

228

scholars and pleased others, but it angered the conservatives, who considered

it an affront to religion. Those conservatives always exerted great efforts

in resisting the book.

Mustaqbal Al-Thaqāfa fī Miṣr is one of Taha Hussein's most important books.

It was published after Egypt had obtained her independence in 1936, and in it

Taha Hussein says: The culture of Europe is man's most magnificent achieve-

ment (lit.: "is the most magnificent of what man has achieved") and it is

incumbent upon Egyptians in their new era to transmit this culture to their

country and to make its benefits available to their children. The author

showed a deep understanding for the problems connected with the system of educ-

ation in Egypt. He said: "Elementary education must be a right belonging to

every Egyptian, and the universities must become independent economically and

academically." Most men in the field of education today believe that Taha

Hussein was right in these views.

Taha Hussein died in 1973 in his eighty-fourth year, and with his death

the Arab world lost a distinguished literary figure and one of the greatest

thinkers.

C. Grammar and drills   جـ — القواعد والتمارين

> 1. Accusative of cause or purpose: تَقْدِيرًا لَهُ

1. Accusative of cause or purpose: تَقْدِيرًا لَهُ

Verbal nouns may be put in the accusative to express the cause, reason or

purpose for an action; the meaning of the construction is "because of, out of,

from" or "in order to". The verbal noun is in the accusative case and with

nunation. If the verbal noun has an object, the object must be placed after a

229

preposition--if there is a preposition usually associated with the object of a verb (as with verb-preposition idioms), that preposition is used; otherwise لِ is used. Illustrations:

شَكَروا الزائِرَ تَقْديرًا لِخَدَماتِهِ الكَثيرَةِ .	'They thanked the visitor in appreciation of his many services' (or: "out of appreciation of", "because of appreciation of").
تَرَكَ بِلادَهُ حُبًّا لِلْحُرِّيَّةِ .	'He left his country out of love for freedom.'
سَمّاهُ عَميدًا لِلأَدَبِ الْعَرَبِيِّ تَكْريمًا لَهُ .	'They named him the "Dean of Arabic literature" in order to honor him.'
قالَ الْوَزيرُ رَدًّا عَلى سُؤالٍ : ...	'The minister said in answer to ("in order to answer") a question,...'
عادَ الى بَيْتِهِ بَحْثًا عَنِ الْمَجَلَّةِ .	'He returned home in search of the magazine.'

Now do Drill 1.

<u>Drill 1</u>. Recognition of accusative of purpose.

Identify the accusatives of purpose and give their meaning.

١ ــ يرحل البدو من مكان الى مكان في الصحراء طلبا للماء .

٢ ــ سافر الى الولايات المتحدة بحثا عن عمل .

٣ ــ قدّم المؤلف كتابه الجديد لوالدته احتراما لها .

٤ ــ عينته الشركة مديرا تقديرا لخدماته .

٥ ــ اقاموا حفلة كبيرة تكريما لاستاذهم .

٦ ــ اجتمع الناس في المطار تكريما للوزير الزائر .

٧ ــ درست الطالبة ساعات طويلة استعدادا للامتحان .

٨ ــ قام الناس اكراما لرجل الدين .

230

٩ ـ بقي مندوبو الدول الاعضاء في اماكنهم انتظارا لوصول السكرتير

العام لمنظمة الامم المتحدة .

١٠ ـ طلب الزواج منها حبّا لها .

(1) Read the following passage and then do Drill Z, which is based on it.

قِصَّةُ حُـــبٍّ

finished **فَرِغا مِــــنْ**   كان فريد وسلوى يشربان القهوة في مقهى الجامعة .

شرب القهوة دون أَن يقولا شيئا ، وبعد دقائق طويلة تكلم فريد :

فريد : لقد أدهشني ما سمعت من والدك أمس ، بل لقد اغضبني .

سلوى : لعلّه اساء اليك بما قاله . انت تعلم أنّ لي رأيا غير رأيه ،

ولكنّ حريّة التصرّف ليست من حقوق الفتاة في بلادنا .

فريد : بل أعلم أنّ للفتاة حقّ التصرّف في أمور حياتها . ألسنا في القرن

العشرين !؟ ولمن تكون حرّية التصرّف اذا لم تكن للمتعلّمات من

بنات العائلات الغنيّة !؟

سلوى : أنت على حقّ ،ولكن ......

parliament   فريد : ولكنّي فقير ، وعائلتي غير معروفة ، ووالدي ليس عضوا فـــــي

<u>الْبَرْلَمانِ</u> ! لقد صار الزواج في هذه الأيّام تجارة !

سلوى : كنت أحبّ ألّا يغضبك كلام والدي الى هذا الحدّ .

فريد : لعلّ هناك رجلا آخر يرغب في أن يتزوّجك ، ولعلّ والدك يفضّله عليّ .

position,
stand,
attitude   سلوى : لست على حق في ذلك . أرجو يا فريد أن تفهم <u>مَوْقِفَ</u> والدي وأن

تفهم <u>مَوْقِفي</u> أنا أيضا . أنا أحبّك كما تحبّني ، لكنّ الحياة لا

تسير دائما في الطريق التي نريدها .

study mission
(group of
students
on fellowship)   فريد : فهمت . أنت تعلمين أنّي مسافر الى فرنسا في <u>بَعْثَةٍ دِراسِيّةٍ</u> عند

231

نهاية هذا العام · كنت أرجو أن نذهب معا ، ولكنّي أرى الآن

أنّ لكلّ منّا طريقا وأنّ الطريقين لن تَلْتَقِيا ·   meet

مضت أعوام أربـعة كان فريد خلالها يدرس العلوم السياسية فـي

باريس · كانت طريقه صعبة ، ولكنه كان يسير بـإصرارٍ ونشاطٍ أدهشـا   persistence

أساتذته وأصدقاءه · فلما حصل على الدكتوراه بـمَرْتَبَةِ الشَّرَفِ الأُولى كان   with Honours first class

أعظم الناس دَهْشَةً ·   surprise

عاد فريد الى بلاده وصار موظفا في مكتب رئيس الوزراء ، وظلّ

يترقى حتى أصبح مديرا للمكتب · وبذل جهودا عظيمة في خدمة بـلاده ،

فاحترمه الناس ووضعوا ثقتهم فيه ، كذلك صادقه الكثيرون من كبـار

رجال الدولة ·

وأقيلت الانتخابات فانتخبه الشعب عضوا في البَرْلَمانِ ·   parliament

وفي حفلة الْتَقَيا : كانت في الحفلة لأنّ والدها كان أحد المدعوّين   met

أما هو فقد كان ضَيْفَ الشَّرَفِ · قالت له :   guest of honor

أخبرتني قبل سفرك الى فرنسا أنّ طريقينا لن تَلْتَقِيا ، لكنّك لم   meet

تكن على حقّ !

قال :

ـ بـل كنت على حقّ ، فما زالت المسافة بـين طريقينا بـعيدة كل

البـعد · لم يتغيّر منّي إلّا وضعي الاجتماعيّ · هل تزوّجت ؟

قالت :

ـ لا ، فانّ لبعض الناس قلوبـا تحبّ مرّة واحدة فقط · وأنت ، هل

تزوّجت ؟

فنظر اليها طويلا قبل أن يقول :

ـ لا ، ولكنني سأتزوّج قريبـا ·

قالت :

لعلّها ابنة صديق لك من أعضاء البرلمان !

قال :

ـ بـل هي طالبة في الجامعة الأمريكية . واود ان تعلمي أنّهـا

من عائلة فقيرة .

Drill 2. Written. Questions.   أسئلـة

met   ١ ـ أين اُلْتَقى فريـد وسلوى ؟

٢ ـ هل عائلة سلوى أغنى من عائلة فريد ؟ كيف علمت ذلك ؟

position, stand on   ٣ ـ ما رأيك في مَوْقِفِ سلوى مِنْ موضوع الزواج ؟ هل يختلف مَوْقِفُ فريـد

position, stand, attitude   من ذلك ؟

٤ ـ ما رأيك في قول فريد : " انّ لكلّ منّا طريقا وانّ الطريقيــن

meet   لن تَلْتَقيا " ؟

٥ ـ كم سنة درس فريد في فرنسا ؟ ماذا درس ؟

٦ ـ أين عمل فريد بعد رجوعه الى بلاده ؟ هل نجح في عمله ؟

٧ ـ كيف كان وضع فريد في المجتمع حين قابل سلوى في الحفلة ؟ هـل

كان رأيه في الزواج قد تغيّر ؟ ورأي سلوى ؟

٨ ـ لماذا قالت سلوى :" ان لبعض الناس قلوبا تحبّ مرّة واحدة فقط" .

(2) Listen to each of the sentences on tape and then do Drill 3.

Drill 3. Written. (On tape) Translate into English the sentences recorded
on tape.

E. Underline Underline __General drills__   هـ ـ التمارين العامة

Drill 4. Written. Completion.

Fill in the empty slots with the correct form of each word.

ACTIVE VERB	PASSIVE VERB	ACTIVE PARTICIPLE	PASSIVE PARTICIPLE	VERBAL NOUN
كَتَبَ				
		واصِفٌ		
				بِناءٌ
	حُدِّدَ			
			مُسَمّى	
شاهَدَ				
		مُغْضِبٌ		
				اِنْتِخابٌ
			مُسْتَخْدَمٌ	
	اُسْتُطيعَ			

Drill 5. Transformation. Perfect passive ◄──► Imperfect passive with   ــ .

١ ـ بُنيت مصانع كثيرة قرب تلك المدينة .

٢ ـ سَيُسمح لهما بالسفر .

٣ ـ أجّل عقد الاجتماع .

٤ ـ سيتّفق على حلّ للمشكلة .

٥ ـ أحترمت احتراما كبيرا .

٦ ـ سيعتمد عليهم كل الاعتماد .

٧ ـ تبودلت الزيارات بين البلدين .

٨ ـ سيدرّسون التاريخ الاسلامي على كبار الاساتذة .

٩ ـ أقيمت في البلاد احتفالات كثيرة تكريما للملك الضيف .

١٠ ـ ستبذل جهود كبيرة لتحسين الاوضاع الاقتصادية .

234

Drill 6. Written. Transformation: Relative clause with verb ⟶ relative

clause with participle.

'He is one of those who are
interested in such subjects
as these.'

هو من الذين يهتمون بمثل هذه المواضيع . ⟵

هو من المهتمين بمثل هذه المواضيع .

١ ـ هذه الدولة من الدول التي تحتاج الى مساعدات كبيرة لتحسين

اوضاعها الاقتصادية .

٢ ـ الجبال التي تحيط بهذه المدينة جبال عالية .

٣ ـ النظام الذي يسود اليوم في معظم البلدان العربية هو النظام

الجمهوري .

٤ ـ ليس هذا الموضوع من المواضيع التي يُسمح ببحثها .

٥ ـ لسنا عادة من الذين يُدعون الى مثل هذه الحفلات .

٦ ـ طه حسين من الذين يعرفون بانتاجهم الادبي الكثير .

٧ ـ هي من الذين يتفقون معي في الرأي .

٨ ـ هو من الذين يشرفون على سير العمل في هذا المصنع .

٩ ـ الدكتورة نوال السعداوي من اللواتي يدعون الى المساواة بين

الرجل والمرأة .

١٠ ـ ليس هذا الحزب من الاحزاب التي تتعاون مع الدولة .

Drill 7. Written. Translation.

1. Rashid had been in love with Widad for a period of five years before he
   married her.

2. The Third World countries are nonaligned states; they neither side with
   the West nor with the East.

3. The three major religions in the Middle East are Islam, Christianity and
   Judaism.

4. She rendered great services to her country; these services were benefited from greatly.

5. They have made great efforts to reach a solution to the problem existing between them.

6. The color of the sea changes from blue to green to white during the day.

7. It is told of (عَنْ) this castle that it had great importance throughout ancient history.

8. This political organization has a black and yellow flag.

9. His beloved is green-eyed and dark-complexioned.

Drill 8. Written. Vocabulary.

Fill in the blanks with the most appropriate word or expression.

(محلية ، يحمّر ، عنوان ، ابيها ، يطلني ، قاموس ، مركز ، عاصمة ،
الميادين ، امّها ، مختلف ، المنحازة ، اقاربها ، المملكة ، دام ،
تبادل ، ردّ ، تحسين ، نسخة ، اقوى) .

١ - الرياض ـــــ ـــــ العربية السعودية .
(kingdom)

٢ - ـــــ رئيسا الجامعتين الزيارات .

٣ - لم ـــــ ـــــ على رسالتي الاخيرة حتى الآن .
(answer)

٤ - اريد الحصول على ـــــ جديدة من ـــــ المنجد .
(copy)

٥ - بيروت ـــــ هام للتجارة الدولية .

٦ - في فرنسا احزاب ـــــ كثيرة .

٧ - يعمل الرئيس الجديد على ـــــ الاوضاع في ـــــ .
(various)

٨ - مصر من الدول غير ـــــ .

٩ - ـــــ وجهه عندما تتحدث معه اي فتاة .

١٠ - ذهبت مع زوجها الى بغداد لزيارة ـــــ و ـــــ و ـــــ .
(mother)

١١ - ـــــ حكمه ثلاثين عاما وهو ـــــ رئيس وزراء عرفته البلاد .
(lasted)

236

أ ـ الجمل التمهيدية	A. Preparatory sentences

جُمَلٌ مُتَفَرِّقَةٌ

Miscellaneous sentences

١ ـ اِشْتَدَّ الْخِلافُ بين الاب وابنه حَوْلَ موضوع زواج الابن .

1. The <u>disagreement</u> between the father and his son <u>over</u> the subject of the son's marriage <u>became intense</u>.

اِشْتَدَّ ، اِشْتِدادٌ

خِلافٌ ـ ات

حَوْلَ

VIII to become harsh, severe, strong, more violent, more intense; to intensify

difference of opinion, disagreement, conflict

about; around, approximately; over, concerning

٢ ـ تَقَعُ مشكلات كثيرة عادة بين الزوجة وامّ زوجها .

2. Usually many problems <u>occur</u> between the wife and her husband's mother.

وَقَعَ يَقَعُ ، وُقوعٌ

to be located; to happen, occur, take place

٣ ـ اجتمع اعضاء ادارة البنك لبحث الاوضاع الاقتصاديّة الحالِيّةِ .

3. The members of the bank's administration met to discuss the <u>present</u> economic conditions.

حالِيٌّ ـ ون

present, current

٤ ـ أَبْدى رئيس الشركة اهتماما كبيرا بالاراءالتي قدّمها له موظفوه .

4. The president of the company <u>showed</u> great interest in the opinions that his employees had presented to him.

أَبْدى ، إِبْداءٌ

IV to reveal, manifest, show, display

٥ ـ أُذيعَ امس في واشنطن ان وزير الخارجية الامريكيّ سيعقـد مؤتمرا صحفيّا لَدى عودته مـن اوروبـا .

5. <u>It was broadcast</u> yesterday in Washington that the American Secretary of State will hold a press conference <u>on</u> his return from Europe.

أَذاعَ ، إِذاعَةٌ (على)

لَدى = عِنْدَ

IV to broadcast, transmit (to)

at, by (place and time); in the presence of, before, with; to have; on, upon (doing s.th.)

٦ ـ استخدمت الجامعة ثلاثـــــة أساتذة سود ولم تكن هـــذه الجامعة قد استخدمـــت أيّ أساتذة سود مِنْ قَبْلُ .

The university employed three black professors; this university had not <u>previously</u> employed any black professors.

مِنْ قَبْلُ

before, previously, earlier, formerly

٧ ـ أرسل رسالة الى أخيه ولكنّ هذا الأخيرَ لـم يُجِبْهُ علــى رسالته .

He sent a letter to his brother, but <u>the latter</u> didn't <u>answer</u> him concerning his letter.

أَجابَ ، إجابَةٌ

IV to answer, respond to s.o.; to comply with (a request)

أَجابَ الى

IV to answer, respond to s.o.

أَجابَ عَنْ ، على

IV to answer, respond (to s.o.) concerning (s.th.)

٨ ـ قدّم الاهل والأصدقاء لهمـــا الهدايا بعد زواجهما فَقَبِلاها بِسُرورٍ .

Relatives and friends presented gifts to them after their marriage, and they <u>accepted</u> them with <u>pleasure</u>.

قَبِلَ ـَ ، قُبولٌ

to accept, approve

سَرَّ ـُ ، سُرورٌ

to please, gladden, make happy

سُرورٌ (بـ)

pleasure, delight (at)

٩ ـ جَرَتْ في الاسبوع الماضي مُحادَثاتٌ هامّة بين الرئيسَيْن السـوريّ والمصريّ .

Important <u>discussions</u> <u>took place</u> last week between the Syrian and Egyptian presidents.

جَرى ـِ ، جَرْيٌ

to take place, occur, happen

مُحادَثَةٌ ـ ات

talk, discussion, conversation

١٠ ـ سأزور لبنان في شهــــر آب (أغُسْطُس) عِوَضًا عن شهــــر كانون الاوّل (ديسمبر) .

I am going to visit Lebanon in August <u>instead of</u> December.

عِوَضًا عَنْ

instead of, in lieu of, in exchange for

[ديسَمبِر]

[December (in the Levant and Iraq: كانونُ الاوّل)]

238

١١ - اِشْتَرى والدي سيّارة بخمسة آلاف دولار ثمّ باعَها بثلاثة آلاف دولار .

My father <u>bought</u> a car for five thousand dollars, then <u>sold</u> it for three thousand.

اِشْتَرى ، شِراءٌ

VIII to buy (note the Form I VN)

باعَ ـِ ، بَيْعٌ

to sell

١٢ - كانَ مَسْرورًا جدّا بوجود جميع أولاده حوله .

He was very pleased to have all his children around him.

سُرَّ ، سُرورٌ (بـ ، من ، لـ)

(passive) to be pleased (at, by), be happy (to)

١٣ - كانت العلاقة بينها وبين أهلها علاقة سَيِّئَةٌ ولكتّها تَحَسَّنَتْ في المدّة الاخيرة وذلك بسبب فهم والدها لها ولزوجها ولتعاونه معهما على حلّ كلّ المشكلات ألتي وقعت بينهم .

The relationship between her and her family was a <u>bad</u> one, but it <u>has improved</u> recently, and that is because of her father's understanding of her and of her husband, and because of his cooperation with them in resolving all the problems that had arisen between them.

سَيِّئٌ – ون

bad, evil

تَحَسَّنَ ، تَحَسُّنٌ

V to improve, get better

١٤ - يحبّ الناس في العالم العربيّ شرب القهوة ولكنّ بعضهم يفضّل الشاي .

People in the Arab World like to drink coffee, but some prefer <u>tea</u>.

شايٌ

tea

ب – النصّ الاساسيّ

مُقْتَطَفاتٌ من جرائد عربيّة

excerpts, selections

١ – اشتدّ الخلاف بين رئيس الوزراء ووزير التربية والتعليم بشأن المناهج الدراسيّة . والمعروف أنّ الخلاف وقع لأنّ وزير التربية

والتعليم يعتبر المناهج الحالية سيّئة ويدعو الى تحسينها؛ أمّا رئيس الوزراء فيرى أن الوضع الاقتصادي لا يسمح الآن بمثل هذا التحسين . وقد أبدى الوزير رغبته في الاجتماع برئيس الوزراء ليبحث الموضوع ، لكنّ رئيس الوزراء رفض ذلك .

٢ - أذيع أمس في <u>المَكسيك</u> أنّ مندوبي منظّمات مختلفة في عشرين دولة Mexico
من دول أمريكا الجنوبيّة عقدوا مؤتمرا في العاصمة المكسيكيّة استمر أربعة أيّام لدراسة الاوضاع الدوليّة . وقيل في نهاية الاجتماع انّ العلاقات بين دول أمريكا الجنوبيّة في تحسّن مستمرّ .

٣ - قام أمس وزير الخارجيّة الامريكيّة بزيارة لدمشق وكان في استقباله لدى وصوله وزير الخارجيّة السوريّ وعدد من كبار موظّفي الدولة . والمعروف أنّ وزير الخارجيّة الامريكيّ ما زار دمشق من قبل .

٤ - قرّر وزير الصناعة تعيين احدى السيّدات اللواتي يعملن في الوزارة رئيسة لمكتبه . والمرأة التي عيّنها الوزير هي السيّدة سُعاد لُطفي وقد أجابت السيّدة سعاد لطفى على سؤال لمندوبنا قائلة " يسرّني أن أكون أوّل امرأة تتمكّن من الحصول على هذه الوظيفة وأنا أقبلها باسم نساء بلادي جميعهنّ " .

٥ - عقد اليوم رئيس الجمهوريّة اجتماعين مع الرئيس السوريّ . وقد وصف <u>مُتَحَدِّثٌ</u> رسميّ المحادثات التي جرت بين الرئيسين بأنّها كانت spokesman
ناجحة .

٦ - أذيع اليوم أنّ وزير الخارجيّة البريطانيّ أرسل رسالة الى وزير خارجيّتنا يطلب فيها أن يعقد الاجتماع القادم بين الوزيرين في لندن عوضا عن باريس .

٧ - اشترت حكومتنا خمسين طائرة حربيّة من دولة غربيّة ، وقد قال <u>مُتَحَدِّثٌ</u> رسميّ انّ الدولة التي باعت الطائرات سوف تنشئ ثلاثة مصانع خلال السنوات الثلاث القادمة .

240

٨ ــ اشتدّ ألخلاف بين البلدين حول مشكلات الشاى لم يستطيعا الوصول

الى اتّفاق بشأنها .

ج ــ القواعد والتمارين :   C. Grammar and drills

```
┌─────────────────────────────────────────────┐
│  1.  Negation of perfect tense with ما       │
│                                              │
│  2.  Particles ending in  ُ u                 │
└─────────────────────────────────────────────┘
```

1. Negation of perfect tense with ما

The perfect tense is normally negated by means of لَمْ with the jussive
mood: دَرَسَ ← لَمْ يَدْرُسْ . The verb زالَ may be negated in this way, but
most often is negated with the negative particle ما : ما زالَ مَوْجوداً 'He
is still present' (see 22.C.2). The particle ما may also be used to negate
the perfect tense of other verbs as well, as in

```
┌─────────────────────────────────────────────────────────────┐
│ 'He had not previously visited    ما كانَ قَدْ زارَ دِمَشْقَ مِنْ قَبْلُ .  │
│  Damascus.'                                                  │
└─────────────────────────────────────────────────────────────┘
```

The choice between ما with perfect and لَمْ with jussive is one of style; since,
however, ما is rather uncommon, it provides some emphasis when it is used.
Now do Drill 1.

Drill 1. Transformation. Negative with لم ⟶ negative with ما .

'I didn't study the history   لم أدرس تاريخ الشرق الاوسط . ⟶
of the Middle East.'
                                       ما درست تاريخ الشرق الاوسط .

١ ــ لم يتزوّجها لأنّه لم يحبّها .

٢ ــ لم اهتمّ بهذا الموضوع اهتماما كبيرا .

٣ ــ لم أقم في سان فرانسيسكو في العام الماضي .

٤ ــ لم يستعدّوا للامتحان .

٥ ــ لم تصل اختي الى هنا حتى الآن .

٦ ــ لم تتعلم مريم اللهجة الكويتية خلال اقامتها في الكويت .

٧ ــ لم يهب لهما ابناء او بنات .

٨ ــ لم يلقيا ترحيبا في المملكة .

2. Particles ending in ُ u

Most parts of speech in Arabic are <u>inflected</u>; nouns and adjectives, for example, show inflections for case depending on their function in the sentence, and verbs are inflected to agree with their subjects. Words that have absolutely no inflections at all are called <u>particles</u>; these include prepositions, e.g. مِنْ 'from'; adverbs, e.g. هُنَا 'here'; conjunctions, e.g. أَنْ 'that' and لِ 'in order that'; etc. We are interested here in particles that end in ُ u: we have now had مُنْذُ, which functions as both a preposition meaning "since; ago" and as a conjunction meaning "since, since the time that" (see L.35.C.3), and the adverbs قَبْلُ 'previously, formerly, earlier, before' and بَعْدُ 'then, thereupon; afterwards, after that, later'; the relative adverb حَيْثُ 'where (the place in which or to which); wherever' will be introduced in Lesson 42.

The important thing to point out is that these particles never change their final vowel regardless of how they are used in the sentence. For example, the adverb قَبْلُ is normally used after the preposition مِنْ , giving the phrase مِنْ قَبْلُ which means the same as قَبْلُ alone; in contrast to the final vowels of prepositions the final vowel of قَبْلُ does not change after مِنْ . As pointed out in L.37.C.5, (p. 183), the <u>preposition</u> قَبْلَ 'before' is in the <u>genitive</u> case when it comes after another preposition but is in the <u>accusative</u> elsewhere. The differing usages are contrasted below:

قَبْلَ كُلِّ شَيْءٍ	'before anything else, first of all'
مِنْ قَبْلِ الْحَرْبِ	'prior to the war, since before the war'
لَمْ أَكُنْ أَعْرِفُهُ مِنْ قَبْلُ .	'I hadn't known him previously.'

Another major difference between adverbs and prepositions is of course that adverbs <u>never</u> take objects while prepositions <u>must</u>.

The adverb بَعْدُ usually occurs in the expression فِيمَا بَعْدُ 'afterwards,

242

later'; a special usage is in the expression أَمَّا بَعْدُ which introduces the body

of a letter (see p.219); finally, after a negative بَعْدُ means "yet, still":

> لَمْ يَجِيءْ بَعْدُ •   'He hasn't come yet.'

D. Comprehension passage

د — نصوص للفهم

(1) Read the following passage and then do Drill 2, which is based on it.

مؤتمر صحفيّ

عقد وزير الخارجيّة المصريّة مؤتمرا صحفيّا حضره عدد غير قليل

من المراسلين العرب والاجانب • وقد تحدّث الوزير في ذلك المؤتمر عـن

العلاقات السياسية بين مصر والولايات المتحدة • بدأ الوزير مؤتمـره

الصحفي بقوله :" يسرني جدا ان اقابلكم اليوم واود ان اشكر لكم حضوركم

هذا المؤتمر كما اود ان اتقدّم بشكري الخاص الى جميع المراسليــن

الاجانب الموجودين بيننا •

سيكون هذا المؤتمر مؤتمرا مفتوحا دون تحديد للوقت • اما الآن

فانا على استعداد للاجابة على اسئلتكم بشأن اي موضوع ترغبون فـــي

السؤال عنه • "

سؤال : حضرة الوزير ، سمعنا انك رفضت ان تقبل دعوة قدّمت اليــــك

لزيارة الولايات المتحدة ، فهل هذا صحيح ؟

اجابة : لا ، لم ارفض الدعوة • لقد قبلتها بكل سرور • كُلُّ ما في الأمْر   ~~the whole story is~~

ان محادثات قد جرت بيننا وبين الولايات المتحدة حول موعــد

الزيارة ، وقد قرّرنا معا ان اقوم بهذه الزيارة في ديسمبـر

عوضا عن القيام بها في اغسطس •

س : اذيع امس في القاهرة وواشنطن ان العلاقات بين البلدين فـــي

تحسّن مستمر ، فما رأيكم في ذلك ؟

ج : حَقًّا انّ العلاقات بين بلدينا في تحسّن مستمرّ • وهدفنا الآن هـو   truly, actually

تحقيق التعاون التامّ بين بلدينا في مختلف الميادين الثقافيّة والاقتصاديّة والسياسيّة .

س : انا مراسل امريكي . تعرف يا حضرة الوزير انّ العلاقات بيــن بلدينا لم تكن دائما حسنة وان الخلاف قد اشتدّ بيننا اكثر مـن مرّة . فهل سيكون لخلافات الماضي تأثير على علاقاتنا فـــي المستقبل ؟

ج : منذ اقدم الازمان تقع الخلافات بين الشعوب والحكومات ، لكنّنـا نعتقد ان الشعبين الامريكي والمصري سيتمكّنان من العمل معا في جوّ يسوده التعاون والثقة المتبادلة .   atmosphere

س : حضرة الوزير ، اودّ ان ارجع بسؤالي الى موضوع زيارتك للولايات المتحدة . ماذا سيبحث خلال هذه الزيارة ؟

ج : سوف اتكلّم عمّا سيبحث خلال هذه الزيارة بعد رجوعي من الولايـات المتحدة ، اما الآن فافضّل ألّا اقول شيئا عن محادثات لم تجـر حتى الآن .

س : شكرا حضرة الوزير .

ج : عفوا .

صَوابٌ أَمْ خَطَأٌ

Drill 2. Written. True-false.

Indicate whether the following sentences are true or false.

١ - بحث وزير الخارجية في مؤتمره الصحفيّ موضوع العلاقات الامريكيـــة المصرية .

٢ - تقدم الوزير بشكره الخاص الى جميع المراسلين الذين حضروا المؤتمر الصحفيّ .

٣ - كل المراسلين الذين حضروا المؤتمر مصريون .

٤ - عقد الوزير مؤتمره الصحفي بعد رجوعه من الولايات المتحدة .

٥ - رفض الوزير دعوة لزيارة الولايات المتحدة .

٦ ــ هدف الوزير ان تبقى العلاقات بين بلاده والولايات المتحدة كما هي الآن .

٧ ــ لم تكن العلاقات بين مصر والولايات المتحدة حسنة دائما لكنّ الخلاف لم يشتدّ بينهما .

٨ ــ يريد الوزير التعاون مع امريكا .

٩ ــ تكلّم الوزير في مؤتمره الصحفيّ عن بعض المواضيع التي ستتناولها المحادثات .

١٠ ــ رفض الوزير ان يجيب على سؤال احد الصحفيّين .

١١ ــ سأل صحفيّ امريكيّ اكثر من سؤال عن موضوع زيارة وزير الخارجيّة لامريكا .

(2) Listen to the passage on tape and then do Drill 3, which is based on it.

(Note حاجّ is a title conferred on the Muslim who has made the pilgrimage to Mecca; it conveys great respect).

<u>Drill 3</u>. Written. (On tape)

Write a brief summary of the short story which is read for you on tape.

E. <u>General drills</u>   هـ ــ التمارين العامّة

<u>Drill 4</u>. Transformation: Statement ⟶ negative.

Note: Use both ما and لم where appropriate.

١ ــ انا من اليمن .

٢ ــ اتفقا على تبادل الزيارات .

٣ ــ سأسافر الى القدس قريبا .

٤ ــ يعتمدون عليهما اعتمادا كبيرا .

٥ ــ جاءني به .

٦ ــ اذهب من هنا .

٧ ــ هما فتاتان سوريتان .

٨ ــ اغضبني اخوك امس .

٩ ــ سنشاهد هذا الفلم غدا .

١٠ ــ يهتمّ باولاده اهتماما كبيرا .

١١ ــ في البيت رجل غريب .

١٢ ــ يحافظ مسؤول المنظمة الثورية على قانون البلد .

<u>Drill 5</u>. Written. Transformation: Singular ⟶ dual ⟶ plural.

'This is the professor who teaches Arabic at our university.'

هذا هو الاستاذ الذي يدرس العربيّة في جامعتنا . ⟵

'These are the professors who teach Arabic at our university.'

هذان هما الاستاذان اللذان يدرّسان العربية في جامعتنا . ⟵

'These are the professors who teach Arabic at our university.'

هؤلاء هم الاساتذة الذين يدرسون العربية في جامعتنا .

١ ــ هذا هو الرجل الذي ألّف هذه الكتب .

٢ ــ هذه هي المرأة التي دعت الى المساواة بين الرجال والنساء .

٣ ــ اجتمعت بالرجل الذي عيّن مديرا للشركة .

٤ ــ قابلت الفتاة التي دعوتها الى حفلتك .

<u>Drill 6</u>. Written. Transformation. Active ⟷ passive.
Supply an appropriate subject where necessary.

١ ــ ستبنى مصانع كثيرة في البلاد .

٢ ــ اقيم احتفال كبير لرئيس الجامعة تقديرا لخدماته .

٣ ــ سوف تسمي المولود الجديد عمر اذا كان ولدا .

٤ ــ دعينا الى حفلة رسمية .

٥ ــ ستذهب السكرتيرة بك الآن الى مكتب رئيس الجامعة .

٦ ــ أجّل الاجتماع الى الاسبوع القادم .

٧ ــ ستؤسّس منظمة جديدة في الشهر القادم .

٨ ــ أستفيد من موارد الزيت استفادة كبيرة .

٩ ــ سيبيع اخي سيارته بثلاثة آلاف دولار .

١٠ ــ حكم عليها بالموت .

١١ ــ منحهم حق الاشتراك في عمل الحزب .

Drill 7. Written translation.

1. We wish to ask you, Sir, about some matters that have to do with social
   life in the United States.

2. The status of the mother in this country is equal to that of the father,
   but her function in the family is different from his.

3. I went with my students yesterday evening to an Arabic restaurant. The
   same night we went together to see the movie Cleopatra.

4. Cars are most numerous in the streets of Beirut, especially in the middle
   of town. Nonetheless, I saw people walking among the cars in the middle
   of the street.

5. The oil companies have built a number of factories in the Arab world and
   the building of these factories was not an easy matter.

6. We found that the reporter painted a generally untrue picture of North
   Africa.

Drill 8. Written. Vocabulary.

Fill in the blanks in the sentences below with the most appropriate word
from among the following:

(أغضه ، منذ ، صدرت ، حاول ، طبعة ، عميقا ، للضيف ، الفتاة ،
صار ، على حقّ ، يوحّدوا ، يترقى ، كافحت ، ثمن ، فهموا ، قابلت ،
دعا ، قواميس ، رأيك ، بالأكرام ، مشكلة) .

١ – لم يعجبني ـــــ ـــــ في تلك ـــــ .
(problem)

٢ – ـــــ ـــــ الشعوب العربية للحصول على استقلالها .

٣ – ـــــ ـــــ جديدة لكتاب " الاغاني " .
(edition)

٤ – بعد ان حصل على شهادته ـــــ استاذا جامعيًّا ثم اخذ ـــــ ـــــ من
(became)
مكانة الى مكانة حتى اصبح رئيسا للجامعة .

٥ – ما ـــــ ـــــ الكتاب الذي اشتريته امس ؟

٦ – ـــــ ـــــ صديقي هذا ـــــ سبع سنوات .
(ago)

٧ – انت ـــــ ـــــ فيما قلته .

٨ – ـــــ بعض القادة العرب أن ـــــ ـــــ الدول العربية .
(tried)

٩ – ـــــ ـــــ ذلك الرجل الى المساواة بين الناس في بلاده .

١٠ – كان بطرس البستاني من الذين ـــــ ـــــ الشعر القديم فهما ـــــ ـــــ .
(understood)

١١ – يعرف العرب ـــــ ـــــ ـــــ .
(guest)

١٢ – ـــــ ـــــ تصرّف ابنه .

Drill 9. Vocabulary. Written.

From the words in parentheses choose the most appropriate one to fill in the blank in each of the following sentences:

١ – يفهم طه حسين الشعر القديم فهما ـــــ . (جميلا، كثيرا، عميقا)

٢ – نوال السعداوي ـــــ المساواة بين (دعت بـ ، دعت الى ،
الرجال والنساء . دعت) .

٣ – قاموا ـــــ ثورة في البلاد . (في ، بـ ، على)

٤ – أسست ـــــ جديدة . (طائرة، منظمة، عائلة)

٥ – تمّ ـــــ الزواج بينهما . (عادة، اخيرا، احيانا)

٦ – سمّى شاعر القطر ـــــ . (ترحيبا به ، تقديرا له ،
حبًّا به)

٧ – اخي ـــــ طالب في صفه . (اصغر، اوضح، اقلّ)

٨ ـ ـ ـ ـ ـ من ـ ـ ـ ـ الحكومة تحسين الاوضاع   (مواضيع، اهداف، آراء)

الاقتصادية فى البلاد ٠

٩ ـ واخذ ـ ـ ـ ـ ـ الى ان اصبح رئيسا للوزراء ٠   (ينجح، يترقى، ينتقل)

١٠ ـ لا يزال الخلاف ـ ـ ـ ـ بين الأب وابنه ٠   (قديما، قائما، مساويا)

Drill 10. Written. Vocabulary.

a. Refer back to Lesson 17 for the meaning relationship between Forms I

and IV. Then check the dictionary for the related meanings of the following

pairs of words and make meaningful sentences out of each pair. Ex.

'He came to the party and brought a   حضر الحفلة واحضر هدية جميلة معه ٠
beautiful gift with him.'

خرج ـ اخرج

صدر ـ اصدر

ظهر ـ اظهر

غضب ـ اغضب

دخل ـ ادخل

b. Use the same dictionary procedure to discover the relationship between

the following pairs of words, and hence the meaning of the unfamiliar word (the

item to the right is the one you already know).

انتج ـ نتج	سكت ـ اسكت	علم ـ اعلم
اذاع ـ ذاع	فقد ـ افقد	ضحك ـ اضحك
ادهش ـ دهش	فهم ـ افهم	مات ـ أمات
اساء ـ ساء	تمّ ـ اتمّ	بقى ـ ابقى
انشأ ـ نشأ	عاد ـ اعاد	سكن ـ اسكن
ابدى ـ بدا	رجع ـ ارجع	مضى ـ امضى
أجلس ـ جلس		جلس ـ أجلس

249

الدرس الثاني والاربعون

أ - الجمل التمهيديّة

A. <u>Preparatory sentences</u>

الشعر العربي

<u>Arabic Poetry</u>

١ - بدأ الشعر العربيّ قبل الاسلام ،
وبَلَغَ مكانة عالية حتّى صار
العرب يعتبرونه اجمل
الفنون .

1 Arabic poetry began before Islam, and it <u>attained</u> such a high position that the Arabs came to consider it the most beautiful of the arts.

بَلَغَ ـُ ، بُلوغٌ

to reach, attain; to come to the ears of

٢ - كانت القَصيدةُ قبل الاسلام
تَنْقَسِمُ الى مواضيع كثيرة
اهمها الحبّ والسياسة ووصف
الصحراءِ والحكم .

2 The <u>ode</u>, before Islam, <u>was divided</u> into many subjects, of which the most important were love, politics, description of the desert, and wise sayings.

قَصيدةٌ ـ قَصائِدُ

qaṣīda, ode

اِنْقَسَمَ ، اِنْقِسامٌ (الى)

VII to be divided, separated (into)

٣ - اِمْرؤُ القَيْسِ من الشعراءِ الذين
عاشوا قبل الاسلام ، وله قصيدة
طويلة تُعَدّ من أجمل الشعر
العربيّ . وقد لُقّبَ بالملك
الضِّلّيلِ لانه كان اميرًا تَرَك
مملكة ابيه واخذ يرحل في
الصحراء من مكان الى مكان .

3 'Imru' al-Qais was one of the poets who lived before Islam. There is a long qaṣīda by him which is considered to be one of the most beautiful Arabic poems. He was <u>given the nickname</u> "The Wandering King" because he was a <u>prince</u> who left his father's kingdom and began to travel around in the desert from place to place.

لَقّبَ ، تَلْقيبٌ (بـ)

II to give s.o. the title, nickname of

[ضِلّيلٌ]

[wandering, errant]

اميرٌ ـ أُمَراءُ

prince, emir, commander

٤ - انتشر الشعر بين العرب في زمن
الاسلام ، وقد حكي أنّ النَبِيّ
محمّدا سمع قصيدة فقامَ من
مكانه وألْقى عَباءَتَهُ على الشاعر

4 Poetry became widespread among the Arabs in the Islamic era. It has been related that the <u>Prophet</u> Muhammad heard a qaṣīda, and then <u>arose</u> from his place and <u>threw</u> his <u>cloak</u> around the poet <u>in admiration of</u> his poem.

250

إعْجابًا بِشعرهِ

نَبِيّ – أَنْبِياءٌ	prophet (nisba = نَبَوِيّ)
قامَ ـُ ، قِيامٌ	to rise up, arise
أَلْقَى ، إِلْقاءٌ	IV to cast, throw; to make, deliver (a speech)
[عَباءَةٌ – ات]	[aba, cloak]
[أُعْجِبَ ، إِعْجابٌ بـ]	[IV (passive) to admire, be proud of]

٥ – وبعد زمن الرَّسول كان لكلّ حاكم شاعرهُ ، بل كان بعض الامراء انفسهم شعراء، وأُدْخِلَتْ على الشعر العربي مواضيع جديدة .

5 — After the era of the Messenger, every governor had his poet; indeed some princes were themselves poets. Thus new topics were introduced into Arabic poetry.

[رَسولٌ – رُسُلٌ] | [messenger; apostle]
أَدْخَلَ ، إِدْخالٌ (على) | IV to introduce, bring in(to)

٦ – كان الشعر العربيّ حتّى نهاية القرن الثامِنَ عَشَرَ غير متأثِّر بالشعر الاوربيّ . فلمّا ازدادت العلاقات بين دول الغرب والدول العربيّة ، أُرسل الطلاب في بَعَثاتٍ علميّة الى اوربّا حَيْثُ اتصلوا بالحَضارَةِ الاوربيّة فبدأ التَّجْديدُ في الشعر العربيّ .

6 — Arabic poetry, until the end of the eighteenth century, was uninfluenced by European poetry. When contacts increased between the countries of the West and the Arab countries, students were sent on academic missions to Europe, where they came in contact with European civilization, and the revival of Arabic poetry began.

بَعْثَةٌ – بَعَثاتٌ | mission, deputation; foreign study mission
حَيْثُ | (relative adverb) where, wherever
حَضارَةٌ – ات | civilization; culture
جَدَّدَ – تَجْديدٌ | II to renew, restore, revive

٧ – يرى بعض الادباء أنّ الشعر العربيّ استفاد من اتّصاله بالشعر الاوربيّ. يقول أولئك الادباء إنّ الشعر العربيّ كادَ يموت في نهاية القرن الثامِنَ عَشَرَ ، وإنّ الشعراء كانوا يكتبون القصائد في مواضيع لا تصوّر المجتمع . فالتجديد إذن انْتِصارٌ للشعر العربيّ .

7 — Some men of letters hold the view that Arabic poetry benefited from its contact with European poetry. Those writers say that Arabic poetry was on the point of dying at the end of the eighteenth century, and that the poets were writing odes on subjects which did not portray society. The revival, then, was a victory for Arabic poetry.

كَادَ ــَ

(no V.N.) to be on the point of, almost (do s.th.)

اِنْتَصَرَ ، اِنْتِصارٌ (على)

VII to be victorious, triumph (over)

٨ ــ يرى ادباء آخرون أنّ تأثّر الشعر العربيّ بالحضارة الغربية ليس تقدّماً ، ويعتقدون أنّ عدداً غير قليل من قصائد المعاصرين لا تصوّر المجتمع العربيّ وإنّما تصوّر أفكار الغرب وحضارته وأساليبه .

8 — Other writers are of the opinion that Arabic poetry's being influenced by western civilization is not progress and believe that not a few qaṣīdas of their contemporaries do not portray Arab society <u>but rather</u> portray the thoughts, civilization, and styles of the West.

إِنَّما

rather, but rather; only

٩ ــ ومن ادباء العرب من يـــرون أنّ التجديد في الادب العربيّ أمر ما زلنا لا نفهمه كل الفهم لاننا لم نُوَفِّهِ حقّه من الدراسة .

9 — And among Arab writers are those who think that modernization in Arabic literature is a matter that we still do not understand completely because we have not <u>given it</u> the study it deserves.

وَفَّى ، تَوْفِيَةٌ

II to give s.o. his full share of

[حقّ] (من)]

truth; right;[(one's) due (of)]

جمل اضافيّة

Additional sentences

١٠ ــ يصل الرئيس الامريكي كلّ يوم عدد كبير من الرسائل مـــن داخل البلاد وخارجها .

10 — Every day the American president receives a large number of letters from <u>within</u> and from outside the country.

دَخَلَ ــُ ، دُخُولٌ

to enter, go in, come in

داخِلٌ

interior; inside, within

١١ ــ عُقد اليوم اجتماع هامّ حضره وزيرا الداخليّةِ والخارجيّةِ .

11 — There was held today an important meeting that was attended by the Secretary of the <u>Interior</u> and the Secretary of State.

الداخِليّةُ

internal affairs

أَحْمَدُ شَوْقِــــي

أحمد شوقي من اشهر شعراء النهضة الادبيّة الحديثة في العالم
العربيّ ٠ ولد بمصر في سنة ١٨٦٩ لعائلة غنيّة معروفة ٠ ولما أكمل
تعليمه في مصر ذهب في بعثة الى فرنسا حيث درس القانون ، وتمكّن
قبل عودته الى مصر من زيارة بريطانيا ٠

عيّن شوقي بعد رجوعه من أوربّا موظّفا بالقصر ، وبعد مـــدّة
قصيرة صار شاعر القصر ٠

تنقسم حياة شوقي الادبيّة الى قسمين : كان في اولهما متأثّرا
بوضعه الاجتماعيّ وثقافته الغربية ووظيفته الرسميّة ، وشعره في هذا
القسم لا يصوّر حياة الشعب وانّما يصوّر حياة القصر وآراء السياسيّين
وحضارة اوربّا ٠ وعلى الرغم من ذلك فقد انتج شيئا من الشعر التاريخيّ
والدينيّ والوطنيّ ٠ وبسبب شعره الوطني أخرجه الانكليز من مصر بعد
قيام الحرب العالميّة الاولى ٠

أمّا القسم الثاني فيبدأ بعد رجوع شوقي الى بلاده ؛ توفّرت له
الحرّية فازداد شعره الوطنيّ وصارت قصائده صورة للمجتمع ٠ والوحدة
العربيّة من اهمّ ما دعا اليه شوقي في هذا القسم من انتاجه ٠

وفي القسم الثاني حقّق شوقي انتصارا عظيما في ميدان التجديد
فقد نجح في ادخال الفَنّ التَّمْثيليّ على الادب العربيّ وبلغ فيه مكانة
عالية
٠

dramatic
arts

وقد عدّ شوقي قائدا للنهضة الشعرية ، ولقّب بأمير الشعراء ٠
فلمّا مات في سنة ١٩٣٢ فقد العرب شاعرا من اعظم شعرائهم ٠ وعنــد
موته ألقى الشاعر حافِظ اِبْراهيم الملقّب بشاعر النيل قصيدة تحدّث فيها

عن مكانة شوقي في عالم الشعر .

ومن شعر شوقي في المعلّم :

كادَ الْمُعَلِّمُ أَنْ يكونَ رَسولا   قُمْ لِلْمُعَلِّمِ وَفِّهِ التَّبْجيلا   respect

Note: By poetic convention, التَّبْجيلَ becomes التَّبْجيلا (alif added to fatḥa)
and رَسولاً becomes رَسولا (loss of nunation) at the end of a line.

أسئلة

١ ـ ما مكانة شوقي بين شعراء النهضة الادبية الحديثة في العالم العربيّ ؟

٢ ـ اين ولد شوقي ؟ متى ولد ؟

٣ ـ ماذا تعرف عن عائلة شوقي ؟

٤ ـ متى ذهب شوقي الى فرنسا ؟

٥ ـ ماذا درس في فرنسا ؟

٦ ـ ما البلد التي تمكّن من زيارتها قبل عودته الى مصر ؟

٧ ـ ماذا عيّن شوقي بعد عودته من اوربا الى مصر ؟ ماذا اصبح بعد ذلك ؟

٨ ـ الى كم قسم تنقسم حياة شوقي الادبية ؟

٩ ـ بماذا تأثّر شوقي في القسم الاول من حياته الادبيّة ؟

١٠ ـ ماذا يصوّر القسم الاول من حياة شوقي الادبية ؟

١١ ـ ماذا انتج شوقي في القسم الاول من حياته الادبية ؟

١٢ ـ متى اخرج الانكليز شوقي من مصر ؟ لماذا ؟

١٣ ـ صف قصائد شوقي في القسم الثاني من حياته الادبية .

١٤ ـ ما الذي استطاع شوقي تحقيقه في القسم الثاني من حياته الادبية ؟

١٥ ـ إلامَ دعا شوقي في القسم الثاني من انتاجه الادبي ؟

١٦ ـ متى مات شوقي ؟

١٧ ـ ماذا فعل حافظ إبراهيم عند موت شوقي ؟

١٨ ـ بماذا لقّب حافظ ابراهيم ؟

١٩ ـ ماذا قال شوقي عن المعلّم شعرا ؟

1. حَيْثُ 'where'

2. كادَ 'almost'

3. Conditional sentences with لَوْ أَنَّ ... لَـ

1. حَيْثُ 'where'

The relative adverb حَيْثُ 'where' is equivalent in meaning to فِي الْمَكانِ الَّذي 'the place in which' or اَلْمَكانُ الَّذي 'the place where', وَهُناكَ 'and there'; the final vowel ُ u never changes. Illustration:

أُرْسِلَ الى أوربّا حَيْثُ اتَّصَلَ بِالْحَضارَةِ الأوربّيةِ . 'He was sent to Europe where he came in contact with European culture.'

The clause with حَيْثُ may also be the object of the prepositions مِنْ or إلى . The combination مِنْ حَيْثُ is equivalent to مِنَ الْمَكانِ 'from where, whence, wherefrom, and...from there'; and إلى حَيْثُ is equivalent to إلى الْمَكانِ وَمِنْ هُناكَ or الَّذي مِنْهُ.. , and may be translated , and وَإلى هُناكَ or الَّذي ... فيهِ 'to where..., to the place where, and... to that place'. Illustration:

هَلْ رَجَعوا مِنْ حَيْثُ ذَهَبوا ؟ 'Did they return from where they had gone?'

يَوَدُّ أَنْ يَرْجِعَ إلى حَيْثُ وُلِدَ . 'He wants to return to where he was born.'

Now do Drill 1.

Drill 1. Combination of sentences using حَيْثُ .

Replace the underlined items with حَيْثُ . Ex.

'He went to France and there he studied French literature.' سافر الى فرنسا وهناك درس الادب الفرنسي. ←

'He went to France, where he studied French literature.' سافر الى فرنسا حيث درس الادب الفرنسيّ.

١ ـ أرسل في بعثة الى بريطانيا وهناك تأثّر بالحضارة الاوربية ٠

٢ ـ رحل النبي محمد الى المدينة ، وهناك صار قائدا سياسيــا

ودينيا مَعًا ٠

at the same time, both

٣ ـ ينتقل البدويّ الى المكان الذى يجد فيه ماء ٠٠

٤ ـ انتقل جُبْران خَليل جُبْران الى الولايات المتحدة ، وهناك كتب

كتاب " النبي " ٠

٥ ـ وصل الوزير الى المطار ، وهناك استقبله عدد من كبار الموظفين٠

٦ ـ رجع من مكان لا يعلمه ٠

٧ ـ أقمت خمس سنوات في واشنطن ، وهناك درست القانون الدوليّ ٠

٨ ـ درست في جامعة القاهرة ، وهناك صادقت عددا كبيرا من المصريين٠

٩ ـ درس في سولت ليك سيتي ، وهناك قابل الفتاة التي تزوّجها ٠

١٠ ـ سكن في عمّان ، وهناك عمل بالتجارة ٠

2. كَادَ 'almost'

The verb كادَ (يَكادُ) means basically "to be on the point of, to be about

to (do s. th.) (would have) almost". It is normally used in either of two

ways: (a) with a following أَنْ -clause or (b) with a following indicative

verb, and in either case is usually translated "almost". Examples:

كادَ أَنْ يَقولَ نَعَمْ ٠	'He almost said "yes".'
يَكادُ أَنْ يَكونَ سَهْلاً ٠	'It is almost easy.'
كِدتُ أَزورُكمْ ٠	'I almost visited you.'
يَكادونَ يَصِلونَ الى العاصِمَةِ ٠	'They will almost reach the capital.'

Now do Drills 2 (on tape) and 3.

Drill 2. (On tape) Conjugation: كاد٠

Drill 3. Transformation.

'The man lost his job.'	أ : فقد الرجل وظيفته ٠ ـــ
'The man was about to lose his job, but he didn't.'	ط : كاد الرجل أن يفقد وظيفته ولكنه لم يفقدها ٠

256

١ ـ حصل على شهادة الدكتوراه .   ٦ ـ أغضبوا والدهم .

٢ ـ حقّقت المنظمة أهدافها .   ٧ ـ وحّدا البلدين .

٣ ـ ماتا عند نهاية الحرب الكبرى ٨ ـ بعت سيارتي .

٤ ـ رفضن طلبها .   ٩ ـ انتصروا علينا .

٥ ـ تزوج الفتاة التي كان يحبها .   ١٠ ـ أغضب الطالب استاذه .

3. Conditional sentences with لَوْ أَنَّ..لَ

In the presentation of conditional sentences in L.37.C.4 it was pointed out that the conditional particles must be followed by a verb in the perfect tense; if, however, an equational sentence (which has no verb) is to be made into a condition clause, then an appropriate form of the perfect tense of كَانَ must be inserted after the condition particle (p. 180). Thus:

أَنا مُسْتَعِدٌّ لِلسَّفَرِ ، إِنْ كانَ فَريد مُسْتَعِدًّا كَذلِكَ فَلْنَذْهَبْ .	'I'm ready to leave; if Farid is also ready, let's go.'

كَانَ must also be inserted before a verbal sentence if the verb in that sentence (a) is not in the perfect tense or (b) does not immediately follow after the conditional particle:

إِذا أَرَدْتَ . إِذا كُنْتَ تُريدُ .	فَلْنَذْهَبْ	(a) 'Let's go if you wish.'
إِنْ سافَرَ أَخوكَ . إِنْ كانَ أَخوكَ قَدْ سافَرَ .	فَلْنَذْهَبْ	(b) 'Let's go if your brother has left.'

The English translations (a) and (b) above each have two possible Arabic equivalents; both are common, the choice being a matter of style.

The discussion above applies to لَوْ ... لَ as well as to إِنْ and إِذا ; When لَوْ is not followed directly by a verb, however, لَوْ أَنَّ ... لَ may replace لَوْ كَانَ ... لَ ; thus:

لَوْ أَنَّ اللُّغَةَ الْعَرَبِيَّةَ صَعْبَةٌ جِدًّا لَما دَرَسْتُها .	'If Arabic were very difficult I would not have studied it.'
لَوْ أَنَّها عَرَبِيَّةٌ لَتَزَوَّجْتُها غَدًا .	'If she were Arab I would marry her tomorrow.'
لَوْ أَنَّ الْأِجابَةَ وَصَلَتْني مِنْ قَبْلُ لَما وَقَعْتُ في هٰذِهِ الْمُشْكِلَةِ .	'If I had received the answer earlier I would not have fallen into this difficulty.'

Note that, as in the last sentence, the perfect tense after لَ ... أَنَّ لَوْ

may be translated with an English past perfect even though قَدْ is not present.

To complete the picture, it should be pointed out that لَوْ used with the

imperfect indicative has <u>optative</u> meaning--"if only, would that..." etc. Example:

| كَمْ سُرِرْتُ لَوْ يَعْلَمُ ذٰلِكَ . | 'How happy I would be if only he knew that!' |

D. <u>Comprehension passages</u>   نصوص للفهم   — د

   Read the following passage; then do Drill 4. Next read the second

passage, and then do Drill 5.

(١)   النبي والشعراء

يعتقد بعض الناس أنّ النبيّ محمدا كان لا يحب الشعر وأنه كان

therefore لِذٰلِكَ يقاوم الشعراء • ويعتقد أولئك الناس أنّ النبي انتصر على

enemies أَعْدائِهِ ثم عمل على اقامة دولة بالمعنى الحديث لهذه الكلمة ، وكان

يرى أنّ الشعر لا يساعد على اقامة دولته ، وانما يسبّب الانقسام بين

العرب ، فمنع الشعر بين المسلمين •

لكنّ الحق بعيد من ذلك كل البعد : فلو أنّ النبيّ قاوم الشعر

لما انتشر الشعر بين المسلمين بعده ، بل في زمنه أيضا، ولما وجدنا

رجالا من أعظم المسلمين يحبون الشعر ويسمعون القصائد •

كان الشعر قد بلغ مكانة عالية بين العرب في زمن النبيّ، وكان لقصائد الشعراء تأثير عظيم في نفوس العرب • وساد الشعر السياسيّ في ذلك الوقت المجتمع العربيّ فاستخدم كما تستخدم الصحف والاذاعة اليوم • وكان النبيّ يعلم هذا كلّه ، ولكنه كان يعلم أيضا أنّ الشعر ليس كلّه سياسة ، كذلك كان يعلم أنّ المسلمين في حاجة الى شعر سياسيّ يقاومون

enemies به الْأَعْدَاءَ وشعر الْأَعْدَاءَ• الحق اذن أنّ النبي كان يقاوم بعض الشعراء• ولكنّه لم يكن مقاوما للشعر نفسه • ألم يكن للنبيّ ثلاثة شعراء أشهرهم حَسّانُ بْنُ ثابِتٍ الذي لقّب بشاعر الرسول ؟

والتاريخ يخبرنا بأنّ النبيّ سمع قصيدة كَعْب بْنُ زُهَيْرٍ فأعجبته

aba, cloak اعجابها جعله يقوم من مكانه ويلقي عَبَاءَتَهُ على الشاعر •

وبعد النبيّ ظهر بين المسلمين عدد كبير من الشعراء منهم جَرير والْفَرَزْدَق وأبو نُواس وبَشّار بْنُ بُرْد وأبو الْعَلاء الْمَعَرّي •

أمّا في القرن العشرين فقد ظهر عدد من الشعراء أشهرهم أمير الشعراء أحمد شوقي وشاعر النيل حافظ ابراهيم •

Drill 4. Written. Multiple choice.

In each item, choose the most appropriate alternative.

١ ـ يرى البعض أنّ النبيّ قاوم الشعر

أ ـ لأنّ الشعر في زمنه كان سياسيّا كلّه •

ب ـ لأنّ الشعر في زمنه كان لا يصور الحضارة العربية •

ج ـ لأنّ الشعر في زمنه كان لا يساعد على التعاون •

٢ ـ كان النبيّ يقاوم

أ ـ الشعر فقط •

ب ـ جميع الشعراء من غير المسلمين •

ج ـ بعض الشعراء السياسيّين •

٣ ـ كان للشعر في زمن النبيّ أهميّة عظيمة

أ ـ لأنه كان يؤثّر في نفوس العرب تأثيرا كبيرا .

ب ـ لأن أكثر الشعراء كانوا من عظماء العرب .

ج ـ لأنّ أكثر الشعر كان سياسيّا .

٤ ـ كان النبيّ في حاجة الى شعر

أ ـ سياسيّ .

ب ـ اجتماعيّ .

ج ـ تاريخيّ .

٥ ـ كان للنبيّ

أ ـ شاعر واحد .

ب ـ ثلاثة شعراء .

ج ـ شعراء كثيرون .

٦ ـ أمير الشعراء هو

أ ـ أبو العَلاء المَعَرّى .

ب ـ حافِظ ابراهيم .

ج ـ أحُمد شَوّقي .

(٢)   من رَحَلاتِ ابْنِ بَطّوطـــــة   trips, travels, journeys

كان للشرق منذ زمن طويل أهمية كبيرة في نظر العالم ، وكان

الناس يرحلون اليه لانه مركز الحضارات القديمة والاديان الكبــــرى

كاليهوديّة والمسيحيّة والاسلام .

great travelers, explorers, globetrotters   من أشهر الرَحّالَةِ العرب ابن بطوطة الذي عاش في القرن الرابع

عشر الميلادى .

Tangiers; North Africa   بدأ ابن بطوطة رَحَلاتِهِ من مكان ولادته طَنْجَة في المَغْرِب ومرّ بالمدن

٢٦٠

الكبرى في الجزائر وتونس ثم وصل الى القاهرة وسافر بعدها الى الحِجازِ

Syria ومن هناك ذهب الى بِلادِ الشّامِ • ثم سافر الى العراق ومنه الى الهِنــدِ India

حيث أقام مدة • وما زال ابن بطوطة يرحل من بلد الى آخر حتى وصل الى

China بلاد الصّينِ •

وصف ابن بطوطة في كتاب مشهور له طَبِيعَةَ البلدان التي زارها ature

وحضارتها والكثير من عادات الناس فيها • يعد الباحثون هذا الكتاب

الذي أصبح مشهورا في الشرق والغرب وترجم الى عدد من اللغات الاجنبية

travels من أعظم ما كتب في أدب الرَّحَلات في القرون الوُسْطى • iddle Ages

Drill 5. Written. Questions.

١ ــ بماذا امتاز الشرق في التاريخ القديم ؟

٢ ــ اذكر ثلاثة من أهمّ الاديان التي ظهرت في الشرق •

٣ ــ في أيّ قرن عاش ابن بطوطة ؟

٤ ــ اذكر الاماكن التي زارها او شاهدها •

٥ ــ ما ابعد بلد غير عربــــيّ وصل اليه ؟

٦ ــ ماذا وصف في كتابه ؟

٧ ــ ما رأي الباحثين في هذا الكتاب ؟

هـ ــ التمارين العامّة E. General drills

Drill 6. Transformation: Singular ⟶ plural.

Give the correct form of the words in parentheses by changing them
from the singular to the plural. Give the meaning of each word.

١ ــ ألّف أحْمد شَوْقي عددا كبيرا من الـ (قصيدة) •

٢ ــ المنطقة التي تسمى اليوم بالشرق الأوسط عرفت (رسول) و (نبيّ)
كثيرين •

261

٣ ـ وصلتني هذا الاسبوع خمس (رسالة) من أهلي وأصدقائي ٠

٤ ـ استقبل مساعد الوزير الـ (مندوبة) العشر في المطار ٠

٥ ـ قابل المراسل عددا من كبار الـ (مسؤول) ٠

٦ ـ في ميشيغان (مقهى) عربية ، بعضها في آن آربر ٠

٧ ـ أحبّ الـ (أغنية) القوميّة ، خاصّة أغنية " سنرجع " ٠

٨ ـ الزيت أهم الـ (مورد) الاقتصادية في الكويت ٠

٩ ـ مضى على رجوعه خمسة (يوم) وخمس (ليلة) ٠

١٠ ـ السدّ العالي من أكبر الـ (سدّ) في العالم ٠

١١ ـ المحافظة على السلام من (هدف) الأمم المتحدة ٠

١٢ ـ تقدّمت مصر في جميع الـ (ميدان) ٠

١٣ ـ لشركتنا (فرع) في معظم الـ (عاصمة) ٠

١٤ ـ تحيط الـ (جبل) بمدينة سولت ليك سيتي ٠

Drill 7. Use of the Ḥāl.

'He returned from school.(walking)'   أ ـ رجع من المدرسة ٠ سائر ٠ ◄━

'How did he return from school?'   طا ـ كيف رجع من المدرسة ؟

'He returned from school walking.'   ط٢ ـ رجع من المدرسة سائرًا ٠

٥ ـ ردّ الوزير على السؤال ٠ هو   ١ ـ خرج من الاجتماع ٠ سعيد ٠
مدهش ٠

٢ ـ عاش في نيويورك ٠ فقير ٠

٦ ـ تكلّمت معهم بعد المؤتمر ٠ ضاحك ٠   ٣ ـ جاء الى الاجتماع ٠ هو مُغْضَب ٠

٧ ـ سار في الشارع الواسع ٠ يغنّي ٠   ٤ ـ تحدّثوا الى والدهم ٠ هم

٨ ـ انتظر امام الباب ٠ هو يفكر ٠   مسرورون ٠

Drill 8. Use of the cognate accusative.

'Their victory was great.'   كان انتصارهم عظيما ٠ ◄━

'They won a great victory.'   انتصروا انتصارا عظيما ٠

262

١ ـ كانت اقامتهنّ في المسيسيبّي
طويلة .

٧ ـ كان نومها عميقا .

٨ ـ كانت رغبتهم في النجاح
قوية .

٢ ـ كان فهمه للمشكلة عميقا .

٣ ـ كانت اساءتنا اليهم عظيمة .

٩ ـ كان احترامنا لرأيك عظيما .

٤ ـ كان اهتمامهم بنا مشكورا .

١٠ ـ كان تعاونكم معنا مشكورا .

٥ ـ كان وصفها للمدينة جميلا .

١١ ـ كانت محاولتهنّ للتأليـــف
ناجحة .

٦ ـ كان ازدياد عدد الطلاب كبيرا .

<u>Drill 9</u>. Written. Translation.

1. Ḥassān b. Thābit, who was nicknamed "Poet of the Messenger", composed many poems in which he spoke of the Prophet and the Moslems.

2. I asked my friend, who recently completed his studies for the Ph.D. degree, to send me a copy of his dissertation; he answered saying: "It will give me great pleasure to send you a copy."

3. The prices of American books have increased greatly; as a result (of that) many professors buy the books they need from Europe.

4. Muṣṭafā Kāmil is a famous Egyptian who struggled for the independence of his country. He also called for the Egyptians to cooperate and to help their country.

5. There is no doubt that the United Nations has helped to solve many political problems; nevertheless, some people believe that it has not succeeded in realizing its goals.

6. It is as though the red-colored hotel which stands near the canal commands (controls) the entire area, and its various inhabitants include an engineer, a doctor and two princes.

7. In this far-away place, the local inhabitants were partial to the ugly prince who had (قَدْ) harmed his older brother the King, and they invited Sindbad to follow the same path (road). (سِنْدُبـاد)

<u>Drill 10</u>. Written. Vocabulary.

Substitute for the underlined words the most appropriate item from those in parentheses.

١ ‏‏- ‏انهى تأليف كتابه في اواخر القرن التاسع عشر .

‏(الربع الثالث من ، نهاية ، بداية)

٢ ‏- ‏أنشأت الدولة المصانع في أوائل القرن العشرين .

‏(النصف الاول من ، بداية ، النصف الثاني من)

٣ ‏- ‏كنا في استقبالها عند وصولها .

‏(بعد ، ساعة ، قبل)

٤ ‏- ‏ظهرت أحزاب كثيرة في العالم العربي بعد الحرب العالمية الثانية .

‏(استمرت ، جرت ، قامت)

٥ ‏- ‏سمّى حافظ ابراهيم " شاعر النيل "

‏(صار ، لقّب ب ، انتخب)

٦ ‏- ‏وصلتني رسالة من اخي امس .

‏(جاءتني ، حضرتني ، ارسلتني)

٧ ‏- ‏استمرّ الاجتماع اربع ساعات .

‏(دام ، مضى ، تمّ)

٨ ‏- ‏" الايّام " من أهمّ كتب طه حسين .

‏(اطول ، اعظم ، اوضح)

٩ ‏- ‏وهبهم الامير قصرا .

‏(باعهم ، منحهم ، اقام لهم)

١٠ ‏- ‏انهى رسالته في العام الماضي .

‏(أكمل ، تابع ، أعدّ)

Drill 11. Written. Vocabulary.

a. Refer back to Lesson 20 for the meaning relationship between Forms II and V, and between III and VI. Then check the dictionary for the related meanings of the following pairs of familiar words and make meaningful sentences out of each pair.

علّم ــ تعلّم

حسّن ــ تحسّن

قدّم ــ تقدّم

أثّر ــ تأثّر

راسل ــ تراسل

b. Use the same procedure to discover the relationship between the following pairs of words, and hence the meaning of the unfamiliar word (the item to the right is the one you already know).

تزوّج ــ زوّج	تأكّد ــ أكّد	أجّل ــ تأجّل	أسّس ــ تأسّس
ترقّى ــ رقّى	تغيّر ــ غيّر	جدّد ــ تجدّد	ألّف ــ تألّف
تناول ــ ناول	تحدّث ــ حدّث	تأخّر ــ أخّر	صوّر ــ تصوّر
تعاون ــ عاون	تكلّم ــ كلّم	وحّد ــ توحّد	قرّر ــ تقرّر
تبادل ــ بادل	تمكّن ــ مكّن	صادق ــ تصادق	حدّد ــ تحدّد
تطوّر ــ طوّر	توفّر ــ وفّر	ساوى ــ تساوى	عيّن ــ تعيّن
		حقّق ــ تحقّق	خرّج ــ تخرّج

Drill 12. Verbs and verb-preposition idioms.

Fill in the blanks with the correct verb or verb-preposition idiom provided. Be sure to insert the preposition in the right place.

١ ــ ـــــ مندوبو المؤتمر ورحّبوا بوزير الخارجية (قام ، قام بـ) .

٢ ــ ـــــ الفتاة اعضاء الحزب الفهم الكامل لوضع المرأة الصعب (دعت ، دعت الى) .

٣ ــ ـــــ قائد الثورة بالموت (حُكِمَ ، حُكِمَ على) .

٤ ــ ـــــ المدينة وهناك اتصلت باصدقائي (حضرت ، حضرت الى) .

٥ ــ ـــــ الاب وجه حبيب بنته وهو لا يعرف ماذا يقول (نظر ، نظر في) .

٦ ــ ــــــ الباحث طويلا كتب قديمة يستفيد منها في كتابته (بحث ،
بحث عن) .

٧ ــ ــــــ النساء محاضرة عن مَيّ زِيادَة (حضرت ، حضرت الى) .

٨ ــ ــــــ رئيس الحزب الوطني واجبه القومي وقاوم الملك (قام ،
قام بـ) .

٩ ــ عندما نجحت المقاومة ــــــ رئيس الحزب البلد (حكم ، حكم على) .

١٠ ــ ــــــ تحسين الوضع الاجتماعي والاقتصادي في بلاده (عمل، عمل على) .

١١ ــ ــــــ و ــــــ في ذلك المصنع نفسه حتى مات (عمل ، عمل على) .

١٢ ــ ــــــ بعيدا وأخذ يفكر في مشكلاته الكثيرة (نظر ، نظر في) .

١٣ ــ ــــــ ها ملك الحب مكانه العالي (دعا ، دعا الى) .

١٤ ــ الوالدان ــــــ ابنهما الى العاصمة لزيارة طبيب القلب (ذهبا ،
ذهبا بـ) .

١٥ ــ ــــــ البنات الى العاصمة معهم (ذهبت ، ذهبت بـ) .

الدرس الثالث والاربعون

أ ـ الجمل التمهيدية

A. <u>Preparatory sentences</u>

جمل متفرّقة

<u>Miscellaneous Sentences</u>

١ ـ لم نشتر حتى الآن تَذاكِرَ السفر للذهاب الى فرنسا .

1 — Up to now we have not bought travel <u>tickets</u> to go to France.

تَذْكِرَةٌ ـ تَذاكِرُ

ticket

٢ ـ اجتمع وزيرا خارجيّة فرنسا وبريطانيا لبحث المواضيع التي تَهُمّ البلدين .

2 — The foreign ministers of France and Great Britain met to discuss the subjects that <u>concern</u> the two countries.

هَمّ ـُ ، هَمّ

to interest, concern, be of importance or concern to

٣ ـ عندما بدأ رئيس الجمهورية مؤتمره الصحفيّ وَقَفَ الناس احتراما له .

3 — When the president began his press conference the people <u>stood up</u> out of respect for him.

وَقَفَ يَقِفُ ، وُقوفٌ

to come to a stop, stop; to stand up, rise to one's feet

٤ ـ لم تُعطَ المرأة العربية جميع حقوقها بَعْدُ .

4 — The Arab woman <u>has not</u> been <u>given</u> all her rights <u>yet</u>.

أَعْطى ، إعْطاءٌ

IV to give (s.o.) (s.th.)

لَمْ ... بَعْدُ .

not yet, still...not

٥ ـ ألّف كثير من الادباء العرب والمستشرقين كتبا كثيرة حول تَفسير القرآن .

5 — Many Arab writers and orientalists have written many books about <u>commentaries</u> on the Koran.

فَسَّرَ ، تَفْسيرٌ

II to explain, expound, interpret, comment on

٦ ‒ ماذا ينفع الانسان لو رَبِحَ
نُقودَ العالَمِ كلّها وخسِرَ
اصدقاءه .

What would it benefit a person were
he to <u>gain</u> all the <u>money</u> in the world
and <u>lose</u> his friends?

رَبِحَ ‒ ، رِبْحٌ (من)

to gain, profit (from); to win

[نَقْدٌ ‒ نُقودٌ]

[cash, money; coins]

خَسِرَ ‒ ، خَسارَةٌ

to lose

٧ ‒ <u>يا لَهُ مِنْ رَجُلٍ كبيرِ القلبِ</u> .

What <u>a</u> big-hearted man he <u>is</u>!

يا لَهُ من ...

what a...he is!

٨ ‒ <u>ما أَعْجَبَ</u> انسانا لا يحترم من
يحترمونه ولا يحبّ من يحبّونه .

<u>How strange</u> is the person who does
not respect those who respect him
and who does not like those who like
him.

ما (أَعْجَبَ)

how (strange) is...

٩ ‒ سوف اتعاون معك كلّ التعاون
اذا شِئْتَ ذلك .

I will cooperate with you fully if
you so <u>wish</u>.

شاءَ ‒ ، مشيئةٌ

to wish, want; will

١٠ ‒ قالت له انّها تحبّه ولكنّه
لم يُصَدِّقْها .

She said that she loved him but he
did not <u>believe</u> her.

صَدَّقَ ، تَصْديقٌ

II to give credence to, believe
(s.o. to be telling the truth
or s.th. to be true)

١١ ‒ من الصعب ان نجد مكانا لِلْجُلوسِ
في هذا المطعم عند الظهر .

It is hard to find a place <u>to sit</u> in
this restaurant at noon.

جَلَسَ ‒ ، جُلوسٌ

to sit, sit down

١٢ ‒ سمعت انّ المصانع قليلة في
مصر . بِالْعَكْسِ هناك مصانع
كثيرة في مصر .

I heard that there are few factories
in Egypt. <u>On the contrary</u>, there are
many factories in Egypt.

بِالْعَكْسِ

on the contrary

268

١٣ - قال إنّه لم يقابل مُطْلَقـًا
فتاة أجمل من الانسة سُهَيْر.

He said that <u>absolutely</u> he had not
met any girl prettier than Miss Suhayr.

مُطْلَقـًا

absolutely, without exception;
(after neg.) at all

١٤ - احببته كاخ لى واخلصت لـه
كلّ الاخلاص ، والعَجيبُ انه لا
يحبّني كما احبّه ولم يخلص
لى كما اخلصت له .

I liked him like a brother of mine
("my own") and I was completely sincere with him, but the <u>strange thing</u>
is that he did not like me as I liked
him nor was he sincere with me as I
was with him.

عَجيبٌ - ون

strange, odd

ب - النص الاساسي

a play

تمثيليّــة

امام شباك التذاكر

لِتَوْفيـق الْحَكيم

هى : سيّدى ! •••• تريد ••••• ؟

هو : لا شيئـا آنسة ! •••• اشكرك !

هى : لا شيء ! ••• ؟

هو : لا شيء •••••••

هى : لا شيء مطلقا ؟ ••••

هو : لا شيء مطلقا ! ••••• ايدهشك ذلك يا آنسة ؟ •••

هى : بعض الشيء يا سيدى ! ••• الا تطلب شيئا ؟ •••

somewhat

هو : وماذا تريدين ان اطلب ؟؟ ••••

هى : اطلب ••• محلّا •••• مثلا ! •••

هو : ليس لديك محلّ ! ••••

هى : ليس لديّ ؟ ! •••

هو : نعم ! ••• ليس لديك ! •••

269

هى : كيف تعرف ذلك ؟ ! ....

هو : اعرف ذلك حَقَّ الْمَعْرِفَةِ .... و انا متأكّد من ذلك ...   I know...very well

هى : نعم ! ...

هو : لا ! ....

هى : نعم ... نعم ...

هو : لا ! لا ! صدّقينى انا ...

هى : كيف اصدّقك يا سيّدى ، و امامى لَوْحَةُ المحلّات ؟ ...   table, chart

هو : لا تهمّني لوحة المحلّات ! ... انى اقول لك ليس لديك محلَ ! ....
و انت متأكّدة من وجوده ... فَلْنَتَراهَنْ! ... وهذه هى مئة فرانك..   let's make a bet!   franc

هى : انا متأكّدة انك ستخسر نُقودَكَ ! ...   money

هو : بالعكس ... وسوف ترين ! ...

هى : هذا عجيب ! ....

هو : لا محلّ لِلْعَجَبِ ! .... انا متأكّد انه ليس لديك محلّ خالٍ .. كلّ   empty, vacant   amazement, surprise
امرأة جميلة ليس لديها محلّ خالٍ في قلبها ! .... افهمت ؟ ....

هى : هذه دُعابَةٌ ظَرِيفَةٌ !! ....   elegant, witty   joke, jest

هو : اعندك حتّى مكان للوقوف ؟ ...

هى : يا لها من دُعابَةٍ ! ...

هو : نعم انّها دُعابة ! ... ولكن اجيبى : اعندك ام لا ؟ ...

هى : مكان للوقوف ؟! ... فى قلبى ! (تضحك) ما اعجب ذلك ! ...

هو : ليس لديك ! ... الم اقل لك ذلك من قبل ؟ ... لقد كنت اذن
على حقّ ... و انغى على ذُلِكَ الرابح !! ...   therefore

هى : بالعكس ! ... لم تربح يا سيّدي ! ...

هو : كيف ! ...

هى : لست انت الرابح ! .... انت تطلب مكانا للوقوف فى آخر الصُّفوفِ !   rows
أليس كذلك ! ...

270

هو : نعم ! ...

هى : حسنا ... عندى طلبك ! ... عندى محلّ ! ... محلّ واحد بقي لِحُسنِ الحَظّ **nately** ... فما رأيك ؟ ...

هو : مكان للوقوف فى آخر الصُّفوف ؟ ... كيف ذلك ؟ ...

هى : الست انت الذى طلبت ؟ ... ومَعَ ذلِكَ ليس هذا صعب التفسير ... أفهمت ؟ ... **pite that**

هو : لا ... لم أفهم ....

هى : إنّ هذا المحلّ يا سيّدى يعطيك الحقّ فى الحضور هنا مَتى شئت: **ever** ترانى وتتحدّث الىّ ... وانت امام شبّاك التذاكر ... واقف كما انت ...الآن ! ...

هو : بِغَيرِ جلوس ؟ ... **hout**

هى : لا جلوس ، ترانى وانت واقف ... هذا هو المحلّ ! ...

هو : اهذا كلّ شيء ؟ ...

هى : كل شيء ... والآن قد اتّفقنا ... وبذلك فقد ربحت ... وهذا حقّ ! ... وانى اضع المئة فرانك فى جَيْبي . **ket**

هو : اذن قد خسرت انا المئة فرانك ! ... ولم اجىء هنا إلّا لاخسرها ...

هى : (ضاحكة) ولكنّك ربحت الوقوف فى آخر الصُّفوف ! ...

هو : كفى يا سيّدتي ! ... ليس من السهل الدّعابة معك ! ... وَداعًا ! **rewell!** يا آنسة ! .... **that's enough!**

هى : (ضاحكة) وَداعًا يا سيّدى ! ...

This is an adaptation of Tawfīq Al-Hakīm's one-act play "At the Ticket Window".
Al-Hakīm (born 1902) is one of Egypt's leading dramatists, novelists and
essayists. A great number of his works have been translated into French,
English and other European languages.

271

C. __Grammar and drills__   ج – القواعد والتمارين

┌───┐
│   1. Adjectival verbs: ما أَجْمَلَهـا   │
└───┘

1. __Adjectival verbs__: ما أَجْمَلَهـا

   The sentence

   ┌───┐
   │   ما أَعْجَبَ ذٰلِكَ !   'How strange that is!'   │
   └───┘

illustrates a common construction. It consists basically of three elements:

(1) the word ما , (2) a Form IV verb derived from an adjective, __always 3 m.s.__

__perfect__, and (3) a pronoun suffix or a noun in the __accusative__. The usual Eng-

lish equivalent is "How (adjective) (subject) is/are...!" Since these verbs are

derived from adjectives, many of them not otherwise existing as verbs, they are

called __adjectival__ verbs. Further examples:

┌──┐
│   ما أَجْمَلَ هٰذِهِ الْمَدِينَةَ !   'How beautiful this city is!'   │
│   │
│   ما أَجْمَلَهـا !   'How beautiful she is!'   │
│   │
│   ما أَصْعَبَ هٰذا الدَّرْسَ الأَخِيرَ !   'How difficult this last lesson │
│   is!'   │
│   ما أَطْوَلَني !   'How tall I am!'   │
└──┘

Now do Drill 1.

__Drill 1__. Transformation: Adjective ⟶ verbal adjective.

'The new lesson is easy.'   الدرس الجديد سهل ←

'How easy the new lesson is!'   • ما أسهل الدرس الجديد

        ٦ – هي عظيمة •   ١ – ابنته جميلة •

        ٧ – بلادكم غنيّة •   ٢ – هذه الجملة صعبة •

        ٨ – أنا قصير •   ٣ – هو قبيح •

        ٩ – نبيل قويّ •   ٤ – قصيدتك طويلة •

        ١٠ – هذا الجبل عال •   ٥ – فهمه للشعر القديم

        ١١ – هذا الشيك كبير •   عميق •

272

Read the following passage and then do Drill 2.

Next read the second passage and then do Drill 3.

(١)   جُحــــــا *

جُحا رجل غير معروف الأَصْلِ تاريخيا • فالأَتْراكُ يقولون انه تُركيّ

والايرانيّون يقولون انه ايراني والعرب يقولون انه عربيّ اسمه ابـو

الغصن من سكان الكوفَةِ في العراق • والناس جميعا في الشرق الاوسط

وشمال افريقيا يخبرون عنه قصصا طريفةً • وعلى الرغم من عدم معرفتنا

أَصْلَهُ التاريخيّ فانه رجل مسلم يُمَثِّلُ الى حد بعيد شيئا عن حياة الناس

وعاداتهم •

وهناك قصص طريفةٌ كثيرة ليس لها علاقة بالعرب او بجحا ولكـــن

الناس يقولون انها جرت مع جحا •

لهذه الاسباب اصبح جحا اليوم رجلا أُسْطوريًّا عند مختلف شعــــوب

الشرق الاوسط وشمال افريقيا •

والقصة التالية هي واحدة من القصص الطريفةِ الكثيرة التي حكيت

عن جحا •

جاء صديق الى جحا يطلب منه حِمارَهُ ليستخدمه في سفر قصير قائـلا

انه سيعود بِالْحِمارِ في المساء • فقال جحا لصديقه : " لا استطيع اجابة

طلبِك لأن الحِمارَ ليس هنا اليوم " • ولَمْ يكمل جحا كلامه حَتَّى بدأ الحِمارُ

يَنْهَقُ في الخارج • فقال صديقه : " اني اسمع حِمارَكَ يا جحا • حِمارُكَ

يَنْهَقُ ! فقال له جحا : " عجيب أَمْرُكَ يا صديقي ! أتصدِّق الحمار ولا

تصدِّقني " !؟ •

origin

Turks

Iranians

Kufa

Sunny

resents

nical

nkey

scarcely had he... when

brays

u: see) below

*This passage is adapted from <u>The Essentials of Arabic</u> By Anis Frayha,
pp. 86-87.

(1) عَجِيبٌ أَمْرُكَ means literally "Strange is your matter." The noun أَمْرٌ ـ أُمُورٌ 'matter, thing, business' is often used with a pronoun suffix as a paraphrase for the independent pronoun; thus, هُوَ = أَمْرُهُ , أَنْتَ = أَمْرُكَ , etc. In this sentence the predicate عَجِيبٌ is placed before the subject أَمْرُكَ for emphasis; the force of this sentence, then, is "How strange you are!"

Drill 2. Written. Questions on reading passage.

أسئـلــة

١ ـ من هو جحا ؟

٢ ـ ما دين جحا ؟

٣ ـ في أيّ منطقة يتحدّث الناس عن جحا ؟

٤ ـ هل يتحدّث الناس عن جحا في المغرب ؟

٥ ـ ماذا طلب صديق جحا منه ؟

٦ ـ اين كان الحمار ؟

٧ ـ كيف عرف صديق جحا ان الحمار في الخارج ؟

٨ ـ ما رأيك بجحا ؟

٩ ـ هل في بلدك رجل تاريخيّ مثل جحا ؟

١٠ ـ أخبرنا شيئا عنه ؟

my dear son

رسالة : أَيْ بُنَيَّ *

لِأَحْمَدَ أَمِين

أَيْ بُنَيَّ :

England — انك الآن تدرس فى إِنْكِلِتَرّا بعد ان أكملت دراستك فى مصر والذين

(various) types, kinds — درسوا قبلك في أوروبا أَشْكالٌ ...

felt — فمنهم من شَعَرَ بأن حريته فى مصر كانت مفقودة ، فرآها فى أوروبا

pleasure, fun / became immersed — متوفرة ... فاَنْغَمَسَ في ... اللَّهْوِ ...

con-trast with — ومن الدارسين فى أوروبا من كانوا عَلى الْعَكْسِ مِنْ ذلك وهم أقل

عددا . هؤلاء اقبلوا على دروسهم باذلين أعظم الجهود ، ولم يعرفوا غير

بيوتهم وكتبهم وجامعاتهم وطريقهم من البيت الى الجامعة ... وظلّوا

يعملون ... حتى حصلوا على شهاداتهم العالية ... ثم عادوا الى بلادهم

يحملون شهاداتهم ويعملون فيما طلب منهم أن يعملوا ...

group — وهناك طائِفَةٌ ثالثةٌ التي تعجبني وهي التي احب ان تَسيرَ على

behave like / character, morals — مَنْهَجِها . هؤلاء ... فهموا انهم انما سافروا ليدرسوا علما ويدرسوا خُلْقًا

... يتعلمون هذه الدروس من الحياة الاجتماعية فى الجامعة ومن الحياة

العائلية فى البيت ، ومن الزيارات ... والحفلات ...

models, examples — كل هؤلاء يا بُنَيَّ قد رأيت نَمازِجَ مِنْهم ... فليكن سفرك أنت للمعرفة

improvement, betterment / will give you success — والعلم وعودتك للإصلاح والنفع والله يُوَفِّقُكَ .

*This is a revised selection from Ahmad Amin's "To My Son" الى ولدي "
pp. 17-27. For the use of أَيّ see L.44.C.1,p. 288.

أسئلة :

Drill 3. Written. Questions.

١ ـ أين درس الابن ؟

٢ ـ الى كم قسم ينقسم الدارسون فى أوروبا فى رأي المؤلف ؟

٣ ـ ماذا تعرف عن القسم الاول ؟

٤ – ماذا تعرف عن القسم الثانى ؟

٥ – ماذا تعرف عن القسم الثالث ؟

٦ – أىّ قسم من هذه الاقسام يفضّل المؤلف ؟

٧ – هل تتفق مع المؤلف فى الرأي ؟ لماذا ؟

٨ – ما رأيك بالطلاب الاجانب الذين يدرسون فى أمريكا ؟

E. **General drills.**   هـ – التمارين العامّة

Drill 4. Use of comparative and superlative.

Fill in the blanks with the proper form of the adjective given in brackets:

(واسع)   هذا الشارع ــــ من ذلك الشارع ٠   – ١

(عميق)   هى ــــ منه فهما للشعر العربىّ القديم ٠   – ٢

(طويل)   المسيسبي ــــ من الامازون ٠   – ٣

(قصير)   أختى ــــ من أختك ٠   – ٤

(كبير)   نبيلٌ أخى ــــ ٠   – ٥

(صغير)   سلْوى ــــ بناته ٠   – ٦

(كثير)   المملكة العربية السعوديّة ــــ البلدان العربية   – ٧

انتاجا للزيت ٠

(واضح)   ترجمة القرآن هذه ــــ من تلك الترجمة ٠   – ٨

(عال)   جبال " روكى " ــــ من جبال " سموكى " ٠   – ٩

(عظيم)   لندن عاصمة بريطانيا ــــ ٠   – ١٠

          اجتمعت بعد الحرب العالمية الثانية بعض الدول   – ١١

(كبير،   ــــ وعدد من الدول ــــ فى مدينة سان

صغير)   فرانسيسكو لتأسيس منظمة الامم المتحدة ٠

Drill 5. Written. Completion.

Active	Passive	Active participle	Passive participle	Verbal noun
رفضت				
يذيع	يهدى			
جدّد	القّوا			
يسرّ	يعطي			
اشترى	فهم			
يلقى	يحاط بـ			
	يوجد			

Drill 6. Written. Translation.

1. The disagreement between the father and his son over the subject of the son's marriage became very intense.

2. There is no doubt that the newspapers here are totally different from our newspapers.

3. The first thing I did last night was to send a letter to my parents, in which I informed them of my new address.

4. Among those who taught her was a well-known French professor who helped her understand French literature and culture.

277

5. At the beginning of this week she received a letter saying that her
brother-in-law had died.

Drill 7. Written. Vocabulary.

Fill in the blanks with the appropriate word from the following

list:

(تحيط ، تحسّنت ، رفضت ، حضارة ، الخلاف ، عاشت ، مضى ، تَلِدَ ، عالية ،

على حق ، حول ، فَقَدَ ، بأمير ، حينَ ، كليّة ، اشتدّ ، جمال ، لُقّب ،

ظهرت ، أساء ، حيّ ، قائمة، من قاوموه) .

١ ــ ـــــ ـــــ على زواجها خمسة اعوام قبل ان ـــــ .
(gave birth)

٢ ــ ـــــ ـــــ احمد شوقى ـــــ الشعراء .
(prince)

٣ ــ هل انتصر صَلاحُ الدّينِ على ـــــ ؟

٤ ــ ـــــ ـــــ والديه وهو فى السابعة من عمره .

٥ ــ ـــــ ـــــ ـــــ بين الزوج وزوجته ـــــ مشكلاتهما العائلية .
(concerning)   (disagreement)

٦ ــ درست الادب الفرنسى فى ـــــ الاداب فى الجامعة اللبنانية .

٧ ــ كان العرب قبل الاسلام اهل ـــــ قبل ان يكونوا اهل حرب .

٨ ــ ـــــ ـــــ الى والده دون ان يعرف انه فعل ذلك .

٩ ــ ـــــ كانت عندما ـــــ ـــــ الزواج منه .
(right)

١٠ ــ ـــــ ـــــ فى لبنان احزاب كثيرة فى النصف الثانى من القرن الحالى .

١١ ــ ـــــ ـــــ الاوضاع فى هذا البلد نتيجة لجهود المخلصين من ابنائه .
(improved)

١٢ ــ كنت ادرس فى جامعة هارفرد ـــــ قابلتها .

١٣ ــ ـــــ ـــــ بهذه المدينة ـــــ عالية .
(mountains)

Drill 8. Vocabulary.

Give the antonyms of the following words or expressions.

عاش	ذهب	جميل
المستقبل	شمال	كثير
اشترى	غرب	صغير
اتّفقا	سيّىء	طويل
خسر	نهاية	قريب
وقف	قَبِلَ	اعطى
قديما	فقير	داخلٌ
حرب	جاء	قَبْلَ
سهل	عدم الانحياز من قَبْلُ	سهل
عامّ	اسود	امام

Drill 9. Written. Dictionary drill.

Look up the following words in the dictionary; indicate the root and the meaning of each word.

يتقصّون	مجاملات	استثقال
عزّ	معتنق	مناورات
مناشير	سخاء	دحرج
تأويل	اشتقاق	راض
تفاؤل	انقلاب	مودّة

279

<u>Drill 10</u>. Vocabulary. Verb-preposition idioms.

Fill in the blank with the preposition usually associated with the verb,
<u>if any</u>, from the following:

بـ ، الى ، فى ، على ، عن ، من

١ ‒ يرغب الاديب العربى ‒‒‒‒ ان تقوم نهضة فكريّة فى مجتمعه .

٢ ‒ يهتم قائد المقاومة ‒‒‒‒‒ الثورة الشعبية .

٣ ‒ يعتمد السلام العالمى ‒‒‒‒‒ تصرف الدول الكبرى .

٤ ‒ ان الامة العربية بحاجة ‒‒‒ الوحدة .

٥ ‒ رأت ‒‒‒‒‒ البنت أخاها الصغير حاملا الكرسى الى الطاولة .

٦ ‒ تحيط جبال خضراء ‒‒‒‒ هذه المدينة الجميلة .

٧ ‒ احتفل اهل القرية كلهم ‒‒‒‒ زواج اخى الكبير .

٨ ‒ تقدم العامل ‒‒‒ طلب للعمل الى المكتب الادارى للمصنع .

٩ ‒ يمتاز لبنان ‒‒‒‒ جباله العالية .

١٠ ‒ حكى ‒‒‒‒ الجاحظ انه قبيح الوجه واسع العينين .

star

١١ ‒ لقّب الشعب العربى أمّ كلثوم ‒‒‒‒‒ "كَوْكَبُ الشرق "

١٢ ‒ أساء ‒‒‒ الاستاذ عندما اخرجنى من الصف .

١٣ ‒ انحاز أهل البلد ‒‒‒ الوزير فى خلافه مع الامير .

<u>Drill 11</u>. Written. Translation.

The American <u>Ambassador</u> in Lebanon

سَفيرٌ

The new American Ambassador arrived in the Lebanese capital last night
to present his <u>credentials</u> to the president of the Republic. This morning

أوراقُ اعْتِمادٍ

at ten o'clock the Ambassador went to the presidential palace to meet the
President, and on his arrival he was met in front of the palace by the Minister
of Foreign Affairs and a number of state officials. Then the Ambassador met
with the President, and presented his credentials in an official ceremony,

280

during which the Ambassador encountered the warmest of welcomes. The

Ambassador remained at the presidential palace for a period of two hours,

after which he returned to the American Embassy. سِفَارَةٌ

The new Ambassador had <u>served</u> his country as a senior official of the خَدَمَ

U.S. State Department for a period of ten years before his appointment as

Ambassador to Lebanon.

<u>Drill 12</u>. Written. Vocabulary.

a. Refer back to Lesson 24 for the meaning of Form X. Then check the dictionary for the related meanings of the following pairs of words. (The familiar word is underlined.)

<u>وقف</u> ــ استوقف	<u>خرج</u> ــ استخرج	<u>خدم</u> ــ استخدم
<u>عاد</u> ــ استعاد	<u>حمل</u> ــ استحمل	<u>مرّ</u> ــ استمرّ
<u>رجع</u> ــ استرجع	<u>انتج</u> ــ استنتج	<u>أعدّ</u> ــ استعدّ
<u>مات</u> ــ استمات	<u>افاد</u> ــ استفاد	<u>عمل</u> ــ استعمل
<u>بقي</u> ــ استبقي	<u>خسر</u> ــ استخسر	<u>فهم</u> ــ استفهم
<u>دل</u> ــ استدلّ	<u>علم</u> ــ استعلم	<u>دعا</u> ــ استدعى
	<u>ردّ</u> ــ استردّ	

b. Refer back to Lesson 21 for the meaning of Form VII. Then check the

dictionary for the related meanings of the following pairs of words.

<u>عقد</u> ــ انعقد	<u>قطع</u> ــ انقطع
<u>قسم</u> ــ انقسم	<u>صرف</u> ــ انصرف
<u>فصل</u> ــ انفصل	<u>قضى</u> ــ انقضى

(Familiar words are underlined.)

c. Refer back to Lesson 21 for the meaning of Form VIII. Then check the dictionary for the related meanings of the following pairs of words:

شدّ ــ اشتدّ   نشر ــ انتشر

زاد ــ ازداد   فقد ــ افتقد

وصل ــ اتصل   ربط ــ ارتبط

هم ــ اهتم   لقي ــ التقى

تبع ــ اتبع

أ - الجمل التمهيدية

A. <u>Preparatory sentences</u>

أحمدُ وكريمة

Ahmad and Karima

١ - تَعَرَّفَ أحمد على كريمة في الجامعة ثم احبّها و احبّته فاتّفقا على ان لا يسمحا لأيّ شيء بالتَفْريق بينهما .

1 Ahmad and Karima <u>met</u> at the university and he fell in l<u>ove</u> with her and she fell in love with him. They agreed that they would let nothing <u>separate</u> them.

[تَعَرَّفَ ، تَعَرُّف على]

[V to become acquainted with (s.o.)]

فَرَّقَ ، تَفْريقٌ ، تَفْرِقَةٌ

II to separate, divide, disperse

٢ - وبعد حبّ دام ثلاثة اعوام تزوّجا وقرر كل منهما ان يبذل كل الجهد لإسْعادِ الآخر .

2 After a love which lasted three years they got married and each one decided to do his or her utmost to <u>make</u> the other one <u>happy</u>.

أسْعَدَ ، إسْعادٌ

IV to make (s.o.) happy

٣ - سرّ الاهل والاصدقاء والأصْحابُ بزواجهما سرورا كبيرا .

3 Their families and <u>friends</u> were very happy over their marriage.

صاحبٌ - أصْحابٌ

friend, comrade

٤ - عمل احمد بجهد عظيم في وظيفته فترقّى وحصل على كثير من المالِ فقدّره رئيس الشركة التي كان يعمل فيها كلّ التقدير .

4 Ahmad worked very hard at his job and was promoted and acquired a lot of <u>money</u>, and he was highly regarded by the president of the company in which he worked.

مالٌ - أمْوالٌ

money, property, wealth

٥ - وبعدئذ اخذ احمد يهتمّ بوظيفته اكثر من اهتمامه بزوجته حتى جعل نفسه مِلْكًا لتلك الوظيفة .

5 <u>Then</u> Ahmad began to concern himself with his position more than with his wife, to the point that he made himself the <u>property</u> of that position.

بعدئذٍ

then, after that, afterwards

مِلْكٌ ـ أَمْلاكٌ

property, possessions

٦ ـ لم يسعد كريمة المال الكثير
الذي كان يحصل عليه احمد
لأنها لم تكن ترى فى الدُّنْيا
الا بيتها " الجميل " لمدة
اربع وعشرين ساعة فى اليوم
ولم يكن لديها ولد تسرّ به •

The large sum of money that Ahmad was earning did not make Karima happy because she saw nothing of the <u>world</u> except her "beautiful" house for twenty-four hours a day. Nor did she have a child in whom she might take pleasure.

دُنْيا

(f.) world; this world (as opposed to الآخِرَة 'the hereafter), worldly existence

دُنْيَوِيّ ، دُنْياوِيّ

(nisba of دُنْيا) wordly, secular, temporal

٧ ـ صَبَرَتْ كريمة طويلا وسَكَتَتْ على
ذلك الوضع •

Karima <u>bore</u> that situation <u>patiently</u> for a long time and <u>said nothing</u>.

صَبَرَ ـِ ، صَبْرٌ (على)
سَكَتَ ـُ سُكوتٌ (عن)

to be patient, forbearing (over s.th.); to endure (s.th.)
to fall silent, say nothing (about)

٨ ـ تحدّثت مع زوجها بالموضوع
قائلة ان المال فقط لايسعدها
لكنّه غَضِبَ غَضَبًا عظيما وقال
لها إنّها لا تقدّر كل ما
يقوم به من عمل لاسعادها •

She spoke with her husband about the subject, saying that money alone did not make her happy. But he <u>became</u> greatly <u>angered</u> and said to her that she did not appreciate all the work he was doing to make her happy.

غَضِبَ ـَ ، غَضَبٌ

to become angry

٩ ـ وبعد انْقِضاءِ خمسة اعوام على
زواجهما عرف الزوجان انهما
وَقَعا فى مشكلة صعبة •

After the <u>passage</u> of five years of their marriage the couple realized that they had <u>fallen</u> into a difficult problem.

انْقَضَى ، انْقِضاءٌ
وَقَعَ يَقَعُ ، وُقوعٌ

VII to elapse, go by, pass (with على : 'over, by')
to fall, fall down; to come to pass, take place, happen; to be located, situated, lie

١٠ ـ طلبت كريمة من احمد الطَّلاقَ
فرفض ان يُطَلِّقَها •

Karima asked Ahmad for a <u>divorce</u>, but he refused to <u>divorce</u> her.

طَلَّقَ ، طَلاقٌ

II to divorce

١١ — تركت كريمة بيت زوجها
وذهبت الى بيت ابيها . عِنْدَئِذٍ
شَعَرَ احمد بانه لا معنى
لحياته بدون زوجته وحبيبته
كريمة . وعلى الرغم من ان
القاضي حكم بينهما بالتفريق
فقد رجعت كريمة الى زوجها
وحبيبها احمد وعاشا معا
سعيدين .

Karima left her husband's house and
went to her father's house. At that point
Ahmad <u>felt</u> that there was no meaning
to his life without his wife and sweetheart Karima, and in spite of the fact
that the <u>judge</u> had ruled in favor of
separation between them Karima returned
to her husband and sweetheart Ahmad
and they lived together happily.

عِنْدَئِذٍ   at that time, then, at that point
شَعَرَ ــُ شُعُورٌ (ب)   to feel, perceive, sense (s.th.)
قاضٍ ــ قُضاةٌ   judge

ب — النص الاساسي

قصّة من كتاب الف ليلة وليلة

slave-girl, maiden   هارون الرَشيد وجَعْفَر والجارية

الليلة التاسعة والعشرون بعد الثلاثمائة

Shahrazad   وحكت شَهْرَزادُ للملك فقالت:

Caliph   " يُحكى ان جَعْفَرَ الْبَرْمَكِي كان في قصر الخَليفَةِ هارون الرَشيد

ليلةً فقال له الرَشيد بـلغني انّك اشتريت سَلامَةَ الجاريةَ السمراءَ اللون

السوداءَ العينين وانا احبّها واطلبها منك منذ مدّة طويلة فهبـها

Commander of   لى . فقال جَعْفَر : لا ابيعها يا أميرَ الْمُؤْمِنينَ . فقال : هبـها لي
the Faithful

thrice   فقال : لا اهبها . فقال الرَشيد : زوجتي زُبَيْدَةُ طالِقٌ ثَلاثَةً ان لـم
divorced

تبعها او تهبها لي . قال جعفر : زوجتي طالِقٌ ثلاثة ان بعتها او

وهبتها لك . ثم عرفا انهما وقعا في مشكلة كبيرة ما استطاعا حلّها .

فأرسل الرشيد يطلب القاضى ابا يوسُفَ ليساعدهما على حلّ هذه المشكلة.

285

جاء القاضي أبو يوسف مسرعًا • فلمّا وصل الى القصر رحّب بـه

such and such الرشيد وقال له : ما طلبناك فى هذا الوقت إلّا لامر هامّ هو كَذا وكَذا

لم نستطع حلّه • فقال • يا امير المؤمنين إنّ هذا الامر اسهل ما

يكون • ثم قال : يا جعفر بع لأمير المؤمنين نصف الجارِيَةِ وهب لـه

admired نصفها فَتَبَرآنِ مِنْ يَمينِكُما بالطلاق • فأُعْجِبَ أميرُ المُؤْمَنينَ بذلك وفعل you will be free of your oath

هو وجعفر ما طلبه القاضي ثم قال الرشيد : أحضروا الجارية فـي

هذا الوقت •

ولمّا احضروا الجارية قال الرشيد للقاضي : اريد ان اتزوّجهـا

probation (Islamic law) فى هذا الوقت فانّى لا استطيع الصبر حتّى تنقضي مدّة الإسْتِبْراءِ فقال

القاضى ابو يوسف : أحضروا الى مَمْلوكًا من مَماليكِ أمير المؤمنيـن mamluke

(before) he con-sumate marr-iage with her; becomes permissible فأزوّجهُ ايّاها ثم يطلّقها قبل ان يَدْخُلَ عَلَيْهَا فَيَحِلَّ زواجها بعدئذ مـن so that I can marry her to him

امير المؤمنين • (2)

فأُعْجِبَ الرشيد بـهذا الحلِّ وطلب إحضار المَمْلوكِ فلمّا حضر قال

للقاضى زوّجه من الجاريةِ ففعل • ثم قال الرَّشيد للمَمْلوكِ : طلّقهـا

he gives him more of ولَك مائة دينارٍ فقال : لا افعل • ولم يزل يَزيدُهُ وهو يرفض حـتّى dinar

by God! اعطاه الف دينارٍ فرفضها وقال : هل الطلاق بيَدى ام بـيَدِكَ ؟ واللّـهِ in my power

لا اطلّقها • فغضب الخَليفةُ وقال : ما الحلّ يا ابا يوسف فقال : يـا

امير المؤمنين : الامر سهل جدا • اجعل هذا المَمْلوك ملكًا للجاريـة.

قال : جعلته ملكا لها • فقال لها القاضى : قولى : قبلت • فقالت

قبلت • فقال القاضى : حكمت بينهما بالتفريق لانه صار ملكا لـهـا

is annulled فانْفَسَخَ الزواج • فسرّ الرشيد بذلك واعطاه عشرة آلاف دينارٍ تقديرا

له فأخذها وانصرف الى بيته •

وفى صباح اليوم التالى قال القاضي لاصحابه : " لا طريق الـى

الدين والدنيا اسهل من طريق العلم فانى اعطيت المال الكثير لانى

استطعت بقليل من العلم حلَّ مشكلة أمير المؤمنين وإسعاده "

permissible   وَأَدْرَكَ شَهْرَزادَ الصَّباحَ ، فسكتت عن الكلام المُباحِ .   overtook

(1) The formula for finalizing a Muslim divorce is the husband's three-fold declaration that his wife is divorced (طالِقٌ; note that this adjective is masculine in form but feminine in gender!). An oath of three-fold divorce cannot be said in jest, for, once uttered, it must necessarily be honored. Thus, this oath is an indication of supreme determination or resolve on the part of the speaker.

(2) The owner of a female slave is forbidden to cohabit with her before he has ascertained that she is not pregnant; if she is pregnant, then it must be clear that he is not the father of her child. Ascertaining that a slave-girl is not pregnant is called اِسْتِبْراءٌ ?istibra'.

Vocabulary note: A special use of فـ 'and then' in reporting conversations is to denote a change of subject. Thus فَقالَ is equivalent to "the other one says", while وَقالَ or ثُمَّ قالَ means "and then he says..."

C. Grammar and drills   ج – القواعد والتمارين

---

1. Vocative: Summary

2. Perfect tense: Performative function

3. Verbs of giving: Summary

4. بَعْدَئِذٍ 'after that'

---

1. Vocative: Summary

a. The noun or adjective following يا is in the __nominative case__ and __does not have nunation__ (see 2.C.4); it refers to a specific person or group of persons:

يا أَميرُ   'O Prince!'

يا يوسُفُ الْكَريمُ   'O generous Yusuf!'

---

b. If, however, the noun or adjective is the first term of an iḍāfa or is followed by a pronoun suffix, it is put in the __accusative case__:

يَا أُمِيرَ الْمُؤْمِنِينَ	'O Commander of the Faithful!'
يَا أُمِيرَنَا	'Our Prince!'
يَا أَبَا يُوسُفَ ، يَا أَخِي الْعَزِيزَ	'O Abu Yusuf, o my dear brother!'

c. The vocative particle أَيُّهَا (f. also أَيَّتُهَا (see 14.C.3) is synonymous to يَا , but is followed by a common noun in the <u>nominative case</u> with the <u>definite article</u>. Examples:

أَيُّهَا السَّيِّدَاتَ وَالسَّادَةُ	'Ladies and gentlemen!'
أَيُّهَا الطُّلَّابُ الْمُحْتَرَمُونَ	'Respected students!'

d. In the cases above a specific person is being addressed. If, on the other hand, there is no specific person being addressed, the vocative noun is in the <u>accusative case</u> and <u>with nunation</u>, as in

يَا رَجُلاً ، سَاعِدْنِي! 'Somebody help me!'

e. The first person singular pronoun suffix ي -ii is sometimes shortened to <u>i</u> in the vocative. Thus يَا أَعِزَّائِي or يَا أَعِزَّاءِ 'my dear ones!' The noun أَبٌ 'father' has a special vocative form with this suffix: يَا أَبَتِ 'O my father!'

f. Another vocative particle is أَيْ found in L.43.D.(2), p. 275; it is quite rare in MSA. It follows the same rules as يَا 'O'.

g. Resume chart:

	SPECIFIC ADDRESSEE nominative case without nunation	NON-SPECIFIC ADDRESSEE accusative case with nunation
يَا (without article)	يَا رَجُلُ	يَا رَجُلاً
أَيُّهَا (with article)	أَيُّهَا الرَّجُلُ	

2. <u>Perfect tense</u>: <u>Performative function</u>

Compare the use of the perfect tense in Arabic as opposed to the use of the present tense in English in the following excerpts from the Basic Text:

قَالَ : إِجْعَلْ هَذَا الْمَمْلُوكَ مِلْكًا لِلْجَارِيَةِ .	'He said, "Make this mameluke the property of the girl."'
قَالَ : جَعَلْتُهُ مِلْكًا لَهَا .	'He said, "I make him her property."'
قَالَ لَها : قُولِي قَبِلْتُ ، فَقالَتْ قَبِلْتُ .	'He said to her, "Say 'I accept'," and she said "I accept".'
حَكَمْتُ بَيْنَهُما بِالتَّفْرِيقِ .	'I declare them separated.'

In these instances the perfects have the meaning of proclamations or formal declarations which are performed by the very act of speaking. English uses the present tense for this purpose, as in "I agree to your terms," "I accept your offer," "I give you my word," "I bet you can't do it," "I pronounce you man and wife," etc. This use of the tenses is referred to as the performative function.

Arabic usage is further illustrated by the following excerpts from a Muslim wedding service:

الإِمامُ لِلْعَروس : قُولِي : زَوَّجْتُكَ نَفْسِي على المَهْرِ المُتَّفَقِ عَلَيْهِ بَيْنَنا على كِتابِ اللَّهِ وَسُنَّةِ رَسُولِهِ (صلعم) .	The Imam to the bride: "Say, 'I wed thee in accordance with the dowry agreed upon between us on the basis of the Book of God and the Sunna of the Prophet (God bless him and grant him salvation!)'."
الإِمامُ لِلْعَرِيس : قُلْ : وَأَنا قَبِلْتُ زَواجَكِ على المَهْرِ المُتَّفَقِ عَلَيْهِ بَيْنَنا على كِتابِ اللَّهِ وَسُنَّةِ رَسُولِهِ (صلعم) .	The Imam to the groom: "Say, 'and I accept marriage to you in accordance with the dowry agreed upon between us on the basis of the Book of God and the Sunna of the Prophet (God bless him and grant him salvation!)'."

In this illustration the acts of marrying and accepting are performed with the uttering of the words themselves; in English these are present tense verbs (underlined) whereas in Arabic they are perfect tense verbs (also underlined).

3. Verbs of giving: Summary

Verbs of giving are followed by two accusatives, the first being the indirect object and the second, the direct object (see 22.C.4). This note deals with two additional features: (a) a pronoun as second accusative and (b) substitution of a ‫ل‬ prepositional phrase for the indirect object. First, here

is a list of all the verbs of giving occurring in this book:

أَعْطَى	IV	to give (s.o.) (s.th.)
وَهَبَ	I	to give (s.o.) (s.th.)
مَنَحَ	I	to grant (s.o.) (s.th.)
زَادَ	I	to give (s.o.) more of (s.th.)
وَفَّى	II	to give (s.o.) (his) due share of (s.th.)
بَاعَ	I	to sell (s.o.) (s.th.)

    a. If the first accusative is a pronoun, it is suffixed to the verb; if

the second accusative is a pronoun, the pronoun is suffixed to the particle

‫إِيَّا‬ - :

<u>Both accusatives are nouns:</u>
أَعْطَى الْخَلِيفَةَ الْهَدِيَّةَ .   'He gave the Caliph the present.'
<u>First accusative is a pronoun:</u>
أَعْطَاهُ الْهَدِيَّةَ .   'He gave him the present.'
<u>Second accusative is a pronoun:</u>
أَعْطَى الْخَلِيفَةَ إِيَّاها .   'He gave it to the Caliph.'
<u>Both accusatives are pronouns:</u>
أَعْطَاهُ إِيَّاها .   'He gave it to him.'

The particle ‫إِيَّا‬ - is used here only with the second of two accusatives

— the direct object — when it is a pronoun.

    b. Compare the following sentences:

وَهَبَنِي الْقَلَمَ .	'He gave <u>me</u> the pencil.'
وَهَبَ الْقَلَمَ لِي .	'He gave the pencil <u>to me</u>.'

290

Certain verbs of giving may express the indirect object not as an accusative noun but as an object of the preposition لِ 'to'. As the illustration above shows, this has an exact parallel in English. The usage in the two languages is different if the direct object is a pronoun:

| هَبْنِي إِيَّاهُ
هَبْهُ لِي | 'Give it to me!' |

The choice between the two constructions is a matter of usage: وَهَبَ often uses the لِ variation, أَعْطَى and بَاعَ do at times, and مَنَحَ , زَادَ and وَفَّى rarely if ever do.

Now do Drill 1.

<u>Drill 1</u>. Substitution: Noun ⟶ pronoun with إِيَّا- .

Substitute the proper form of the pronoun for the underlined noun. <u>Ex.</u>
'He taught them history.'   درّسهم <u>التاريخ</u> . ⟵

'He taught it to them.'   درّسهم ايّاه .

٥ ــ أعطانا <u>الجرائد</u> .	١ ــ أعطانى <u>الكتابين</u> .
٦ ــ أعطاهن <u>الرسائل</u> .	٢ ــ أعطيته <u>الرسالة</u> .
٧ ــ درّسنى <u>الأدب العربيّ</u> .	٣ ــ درّستهنّ <u>اللّغة العربيّة</u> .
٨ ــ منحته <u>قلبها</u> .	٤ ــ وهبتكما <u>الكتب</u> .

4. بَعْدَئِذٍ 'after that'

The word بَعْدَئِذٍ , which occurs in the Basic text, is an adverb meaning "after that, afterwards". It consists of the preposition بَعْدَ 'after' and suffix ئِذٍ with the general meaning "that time". This suffix is found with several prepositions and nouns referring to time or a period of time; these all take the adverbial accusative ending -<u>a</u>. Examples:

يَوْمَئِذٍ 'on that day'	عِنْدَئِذٍ 'at that time, then'
حِينَئِذٍ 'at that time'	بَعْدَئِذٍ 'after that'
سَاعَتَئِذٍ 'in that hour	وَقْتَئِذٍ 'at that time'

D. Comprehension passages

(1) Read the following passage and then do Drill 2.

Next read the second passage and do Drill 3.

(١)
الآ ـــــــــاء

جلست أمام والدها ... وقالت في صوت قوّي ... :

ـ اني أحبّه ...

فأُدهش قولها والدها وشعر أنّ ابنته ضَرَبَتْهُ على وجهه واراد أن يَصْرُخَ

في وجهها ؛ ولكنّه تَمالَكَ نفسه ... وقال :

ـ منذ متى ؟

ـ منذ عام وأكثر .

ـ وكنت تقابلينه ؟

ـ نعم ... كثيرا .

ـ أين ؟

ـ في بيته !!

ـ في بيته ... وَحْدَكُما ؟

ـ لقد قَدَّمَني الى اخواته ... وأمّه !

ـ هل قبّلَكِ ؟

ـ نعم ...

ـ ولَمْ تَخْجَلي ... ؟

ـ لم أشعر بالخَجَلِ ... شعرت بالحب !

ـ هل طلبك للزواج ؟

ـ سنتزوّج ، ولكن لا يستطيع ان يطلبني للزواج الآن ... انّه لا يزال

طالبا ، ولا يستطيع أن يعدّ لي بيتا .

ـ هل أخبرت أمّك بكل ذلك ؟

ـ لا ... خِفْتُ ألا تفهميني !

voice

scream   she stru[ck]

he gained control over

alone, by yourselves

he introduced

he kissed

you were not ashamed

shame

I feared, was afraid

292

- ولماذا تخبرينى أنا ؟

- لأنّي أحترمك ... ولأنى واثقة أنّك ستفهمنى .

وسكت الأب قليلا كأنّه يفكّر ، ثم قال :

- هل أستطيع أن اعرفه ؟

فقالت فى سرور :

naturally, of course   - نعم ... طبعًا ...

eat, drink, have   - ادعيه لِتَناوُلِ الشاى معنا ، غدا ...

members   وجاء الشابّ فى الغد ... وجلس بين أفرادِ العائلة كلّهم ...   young man

searching   الأب والأم والاخوة ... وكان الأب ينظر اليه مُتَفَحِّصًا كأنّه يبحث فى   traces; crime

convince   قلبه عن آثارِ الجَريمَةِ ... ولكنّه لم يستطع أن يُقنِعَ نفسه بأن هناك

devoted themselves to   جَريمَةً أو أثرًا لها ... ضحك وهو يجد أبناءه وقد انْصَرَفوا الى الشابّ

the young man   فى حديثٍ طويل .   conversation

became friends with each other   وأصبح صديقا للعائلة وحبيبا للابنة ... ثم تَصادَقَتِ العائلتان

... الاب والاب ... والأم والأم ... والاخوة والاخوة ....

وبعد عامين ... تم الزواج !

This short story is adapted from مُنتَهى الحُبّ (pp. 119-121) by Ihsan Abdul-Quddūs.

Drill 2.   Written. Question/answer.

١ ‑ لماذا غضب الوالد ؟

٢ ‑ لماذا أخبرت الفتاة والدها عن حبّها عوضا عن أمّها ؟

٣ ‑ هل قابلت الفتاة حبيبها ؟ أين ؟

٤ ‑ لماذا لم يستطع الحبيبان أن يتزوّجا ؟

٥ ‑ هل دعت الفتاة حبيبها الى بيتها ؟ ومن قابل هناك ؟

convinced   ٦ ‑ بماذا اقتنع الوالد نفسه ؟

٧ ‑ ماذا كانت نتيجة لقاء الحبيب بالعائلة ؟

٨ ‑ متى تزوّج الحبيبان ؟

293

المعلّم الأُمّــــي

illiterate

(من كتاب ألف ليلة وليلة)

قالت شَهْرَزادُ للملك شَهْريار :   Shahrazad

Shahriyar

يحكى أيّها الملك أنّ رجلا لا يعرف القراءة والكتابة لم يجـــد

عملا يعيش منه ••• ففتح مكتبا لتعليم الاولاد ••• وكان يطلب من كبارهم

تعليم صغارهم ، ويَكْتَفي بالاشراف عليهم •   contented himself with

وفي يوم من الايّام جاءت الى أحد الاولاد الذين في المكتب

رسالة من زوجها الغائِبِ في سفر بعيد ، فأخذت الرسالة وذهبت الـــى   absent

المكتب واعطتها للمعلّم كي يقرأها لها • فلمّا أخذ الرسالة منهـــــا

وقع في حَرَجٍ شَديدٍ ••• ولكنه قال لنفسه من الأحسن أن أتَظاهَـــــرَ   great embarrassment / I pretend

يقراءتها وأخبرها بأيّ شيءٍ مِنْ عِنْدي ••• وعلى هذا فتحها ووجد فيها قِطْعَةً   a piece of my own

قُماشٍ ثم أمْسَكَ الرسالة مَقْلوبَةً، مُتَظاهِرًا بأنّه يقرأ ما فيها • وانقضت   upside down / cloth; took hold of

مدّة وهو ساكت ••• فلمّا رأت المرأة ذلك ظَنَّتْ أنّ زوجها قد مات •• فقالت   she thought

للمعلّم وهي تَبْكي : أرجوك يا سيّدي : قل لى الحق • اذا كان زوجي قـــد   crying

مات اخبرني بذلك حتى أقوم بالواجب • فلمّا سمع كلامها ••• قال لهـا :

يا سيّدتي أنا لا أريد أن أُعْلِمَكِ بمثل هذا الخبر المُحْزِنِ • فحين سمعت   notify / saddening, sad

كلامه عرفت أنّ زوجها مات وخرجت من عنده وهي تَبْكي حُزْنًا على زوجهـا •   cries / out of sadness for

ولمّا وصلت بيتها اجتمع عندها الجيران لِتَعْزِيَتِها •••   to offer her their condolences

وكان زوجها قد أرسل مع رسالته اليها رسالة أخرى الى أحـــد

أصدقائه وفيها أنّه بخير ••• وأنّه عائد الى بلده وأهله وسيصل بعـــد

أيّام • فلمّا سمع صديقه هذا بما جرى لزوجته تَعَجَّبَ ••• وذهب اليهـا   he was amazed

وسألها : من الذي أخبرك بموت زوجك ؟ فأخبرته بما قال لها المعلّـــم

وأعطته الرسالة ••• فلمّا قرأها ضحك وقال لها : انّ هذه الرسالة ليس

فيها أيّ شيءٍ عن موت زوجك فقد أرسل لى زوجك رسالة أخرى وفيها أنّـــه

بـخير ••• وسيكون عندنا هنا بَعْدَ أيّام ، وقد حَمَلَ لَكِ معه كثيرا مـــن الـهـدايا ••••

عند ذلك ذهبت المرأة مع صديق زوجها الى المعلّم وقالت لـه :

كيف أخبرتنى بموت زوجى مَعَ أنَّهُ سيحضر قريبـا ••• ومعه الـهـدايـا الكثيرة ؟

فلمّا سمع المعلّم كلامها وقع فى حَرَجٍ شَديدٍ ولكنّه اعْتَذَرَ قائلا : انّى لمّا

رأيت الرسالة فيها قِطْعَةُ قُماشٍ رأيتـك تَبْكينَ ، اعتقدت أنّ زوجك مات وأنّ

تلك هى قِطْعَةٌ من القُماشِ الذى كُفِّنَّ بـه •

Drill 3. Written. Indicate whether the statement is true or false.

١ – أخذت قصّة " المعلّم الأُمّيّ " من كتاب " ألف ليلة وليلة " •

٢ – كان المعلّم يعرف القراءة والكتابة جيّدا •

٣ – كان بعض الطلّاب يعلّمون البعض الآخر •

٤ – جاءت الى المعلّم رسالة من زوج المرأة الغائِبِ •

٥ – قال المعلّم للمرأة انّه لا يعرف القراءة والكتابة •

٦ – أخبر المعلّم المرأة أنّ زوجها مات •

٧ – أسعد موت زوج المرأة المعلّم •

٨ – زار الجيران المرأة فى بيتها •

٩ – أخبر المرأة صديق زوجها أنّ زوجها لم يمت •

١٠ – لا يعرف صديق زوج المرأة القراءة والكتابة •

١١ – قال الزوج فى احدى رسالتيه انّه سوف يَحْمِلُ معه كثيرا من الـهـدايـا الى عائلته •

١٢ – أرسل الزوج رسالتين : واحدة الى زوجته وأخرى الى صديقه •

١٣ – قدّم المعلّم اعْتِذارَهُ لصديق الزوج •

(2) Listen to the passage on tape, then do Drill 4, which is based on it.

<u>Drill 4</u>. Written. Write a brief summary in English of the story on tape.

E. <u>General drills</u>.   هـ ـ   التمارين العامّة

<u>Drill 5</u>. Written. Cardinal and ordinal numbers.

    Write out the correct form of the numbers. <u>Ex</u>.

'I received the <u>three</u>
letters, but I read
the <u>third one</u> only.'

وصلتني الرسائل ألـ ٣ ، ولكنّى لم أقرأ

الّا الرسالة ألـ ٣ . ←

وصلتني الرسائل <u>الثلاث</u> ، ولكتّي لم أقرأ

الّا الرسالة <u>الثالثة</u> .

١ ـ قرأت الجمل ألـ ٥ ، فلم أفهم غير الجملة ألـ ٥ .

٢ ـ سمعت المحاضرات ألـ ٩ ، فلم تعجبنى الّا المحاضرة ألـ ٩ .

٣ ـ حكم البلاد ١٣ عاما ، وفى نهاية العام ألـ ١٣ مات .

٤ ـ عمل في الكلّية ٢٣ سنة ، ولكتّه لم يترقّ الّا فى نهاية السنة ألـ ٢٠ .

٥ ـ قاوم الشعب الحكم الاجنبيّ ٤٨ سنة ، وفى ألسنة ألـ ٤٨ حصل علـــــى

أستقلاله .

٦ ـ في الكتاب ١٦٩ درسا أهمّها الدرس ألـ ٦٩ .

<u>Drill 6</u>. Written. Question formation.

    Form questions using the following items, then write the answer to each
question.

هل ، أ ، أَلَمْ ، ألن ، لِمَ ، فيمَ ، مِمَّ ، عَمَّنْ ، كيف ، أين ، لماذا ،

متى ، حتّى متى ، مَنْ ، الى أين .

Transformation: Perfect passive ⟶ لـم + jussive passive.

فرّق بينهم • ⟶	'They were separated.' ⟶
لم يفرّق بينهم •	'They were not separated.'

٧ ــ احتيج الى عدد كبير من
العمّال •

٨ ــ صودقن •

٩ ــ أجّل الاجتماع •

١٠ ــ انتخب رئيسا للجمهوريّة •

١١ ــ استقبلت في المطار •

١ ــ أعطوا كتبا علميّة •

٢ ــ صدّق الخبر •

٣ ــ أذيعت الأخبار.

٤ ــ لقّب بالشاعر الوطنيّ •

٥ ــ سمّي بشيرا •

٦ ــ أقيمت حفلات كثيرة •

Drill 8. أنّ / أن clauses ⟶ verbal noun construction.

ذكر لي أنّه يرغب في زيارة اليمن، ⟵

ذكر لي رغبته في زيارة اليمن •

'He mentioned to me his desire
to visit Yemen.'

٩ ــ لا تحبّهم على الرغم من
أنّهم يهتمّون بأمرها •

١٠ ــ أنّكم تحتاجون الينا أمر
معروف •

١١ ــ لم يسمع بأن يحضر الاجتماع •

١٢ ــ ما السبب في أنّك أخرجتها
من المكتب ؟

١٣ ــ سافرت الى الشرق الاوسط قبل
أن أتعلّم اللغة العربية •

١٤ ــ يحتاج حلّ المشكلة الى أن
يتعاونوا •

١ ــ تغيّرت حياتها بعد أن قابلت
الرجل الذي تزوّجته •

٢ ــ سمعت بأنّهم غضبوا •

٣ ــ لم يغضبنا أنّكم أسأتم
الينا •

٤ ــ أدهشنا أنّكم رفضتم دعوتنا •

٥ ــ تحترمهم لانّهم يكافحون •

٦ ــ لم أكن أعلم بأنّهم أستقلّوا •

٧ ــ قابلت الأستاذ بعد أن انصرف
الطلّاب •

٨ ــ لا يعجبني أن يبقوا هنا •

<u>Drill 9</u>. Vocabulary.

Replace each of the expressions in parentheses by a single word having the same meaning.

١ – حكم القاضى بـ (التفريق بين الزوج وزوجته) .

٢ – أعجبته السيّارة ، <u>لِذُلِكَ</u> (قدّم المال ثمنًا لها وأخذها) . therefore

٣ – سمعت أنّ صديقك (حصل على وظيفة أعلى من الوظيفة التى كانت له) .

٤ – سوف يزداد عدد المصانع فى (السنوات القادمة) .

٥ – كان لى مال كثير ، ولكنّى (لم أستطع ان أجده) .

٦ – أكملت كتابة (بحث قدّمته الى الجامعة للحصول على شهادة) .

٧ – مصر دولة (يحكمها أبناؤها) .

٨ – نظام الحكم فى الأردن نظام (دولة يحكمها ملك) .

٩ – هذا (رجل يؤلّف الأشعار) .

١٠ – ألسيّد فَريد وَجْدي (متحدّث باسم بلاده) فى منظمة الامم المتحدة .

<u>Drill 10</u>. Written. Translation.

Some people in the West think that divorce is an easy matter in the Middle East; this is not true. If the husband and the wife encounter a serious family problem, and if they decide as a result to ask for a divorce, they must go to a judge. The judge looks into the matter and tries to resolve the problem. If he does not succeed, he grants the husband and the wife a divorce which protects (= "preserves") the rights of the sons and daughters.

 مَبْلَغ As for the <u>amount of money</u> which the wife gets at the time of the divorce, it is determined before the marriage. That money is called the dowry (أَلْمَهْرُ). The woman has the right to take all of her dowry before the marriage, or after the divorce, if divorce should take place.

298

Fill in the blanks in the following sentences with an appropriate word.

(ينفع ، عوضا عن ، وقف ، قرية ، أنقسم،أسعدني ، نشاط ، يغضب ، تضع،

قوانين ، سكت ، كاد ، بصر ، ربح ، الانسان ، القاضي ، أغضبه ، أمواله ،

الدنيا ، حول ، أرسل ، يخسر ، التفريق ، عهد ، قاموس) .

١ ــ حاولت ـــــــ ولكنّه لم ـــــــ .
   (get angry)

٢ ــ ألأمريكيّون يحترمون ـــــــ بلدهم .

٣ ــ حكم ـــــــ بينهما بـ ـــــــ .
   (separation)

٤ ــ ـــــــ خبر زواج ابنك .

٥ ــ ـــــــ عدد من الطلاب المصريّين للدراسة الى فرنسا .

٦ ــ ذلك الرجل الغنيّ أن ـــــــ ـــــــ كل ـــــــ .
   (almost)   (money)

٧ ــ عقد الأجتماع في القاهرة ـــــــ بيروت .

٨ ــ ـــــــ مدّة قصيرة ثم قالت لوالدتها أتّها تحب ابن الجيران .

٩ ــ ماذا ـــــــ الانسان لو ـــــــ ـــــــ وخسر نفسه .
   (the world)

١٠ ــ الرأي العام العالمى ـــــــ مشكلة الشرق الأوسط .
   (concerning)

١١ ــ المراسلون مدّة دقيقة احتراما لرئيس الجمهوريّة عندما

   بدأ مؤتمره الصحفى .

١٢ ــ ولد فى ـــــــ صغيرة وفقد ـــــــ ـه ـــــــ وهو في الخامسة من عمره .

١٣ ــ تقوم الأمم المتحدة بـ ـــــــ ثقافى واسع . لذلك ـــــــ الدول الصغرى

   ثقتها الكبيرة فيها .

أوستن ــ تكساس ٢٥ آب (أغسطس)١٩٧٥.

عزيزي سليم :

تحيّة أخويّة وبعد ، وصلتني رسالتك أمس ولم تكن قد وصلتنى منـك

(now to our topic: see p. 243)

أيّ رسائل منذ أكثر من ستة أشهر • لقد سررت جدّا برسالتك هذه كما

سرّني أيضا خبر نجاحك فى الامتحانات الحكومية وحصولك على شهــــادة

البكالوريوس بامْتِيازٍ • أرجو لك النجاح فى كل ما تقوم به من أعمال   with ho...

distinc...

وكلّى ثقة أنّك ستتابع دراستك للحصول على شهادة الماجستير فــــى

الجامعة الأمريكيّة فى بيروت • لقد أسعدني جدّا قولك انّ لك خَطيبَـــةً   fiancée

الآن تحبّـــك وتحبّـهــــا وتهتم بك وتهتم بـها • ألف سلام منّى اليها

على غَيْرِ مَعْرِفَةٍ •   even though I do not know her

نحن هنا مسرورون فى حياتنا الاجتماعيّة والدراسيّة على الرغم

من أنّ أوضاعنا الماليّة ليست حسنة جدّا • أنا أدرس العُلومَ اللّغويّة   linguis-tics

وأدرّس اللّغة العربيّة هنا فى جامعة تكساس وزوجتى تدرس العلـــوم

السياسيّة • لقد قابلنا كثيرا من الناس هنا واصبح لنا أصدقاءكثيرون •

وأود أن اخبرك أنّ الشعب الأمريكى كالشعب العربىّ شعب يمتاز بالكَرَمِ   generosity

فالأمريكى يكرم الضيف ويقدّم للأجنبى كل ما يستطيع تقديمه مـــــن

مساعدة •

الأساتذة الذين يدرسوننى من كبار الاساتذة فى الولايات المتحدة

وهم يقومون بكل ما يجب القيام به لمساعدتى فى مختلف الميادين • انّى

اشعر أنّ معرفتى بالمواضيع التى ادرسها تزداد يوما بعد يوم وهـــذا

بسبب مساعدة اساتذتي لي • لقد بدأت منذ مدة قصيرة بكتابة رسالـــة

الدكتوراه وانا أبذل الآن كل الجهود فى انهاء هذه الرسالة وجعلهــا

رسالة تعجب اساتذتى •

ارجو أن تجيبنى على رسالتى هذه عندما يسمح لك الوقت بـذلـــك

كما ارجو ان تبقى على اتصال وأن لا تنقطع الرسائل بيننا يا صديقـــى

العزيز •

سلامى الى جميع الاهل والاصدقاء٠ من عندنا جميع أصدقاؤك يرسلون

لك سلامهم ٠   المخلص

أحمد امـــــــام

Drill 13. Written. Vocabulary.

Taking into consideration the meanings of the various patterns of the
verb, and with the help of the dictionary, show how the following groups
of words are related:

١ـ علـم ـ علّم ـ اعلم ـ تعلّم ـ استعلم

٢ـ عجب ـ أعجب ـ تعجّب

٣ـ خرج ـ خرّج ـ تخرّج ـ استخرج

٤ـ بدل ـ بادل ـ تبادل ـ استبدل

٥ـ فقد ـ افقد ـ افتقد ـ استفقد

٦ـ قطع ـ قطّع ـ قاطع ـ أقطع ـ تقطّع ـ انقطع ـ اقتطع ـ استقطع

الدرس الخامس والاربعون

أ ـ آيات وأحاديث

(١) ـ آيات

١ ـ وإذا قرىء القرآن فاستمعوا له وانصتوا لعلكم ترحمون (٢٠٤ الأعراف)

٢ ـ وإذا حييتم بتحيّة فحيّوا بأحسن منها او ردّوها (٨٦ النساء)

٣ ـ انّ الذين آمنوا والذين هادوا والنصارى والصابـئين مــن آمن بالله واليوم الآخر وعمل صالحا فلـهم أجرهم عند ربّهم ولا خوف عليـهم ولا هم يحزنون (٦٢ البقرة)

٤ ـ ولو شاء ربّك لجعل الناس أمّة واحدة (١١٨ هود)

٥ ـ ان تقرضوا الله قرضا حسنا يضاعفه لكم (١٧ التغابـن)

٦ ـ ان ينصركم الله فلا غالب لكم (١٦٠ آل عمران)

٧ ـ فأمّا اليتيم فلا تقـهر

وأمّا السائل فلا تنـهر

وأمّا بـنعمة ربّك فحدّث (٩ ، ١٠ ، ١١ الضحى)

٨ ـ من عمل صالحا فلنفسه ومن أساء فعليها (٤٦ فصّلت)

٩ ـ وقضى ربّك ألّا تعبدوا الّا ايّاه وبالوالدين احسانا .... فـلا تقل لـهما أفّ ولا تنهرهما وقل لـهما قولا كريما. واخفض لهما جناح الذلّ من الرحمة وقل ربّ ارحمهما كما ربّياني صغيرا.
(٢٣ و ٢٤ بني اسرائيل)

(٢) ـ أحاديث

١٠ ـ من مات وهو يعلم أنّه لا اله الا الله دخل الجنّة .

١١ ـ لا يؤمن أحدكم حتى يحبّ لأخيه ما يحب لنفسه .

A. Qur'anic Verses and Hadiths

Qur'anic Verses and Sayings of the Prophet

(1). Verses from the Qur'an (1)

1. When the Koran is recited listen to it attentively and perhaps you will find mercy.* (Sura VII, "The Heights", verse 204)

2. And when you are greeted with a greeting, answer with a nicer greeting, or with the same one. (Sura IV, "Women", verse 86)

3. Those who believe (in the Qur-an),/ And those who follow the Jewish (scriptures),/ And the Christians and the Sabians,-/ Any who believe in God/ And the Last Day,/ And work righteousness,/ Shall have their reward/ With their Lord: on them/ Shall be no fear, nor shall they grieve.* (Sura II, "The Heifer", verse 62)

4. If your Lord had willed he would have made all people one nation. (Sura XI, "Hūd", verse 118)

5. If you make a good loan to God, He will double it for you. (Sura LXIV, "Mutual Fraud", verse 17)

6. If God helps you no one can overcome you. (Sura III, "The Family of Imran", verse 160)

7. Therefore, treat not/ The orphan with harshness,/* Nor repulse the petitioner/ (unheard);/* But the Bounty/ Of Thy Lord-/ Rehearse and proclaim!* (Sura XCIII, "The Glorious Morning Light", verses 9-11)

8. Whoever does what is right gains by it; he who does evil pays for it. (Sura XLI, "Distinguished", verse 46)

---

(1) Abdullah Yusuf Ali, The Holy Quran. Text, Translation and Commentary. Vol. I. McGregor & Werner, Inc., 1946 is the source for the translation of Suras 3, 7 and 9.

9. Thy Lord hath decreed/ That ye worship none but Him,/ And that ye be kind/ To parents.../ Say not to them a word/ Of contempt, nor repel them,/ But address them/ In terms of honour.* And, out of kindness,/ Lower to them the wing/ Of humility, and say:/ "My Lord! bestow on them/ Thy Mercy even as they/ Cherished me in childhood."* (Sura XVII "The Children of Israel", verses 23-24)

(2). <u>Sayings of the Prophet</u>

10. He who dies knowing that there is no god but God will enter Paradise.

11. No one among you is a believer until he wants for his brother what he wants for himself.

ب – شعر

العـــــراك

لِمِخائيل نُعَيْمَة

دخل الشيطان قلبى فرأى فيه مـــلاك
وبلمح الطّرف ما بينهما اشتدّ العراك
ذا يقول: البيت بيتى ! فيعيد القول ذاك
وانا اشهد ما يجرى ولا ابدى حــراك
سائلا ربّى : " أفى الاكوان من ربّ سواك "
جبلت قلبى من الهدء يداه ويــداك " ؟
والى اليوم أرانى فى شكوك وارتبـاك
لست أدرى أرجيم فى فؤادى أم مــلاك •

304

The Struggle

by Mikha'īl Nuᶜaymi

The Devil entered my heart, and in it saw an angel.

And in the twinkling of an eye a violent fight broke out between them.

One says, "This house is mine!" and the other says it's his,

While I witness what goes on, without moving a muscle,

Asking my Lord: "Is there in all creation a god besides You,

Whose hand, together with yours, fashioned my heart from the beginning?"

And until today I see myself in doubt and confusion,

Not knowing whether in my heart is a demon or an angel.

<u>Meter</u>. The meter of this poem is رَمَلْ Ramal, one of the sixteen traditional meters of Arabic poetry. The pattern for this poem is

‿ ⌣ — — | ‿ ⌣ — — ‖ ‿ ⌣ — — | ‿ ⌣ —

in which ⌣ is a "light" syllable (ending in a short vowel, e.g. دَخَلَ = ⌣ ⌣ ⌣) and — is a "heavy" syllable (anything else, e.g. قَلْبِـي = — —). The first hemistich of each line contains two feet of four syllables: the first is long or short (‿), the second must be short (⌣), and the last two must be long (— —), giving ‿ ⌣ — — . The last foot of the line has only three syllables. Elision (waṣla) must be rigidly observed; and the end of the line is in pausal form (الـمَلاك، الـجِـراك , etc.) to facilitate the rhyme.

B. <u>Grammar and drills</u>   ج ‑ الـقواعد والـتمارين

---

1. The particle إِيّا‑ : Summary

---

1. The particle إيّا‑ : Summary

The particle إيّا‑ only occurs with a pronoun suffix and is equivalent to putting that suffix in the accusative case: إِيّاهُ 'him', إِيّاكَ 'you', إِيّايَ

305

'me', إِيَّانَا 'us', etc. This pronoun is the object of a verb but is not suffix-ed to the verb. One instance of this is as the second accusative object of a verb (see L.44.C.3), as in

| أَعْطَى الْجَارِيَةَ إِيَّاهُ . | 'He gave it to the slave girl.' |

Two other uses are found in the Koran:

(1) <u>Pronoun object preceding verb for emphasis</u>:

| إِيَّاكَ نَعْبُدُ وَإِيَّاكَ نَسْتَعِينُ . | <u>Thee</u> we worship and <u>Thee</u> we turn to for help.' (Sura I, "The Opening", verse 4) |

(2) <u>Pronoun object separated from verb</u> (see Text A, 9 above):

| وَقَضَى رَبُّكَ أَلَّا تَعْبُدُوا إِلَّا إِيَّاهُ . | 'And your Lord has decreed that you worship only Him.' (Sura XVII, "The Children of Israel", verse 23) |

The final two uses given here are common in Modern Standard Arabic:

(3) The particle - إِيَّا with a following أَنْ clause means "be careful not to...", as in

| إِيَّاكَ أَنْ تَقُولَ ذَلِكَ ! | 'Take care not to say that!' |

(4) When a verb with an accusative object is nominalized (transformed into a verbal noun) the object remains in the accusative case:

| أَغْضَبَهَا أَنَّهُمْ رَفَضُوا دَعْوَتَهَا . | 'It angered her that they rejected her invitation.' |
| أَغْضَبَهَا رَفْضُهُمْ دَعْوَتَهَا . | 'Their rejecting her invitation angered her.' |

If the object of the verb is a pronoun suffix, that pronoun suffix is attached to إِيَّا - after the verbal noun:

> أغضبها انهم رفضوها .   'It angered her that they rejected it.'
>
> اغضبها رفضهم اياها .   'Their rejecting it angered her.'

This matter does not arise with verb-preposition idioms, since the object--
whether noun or pronoun--will be the object of the preposition, as in

> سرّنا حصوله عليها .   'His obtaining it pleased us.'

Now do Drill 1.

Drill 1. Transformation: Noun object ➔ pronoun object.

'Your rejecting our invitation   ➔   أدهشنا رفضكم دعوتنا .
amazed us.'

'Your rejecting it amazed us.'   أدهشنا رفضكم اياها .

١ ـ متى موعد طبعكم الكتاب الجديد ؟

٢ ـ ما سبب ادخالهم المفردات على هذا الدرس ؟

٣ ـ هل تمكّنت من بيعهم الهدية ؟

٤ ـ طالبنا بمنحهم سليم المال .

٥ ـ سمعت باعدادهم الامتحانات القادمة .

Table 1. Sound verbs: Form I. دَرَسَ (ُ) 'to study'

| | ACTIVE | | | | | PASSIVE | |
	Perfect	Indicative	Subjunctive	Jussive	Imperative	Perfect	Indicative
3 MS	دَرَسَ	يَدْرُسُ	يَدْرُسَ	يَدْرُسْ		دُرِسَ	يُدْرَسُ
FS	دَرَسَتْ	تَدْرُسُ	تَدْرُسَ	تَدْرُسْ		دُرِسَتْ	تُدْرَسُ
2 MS	دَرَسْتَ	تَدْرُسُ	تَدْرُسَ	تَدْرُسْ	أُدْرُسْ	دُرِسْتَ	تُدْرَسُ
FS	دَرَسْتِ	تَدْرُسِينَ	تَدْرُسِي	تَدْرُسِي	أُدْرُسِي	دُرِسْتِ	تُدْرَسِينَ
1 S	دَرَسْتُ	أَدْرُسُ	أَدْرُسَ	أَدْرُسْ		دُرِسْتُ	أُدْرَسُ
3 MD	دَرَسَا	يَدْرُسَانِ	يَدْرُسَا	يَدْرُسَا		دُرِسَا	يُدْرَسَانِ
FD	دَرَسَتَا	تَدْرُسَانِ	تَدْرُسَا	تَدْرُسَا		دُرِسَتَا	تُدْرَسَانِ
2 D	دَرَسْتُمَا	تَدْرُسَانِ	تَدْرُسَا	تَدْرُسَا	أُدْرُسَا	دُرِسْتُمَا	تُدْرَسَانِ
3 MP	دَرَسُوا	يَدْرُسُونَ	يَدْرُسُوا	يَدْرُسُوا		دُرِسُوا	يُدْرَسُونَ
FP	دَرَسْنَ	يَدْرُسْنَ	يَدْرُسْنَ	يَدْرُسْنَ		دُرِسْنَ	يُدْرَسْنَ
2 MP	دَرَسْتُمْ	تَدْرُسُونَ	تَدْرُسُوا	تَدْرُسُوا	أُدْرُسُوا	دُرِسْتُمْ	تُدْرَسُونَ
FP	دَرَسْتُنَّ	تَدْرُسْنَ	تَدْرُسْنَ	تَدْرُسْنَ	أُدْرُسْنَ	دُرِسْتُنَّ	تُدْرَسْنَ
1 P	دَرَسْنَا	نَدْرُسُ	نَدْرُسَ	نَدْرُسْ		دُرِسْنا	تُدْرَسُ

Participles: دَارِسٌ مَدْرُوسٌ

Verbal noun: دِرَاسَةٌ دَرْسٌ

Other Form I stem vowel patterns are:

a - a, e.g. ذَهَبَ 'to go'

a - i, e.g. رَجَعَ 'to return'

i - a, e.g. شَرِبَ 'to drink'

u - u, e.g. كَرُمَ 'to be noble'

Table 2. Sound verbs: Form II. دَرَّسَ 'to instruct'

	ACTIVE					PASSIVE	
	Perfect	Indicative	Subjunctive	Jussive	Imperative	Perfect	Indicative
3 MS	دَرَّسَ	يُدَرِّسُ	يُدَرِّسَ	يُدَرِّسْ		دُرِّسَ	يُدَرَّسُ
FS	دَرَّسَتْ	تُدَرِّسُ	تُدَرِّسَ	تُدَرِّسْ		دُرِّسَتْ	تُدَرَّسُ
2 MS	دَرَّسْتَ	تُدَرِّسُ	تُدَرِّسَ	تُدَرِّسْ	دَرِّسْ	دُرِّسْتَ	تُدَرَّسُ
FS	دَرَّسْتِ	تُدَرِّسِينَ	تُدَرِّسِي	تُدَرِّسِي	دَرِّسِي	دُرِّسْتِ	تُدَرَّسِي
1 S	دَرَّسْتُ	أُدَرِّسُ	أُدَرِّسَ	أُدَرِّسْ		دُرِّسْتُ	أُدَرَّسُ
3 MD	دَرَّسا	يُدَرِّسانِ	يُدَرِّسا	يُدَرِّسا		دُرِّسا	يُدَرَّسانِ
FD	دَرَّسَتا	تُدَرِّسانِ	تُدَرِّسا	تُدَرِّسا		دُرِّسَتا	تُدَرَّسانِ
2 D	دَرَّسْتُما	تُدَرِّسانِ	تُدَرِّسا	تُدَرِّسا	دَرِّسا	دُرِّسْتُما	تُدَرَّسانِ
3 MP	دَرَّسوا	يُدَرِّسونَ	يُدَرِّسوا	يُدَرِّسوا		دُرِّسوا	يُدَرَّسونَ
FP	دَرَّسْنَ	يُدَرِّسْنَ	يُدَرِّسْنَ	يُدَرِّسْنَ		دُرِّسْنَ	يُدَرَّسْنَ
2 MP	دَرَّسْتُمْ	تُدَرِّسونَ	تُدَرِّسوا	تُدَرِّسوا	دَرِّسوا	دُرِّسْتُمْ	تُدَرَّسونَ
FP	دَرَّسْتُنَّ	تُدَرِّسْنَ	تُدَرِّسْنَ	تُدَرِّسْنَ	دَرِّسْنَ	دُرِّسْتُنَّ	تُدَرَّسْنَ
1 P	دَرَّسْنا	نُدَرِّسُ	نُدَرِّسَ	نُدَرِّسْ		دُرِّسْنا	نُدَرَّسُ

Participles: مُدَرِّسٌ   مُدَرَّسٌ

Verbal noun: تَدْريسٌ

309

Table 3. Sound verbs: Form III. شَاهَدَ 'to witness'

	ACTIVE					PASSIVE	
	Perfect	Indicative	Subjunctive	Jussive	Imperative	Perfect	Indicative
3 MS	شَاهَدَ	يُشَاهِدُ	يُشَاهِدَ	يُشَاهِدْ		شُوهِدَ	يُشَاهَدُ
FS	شَاهَدَتْ	تُشَاهِدُ	تُشَاهِدَ	تُشَاهِدْ		شُوهِدَتْ	تُشَاهَدُ
2 MS	شَاهَدْتَ	تُشَاهِدُ	تُشَاهِدَ	تُشَاهِدْ	شَاهِدْ	شُوهِدْتَ	تُشَاهَدُ
FS	شَاهَدْتِ	تُشَاهِدِينَ	تُشَاهِدِي	تُشَاهِدِي	شَاهِدِي	شُوهِدْتِ	تُشَاهَدِينَ
1 S	شَاهَدْتُ	أُشَاهِدُ	أُشَاهِدَ	أُشَاهِدْ		شُوهِدْتُ	أُشَاهَدُ
3 MD	شَاهَدَا	يُشَاهِدَانِ	يُشَاهِدَا	يُشَاهِدَا		شُوهِدَا	يُشَاهَدَانِ
FD	شَاهَدَتَا	تُشَاهِدَانِ	تُشَاهِدَا	تُشَاهِدَا		شُوهِدَتَا	تُشَاهَدَانِ
2 D	شَاهَدْتُمَا	تُشَاهِدَانِ	تُشَاهِدَا	تُشَاهِدَا	شَاهِدَا	شُوهِدْتُمَا	تُشَاهَدَانِ
3 MP	شَاهَدُوا	يُشَاهِدُونَ	يُشَاهِدُوا	يُشَاهِدُوا		شُوهِدُوا	يُشَاهَدُونَ
FP	شَاهَدْنَ	يُشَاهِدْنَ	يُشَاهِدْنَ	يُشَاهِدْنَ		شُوهِدْنَ	يُشَاهَدْنَ
2 MP	شَاهَدْتُمْ	تُشَاهِدُونَ	تُشَاهِدُوا	تُشَاهِدُوا	شَاهِدُوا	شُوهِدْتُمْ	تُشَاهَدُونَ
FP	شَاهَدْتُنَّ	تُشَاهِدْنَ	تُشَاهِدْنَ	تُشَاهِدْنَ	شَاهِدْنَ	شُوهِدْتُنَّ	تُشَاهَدْنَ
1 P	شَاهَدْنَا	نُشَاهِدُ	نُشَاهِدَ	نُشَاهِدْ		شُوهِدْنَا	نُشَاهَدُ

Participles: مُشَاهِدٌ   مُشَاهَدٌ

Verbal noun: مُشَاهَدَةٌ

Table 4. Sound verbs: Form IV. أَكْرَمَ 'to honor'

	Perfect	Indicative	Subjunctive	Jussive	Imperative	Perfect	Indicative
		ACTIVE				PASSIVE	
3 MS	أَكْرَمَ	يُكْرِمُ	يُكْرِمَ	يُكْرِمْ		أُكْرِمَ	يُكْرَمُ
FS	أَكْرَمَتْ	تُكْرِمُ	تُكْرِمَ	تُكْرِمْ		أُكْرِمَتْ	تُكْرَمُ
2 MS	أَكْرَمْتَ	تُكْرِمُ	تُكْرِمَ	تُكْرِمْ	أَكْرِمْ	أُكْرِمْتَ	تُكْرَمُ
FS	أَكْرَمْتِ	تُكْرِمِينَ	تُكْرِمِي	تُكْرِمِي	أَكْرِمِي	أُكْرِمْتِ	تُكْرَمِينَ
1 S	أَكْرَمْتُ	أُكْرِمُ	أُكْرِمَ	أُكْرِمْ		أُكْرِمْتُ	أُكْرَمُ
3 MD	أَكْرَمَا	يُكْرِمَانِ	يُكْرِمَا	يُكْرِمَا		أُكْرِمَا	يُكْرَمَانِ
FD	أَكْرَمَتَا	تُكْرِمَانِ	تُكْرِمَا	تُكْرِمَا		أُكْرِمَتَا	تُكْرَمَانِ
2 D	أَكْرَمْتُمَا	تُكْرِمَانِ	تُكْرِمَا	تُكْرِمَا	أَكْرِمَا	أُكْرِمْتُمَا	تُكْرَمَانِ
3 MP	أَكْرَمُوا	يُكْرِمُونَ	يُكْرِمُوا	يُكْرِمُوا		أُكْرِمُوا	يُكْرَمُونَ
FP	أَكْرَمْنَ	يُكْرِمْنَ	يُكْرِمْنَ	يُكْرِمْنَ		أُكْرِمْنَ	يُكْرَمْنَ
2 MP	أَكْرَمْتُمْ	تُكْرِمُونَ	تُكْرِمُوا	تُكْرِمُوا	أَكْرِمُوا	أُكْرِمْتُمْ	تُكْرَمُونَ
FP	أَكْرَمْتُنَّ	تُكْرِمْنَ	تُكْرِمْنَ	تُكْرِمْنَ	أَكْرِمْنَ	أُكْرِمْتُنَّ	تُكْرَمْنَ
1 P	أَكْرَمْنَا	نُكْرِمُ	نُكْرِمَ	نُكْرِمْ		أُكْرِمْنَا	نُكْرَمُ

Participles: مُكْرِمٌ مُكْرَمٌ

Verbal noun: إِكْرَامٌ

311

Table 5. Sound verbs: Form V.   تَقَدَّمَ   'to advance, progress'

| | ACTIVE | | | | | PASSIVE | |
	Perfect	Indicative	Subjunctive	Jussive	Imperative	Perfect	Indicative
3 MS	تَقَدَّمَ	يَتَقَدَّمُ	يَتَقَدَّمَ	يَتَقَدَّمْ			
FS	تَقَدَّمَتْ	تَتَقَدَّمُ	تَتَقَدَّمَ	تَتَقَدَّمْ			
2 MS	تَقَدَّمْتَ	تَتَقَدَّمُ	تَتَقَدَّمَ	تَتَقَدَّمْ	تَقَدَّمْ		
FS	تَقَدَّمْتِ	تَتَقَدَّمِينَ	تَتَقَدَّمِي	تَتَقَدَّمِي	تَقَدَّمِي		
1 S	تَقَدَّمْتُ	أَتَقَدَّمُ	أَتَقَدَّمَ	أَتَقَدَّمْ			
3 MD	تَقَدَّما	يَتَقَدَّمانِ	يَتَقَدَّما	يَتَقَدَّما			
FD	تَقَدَّمَتا	تَتَقَدَّمانِ	تَتَقَدَّما	تَتَقَدَّما			
2 D	تَقَدَّمْتُما	تَتَقَدَّمانِ	تَتَقَدَّما	تَتَقَدَّما	تَقَدَّما		
3 MP	تَقَدَّموا	يَتَقَدَّمُونَ	يَتَقَدَّموا	يَتَقَدَّموا			
FP	تَقَدَّمْنَ	يَتَقَدَّمْنَ	يَتَقَدَّمْنَ	يَتَقَدَّمْنَ			
2 MP	تَقَدَّمْتُمْ	تَتَقَدَّمُونَ	تَتَقَدَّموا	تَتَقَدَّموا	تَقَدَّموا		
FP	تَقَدَّمْتُنَّ	تَتَقَدَّمْنَ	تَتَقَدَّمْنَ	تَتَقَدَّمْنَ	تَقَدَّمْنَ		
1 P	تَقَدَّمْنا	نَتَقَدَّمُ	نَتَقَدَّمَ	نَتَقَدَّمْ			

Participles: مُتَقَدِّمٌ

Verbal noun: تَقَدُّمٌ

The verb has no passive; the passive of   تَعَلَّمَ   'to learn' is   تُعُلِّمَ   'it was learned'.

Table 6. Sound verbs: Form VI.   تَنَاوَلَ   'to take up; deal with'

	Perfect	Indicative	Subjunctive	Jussive	Imperative	Perfect	Indicative
		ACTIVE				PASSIVE	
3 MS	تَنَاوَلَ	يَتَنَاوَلُ	يَتَنَاوَلَ	يَتَنَاوَلْ			
FS	تَنَاوَلَتْ	تَتَنَاوَلُ	تَتَنَاوَلَ	تَتَنَاوَلْ			
2 MS	تَنَاوَلْتَ	تَتَنَاوَلُ	تَتَنَاوَلَ	تَتَنَاوَلْ	تَنَاوَلْ		
FS	تَنَاوَلْتِ	تَتَنَاوَلِينَ	تَتَنَاوَلِي	تَتَنَاوَلِي	تَنَاوَلِي		
1 S	تَنَاوَلْتُ	أَتَنَاوَلُ	أَتَنَاوَلَ	أَتَنَاوَلْ			
3 MD	تَنَاوَلَا	يَتَنَاوَلَانِ	يَتَنَاوَلَا	يَتَنَاوَلَا			
FD	تَنَاوَلَتَا	تَتَنَاوَلَانِ	تَتَنَاوَلَا	تَتَنَاوَلَا			
2 D	تَنَاوَلْتُمَا	تَتَنَاوَلَانِ	تَتَنَاوَلَا	تَتَنَاوَلَا	تَنَاوَلَا		
3 MP	تَنَاوَلُوا	يَتَنَاوَلُونَ	يَتَنَاوَلُوا	يَتَنَاوَلُوا			
FP	تَنَاوَلْنَ	يَتَنَاوَلْنَ	يَتَنَاوَلْنَ	يَتَنَاوَلْنَ			
2 MP	تَنَاوَلْتُمْ	تَتَنَاوَلُونَ	تَتَنَاوَلُوا	تَتَنَاوَلُوا	تَنَاوَلُوا		
FP	تَنَاوَلْتُنَّ	تَتَنَاوَلْنَ	تَتَنَاوَلْنَ	تَتَنَاوَلْنَ	تَنَاوَلْنَ		
1 P	تَنَاوَلْنَا	نَتَنَاوَلُ	نَتَنَاوَلَ	نَتَنَاوَلْ			

Participles: مُتَنَاوِلٌ

Verbal noun: تَنَاوُلٌ

The passive of this verb is rare; its form is   تُنُووِلَ   'it was taken'.

313

Table 7. Sound verbs: Form VII. اِنْصَرَفَ 'to go away'

| | ACTIVE | | | | | PASSIVE | |
	Perfect	Indicative	Subjunctive	Jussive	Imperative	Perfect	Indicative
3 MS	اِنْصَرَفَ	يَنْصَرِفُ	يَنْصَرِفَ	يَنْصَرِفْ			
FS	اِنْصَرَفَتْ	تَنْصَرِفُ	تَنْصَرِفَ	تَنْصَرِفْ			
2 MS	اِنْصَرَفْتَ	تَنْصَرِفُ	تَنْصَرِفَ	تَنْصَرِفْ	اِنْصَرِفْ		
FS	اِنْصَرَفْتِ	تَنْصَرِفِينَ	تَنْصَرِفِي	تَنْصَرِفِي	اِنْصَرِفِي		
1 S	اِنْصَرَفْتُ	أَنْصَرِفُ	أَنْصَرِفَ	أَنْصَرِفْ			
3 MD	اِنْصَرَفَا	يَنْصَرِفَانِ	يَنْصَرِفَا	يَنْصَرِفَا			
FD	اِنْصَرَفَتَا	تَنْصَرِفَانِ	تَنْصَرِفَا	تَنْصَرِفَا			
2 D	اِنْصَرَفْتُمَا	تَنْصَرِفَانِ	تَنْصَرِفَا	تَنْصَرِفَا	اِنْصَرِفَا		
3 MP	اِنْصَرَفُوا	يَنْصَرِفُونَ	يَنْصَرِفُوا	يَنْصَرِفُوا			
FP	اِنْصَرَفْنَ	يَنْصَرِفْنَ	يَنْصَرِفْنَ	يَنْصَرِفْنَ			
2 MP	اِنْصَرَفْتُمْ	تَنْصَرِفُونَ	تَنْصَرِفُوا	تَنْصَرِفُوا	اِنْصَرِفُوا		
FP	اِنْصَرَفْتُنَّ	تَنْصَرِفْنَ	تَنْصَرِفْنَ	تَنْصَرِفْنَ	اِنْصَرِفْنَ		
1 P	اِنْصَرَفْنَا	نَنْصَرِفُ	نَنْصَرِفَ	نَنْصَرِفْ			

Participles: مُنْصَرِفٌ

Verbal noun: اِنْصِرَافٌ

Form VII has no passive.

314

Table 8. Sound verbs: Form VIII. اِنْتَخَبَ 'to elect'

	ACTIVE					PASSIVE	
	Perfect	Indicative	Subjunctive	Jussive	Imperative	Perfect	Indicative
3 MS	اِنْتَخَبَ	يَنْتَخِبُ	يَنْتَخِبَ	يَنْتَخِبْ		أُنْتُخِبَ	يُنْتَخَبُ
FS	اِنْتَخَبَتْ	تَنْتَخِبُ	تَنْتَخِبَ	تَنْتَخِبْ		أُنْتُخِبَتْ	تُنْتَخَبُ
2 MS	اِنْتَخَبْتَ	تَنْتَخِبُ	تَنْتَخِبَ	تَنْتَخِبْ	اِنْتَخِبْ	أُنْتُخِبْتَ	تُنْتَخَبُ
FS	اِنْتَخَبْتِ	تَنْتَخِبِينَ	تَنْتَخِبِي	تَنْتَخِبِي	اِنْتَخِبِي	أُنْتُخِبْتِ	تُنْتَخَبِينَ
1 S	اِنْتَخَبْتُ	أَنْتَخِبُ	أَنْتَخِبَ	أَنْتَخِبْ		أُنْتُخِبْتُ	أُنْتَخَبُ
3 MD	اِنْتَخَبَا	يَنْتَخِبَانِ	يَنْتَخِبَا	يَنْتَخِبَا		أُنْتُخِبَا	يُنْتَخَبَانِ
FD	اِنْتَخَبَتَا	تَنْتَخِبَانِ	تَنْتَخِبَا	تَنْتَخِبَا		أُنْتُخِبَتَا	تُنْتَخَبَانِ
2 D	اِنْتَخَبْتُمَا	تَنْتَخِبَانِ	تَنْتَخِبَا	تَنْتَخِبَا	اِنْتَخِبَا	أُنْتُخِبْتُمَا	تُنْتَخَبَانِ
3 MP	اِنْتَخَبُوا	يَنْتَخِبُونَ	يَنْتَخِبُوا	يَنْتَخِبُوا		أُنْتُخِبُوا	يُنْتَخَبُونَ
FP	اِنْتَخَبْنَ	يَنْتَخِبْنَ	يَنْتَخِبْنَ	يَنْتَخِبْنَ		أُنْتُخِبْنَ	يُنْتَخَبْنَ
2 MP	اِنْتَخَبْتُمْ	تَنْتَخِبُونَ	تَنْتَخِبُوا	تَنْتَخِبُوا	اِنْتَخِبُوا	أُنْتُخِبْتُمْ	تُنْتَخَبُونَ
FP	اِنْتَخَبْتُنَّ	تَنْتَخِبْنَ	تَنْتَخِبْنَ	تَنْتَخِبْنَ	اِنْتَخِبْنَ	أُنْتُخِبْتُنَّ	تُنْتَخَبْنَ
1 P	اِنْتَخَبْنَا	نَنْتَخِبُ	نَنْتَخِبَ	نَنْتَخِبْ		أُنْتُخِبْنَا	نُنْتَخَبُ

Participles: مُنْتَخِبٌ   مُنْتَخَبٌ

Verbal noun: اِنْتِخَابٌ

Table 9. Sound verbs: Form IX. اِحْمَرَّ 'to turn red'

| | ACTIVE | | | | | PASSIVE | |
	Perfect	Indicative	Subjunctive	Jussive	Imperative	Perfect	Indicative
3 MS	اِحْمَرَّ	يَحْمَرُّ	يَحْمَرَّ	يَحْمَرَّ			
FS	اِحْمَرَّتْ	تَحْمَرُّ	تَحْمَرَّ	تَحْمَرَّ			
2 MS	اِحْمَرَرْتَ	تَحْمَرُّ	تَحْمَرَّ	تَحْمَرَّ	اِحْمَرَّ		
FS	اِحْمَرَرْتِ	تَحْمَرِّينَ	تَحْمَرِّي	تَحْمَرِّي	اِحْمَرِّي		
1 S	اِحْمَرَرْتُ	أَحْمَرُّ	أَحْمَرَّ	أَحْمَرَّ			
3 MD	اِحْمَرَّا	يَحْمَرَّانِ	يَحْمَرَّا	يَحْمَرَّا			
FD	اِحْمَرَّتَا	تَحْمَرَّانِ	تَحْمَرَّا	تَحْمَرَّا			
2 D	اِحْمَرَرْتُمَا	تَحْمَرَّانِ	تَحْمَرَّا	تَحْمَرَّا	اِحْمَرَّا		
3 MP	اِحْمَرُّوا	يَحْمَرُّونَ	يَحْمَرُّوا	يَحْمَرُّوا			
FP	اِحْمَرَرْنَ	يَحْمَرِرْنَ	يَحْمَرِرْنَ	يَحْمَرِرْنَ			
2 MP	اِحْمَرَرْتُمْ	تَحْمَرُّونَ	تَحْمَرُّوا	تَحْمَرُّوا	اِحْمَرُّوا		
FP	اِحْمَرَرْتُنَّ	تَحْمَرِرْنَ	تَحْمَرِرْنَ	تَحْمَرِرْنَ	اِحْمَرِرْنَ		
1 P	اِحْمَرَرْنا	نَحْمَرُّ	نَحْمَرَّ	نَحْمَرَّ			

Participles: مُحْمَرٌّ

Verbal noun: اِحْمِرارٌ

Form IX has no passive.

316

Table 10. Strong verbs: Form X. اِسْتَقْبَلَ 'to receive'

	ACTIVE					PASSIVE	
	Perfect	Indicative	Subjunctive	Jussive	Imperative	Perfect	Indicative
3 MS	اِسْتَقْبَلَ	يَسْتَقْبِلُ	يَسْتَقْبِلَ	يَسْتَقْبِلْ		أُسْتُقْبِلَ	يُسْتَقْبَلُ
FS	اِسْتَقْبَلَتْ	تَسْتَقْبِلُ	تَسْتَقْبِلَ	تَسْتَقْبِلْ		أُسْتُقْبِلَتْ	تُسْتَقْبَلُ
2 MS	اِسْتَقْبَلْتَ	تَسْتَقْبِلُ	تَسْتَقْبِلَ	تَسْتَقْبِلْ	اِسْتَقْبِلْ	أُسْتُقْبِلْتَ	تُسْتَقْبَلُ
FS	اِسْتَقْبَلْتِ	تَسْتَقْبِلينَ	تَسْتَقْبِلي	تَسْتَقْبِلي	اِسْتَقْبِلي	أُسْتُقْبِلْتِ	تُسْتَقْبَلينَ
1 S	اِسْتَقْبَلْتُ	أَسْتَقْبِلُ	أَسْتَقْبِلَ	أَسْتَقْبِلْ		أُسْتُقْبِلْتُ	أُسْتَقْبَلُ
3 MD	اِسْتَقْبَلا	يَسْتَقْبِلانِ	يَسْتَقْبِلا	يَسْتَقْبِلا		أُسْتُقْبِلا	يُسْتَقْبَلانِ
FD	اِسْتَقْبَلَتا	تَسْتَقْبِلانِ	تَسْتَقْبِلا	تَسْتَقْبِلا		أُسْتُقْبِلَتا	تُسْتَقْبَلانِ
2 D	اِسْتَقْبَلْتُما	تَسْتَقْبِلانِ	تَسْتَقْبِلا	تَسْتَقْبِلا	اِسْتَقْبِلا	أُسْتُقْبِلْتُما	تُسْتَقْبَلانِ
3 MP	اِسْتَقْبَلوا	يَسْتَقْبِلونَ	يَسْتَقْبِلوا	يَسْتَقْبِلوا		أُسْتُقْبِلوا	يُسْتَقْبَلونَ
FP	اِسْتَقْبَلْنَ	يَسْتَقْبِلْنَ	يَسْتَقْبِلْنَ	يَسْتَقْبِلْنَ		أُسْتُقْبِلْنَ	يُسْتَقْبَلْنَ
2 MP	اِسْتَقْبَلْتُمْ	تَسْتَقْبِلونَ	تَسْتَقْبِلوا	تَسْتَقْبِلوا	اِسْتَقْبِلوا	أُسْتُقْبِلْتُمْ	تُسْتَقْبَلونَ
FP	اِسْتَقْبَلْتُنَّ	تَسْتَقْبِلْنَ	تَسْتَقْبِلْنَ	تَسْتَقْبِلْنَ	اِسْتَقْبِلْنَ	أُسْتُقْبِلْتُنَّ	تُسْتَقْبَلْنَ
1 P	اِسْتَقْبَلْنا	نَسْتَقْبِلُ	نَسْتَقْبِلَ	نَسْتَقْبِلْ		أُسْتُقْبِلْنا	نُسْتَقْبَلُ

Participles: مُسْتَقْبِلٌ   مُسْتَقْبَلٌ

Verbal noun: اِسْتِقْبالٌ

317

Table 11. Quadriliteral verbs. تَرْجَمَ 'to translate'

| | ACTIVE | | | | | PASSIVE | |
	Perfect	Indicative	Subjunctive	Jussive	Imperative	Perfect	Indicative
3 MS	تَرْجَمَ	يُتَرْجِمُ	يُتَرْجِمَ	يُتَرْجِمْ		تُرْجِمَ	يُتَرْجَمُ
FS	تَرْجَمَتْ	تُتَرْجِمُ	تُتَرْجِمَ	تُتَرْجِمْ		تُرْجِمَتْ	تُتَرْجَمُ
2 MS	تَرْجَمْتَ	تُتَرْجِمُ	تُتَرْجِمَ	تُتَرْجِمْ	تَرْجِمْ		
FS	تَرْجَمْتِ	تُتَرْجِمِينَ	تُتَرْجِمِي	تُتَرْجِمِي	تَرْجِمِي		
1 S	تَرْجَمْتُ	أُتَرْجِمُ	أُتَرْجِمَ	أُتَرْجِمْ			
3 MD	تَرْجَمَا	يُتَرْجِمَانِ	يُتَرْجِمَا	يُتَرْجِمَا		تُرْجِمَا	يُتَرْجَمَانِ
FD	تَرْجَمَتَا	تُتَرْجِمَانِ	تُتَرْجِمَا	تُتَرْجِمَا		تُرْجِمَتَا	تُتَرْجَمَانِ
2 D	تَرْجَمْتُمَا	تُتَرْجِمَانِ	تُتَرْجِمَا	تُتَرْجِمَا	تَرْجِمَا		
3 MP	تَرْجَمُوا	يُتَرْجِمُونَ	يُتَرْجِمُوا	يُتَرْجِمُوا			
FP	تَرْجَمْنَ	يُتَرْجِمْنَ	يُتَرْجِمْنَ	يُتَرْجِمْنَ			
2 MP	تَرْجَمْتُمْ	تُتَرْجِمُونَ	تُتَرْجِمُوا	تُتَرْجِمُوا	تَرْجِمُوا		
FP	تَرْجَمْتُنَّ	تُتَرْجِمْنَ	تُتَرْجِمْنَ	تُتَرْجِمْنَ	تَرْجِمْنَ		
1 P	تَرْجَمْنَا	نُتَرْجِمُ	نُتَرْجِمَ	نُتَرْجِمْ			

Participles: مُتَرْجِمٌ   مُتَرْجَمٌ

Verbal noun: تَرْجَمَةٌ

Table 12. Doubled verbs: Form I. عَدَّ (ُ) 'to count'

| | ACTIVE | | | | | PASSIVE | |
	Perfect	Indicative	Subjunctive	Jussive	Imperative	Perfect	Indicative
3 MS	عَدَّ	يَعُدُّ	يَعُدَّ	يَعُدَّ		عُدَّ	يُعَدُّ
FS	عَدَّتْ	تَعُدُّ	تَعُدَّ	تَعُدَّ		عُدَّتْ	تُعَدُّ
2 MS	عَدَدْتَ	تَعُدُّ	تَعُدَّ	تَعُدَّ	عُدَّ، أُعْدُدْ	عُدِدْتَ	تُعَدُّ
FS	عَدَدْتِ	تَعُدِّينَ	تَعُدِّي	تَعُدِّي	عُدِّي	عُدِدْتِ	تُعَدِّينَ
1 S	عَدَدْتُ	أَعُدُّ	أَعُدَّ	أَعُدَّ		عُدِدْتُ	أُعَدُّ
3 MD	عَدَّا	يَعُدَّانِ	يَعُدَّا	يَعُدَّا		عُدَّا	يُعَدَّانِ
FD	عَدَّتا	تَعُدَّانِ	تَعُدَّا	تَعُدَّا		عُدَّتا	تُعَدَّانِ
2 D	عَدَدْتُما	تَعُدَّانِ	تَعُدَّا	تَعُدَّا	عُدَّا	عُدِدْتُما	تُعَدَّانِ
3 MP	عَدُّوا	يَعُدُّونَ	يَعُدُّوا	يَعُدُّوا		عُدُّوا	يُعَدُّونَ
FP	عَدَدْنَ	يَعْدُدْنَ	يَعْدُدْنَ	يَعْدُدْنَ		عُدِدْنَ	يُعْدَدْنَ
2 MP	عَدَدْتُمْ	تَعُدُّونَ	تَعُدُّوا	تَعُدُّوا	عُدُّوا	عُدِدْتُمْ	تُعَدُّونَ
FP	عَدَدْتُنَّ	تَعْدُدْنَ	تَعْدُدْنَ	تَعْدُدْنَ	أُعْدُدْنَ	عُدِدْتُنَّ	تُعْدَدْنَ
1 P	عَدَدْنا	نَعُدُّ	نَعُدَّ	نَعُدَّ		عُدِدْنا	نُعَدُّ

Participles: عَادٌّ   مَعْدُودٌ

Verbal noun: عَدٌّ

Other doubled I stem vowel patterns are:

a - i, e.g. تَمَّ ـِـ 'to be completed'

i - a, e.g. وَدَّ ـَـ 'to want' ('I wanted' = وَدِدْتُ)

319

Table 13. Doubled verbs: Form IV. أحَبَّ 'to love'

	ACTIVE					PASSIVE	
	Perfect	Indicative	Subjunctive	Jussive	Imperative	Perfect	Indicative
3 MS	أَحَبَّ	يُحِبُّ	يُحِبَّ	يُحِبَّ		أُحِبَّ	يُحَبُّ
FS	أَحَبَّتْ	تُحِبُّ	تُحِبَّ	تُحِبَّ		أُحِبَّتْ	تُحَبُّ
2 MS	أَحْبَبْتَ	تُحِبُّ	تُحِبَّ	تُحِبَّ	أَحِبَّ	أُحْبِبْتَ	تُحَبُّ
FS	أَحْبَبْتِ	تُحِبِّينَ	تُحِبِّي	تُحِبِّي	أَحِبِّي	أُحْبِبْتِ	تُحَبِّينَ
1 S	أَحْبَبْتُ	أُحِبُّ	أُحِبَّ	أُحِبَّ		أُحْبِبْتُ	أُحَبُّ
3 MD	أَحَبَّا	يُحِبَّانِ	يُحِبَّا	يُحِبَّا		أُحِبَّا	يُحَبَّا
FD	أُحِبَّتَا	تُحِبَّانِ	تُحِبَّا	تُحِبَّا		أُحِبَّتَا	تُحَبَّا
2 D	أَحْبَبْتُمَا	تُحِبَّانِ	تُحِبَّا	تُحِبَّا	أَحِبَّا	أُحْبِبْتُمَا	تُحَبَّا
3 MP	أَحَبُّوا	يُحِبُّونَ	يُحِبُّوا	يُحِبُّوا		أُحِبُّوا	يُحَبُّوا
FP	أَحْبَبْنَ	يُحْبِبْنَ	يُحْبِبْنَ	يُحْبِبْنَ		أُحْبِبْنَ	يُحْبَبْنَ
2 MP	أَحْبَبْتُمْ	تُحِبُّونَ	تُحِبُّوا	تُحِبُّوا	أَحِبُّوا	أُحْبِبْتُمْ	تُحَبُّوا
FP	أَحْبَبْتُنَّ	تُحْبِبْنَ	تُحْبِبْنَ	تُحْبِبْنَ	أَحْبِبْنَ	أُحْبِبْتُنَّ	تُحْبَبْنَ
1 P	أَحْبَبْنَا	نُحِبُّ	نُحِبَّ	نُحِبَّ		أُحْبِبْنَا	نُحَبُّ

Participles: مُحِبٌّ　　　　　　مُحَبٌّ

Verbal noun: إِحْبَابٌ

Table 14. Doubled verbs: Form VII. اِنْضَمَّ اِلَى 'to join'

| | ACTIVE | | | | | PASSIVE | |
	Perfect	Indicative	Subjunctive	Jussive	Imperative	Perfect	Indicative
3 MS	اِنْضَمَّ	يَنْضَمُّ	يَنْضَمَّ	يَنْضَمَّ			
FS	اِنْضَمَّتْ	تَنْضَمُّ	تَنْضَمَّ	تَنْضَمَّ			
2 MS	اِنْضَمَمْتَ	تَنْضَمُّ	تَنْضَمَّ	تَنْضَمَّ	اِنْضَمِمْ، اِنْضَمَّ		
FS	اِنْضَمَمْتِ	تَنْضَمِّينَ	تَنْضَمِّي	تَنْضَمِّي	اِنْضَمِّي		
1 S	اِنْضَمَمْتُ	أَنْضَمُّ	أَنْضَمَّ	أَنْضَمَّ			
3 MD	اِنْضَمَّا	يَنْضَمَّانِ	يَنْضَمَّا	يَنْضَمَّا			
FD	اِنْضَمَّتَا	تَنْضَمَّانِ	تَنْضَمَّا	تَنْضَمَّا			
2 D	اِنْضَمَمْتُمَا	تَنْضَمَّانِ	تَنْضَمَّا	تَنْضَمَّا	اِنْضَمَّا		
3 MP	اِنْضَمُّوا	يَنْضَمُّونَ	يَنْضَمُّوا	يَنْضَمُّوا			
FP	اِنْضَمَمْنَ	يَنْضَمِمْنَ	يَنْضَمِمْنَ	يَنْضَمِمْنَ			
2 MP	اِنْضَمَمْتُمْ	تَنْضَمُّونَ	تَنْضَمُّوا	تَنْضَمُّوا	اِنْضَمُّوا		
FP	اِنْضَمَمْتُنَّ	تَنْضَمِمْنَ	تَنْضَمِمْنَ	تَنْضَمِمْنَ	اِنْضَمِمْنَ		
1 P	اِنْضَمَمْنا	نَنْضَمُّ	نَنْضَمَّ	نَنْضَمَّ			

Participles: مُنْضَمٌّ

Verbal noun: اِنْضِمَامٌ

Form VII has no passive.

Table 15. Doubled verbs: Form VIII.　　إِحْتَلَّ　　'to occupy'

| | ACTIVE | | | | | PASSIVE | |
	Perfect	Indicative	Subjunctive	Jussive	Imperative	Perfect	Indicative
3 MS	اِحْتَلَّ	يَحْتَلُّ	يَحْتَلَّ	يَحْتَلَّ		أُحْتُلَّ	يُحْتَلُّ
FS	اِحْتَلَّتْ	تَحْتَلُّ	تَحْتَلَّ	تَحْتَلَّ		أُحْتُلَّتْ	تُحْتَلُّ
2 MS	اِحْتَلَلْتَ	تَحْتَلُّ	تَحْتَلَّ	تَحْتَلَّ	اِحْتَلَّ		
FS	اِحْتَلَلْتِ	تَحْتَلِّينَ	تَحْتَلِّي	تَحْتَلِّي	اِحْتَلِّي		
1 S	اِحْتَلَلْتُ	أَحْتَلُّ	أَحْتَلَّ	أَحْتَلَّ			
3 MD	اِحْتَلَّا	يَحْتَلَّانِ	يَحْتَلَّا	يَحْتَلَّا		أُحْتُلَّا	يُحْتَلَّانِ
FD	اِحْتَلَّتا	تَحْتَلَّانِ	تَحْتَلَّا	تَحْتَلَّا		أُحْتُلَّتا	تُحْتَلَّانِ
2 D	اِحْتَلَلْتُما	تَحْتَلَّانِ	تَحْتَلَّا	تَحْتَلَّا	اِحْتَلَّا		
3 MP	اِحْتَلُّوا	يَحْتَلُّونَ	يَحْتَلُّوا	يَحْتَلُّوا			
FP	اِحْتَلَلْنَ	يَحْتَلِلْنَ	يَحْتَلِلْنَ	يَحْتَلِلْنَ			
2 MP	اِحْتَلَلْتُمْ	تَحْتَلُّونَ	تَحْتَلُّوا	تَحْتَلُّوا	اِحْتَلُّوا		
FP	اِحْتَلَلْتُنَّ	تَحْتَلِلْنَ	تَحْتَلِلْنَ	تَحْتَلِلْنَ	اِحْتَلِلْنَ		
1 P	اِحْتَلَلْنا	نَحْتَلُّ	نَحْتَلَّ	نَحْتَلَّ			

Participles:　مُحْتَلٌّ　　　　　　　　　　　مُحْتَلٌّ

Verbal noun:　اِحْتِلَالٌ

This verb occurs passive in the third-person only.

322

Table 16. Doubled verbs: Form X. اِسْتَمَرَّ 'to continue'

| | ACTIVE | | | | | PASSIVE | |
	Perfect	Indicative	Subjunctive	Jussive	Imperative	Perfect	Indicative
3 MS	اِسْتَمَرَّ	يَسْتَمِرُّ	يَسْتَمِرَّ	يَسْتَمِرَّ			
FS	اِسْتَمَرَّتْ	تَسْتَمِرُّ	تَسْتَمِرَّ	تَسْتَمِرَّ			
2 MS	اِسْتَمَرَرْتَ	تَسْتَمِرُّ	تَسْتَمِرَّ	تَسْتَمِرَّ	اِسْتَمِرَّ		
FS	اِسْتَمَرَرْتِ	تَسْتَمِرِّينَ	تَسْتَمِرِّي	تَسْتَمِرِّي	اِسْتَمِرِّي		
1 S	اِسْتَمَرَرْتُ	أَسْتَمِرُّ	أَسْتَمِرَّ	أَسْتَمِرَّ			
3 MD	اِسْتَمَرَّا	يَسْتَمِرَّانِ	يَسْتَمِرَّا	يَسْتَمِرَّا			
FD	اِسْتَمَرَّتَا	تَسْتَمِرَّانِ	تَسْتَمِرَّا	تَسْتَمِرَّا			
2 D	اِسْتَمْرَرْتُما	تَسْتَمِرَّانِ	تَسْتَمِرَّا	تَسْتَمِرَّا	اِسْتَمِرَّا		
3 MP	اِسْتَمَرُّوا	يَسْتَمِرُّونَ	يَسْتَمِرُّوا	يَسْتَمِرُّوا			
FP	اِسْتَمْرَرْنَ	يَسْتَمْرِرْنَ	يَسْتَمْرِرْنَ	يَسْتَمْرِرْنَ			
2 MP	اِسْتَمْرَرْتُمْ	تَسْتَمِرُّونَ	تَسْتَمِرُّوا	تَسْتَمِرُّوا	اِسْتَمِرُّوا		
FP	اِسْتَمْرَرْتُنَّ	تَسْتَمْرِرْنَ	تَسْتَمْرِرْنَ	تَسْتَمْرِرْنَ	اِسْتَمْرِرْنَ		
1 P	اِسْتَمْرَرْنا	نَسْتَمِرُّ	نَسْتَمِرَّ	نَسْتَمِرَّ			

Participles: مُسْتَمِرٌّ

Verbal noun: اِسْتِمْرَارٌ

This verb has no passive.

Table 17. Hollow verbs: Form I. قَالَ – يَقُولُ 'to say'

| | ACTIVE | | | | | PASSIVE | |
	Perfect	Indicative	Subjunctive	Jussive	Imperative	Perfect	Indicative
3 MS	قَالَ	يَقُولُ	يَقُولَ	يَقُلْ		قِيلَ	يُقَالُ
FS	قَالَتْ	تَقُولُ	تَقُولَ	تَقُلْ		قِيلَتْ	تُقَالُ
2 MS	قُلْتَ	تَقُولُ	تَقُولَ	تَقُلْ	قُلْ		
FS	قُلْتِ	تَقُولِينَ	تَقُولِي	تَقُولِي	قُولِي		
1 S	قُلْتُ	أَقُولُ	أَقُولَ	أَقُلْ			
3 MD	قَالَا	يَقُولَانِ	يَقُولَا	يَقُولَا		قِيلَا	يُقَالَا
FD	قَالَتَا	تَقُولَانِ	تَقُولَا	تَقُولَا		قِيلَتَا	تُقَالَا
2 D	قُلْتُمَا	تَقُولَانِ	تَقُولَا	تَقُولَا	قُولَا		
3 MP	قَالُوا	يَقُولُونَ	يَقُولُوا	يَقُولُوا			
FP	قُلْنَ	يَقُلْنَ	يَقُلْنَ	يَقُلْنَ			
2 MP	قُلْتُمْ	تَقُولُونَ	تَقُولُوا	تَقُولُوا	قُولُوا		
FP	قُلْتُنَّ	تَقُلْنَ	تَقُلْنَ	تَقُلْنَ	قُلْنَ		
1 P	قُلْنَا	نَقُولُ	نَقُولَ	نَقُلْ			

Participles: قَائِلٌ   مَقُولٌ

Verbal noun: قَوْلٌ

This verb occurs passive in the third-person only.

Table 18. Hollow verbs: Form I. سارَ — يَسِيرُ 'to move along'

| | ACTIVE | | | | | PASSIVE | |
	Perfect	Indicative	Subjunctive	Jussive	Imperative	Perfect	Indicative
3 MS	سارَ	يَسِيرُ	يَسِيرَ	يَسِرْ			
FS	سارَتْ	تَسِيرُ	تَسِيرَ	تَسِرْ			
2 MS	سِرْتَ	تَسِيرُ	تَسِيرَ	تَسِرْ	سِرْ		
FS	سِرْتِ	تَسِيرِينَ	تَسِيرِي	تَسِيرِي	سِيرِي		
1 S	سِرْتُ	أَسِيرُ	أَسِيرَ	أَسِرْ			
3 MD	سارا	يَسِيرانِ	يَسِيرا	يَسِيرا			
FD	سارَتا	تَسِيرانِ	تَسِيرا	تَسِيرا			
2 D	سِرْتُما	تَسِيرانِ	تَسِيرا	تَسِيرا	سِيرا		
3 MP	ساروا	يَسِيرونَ	يَسِيروا	يَسِيروا			
FP	سِرْنَ	يَسِرْنَ	يَسِرْنَ	يَسِرْنَ			
2 MP	سِرْتُمْ	تَسِيرونَ	تَسِيروا	تَسِيروا	سِيروا		
FP	سِرْتُنَّ	تَسِرْنَ	تَسِرْنَ	تَسِرْنَ	سِرْنَ		
1 P	سِرْنا	نَسِيرُ	نَسِيرَ	نَسِرْ			

Participles: سائِرٌ

Verbal noun: سَيْرٌ

This verb has no passive.

Table 19. Hollow verbs: Form I. خافَ ـ يَخافُ 'to fear'

	ACTIVE					PASSIVE	
	Perfect	Indicative	Subjunctive	Jussive	Imperative	Perfect	Indicative
3 MS	خافَ	يَخافُ	يَخافَ	يَخَفْ		خيفَ	يُخافُ
FS	خافَتْ	تَخافُ	تَخافَ	تَخَفْ		خيفَتْ	تُخافُ
2 MS	خِفتَ	تَخافُ	تَخافَ	تَخَفْ	خَفْ		
FS	خِفتِ	تَخافينَ	تَخافي	تَخافي	خافي		
1 S	خِفتُ	أَخافُ	أَخافَ	أَخَفْ			
3 MD	خافا	يَخافانِ	يَخافا	يَخافا		خيفا	يُخافانِ
FD	خافَتا	تَخافانِ	تَخافا	تَخافا		خيفَتا	تُخافانِ
2 D	خِفتُما	تَخافانِ	تَخافا	تَخافا	خافا		
3 MP	خافوا	يَخافونَ	يَخافوا	يَخافوا			
FP	خِفنَ	يَخَفْنَ	يَخَفْنَ	يَخَفْنَ			
2 MP	خِفتُمْ	تَخافونَ	تَخافوا	تَخافوا	خافوا		
FP	خِفتُنَّ	تَخَفْنَ	تَخَفْنَ	تَخَفْنَ	خَفْنَ		
1 P	خِفنا	نَخافُ	نَخافَ	نَخَفْ			

Participles: خائِفٌ مَخوفٌ

Verbal noun: خَوْفٌ

This verb normally occurs passive in the third-person only.

Table 20. Hollow verbs: Form IV. أَجَابَ 'to answer'

| | ACTIVE | | | | | PASSIVE | |
	Perfect	Indicative	Subjunctive	Jussive	Imperative	Perfect	Indicative
3 MS	أَجَابَ	يُجِيبُ	يُجِيبَ	يُجِبْ		أُجِيبَ	يُجَابُ
FS	أَجَابَتْ	تُجِيبُ	تُجِيبَ	تُجِبْ		أُجِيبَتْ	تُجَابُ
2 MS	أَجَبْتَ	تُجِيبُ	تُجِيبَ	تُجِبْ	أَجِبْ	أُجِبْتَ	تُجَابُ
FS	أَجَبْتِ	تُجِيبِينَ	تُجِيبِي	تُجِيبِي	أَجِيبِي	أُجِبْتِ	تُجَابِينَ
1 S	أَجَبْتُ	أُجِيبُ	أُجِيبَ	أُجِبْ		أُجِبْتُ	أُجَابُ
3 MD	أَجَابَا	يُجِيبَانِ	يُجِيبَا	يُجِيبَا		أُجِيبَا	يُجَابَانِ
FD	أَجَابَتَا	تُجِيبَانِ	تُجِيبَا	تُجِيبَا		أُجِيبَتَا	تُجَابَانِ
2 D	أَجَبْتُمَا	تُجِيبَانِ	تُجِيبَا	تُجِيبَا	أَجِيبَا	أُجِبْتُمَا	تُجَابَانِ
3 MP	أَجَابُوا	يُجِيبُونَ	يُجِيبُوا	يُجِيبُوا		أُجِيبُوا	يُجَابُونَ
FP	أَجَبْنَ	يُجِبْنَ	يُجِبْنَ	يُجِبْنَ		أُجِبْنَ	يُجَبْنَ
2 MP	أَجَبْتُمْ	تُجِيبُونَ	تُجِيبُوا	تُجِيبُوا	أَجِيبُوا	أُجِبْتُمْ	تُجَابُونَ
FP	أَجَبْتُنَّ	تُجِبْنَ	تُجِبْنَ	تُجِبْنَ	أَجِبْنَ	أُجِبْتُنَّ	تُجَبْنَ
1 P	أَجَبْنَا	نُجِيبُ	نُجِيبَ	نُجِبْ		أُجِبْنَا	نُجَابُ

Participles: مُجِيبٌ   مُجَابٌ

Verbal noun: إِجَابَةٌ

327

Table 21. Hollow verbs: Form VII إنْقَادَ 'to be led'

| | ACTIVE | | | | | PASSIVE | |
	Perfect	Indicative	Subjunctive	Jussive	Imperative	Perfect	Indicative
3 MS	إنْقَادَ	يَنْقَادُ	يَنْقَادَ	يَنْقَدْ			
FS	إنْقَادَتْ	تَنْقَادُ	تَنْقَادَ	تَنْقَدْ			
2 MS	إنْقَدْتَ	تَنْقَادُ	تَنْقَادَ	تَنْقَدْ	إنْقَدْ		
FS	إنْقَدْتِ	تَنْقَادِينَ	تَنْقَادِي	تَنْقَادِي	إنْقَادِي		
1 S	إنْقَدْتُ	أَنْقَادُ	أَنْقَادَ	أَنْقَدْ			
3 MD	إنْقَادَا	يَنْقَادَانِ	يَنْقَادَا	يَنْقَادَا			
FD	إنْقَادَتَا	تَنْقَادَانِ	تَنْقَادَا	تَنْقَادَا			
2 D	إنْقَدْتُما	تَنْقَادَانِ	تَنْقَادَا	تَنْقَادَا	إنْقَادَا		
3 MP	إنْقَادُوا	يَنْقَادُونَ	يَنْقَادُوا	يَنْقَادُوا			
FP	إنْقَدْنَ	يَنْقَدْنَ	يَنْقَدْنَ	يَنْقَدْنَ			
2 MP	إنْقَدْتُمْ	تَنْقَادُونَ	تَنْقَادُوا	تَنْقَادُوا	إنْقَادُوا		
FP	إنْقَدْتُنَّ	تَنْقَدْنَ	تَنْقَدْنَ	تَنْقَدْنَ	إنْقَدْنَ		
1 P	إنْقَدْنا	نَنْقَادُ	نَنْقَادَ	نَنْقَدْ			

Participles: مُنْقَادٌ

Verbal noun: إنْقِيَادٌ

Form VII has no passive.

328

Table 22. Hollow verbs: Form VIII. اِخْتَارَ 'to choose'

| | ACTIVE | | | | | PASSIVE | |
	Perfect	Indicative	Subjunctive	Jussive	Imperative	Perfect	Indicative
3 MS	اِخْتَارَ	يُخْتَارُ	يُخْتَارَ	يَخْتَرْ		اُخْتِيرَ	يُخْتَارُ
FS	اِخْتَارَتْ	تُخْتَارُ	تُخْتَارَ	تَخْتَرْ		اُخْتِيرَتْ	تُخْتَارُ
2 MS	اِخْتَرْتَ	تُخْتَارُ	تُخْتَارَ	تَخْتَرْ	اِخْتَرْ		
FS	اِخْتَرْتِ	تُخْتَارِينَ	تُخْتَارِي	تَخْتَارِي	اِخْتَارِي		
1 S	اِخْتَرْتُ	أُخْتَارُ	أُخْتَارَ	أَخْتَرْ			
3 MD	اِخْتَارَا	يُخْتَارَانِ	يُخْتَارَا	يُخْتَارَا		اُخْتِيرَا	يُخْتَارَانِ
FD	اِخْتَارَتَا	تُخْتَارَانِ	تُخْتَارَا	تُخْتَارَا		اُخْتِيرَتَا	تُخْتَارَانِ
2 D	اِخْتَرْتُمَا	تُخْتَارَانِ	تُخْتَارَا	تُخْتَارَا	اِخْتَارَا		
3 MP	اِخْتَارُوا	يُخْتَارُونَ	يُخْتَارُوا	يُخْتَارُوا			
FP	اِخْتَرْنَ	يَخْتَرْنَ	يَخْتَرْنَ	يَخْتَرْنَ			
2 MP	اِخْتَرْتُمْ	تُخْتَارُونَ	تُخْتَارُوا	تُخْتَارُوا	اِخْتَارُوا		
FP	اِخْتَرْتُنَّ	تَخْتَرْنَ	تَخْتَرْنَ	تَخْتَرْنَ	اِخْتَرْنَ		
1 P	اِخْتَرْنَا	نُخْتَارُ	نُخْتَارَ	نَخْتَرْ			

Participles: مُخْتَارٌ   مُخْتَارٌ

Verbal noun: اِخْتِيَارٌ

This verb normally occurs passive only in the third-person.

329

Table 23. Hollow verbs: Form X. اِسْتَفَادَ (مِنْ) 'to benefit from'

		ACTIVE				PASSIVE	
	Perfect	Indicative	Subjunctive	Jussive	Imperative	Perfect	Indicative
3 MS	اِسْتَفَادَ	يَسْتَفِيدُ	يَسْتَفِيدَ	يَسْتَفِدْ		أُسْتُفِيدَ	يُسْتَفَادُ
FS	اِسْتَفَادَتْ	تَسْتَفِيدُ	تَسْتَفِيدَ	تَسْتَفِدْ			
2 MS	اِسْتَفَدْتَ	تَسْتَفِيدُ	تَسْتَفِيدَ	تَسْتَفِدْ	اِسْتَفِدْ		
FS	اِسْتَفَدْتِ	تَسْتَفِيدِينَ	تَسْتَفِيدِي	تَسْتَفِيدِي	اِسْتَفِيدِي		
1 S	اِسْتَفَدْتُ	أَسْتَفِيدُ	أَسْتَفِيدَ	أَسْتَفِدْ			
3 MD	اِسْتَفَادَا	يَسْتَفِيدَانِ	يَسْتَفِيدَا	يَسْتَفِيدَا			
FD	اِسْتَفَادَتَا	تَسْتَفِيدَانِ	تَسْتَفِيدَا	تَسْتَفِيدَا			
2 D	اِسْتَفَدْتُما	تَسْتَفِيدَانِ	تَسْتَفِيدَا	تَسْتَفِيدَا	اِسْتَفِيدَا		
3 MP	اِسْتَفَادُوا	يَسْتَفِيدُونَ	يَسْتَفِيدُوا	يَسْتَفِيدُوا			
FP	اِسْتَفَدْنَ	يَسْتَفِدْنَ	يَسْتَفِدْنَ	يَسْتَفِدْنَ			
2 MP	اِسْتَفَدْتُمْ	تَسْتَفِيدُونَ	تَسْتَفِيدُوا	تَسْتَفِيدُوا	اِسْتَفِيدُوا		
FP	اِسْتَفَدْتُنَّ	تَسْتَفِدْنَ	تَسْتَفِدْنَ	تَسْتَفِدْنَ	اِسْتَفِدْنَ		
1 P	اِسْتَفَدْنا	نَسْتَفِيدُ	نَسْتَفِيدَ	نَسْتَفِدْ			

Participles: مُسْتَفِيدٌ   مُسْتَفَادٌ

Verbal noun: اِسْتِفَادَةٌ

This verb occurs passive in the third-person masculine singular only.

330

Table 24. Assimilated verbs: Form I وَعَدَ (يَ) ب 'to promise (s.o.) s.th.'

| | ACTIVE | | | | | PASSIVE | |
	Perfect	Indicative	Subjunctive	Jussive	Imperative	Perfect	Indicative
3 MS	وَعَدَ	يَعِدُ	يَعِدَ	يَعِدْ		وُعِدَ	يُوعَدُ
FS	وَعَدَتْ	تَعِدُ	تَعِدَ	تَعِدْ		وُعِدَتْ	تُوعَدُ
2 MS	وَعَدْتَ	تَعِدُ	تَعِدَ	تَعِدْ	عِدْ	وُعِدْتَّ	تُوعَدُ
FS	وَعَدْتِ	تَعِدِينَ	تَعِدِي	تَعِدِي	عِدِي	وُعِدْتِّ	تُوعَدِينَ
1 S	وَعَدْتُ	أَعِدُ	أَعِدَ	أَعِدْ		وُعِدْتُّ	أُوعَدُ
3 MD	وَعَدَا	يَعِدَانِ	يَعِدَا	يَعِدَا		وُعِدَا	يُوعَدَانِ
FD	وَعَدَتَا	تَعِدَانِ	تَعِدَا	تَعِدَا		وُعِدَتَا	تُوعَدَانِ
2 D	وَعَدْتُمَا	تَعِدَانِ	تَعِدَا	تَعِدَا	عِدَا	وُعِدْتُمَا	تُوعَدَانِ
3 MP	وَعَدُوا	يَعِدُونَ	يَعِدُوا	يَعِدُوا		وُعِدُوا	يُوعَدُونَ
FP	وَعَدْنَ	يَعِدْنَ	يَعِدْنَ	يَعِدْنَ		وُعِدْنَ	يُوعَدْنَ
2 MP	وَعَدْتُمْ	تَعِدُونَ	تَعِدُوا	تَعِدُوا	عِدُوا	وُعِدْتُمْ	تُوعَدُونَ
FP	وَعَدْتُنَّ	تَعِدْنَ	تَعِدْنَ	تَعِدْنَ	عِدْنَ	وُعِدْتُنَّ	تُوعَدْنَ
1 P	وَعَدْنَا	نَعِدُ	نَعِدَ	نَعِدْ		وُعِدْنَا	نُوعَدُ

Participles: وَاعِدٌ   مَوْعُودٌ

Verbal noun: وَعْدٌ

Table 25. Assimilated verbs: Form VIII.   اِتَّفَقَ على 'to agree on'

| | ACTIVE | | | | | PASSIVE | |
	Perfect	Indicative	Subjunctive	Jussive	Imperative	Perfect	Indicative
3 MS	اِتَّفَقَ	يَتَّفِقُ	يَتَّفِقَ	يَتَّفِقْ		اُتُّفِقَ	يُتَّفَقُ
FS	اِتَّفَقَتْ	تَتَّفِقُ	تَتَّفِقَ	تَتَّفِقْ			
2 MS	اِتَّفَقْتَ	تَتَّفِقُ	تَتَّفِقَ	تَتَّفِقْ	اِتَّفِقْ		
FS	اِتَّفَقْتِ	تَتَّفِقِينَ	تَتَّفِقِي	تَتَّفِقِي	اِتَّفِقِي		
1 S	اِتَّفَقْتُ	أَتَّفِقُ	أَتَّفِقَ	أَتَّفِقْ			
3 MD	اِتَّفَقَا	يَتَّفِقَانِ	يَتَّفِقَا	يَتَّفِقَا			
FD	اِتَّفَقَتَا	تَتَّفِقَانِ	تَتَّفِقَا	تَتَّفِقَا			
2 D	اِتَّفَقْتُمَا	تَتَّفِقَانِ	تَتَّفِقَا	تَتَّفِقَا	اِتَّفِقَا		
3 MP	اِتَّفَقُوا	يَتَّفِقُونَ	يَتَّفِقُوا	يَتَّفِقُوا			
FP	اِتَّفَقْنَ	يَتَّفِقْنَ	يَتَّفِقْنَ	يَتَّفِقْنَ			
2 MP	اِتَّفَقْتُمْ	تَتَّفِقُونَ	تَتَّفِقُوا	تَتَّفِقُوا	اِتَّفِقُوا		
FP	اِتَّفَقْتُنَّ	تَتَّفِقْنَ	تَتَّفِقْنَ	تَتَّفِقْنَ	اِتَّفِقْنَ		
1 P	اِتَّفَقْنَا	نَتَّفِقُ	نَتَّفِقَ	نَتَّفِقْ			

Participles: مُتَّفِقٌ   مُتَّفَقٌ

Verbal noun: اِتِّفَاقٌ

This verb occurs passive in the third-person masculine singular only.

Table 26. Defective verbs: Form I. (´) لَقِيَ 'to find, meet'

| | ACTIVE | | | | | PASSIVE | |
	Perfect	Indicative	Subjunctive	Jussive	Imperative	Perfect	Indicative
3 MS	لَقِيَ	يَلْقَى	يَلْقَى	يَلْقَ		لُقِيَ	يُلْقَى
FS	لَقِيَتْ	تَلْقَى	تَلْقَى	تَلْقَ		لُقِيَتْ	تُلْقَى
2 MS	لَقِيتَ	تَلْقَى	تَلْقَى	تَلْقَ	اِلْقَ	لُقِيتَ	تُلْقَى
FS	لَقِيتِ	تَلْقَيْنَ	تَلْقَيْ	تَلْقَيْ	اِلْقَيْ	لُقِيتِ	تُلْقَيْنَ
1 S	لَقِيتُ	أَلْقَى	أَلْقَى	أَلْقَ		لُقِيتُ	أُلْقَى
3 MD	لَقِيا	يَلْقَيانِ	يَلْقَيا	يَلْقَيا		لُقِيا	يُلْقَيانِ
FD	لَقِيَتا	تَلْقَيانِ	تَلْقَيا	تَلْقَيا		لُقِيَتا	تُلْقَيانِ
2 D	لَقِيتُما	تَلْقَيانِ	تَلْقَيا	تَلْقَيا	اِلْقَيا	لُقِيتُما	تُلْقَيانِ
3 MP	لَقُوا	يَلْقَوْنَ	يَلْقَوْا	يَلْقَوْا		لُقُوا	يُلْقَوْنَ
FP	لَقِينَ	يَلْقَيْنَ	يَلْقَيْنَ	يَلْقَيْنَ		لُقِينَ	يُلْقَيْنَ
2 MP	لَقِيتُمْ	تَلْقَوْنَ	تَلْقَوْا	تَلْقَوْا	اِلْقَوْا	لُقِيتُمْ	تُلْقَوْنَ
FP	لَقِيتُنَّ	تَلْقَيْنَ	تَلْقَيْنَ	تَلْقَيْنَ	اِلْقَيْنَ	لُقِيتُنَّ	تُلْقَيْنَ
1 P	لَقِينا	نَلْقَى	نَلْقَى	نَلْقَ		لُقِينا	نُلْقَى

Participles: لاقٍ مُلْقِيّ

Verbal noun: لِقاءٌ

333

Table 27. Defective verbs: Form I. دَعَا (ُ) 'to call'

| | | ACTIVE | | | | PASSIVE | |
	Perfect	Indicative	Subjunctive	Jussive	Imperative	Perfect	Indicative
3 MS	دَعَا	يَدْعو	يَدْعُوَ	يَدْعُ		دُعِيَ	يُدْعَى
FS	دَعَتْ	تَدْعو	تَدْعُوَ	تَدْعُ		دُعِيَتْ	تُدْعَى
2 MS	دَعَوْتَ	تَدْعو	تَدْعُوَ	تَدْعُ	اُدْعُ	دُعِيتَ	تُدْعَى
FS	دَعَوْتِ	تَدْعينَ	تَدْعي	تَدْعي	اُدْعي	دُعِيتِ	تُدْعَيْنَ
1 S	دَعَوْتُ	أَدْعو	أَدْعُوَ	أَدْعُ		دُعِيتُ	أُدْعَى
3 MD	دَعَوَا	يَدْعُوانِ	يَدْعُوَا	يَدْعُوَا		دُعِيا	يُدْعَوانِ
FD	دَعَتا	تَدْعُوانِ	تَدْعُوَا	تَدْعُوَا		دُعِيَتا	تُدْعَوانِ
2 D	دَعَوْتُما	تَدْعُوانِ	تَدْعُوَا	تَدْعُوَا	اُدْعُوَا	دُعِيتُما	تُدْعَوانِ
3 MP	دَعَوْا	يَدْعونَ	يَدْعوا	يَدْعوا		دُعوا	يُدْعَوْنَ
FP	دَعَوْنَ	يَدْعونَ	يَدْعونَ	يَدْعونَ		دُعينَ	يُدْعَوْنَ
2 MP	دَعَوْتُمْ	تَدْعونَ	تَدْعوا	تَدْعوا	اُدْعوا	دُعيتُمْ	تُدْعَوْنَ
FP	دَعَوْتُنَّ	تَدْعونَ	تَدْعونَ	تَدْعونَ	اُدْعونَ	دُعيتُنَّ	تُدْعَوْنَ
1 P	دَعَوْنا	تَدْعو	نَدْعُوَ	نَدْعُ		دُعينا	تُدْعَى

Participles: داعٍ   مَدْعُوٌّ

Verbal noun: دُعاءٌ

Table 28. Defective verbs: Form I. بَنَى حَ 'to build'

	ACTIVE					PASSIVE	
	Perfect	Indicative	Subjunctive	Jussive	Imperative	Perfect	Indicative
3 MS	بَنَى	يَبْنِي	يَبْنِيَ	يَبْنِ		بُنِيَ	يُبْنَى
FS	بَنَتْ	تَبْنِي	تَبْنِيَ	تَبْنِ		بُنِيَتْ	تُبْنَى
2 MS	بَنَيْتَ	تَبْنِي	تَبْنِيَ	تَبْنِ	اِبْنِ	بُنِيتَ	تُبْنَى
FS	بَنَيْتِ	تَبْنِينَ	تَبْنِي	تَبْنِي	اِبْنِي	بُنِيتِ	تُبْنَيْنَ
1 S	بَنَيْتُ	أَبْنِي	أَبْنِيَ	أَبْنِ		بُنِيتُ	أُبْنَى
3 MD	بَنَيَا	يَبْنِيَانِ	يَبْنِيَا	يَبْنِيَا		بُنِيَا	يُبْنَيَانِ
FD	بَنَتَا	تَبْنِيَانِ	تَبْنِيَا	تَبْنِيَا		بُنِيَتَا	تُبْنَيَانِ
2 D	بَنَيْتُمَا	تَبْنِيَانِ	تَبْنِيَا	تَبْنِيَا	اِبْنِيَا	بُنِيتُمَا	تُبْنَيَانِ
3 MP	بَنَوْا	يَبْنُونَ	يَبْنُوا	يَبْنُوا		بُنُوا	يُبْنَوْنَ
FP	بَنَيْنَ	يَبْنِينَ	يَبْنِينَ	يَبْنِينَ		بُنِينَ	يُبْنَيْنَ
2 MP	بَنَيْتُمْ	تَبْنُونَ	تَبْنُوا	تَبْنُوا	اِبْنُوا	بُنِيتُمْ	تُبْنَوْنَ
FP	بَنَيْتُنَّ	تَبْنِينَ	تَبْنِينَ	تَبْنِينَ	اِبْنِينَ	بُنِيتُنَّ	تُبْنَيْنَ
1 P	بَنَيْنَا	نَبْنِي	نَبْنِيَ	نَبْنِ		بُنِينَا	نُبْنَى

Participles: بَانٍ   مَبْنِيٌّ

Verbal noun: بُنْيَانٌ، بِنَاءٌ

All derived defective verbs are conjugated like this verb.

335

APPENDIX II   DAYS AND MONTHS

A. Days of the Week   أَيّامُ الأُسْبُوعِ

                    Sunday   اَلأَحَدُ

                    Monday   اَلإِثْنَيْنِ

                    Tuesday   الثَّلاثاءُ

                    Wednesday   اَلأَرْبِعاءُ

                    Thursday   الخَمِيسُ

                    Friday   الجُمْعَةُ

                    Saturday   السَّبْتُ

B. Months of the Year   شُهُورُ السَّنَةِ

    1. Western Calendar:

	Used in Iraq and the Levant	Used in Egypt and North Africa
January	كانونُ الثّاني	يَنايِر
February	شُباطُ	فَبْرايِر
March	آذارُ	مارس
April	نيسانُ	إبْريل
May	أَيّارُ	مايو
June	حَزِيرانُ	يونِيو
July	تَمّوزُ	يولِيو
August	آبُ	أُغْسْطُس
September	أَيْلولُ	سِبْتَمْبِر
October	تِشْرينُ الأَوَّلُ	أُكْتوبِر
November	تِشْرينُ الثّاني	نوفَمْبِر
December	كانونُ الأَوَّلُ	ديسَمْبِر

336

2. Islamic Calendar (Lunar Year)

١ ــ مُحَرَّمٌ

٢ ــ صَفَر

٣ ــ رَبِيعُ الأَوَّلُ

٤ ــ رَبِيعُ الثَّاني

٥ ــ جُمادَى الأُوَّلُ

٦ ــ جُمادَى الآخِرُ

٧ ــ رَجَب

٨ ــ شَعْبان

٩ ــ رَمَضان

١٠ ــ شَوّال

١١ ــ ذو الْقَعْدَةِ

١٢ ــ ذو الْحِجَّةِ

C. <u>Seasons of the Year</u>   فُصولُ السَّنَةِ

Spring	الرَّبِيعُ
Summer	الصَّيْفُ
Fall	الْخَرِيفُ
Winter	الشِّتاءُ

Included are the Arab states, with their official names in parentheses,
the capital city, and their major cities, including cities mentioned in this
book. All names are feminine except those marked (m.).

(m.) Jordan (The Hashemite Kingdom of
Jordan)
  اَلْأُرْدُنُّ (اَلْمَمْلَكَةُ الْأُرْدُنِّيَّةُ الْهَاشِمِيَّةُ)

  Amman (capital)
  عَمَّانُ

  Petra
  الْبَتْرَاءُ

  Jerash
  جَرَش

United Arab Emirates:
  الْإِمَارَاتُ الْعَرَبِيَّةُ الْمُتَّحِدَةُ (دَوْلَةُ الْإِمَارَاتِ الْعَرَبِيَّةِ الْمُتَّحِدَةِ)

  Abu Dhabi
  أَبُو ظَبِي

  Dubai
  دُبَيّ

  Ras Al Khaima
  رَأْسُ الْخَيْمَةِ

  Al-Sharja
  الشَّارِقَةُ

  Ajman
  عَجْمان

  Fujeira
  الْفُجَيْرَةُ

  Umm Al Qiwain
  أُمُّ الْقِيوَيْنِ

  Abu Dhabi (capital)
  أَبُو ظَبِي

Bahrain (The State of Bahrain)
  الْبَحْرَيْنِ (دَوْلَةُ الْبَحْرَيْنِ)

  Manama (capital)
  الْمَنَامَةُ

Tunisia (The Tunisian Republic)
  تُونِسُ (الْجُمْهُورِيَّةُ التُّونِسِيَّةُ)

  Tunis (capital)
  تُونِسُ

  Carthage
  قَرْطَجَنَّةُ ، قَرْطاجَةُ

Algeria (The Algerian Popular Democratic
Republic)
  الْجَزَائِرُ (الْجُمْهُورِيَّةُ الْجَزَائِرِيَّةُ الدِّيمُقْراطِيَّةُ الشَّعْبِيَّةُ)

  Algiers (capital)
  اَلْجَزَائِرُ

  Constantine
  الْقُسْطَنْطِنِيَّةُ

Saudi Arabia (The Saudi Arabian
Kingdom)
  اَلسَّعُودِيَّةُ (اَلْمَمْلَكَةُ الْعَرَبِيَّةُ السَّعُودِيَّةُ)

  Riyadh (capital)
  اَلرِّياضُ

  Jidda
  جَدَّةُ

  Dhahran
  اَلظَّهْرَانُ

Medina	أَلْمَدِينَةُ
Mecca	مَكَّةُ
(m.) Sudan (The Democratic Republic of the Sudan)	السُّودانُ (جُمْهُورِيَّةُ السُّودانِ الدِّيمُقْراطِيَّةِ)
Khartoum (capital)	أَلْخَرْطومُ
Omdurman	أَمُّ دُرْمانَ
Syria (The Syrian Arab Republic)	سوريا ، سورِيَةُ (الْجُمْهورِيَّةُ الْعَرَبِيَّةُ السّورِيَّةُ)
Syria	الشّامُ ، بِلادُ الشّامِ
Damascus (capital)	دِمَشْقُ ، دِمَشْقُ الشّامِ ، الشّامُ
Palmyra	تَدْمُرُ
Aleppo	حَلَبُ
Hama	حَماه
Homs	حُمْص
Somalia (Somali Democratic Republic)	أَلصّومالُ ، صوماليا (الْجُمْهورِيَّةُ الدِّيمُقْراطِيَّةُ الصّوماليَّةُ)
Mogadishu (capital)	موغاديشو ، مقديشو
(m.) Iraq (The Iraqi Republic)	أَلْعِراقُ (الْجُمْهورِيَّةُ الْعِراقِيَّةُ)
Baghdad (capital)	بَغْدادُ
Arbil	أَرْبِيلُ
Basra	أَلْبَصْرَةُ
Kerkuk	كَرْكوك
Kufa	أَلْكوفَةُ
Mosul	أَلْموصِلُ
Oman (Sultanate of Oman)	عُمانُ (سَلْطَنَةُ عُمانَ)
Muscat (capital)	مَسْقَط
(m.) Morocco (The Kingdom of Morocco)	أَلْمَغْرِبُ (الْمَمْلَكَةُ الْمَغْرِبِيَّةُ)
Rabat (capital)	أَلرِّباطُ
Casablanca	أَلدّارُ الْبَيْضاءُ
Tangiers	طَنْجَةُ
Fez	فاس
Marrakesh	مَرّاكِشُ

Palestine	فِلَسْطِينُ
Bethlehem	بَيْتَ لَحْمُ
Jerusalem	أَلْقُدْسُ
Nazareth	أَلنّاصِرَةُ
Qatar (The State of Qatar)	قَطَر (دَوْلَةُ قَطَر)
Doha (capital)	أَلدَّوْحَةُ
Kuwait	أَلْكُوَيْتُ (دَوْلَةُ الْكُوَيْتِ)
Kuwait City (capital)	أَلْكُوَيْتُ
(m.) Lebanon (The Republic of Lebanon)	لُبْنانُ (أَلْجُمْهُورِيَّةُ اللُّبْنانِيَّةُ)
Beirut (capital)	بَيْروتُ
Baskinta	بِسْكِنْتا
Baalbak	بَعْلَبَكُ
Sidon	صَيْدا
Tyr	صور
Tripoli	طَرابُلَسُ (طرابُلس الشّامِ)
Libya (Libyan Arab Republic)	ليبِيا (أَلْجُمْهُورِيَّةُ الْعَرَبِيَّةُ اللّيبِيَّةُ)
Benghazi (capital)	بَنْغازي
Tripoli (capital)	طَرابُلُسُ (طَرابُلُسُ الْغَرْبِ)
Egypt (The Arab Republic of Egypt)	مِصْرُ (جُمْهُورِيَّةُ مِصْرَ الْعَرَبِيَّةُ)
Cairo (capital)	أَلْقاهِرَةُ
Alexandria	أَلْإِسْكَنْدَرِيَّةُ
Aswan	أَسْوانُ
Port Said	بور سَعيد
Suez	أَلسُّوَيْسُ
Luxor	أَلْأَقْصُرُ
Mauritania (The Islamic Republic of Mauritania)	موريتانِيا (أَلْجُمْهُورِيَّةُ الْإِسْلامِيَّةُ الْموريتانِيَّةُ)
Nouakchott (capital)	نُواكْشوت ، نواخشوت
(South) Yemen (The People's Democratic Republic of Yemen)	أَلْيَمَنُ (أَلْجُنوبِيَّةُ) (جُمْهُورِيَّةُ أَلْيَمَن الدّيمُقْراطِيَّةُ الشّعْبِيَّةُ)
Aden (capital)	عَدَنُ
Medina Al-Shaab (capital)	مَدينَةُ الشّعْبِ

(North) Yemen (The Yemen Arab Republic) أَلْيَمَنُ (الشَّمَالِيَّةُ) (اَلْجُمْهُورِيَّةُ الْعَرَبِيَّةُ الْيَمَنِيَّةُ)

    Sanaa (capital)   صَنْعَاءُ

    Taizz   تَعِزُّ

ADJECTIVES BY LESSON

Lesson 1.	أَوَّلُ	first
	أَساسيّ	basic
Lesson 2.	أَلثَّانِي	the second
Lesson 3.	ثالِثٌ	third
	عَرَبِيٌّ – عَرَبٌ	Arabic, Arabian, Arab
	جَديدٌ	new
Lesson 4.	رابِعٌ	fourth
	مَوْجودٌ	present
	بَعيدٌ (مِنْ)	far (from)
Also:	بِخَيْرٍ	(prep. phrase) fine, well
Lesson 5.	خامِسٌ	fifth
nisba	وَطَنيّ	national, nationalistic
	زائِرٌ	visiting
	قَديمٌ	old, ancient
	حَديثٌ	modern, new
	أَمْريكيّ	American
	أَجْنَبيّ	foreign
	فَرَنْسيّ	French
	كَبيرٌ	big, large
	قَريبٌ (مِنْ)	near (to)
Lesson 6.	سادِسٌ	sixth
	لُغَويّ	linguistic, language
	اِنْكِليزيّ	English
	ثانَويّ	secondary
	سَنَويّ	yearly, annual
Lesson 7.	سابِعٌ	seventh
	خاصّ	special, private
Lesson 8.	ثامِنٌ	eighth
	جُدُدٌ	new (plural)
Lesson 9.	تاسِعٌ	ninth
	نِسائيّ	female, womanly, women's
Also:	بَعْضٌ	(noun) some
	كلّ	(noun) all; each; the whole
Lesson 10.	عاشِرٌ	tenth
	ذاهِبٌ – ون	going

L. 10 (con't.)	قَصِيرٌ – قِصارٌ	short
Lesson 11.	الحادِيَ عَشَرَ	the eleventh
	بَلَدِيّ	native, indigenous, home (not alien)
Lesson 12.	الثّانِيَ عَشَرَ	the twelfth
Lesson 13.	عَزِيزٌ – أَعِزّاءُ	dear
	مَدَنِيّ	city-dwelling, urban; civilized
	قادِمٌ – ون	coming; next (week, etc.)
	مُخْلِصٌ – ون	sincere
	مُشْتاقٌ الى	longing for, looking forward to
Lesson 14.	سِياسِيّ	political
	حاضِرٌ – ون	present, current
Lesson 15.	مُسْتَعِدّ – ون (ل)	ready, prepared (for)
	سَهْلٌ (على)	easy (for)
	فِكْرِيّ	mental, intellectual, speculative
	جَمِيلٌ – ون	beautiful, handsome
	أَخِيرٌ	last, latest; final; recent
Also:	مُعْظَمٌ	(noun) most (of)
Lesson 16.	هامّ	important
	عالِيَةٌ	(f.) high
Lesson 17.	آخَرُ – ون	other; another
	أُخْرى – أُخْرَياتٌ	fem. of آخَر
Lesson 18.	طَوِيلٌ – طِوالٌ	long; tall
	كَبِيرٌ – كِبارٌ ، كُبَراءُ	big; old (person)
	عَظِيمٌ – عِظامٌ ، عُظَماءُ	great, huge, grand, enormous
	صَغِيرٌ – صِغارٌ	little, small, young (person)
	كَثِيرٌ – ون ، كِثارٌ	much; many
Lesson 19.	بَدَوِيّ	bedouin
	صَحْراوِيّ	desert, desolate
	حَيَوِيّ	lively, vital
Lesson 20. None		
Lesson 21.	رَئِيسِيّ	main, chief, principal, leading
Lesson 22.	مُساوِيَةٌ (ل)	(f.) equal (to)
	صَعْبٌ – صِعابٌ	difficult, hard
	اِجْتِماعِيّ	sociological, societal, social
Lesson 23.	مُسْلِمٌ – ون	Muslim
	قَوْمِيّ	national(ist), nationalistic

Lesson 24.	دُوَلِيّ	international
	ثَوْرِيّ	revolutionary
Lesson 25.	غَرِيبٌ ــ غُرَبَاءُ	strange
	يَدَوِيّ	manual
Lesson 26.	فَنِّيّ	artistic(al); technical; professional
	حَبِيبٌ ــ أَحِبَّاءُ	beloved, dear
Also:	غَالِبٌ	(AP) most of (with foll. genitive)
Lesson 27.	سَعِيدٌ ــ سُعَدَاءُ (ب)	happy (about, at, with)
	مُنْتَشِرٌ	scattered, spread out, widespread, prevailing
	أَخَوِيّ	brotherly, fraternal
	حَاصِلٌ ــ ون على	having obtained
	سَاكِنٌ ــ ون	living (in a place), dwelling, residing
	صُحُفِيّ	journalistic
	مُقْبِلٌ ــ ون على	approaching; embarking on; devoting o.s. to
	مُخْتَلِفٌ ــ ون (عن ، من)	differing, different (from)
	خَارِجِيّ	external, outer
	أَبَوِيّ	fatherly, paternal
Also:	نَفْسُ الـ	(noun) the same
Lesson 28.	مُتَنَاوِلٌ ــ ون	dealing with, treating
	مُظْهِرٌ ــ ون	showing, demonstrating; revealing
	مُتَأَكِّدٌ ــ ون (من)	certain, convinced (of)
	مَعْرُوفٌ (ون) (ب)	known; well-known, famous (for)
Also:	جَمِيعُ	(noun) all
Lesson 29.	مِيلَادِيّ	A.D., of the Christian era
	قَبِيحٌ ــ قِبَاحٌ	ugly
Lesson 20.	عَامِّيّ	common, popular; colloquial
	مُسْتَخْدَمٌ ــ ون	used, utilized
	رَسْمِيّ	official; formal
	مُتَّبَعٌ ــ ون	followed, observed, adhered to
	مُتَّفَقٌ عليه	agreed upon (m.s.)
Lesson 31.	قَلِيلٌ ــ قَلَائِلُ ، قِلَالٌ	few, small (in number), scant
	نَائِمٌ ــ ون	asleep, sleeping
	مُتَأَخِّرٌ ــ ون	delayed, late
Lesson 32.	غَنِيّ ــ أَغْنِيَاءُ (ب)	rich, wealthy (in)
	فَقِيرٌ ــ فُقَرَاءُ (في)	poor (in)

L. 32 (con't.)	مُقِيمٌ – ون (فِي)	residing, living (in)
	مُمْتازٌ – ون	excellent,
Lesson 33.	صَحِيحٌ – صِحاحٌ	right, true, correct
Also:	كِلا (كِلْتا)	(noun) both
AP Lesson 34.	واضِحٌ	clear, evident
	مائِتٌ	dying
	عائِشٌ	living, alive
Lesson 35.	مُقَدَّسٌ – ون	holy, sacred
	حَسَنٌ – حِسانٌ	good, fine, excellent, beautiful
	ماضٍ – ماضونَ	past, last (time)
	مَسِيحِيٌّ – ون	Christian
	يَهُودِيٌّ – يَهُودٌ	Jewish
	تالٍ	following, subsequent, next
	عامٌّ	general, common
Lesson 36.	مَلَكِيٌّ – ون	royal; royalist
	أَحْمَرُ (حَمْراءُ) حُمْرٌ	red
	حاكِمٌ – ون	governing; ruling
Lesson 37.	سائِدٌ – ون	prevailing
	مَسْؤُولٌ – ون (عَن)	responsible (for)
	قَوِيٌّ – أَقْوِياءُ	strong, powerful
	مُسَمّىً – ون	named, called
	مُتَساوٍ – ون (لِ)	equal, equivalent, similar (to)
	مُسْتَقِلٌّ – ون	independent
Lesson 38.	واسِعٌ – ون	wide, spacious; extensive
	آخِرُ – ون ، أَواخِرُ	last, final; latter; (foll. by noun of time) the latter part of, the end of
	مُكافِحٌ – ون	fighting, combatting
	قائِمٌ – ون	standing; existing
	مَرْكَزِيٌّ – ون	central
	مَحَلِّيٌّ – ون	local; indigenous; native
	مُخْتَلِفٌ	(with foll. genitive) various
Lesson 39.	جَيِّدٌ – جِيادٌ	good; excellent
Lesson 40.	مَفْقُودٌ – ون	missing, lost
	مَفْتُوحٌ	opened, open
	مَفْهُومٌ	understood
	عَمِيقٌ	deep, profound

345

L. 40 (con't.)	مُدْهِشٌ – ون	surprising, astonishing, amazing
Also:	عَلى حَقٍّ	(prep. phrase) (to be) right
Lesson 41.	واقِعٌ	located, situated
	حالِيٌّ – ون	present, current
	سَيِّئٌ – ون	bad, evil
	مَقْبولٌ – ون	acceptable
	مَسْرورٌ – ون (بـ)	glad, happy, delighted (at), pleased (with)
Lesson 42.	نَبَوِيٌّ	prophetic; pertaining to the Prophet Muhammad
Lesson 43.	مُهِمٌّ	important, significant
	واقِفٌ – ون	standing
	جالِسٌ – ون	sitting
	عجيب – ون	strange, odd
Lesson 44.	دُنْيَوِيٌّ ، دُنْياوِيٌّ	worldly, secular, temporal
	صابِرٌ	patient, forbearing, steadfast
	ساكِتٌ	silent, quiet; calm
	غاضِبٌ – ون	angry; annoyed
	طالِقٌ	(f.) divorced
	شاعِرٌ (بـ)	feeling, perceiving, sensing (s.th.)
Lesson 45.	نَصْرانِيٌّ – نَصارى	Christian
	صابِىءٌ – ون	Sabian
	صالِحٌ – ون	good, righteous, pious
	غالِبٌ – ون	winning; conquering
	كَريمٌ – كُرَماءُ ، كِرامٌ	noble; generous

Particles are words that show no inflection for case regardless of their syntactic function in the sentence. For example, اَلآنَ 'now' remains unchanged in

وَصَلوا الآنَ .	'They arrived (just) now.'

where it modifies the verb; in

لِنَتَعاوَنْ كُلَّ التَّعاوُنِ بَعْدَ الآنَ .	'Let's cooperate fully from now on.'

where it is the object of a preposition, and in

اَلإمْتِحانُ الآنَ يا خَليلُ .	'The exam is (right) now, Khalil.'

where it is a predicate. Nouns or adjectives, on the other hand, do show case inflections according to their function; for example اَلْيَوْمُ 'today' in

وَصَلَ الْيَوْمَ	'He arrived today.'
مُنْذُ الْيَوْمِ	'from today on'

is accusative as a modifier of the verb but is genitive as the object of a preposition. Since nouns and adjectives perform some of the functions of particles, such words will also be listed here but after the heading "Also:".

The particles are subdivided according to their syntactic function. Further information about their meanings, forms, or uses can be obtained from the Arabic-English Glossary or from the Grammatical Notes.

PARTICLES

1. Adverbs

هُنا	'here'	Also: اَلْيَوْمَ	'today'
هُناكَ	'there'	اَللَّيْلَةَ	'tonight'
مَعًا	'together'	غَدًا	'tomorrow'
اَلْآنَ	'now'	صَباحًا	'in the morning'
أَمْسِ	'yesterday'	مَساءٌ	'in the evening
مِنْ قَبْلُ	'before, earlier'	أَحْيانًا	'sometimes'
ثُمَّ	'then'	جِدًّا	'very'
مِنْ ثَمَّ	'thereupon'	كَثيرًا	'a lot; often'
بَعْدُ	'afterward, later'	دائِمًا	'always'
إِذَنْ ، إِذًا	'then, in that case'	قَديمًا	'formerly; of old'
فَقَطْ	'only'	مُطْلَقًا	'absolutely'
أَيْضًا	'also'	عادَةً	'usually'
حَتَّى	'even'	خاصَّةً	'especially'
بَعْدَئِذٍ	'after that'	عامَّةً	'generally'
عِنْدَئِذٍ	'at that time'	قَريبًا	'soon'
حينَئِذٍ	'at that time'	طَويلاً	'at length'
ساعَتَئِذٍ	'at that time'	أَخيرًا	'recently'
يَوْمَئِذٍ	'on that day'	حَقًّا	'truly'
وَقْتَئِذٍ	'at that time'	عَوَضًا عَنْ	'instead of'
		مَثَلاً	'for example'
		كَذٰلِكَ	'likewise; also'
		لِذٰلِكَ	'therefore'

2. Conjunctions

وَ	'and'		أَنَّ	'that'
فَ	'and, and so'		إِنَّ	'that'
وَ	'while, as' (ḥaal)		أَنْ	'that'
أَوْ	'or'		مَا	(nominalizer) 'that'
أَمْ	'or'		إِنْ	'if'
أَمَّا .. فَ	'as for'		إِذَا	'if'
أَيْ	'that is to say'		لَوْ	'if'
بَلْ	'but, rather'		حَتَّى	'until'
إِنَّمَا	'but, on the contrary'		إِلَى أَنْ	'until'
لَعَلَّ	'perhaps'		كَيْ	'in order that'
لَكِنَّ	'but'		لِ	'in order that'
لَكِنْ	'but'		لِكَيْ	'in order that'
لِأَنَّ	'because'		لِأَنْ	'in order that'
كَأَنَّ	'as, as if'		حَتَّى	'in order that'
كَمَا	'as, and also'		كَيْلَا	'in order that not'
مِثْلَمَا	'as, just as'		لِكَيْلَا	'in order that not'
لَمَّا	'when'		لِئَلَّا	'in order that not'
حَيْثُ	'where'		بَعْدَ أَنْ	'after'
مُنْذُ	'since'		قَبْلَ أَنْ	'before'

Also:

حِينَ	'when'
عِنْدَمَا	'when'
كَمَا	'as, and also
مِثْلَمَا	'as'

3. **Exceptive**

إِلّا 'except'

4. **Intensifying**

إِنَّ 'indeed, verily'

لَ 'indeed, truly'

5. **Interjections**

نَعَمْ 'yes'   Also: طَبْعًا 'of course!'

لا 'no'

مَا (أَعْجَبَ) 'how (strange)...!'

يَا لَهُ مِنْ 'what a...he is!'

أُفٍّ (expression of anger or displeasure)

6. **Interrogatives**

أَ (sign of question)   Also: مَنْ 'who?'

هَلْ (sign of question)   مَا 'what?'

أَيْنَ 'where?'   مَاذا 'what?'

مَتى 'when?'   أَيّ 'which?'

كَيْفَ 'how?'   كَمْ 'how much? how many?'

لِمَاذا 'why?'

7. **Negatives**

لا 'no; not'   Also: غَيْرٌ 'non-' (noun)

مَا 'not'   عَدَمٌ 'non-' (noun)

لَنْ 'will not'   لَيْسَ 'is not' (verb)

لَمْ 'did not'

350

8. Prepositions

بِ 'in; by (means of); for (price)'

فِي 'in'

لِ 'to, for, of'

كَ 'like, as'

مَعَ 'with; in spite of'

مِنْ 'from'

عَنْ 'from; concerning'

إِلَى 'to'

عَلَى 'on'

لَدَى 'at (time or place of)'

سِوَى 'except'

حَتَّى 'up to, as far as'

وَ 'by' (oaths)

Also:

بَعْدَ 'after'

قَبْلَ 'before'

فَوْقَ 'over, above'

تَحْتَ 'under, below'

وَرَاءَ 'behind'

وَسْطَ 'amidst'

أَمَامَ 'in front of'

عِنْدَ 'at (time or place)'

أَثْنَاءَ 'during'

خِلالَ 'during'

خَارِجَ 'outside of'

دَاخِلَ 'inside of'

دُونَ 'without'

بِدُونِ 'without'

مِثْلَ 'like'

بَيْنَ 'between, among'

حَوْلَ 'about, concerning, approximatly'

قُرْبَ 'near, in the vicinity of'

بِسَبَبِ 'because of'

بِشَأْنِ 'concerning'

351

9. Verbal

لِ (indirect command) 'let...'

سَوْفَ 'will, going to...'

سَ 'will, going to...'

قَدْ (with perfect tense) 'has (done), had (done),' etc. (with imperfect indicative) 'perhaps, sometimes'

‑إِيّا‑ (sign of pronominal direct object)

10. Vocative

يا 'o'

أَيُّها (أَيَّتُها) 'o'

أَيْ 'o'

352

Listed below are all verbs found in this book, listed by lesson in order

of occurrence. They are arranged vertically by Form number (Q = quadriliteral)

and horizontally by root-type. All verbs are given in their citation form

(3 MS Perfect) unless that form does not normally occur. Parentheses ( ) indi-

cate an active verb that occurs only in the form given as of that lesson; its

complete paradigm will be given in a subsequent lesson. Inactive vocabulary

items (words that occur only in grammatical notes or are glossed in the margins

of Arabic texts) are marked by an asterisk *; an inactive verb is repeated in the

lesson in which it becomes active. Verbs are <u>not</u> repeated in subsequent lessons

if they are used in additional meanings. Verbs are given with their character-

istic prepositions; verb-preposition idioms are listed separately from the corres-

ponding verbs used without prepositions.

	Form	Strong	Doubled	Assimilated	Hollow	Detective
Lesson 4					لَيْسَ	
Lesson 6 Perfect 3s	I II VIII	دَرَسَ ُ رَجَعَ ِ حَضَرَ ُ الى دَرَّسَ اِنْتَقَلَ				
Lesson 7	I III IV V	بَدَأَ َ َ قَرَأَ َ تَابَعَ أَكْمَلَ تَعَلَّمَ				
Lesson 8 Perfect plural	IV VIII X	أَصْدَرَ اِسْتَمَعَ ل اِسْتَقْبَلَ				
Lesson 9 Perfect plural	I III	فَعَلَ َ شَرِبَ َ ذَهَبَ َ أَكَلَ و َ شَاهَدَ				
Lesson 10	I IV	تَرَكَ ُ أَعَدَّ *			*حانَ	
Lesson 11 Jussive singular	I III	عَمِلَ َ حَصَلَ ُ على سَافَرَ			(كانَ)	
Lesson 12 Jussive plural	I IV V	سَأَلَ َ سَمِعَ َ ل بـ أَعْجَبَ أَخْبَرَ بـ تَحَدَّثَ (الى)			(قالَ)	

354

	Form	Strong	Doubled	Assimilated	Hollow	Defective
Lesson 13 Imperfect Indicative Singular	I	بَحَثَ ـَ عن سَكَنَ ـُ كَتَبَ ـُ ذَكَرَ ـُ				
	IV	أَرْسَلَ				
Lesson 14 Imperfect Indicative Plural	I	بَحَثَ ـَ نَقَلَ ـُ نَشَرَ ـُ سَمِعَ ـَ (بـ) حَضَرَ ـُ				
	III	قابَلَ				
Lesson 15	I	شَمَلَ ـُ				
Lesson 16	I	عَمِلَ ـَ على * حَمِدَ ـَ * شَكَرَ ـُ * سَلِمَ ـَ * شَهِدَ ـَ * خَدَمَ ـِ		* وَصَلَ	* عادَ * زارَ	* بَنى * بَقِيَ
	II	قَدَّمَ				
Lesson 17	I	* صَدَقَ * كَسَرَ * كَذَبَ * قَتَلَ خَرَجَ عَلِمَ * سَمِعَ * رَجَعَ				
	II	* صَدَّقَ * كَسَّرَ * مَرَّضَ * كَذَّبَ * قَتَّلَ * سَلَّمَ على	حَدَّدَ قَرَّرَ		عَيَّنَ * خَيَّمَ * عَيَّدَ	* سَمَّى

	Form	Strong	Doubled	Assimilated	Hollow	Defective
Lesson 18 Form III	I	بَذَلَ ُ		*تَقَعُ		
	III	سَاعَدَ				
		شَارَكَ في				
		حَاضَرَ				
	VIII	اِعْتَمَدَ على				
Lesson 19 Form IV	I	رَحَلَ ـَ				
	II	رَحَّبَ بـ * فَضَّلَ (على)				
	IV	أَظْهَرَ أَقْبَلَ على أَسْرَعَ الى أَكْرَمَ				
	VIII	اِخْتَلَفَ(عن)				
Lesson 20 Subjunctive Form V Form VI	I	نَظَرَ ُ في عَرَفَ اَ طَلَبَ اَ				
	II	* عَلَّمَ * مَكَّنَ من * كَلَّمَ				
	III	* عَاوَنَ * قَابَلَ				
	V	تَمَكَّنَ من تَكَلَّمَ تَقَدَّمَ تَقَدَّمَ بـ * تَقَرَّرَ * تَمَصَّرَ * تَعَلَّقَ بـ				
	VI	* تَقابَلَ * تَراسَلَ			تَعَاوَنَ	
Lesson 21 Dual Form VII Form VIII	I	عَقَدَ ـِ * صَرَفَ ـِ * قَصَرَ ُ * سَحَبَ ـَ * فَتَحَ ـَ	*ضَرَّ ُ		*زادَ ـِ	* تَجْري * دَعا ُ * لَقِيَ ـَ

Form	Strong	Doubled	Assimilated	Hollow	Defective
(Lesson 21)	* كَسَرَ ـِ * تَبِعَ ـَ * صَدَمَ ـِ		* وَصَلَ ـِ * وَجَدَ ـِ		
	* جَمَعَ ـَ * عَمِدَ ـَ * نَقَلَ ـُ * طَلَعَ ـُ * ثَأَرَ ـَ * ظَلَمَ ـِ * خَتَمَ ـِ * أَمَرَ ـُ				
II	أَثَّرَ على				
VII	اِنْصَرَفَ اِنْعَقَدَ * اِنْقَطَعَ * اِنْكَسَرَ * اِنْسَحَبَ * اِنْفَتَحَ				
VIII	اِنْتَخَبَ اِعْتَبَرَ اِجْتَمَعَ اِنْتَظَرَ اِخْتَلَفَ * اِدَّكَرَ * اِتَّبَعَ * اِفْتَتَحَ * اِعْتَرَفَ * اِصْطَدَمَ * اِطَّلَعَ * اِثَّأَرَ	* اِضْطَرَّ	* اِتَّصَلَ ـِ * اِتَّحَدَ	* اِزْدَانَ	* اِدَّعَى * اِلْتَقَى

357

	Form	Strong	Doubled	Assimilated	Hollow	Defective
(Lesson 21)		* اِخْتَتَمَ				
		* اِئْتَمَرَ				
		* اِظَّلَمَ				
		* اِتَّحَدَ				
Lesson 22	I	مَنَحَ ـَ	(ظَلَّ) ـَ	(يَجِبُ)	زالَ ـَ	* يَـقِيَ
		جَمَعَ ـَ ـِين				
	II		حَقَّقَ			
	III	طالَبَ ـ				
	IV	أَصْبَحَ				
	V	تَصَرَّفَ		تَوَفَّرَ		
		تَقَدَّمَ				
	VIII	اِعْتَقَدَ				
Lesson 23	I	فَتَحَ ـَ				* يَقولُ
		جَمَعَ ـَ				
		* خَدَمَ ـ				
		* حَكَمَ ـُ				
	IV	أَنْشَأَ				
	V	تَأَثَّرَ ـ			تَطَوَّرَ	
	VIII	اِحْتَرَمَ				
Lesson 24	I	حَكَمَ ـُ		* وَطَنَ ـِ	* عادَ ـُ	* مَشى ـِ
		رَبَطَ ـِ ـين				
		حَفَرَ ـِ				
		نَجَحَ ـَ				
		* غَرُبَ ـَ				
		* حَسُنَ ـُ				
		* نَجَدَ ـُ				
		* فَهِمَ ـَ				
		* حَلَفَ ـِ				
		* قَصَرَ				
	II					
	IV	أَشْرَفَ على	* أَعَدَّ		* أَعادَ	
		* أَعْمَلَ			* أَفادَ	
		* آجَرَ			* أَعارَ	
		* أَفْهَمَ				

	Form	Strong	Doubled	Assimilated	Hollow	Defective
(Lesson 24)	V					*اِنْتَهى
	VIII					
	IX	* اِحْمَرَّ			* اِسْوَدَّ * اِحْوَلَّ	
	X	* اِسْتَغْرَبَ * اِسْتَحْسَنَ * اِسْتَنْجَدَ * اِسْتَأْجَرَ * اِسْتَفْهَمَ * اِسْتَخْلَفَ * اِسْتَحْجَرَ * اِسْتَعْمَلَ		* اِسْتَوْطَنَ * اِسْتَوْزَرَ	* اِسْتَفَادَ * اِسْتَعَادَ * اِسْتَعَارَ	
Lesson 25 Imperative	I	مَنَعَ ـَ جَعَلَ ـَ حَكَمَ ـُ على أَخَذَ ـُ * مَدَحَ ـَ * فَرَضَ ـِ على				*رَجا ـُ
	II	أَجَّلَ * فَتَّشَ عن				* أَدّى
	III				قاوم	
Lesson 26	I	رَغِبَ ـَ في عَلِمَ ـَ (ب)			(قالَ، يَقولُ) (عادَ ـُ)	
	II	فَكَّرَ			* غَيَّرَ	
	IV		(أحبَّ، أحبّ)			
	V				تَزَوَّجَ	
	VI	تَراسَلَ				
	VII	اِنْقَطَعَ				
Lesson 27 AP: I	I	خَرَجَ ـُ				
	III	راسَلَ صادَقَ				
	IV	أَخْرَجَ				

	Form	Strong	Doubled	Assimilated	Hollow	Defective
Lesson 28 AP: Derived	I	* فَقَدَ ـِ		(وَصَلَ ـِ)	* جاءَ ـِ في	
		حَمَلَ ـِ			* قامَ ـِ ـُ	
	III	حافَظَ على				
	IV	أَخْلَصَ لـ				
		أَسْلَمَ				
	V	تَأَكَّدَ من				
		تَطَلَّبَ				
	VIII	اِنْتَشَرَ				
Lesson 29 Passive: Perfect QUADRI-LITERALS	I	ذَهَبَ ـَ ـَ		وُلِدَ		* يَـنى ـِ
		ضَحِكَ ـَ				
		عُرِفَ بـ				
		رَسَمَ ـُ				
		* طَرَدَ ـُ				
	II	* غَيَّرَ				
		* طَوَّرَ				
		* زَوَّجَ				
	III	* بارَكَ				
	IV	* أَنْتَجَ				
	V	* تَغَيَّرَ			* تَجَوَّلَ	
		* تَطَوَّرَ				
	VI	* تَبارَكَ				
	X	* اِسْتَنْبَطَ				
	Q I	سَيْطَرَ على				
		تَرْجَمَ				
	Q II	* تَأَمْرَكَ				
		* تَشَيْطَنَ				
		* تَفَلْسَفَ				
Lesson 30 Passive: Imperfect Passive Participles	II	فَضَّلَ على				
		* عَبَّرَ عن				
	III	عاصَرَ				
	IV		* (يُحِبّون)			
	V	تَغَيَّرَ				
	VIII	اِتَّبَعَ				
	X	اِسْتَخْدَمَ				

	Form	Strong	Doubled	Assimilated	Hollow	Defective
Lesson 31 Hollow: I	I				نامَ -َ دامَ -ُ سارَ -ِ سارَ -ِ جاءَ -ِ عادَ -ُ عادَ -ِ زارَ -ُ	* غَنّى
	II	* هَنّأَ -				
	IV	أَجْلَسَ أَحْضَرَ			* أَجابَ	
	V	تأَخّرَ				
	VIII	اِحْتَفَلَ -				
Lesson 32 Hollow: Derived	II	حَسّنَ	سَبّبَ			
	IV				أَدارَ أَرادَ أَقامَ	
	VIII	اِشْتَرَكَ في			اِمْتازَ - اِحْتاجَ الى اِزْدادَ	
	X				اِسْتَفادَ من اِسْتَطاعَ	
Lesson 33 Assimilated	I	* سَقَطَ -ُ * فَقَدَ -ِ		وَضَعَ -َ وَصَفَ -ِ وَجَدَ -ِ وَثِقَ -َ في وَقَعَ -َ	* عاشَ -ِ * ماتَ -ُ	
	II		أَسّسَ * أَمّمَ			
	VIII			اِتّفَقَ على اِتّصَلَ - اِتّحَدَ		

	Form	Strong	Doubled	Assimilated	Hollow	Defective
Lesson 34 Doubled: I	I	طَبَعَ ـَ	دَلَّ ـُ على شَكَّ ـُ في عَدَّ ـُ حَلَّ ـُ وَدَّ ـَ ظَلَّ ـَ * لَبَّ ـَ * تَمَّ ـِ	وَضَح ـ وَهَبَ ـَ	ماتَ ـُ عاشَ ـِ	
	II	أَلَّفَ			صَوَّرَ	
	V		* تَعَدَّدَ			
Lesson 35 Doubled: Derived	I	شَكَرَ ـُ (على)	مَرَّ ـُ ـ	وَعَدَ ـِ ـ	* زادَ ـِ على	
	IV		أَعَدَّ			
	VII		* اِنْضَمَّ الى			
	VIII		اِهْتَمَّ ـ			
	IX		* اِحْمَرَّ			
	X		اِسْتَمَرَّ * اِسْتَرَدَّ			
Lesson 36 Defective: I	I	* عَرَضَ ـِ على				دَعا ـُ تَلا ـُ حَكى ـِ لَقِيَ ـَ رَأَي ـَ بَنى ـِ بَقِيَ ـَ
	IV				أَحاطَ ـ	
Lesson 37 Defective: Derived	I				سادَ ـُ قامَ ـُ ـ * قالَ ـُ ـ * قامَ ـُ	دَعا ـُ ـ
	II	* ثَبَّتَ		* وَفَّرَ		غَنّى سَمّى
	III					ساوى
	IV					* نادى * أَلْغى * أَعْطى
	V					* تَمَنّى

362

	Form	Strong	Doubled	Assimilated	Hollow	Defective
(Lesson 37)	VI	تَبادَلَ				* تَلاقى
	VII	* اِنْفَصَلَ				* اِنْقَضى
	VIII					* اِشْتَرى
	X		اِسْتَقَلَّ			* اِسْتَثْنى
Lesson 38	I	ظَهَرَ ـَ	حَدَّ ـُ			دعا ـُ الى
	II			وَحَّدَ		
	III	كافَحَ			حاوَلُ	
	VII				اِنْحازَ الى	
Lesson 39	I	صَدَرَ ـُ	رَدَّ ـُ			رَجا ـُ
		رَفَضَ ـُ				
	II					أدّى
	IV	* أَرْفَقَ ـ			* أَضافَ	
		* آسَفَ				
Lesson 40	I	فَهِمَ ـَ			صارَ ـِ	
		دَفَعَ ـَ				
		فَقَدَ ـِ				
		* فَرَغَ ـَ من				
	II	قَدَّرَ				
	IV	أَدْهَشَ			أَساءَ الى	أَنْهى
		أَغْضَبَ				
	V					تَرَقّى
	VIII					* اِلْتَقى
Lesson 41	I	قَبِلَ ـَ	سَرَّ ـُ		باعَ ـِ	جَرى ـِ
	IV				أَذاعَ	أَبْدى
					أَجابَ على	
	V	تَحَسَّنَ				
	VIII		اِشْتَدَّ			اِشْتَرى
Lesson 42	I	بَلَغَ ـُ			كادَ ـَ	
		دَخَلَ ـُ			قامَ ـُ	
	II	لَقَّبَ ـ	جَدَّدَ			وَفّى
	IV	أَدْخَلَ				أَلْقى

363

	Form	Strong	Doubled	Assimilated	Hollow	Defective
(Lesson 42)	VII	اِنْقَسَمَ				
	VIII	اِنْتَصَرَ				
Lesson 43	I	جَلَسَ ـِ	هَمَّ ـُ	وَقَفَ ـِ	شاءَ ـَ	
		خَسِرَ ـَ	* كَفَّ ـُ			
		رَبِحَ ـَ				
		* نَهَقَ ـَ				
		* شَعَرَ ـُ ـِ				
	II	فَسَّرَ		* وَفَّقَ		
		صَدَّقَ				
		* مَثَّلَ				
	IV	* أَصْلَحَ				أَعْطى
	VI	* تَراهَنَ				
	VII	* اِنْغَمَسَ				
Lesson 44	I	غَضِبَ ـَ	* ظَنَّ ـُ		* زادَ ـِ	* بَكى ـِ
		صَبَرَ ـِ على	* حَلَّ ـِ		* خافَ ـَ	
		شَعَرَ ـُ ـِ				
		سَكَتَ ـُ				
		* يَرى ـَ				
		* خَجِلَ ـَ				
		* دَخَلَ ـُ عليها				
		* صَرَخَ ـُ				
		* ضَرَبَ ـِ				
		* قَبِلَ ـَ				
	II	طَلَّقَ			زَوَّجَ *	عَزّى *
		فَرَّقَ				
		* كَفَّنَ				
		* قَبَّلَ				
	IV	أَسْعَدَ				
		* أَدْرَكَ				
		* أَمْسَكَ				
		* أَقْنَعَ				
		* أَحْزَنَ				
	V	* تَعَجَّبَ				

	Form	Strong	Doubled	Assimilated	Hollow	Defective
(Lesson 44)	VI	* تَمَالَكَ				
		* تَظاهَرَ				
		* تَصادَقَ				
	VII	* اِنْفَسَخَ				اِنْقَضى
		* اِنْصَرَفَ الى				
	VIII	* اِعْتَذَرَ				* اِكْتَفى بـ
Lesson 45	I	* جَبَلَ ُ			* هانَ ِ	* قَضى ِ
		* شَهِدَ َ				* دَرى ِ
		* خَفَضَ ِ				
		* لَمَحَ َ				
		* عَبَدَ ِ				
		* رَحِمَ َ				
		* نَهَرَ َ				
		* قَهَرَ َ				
		* نَصَرَ ُ				
		* حَزِنَ َ				
	II	* حَدَّثَ				* حَيِيَ
	III	* ضاعَفَ				
	IV	* أَحْسَنَ				
		* أَنْصَتَ				
		* أَقْرَضَ				
		* آمَنَ				
	VIII	* اِرْتَبَكَ				

ENGLISH-ARABIC GLOSSARY

This glossary is arranged in order of English words used to translate the Arabic vocabulary of this book. Most English words so used are included herein. Not all Arabic words, however, are included here; omitted are proper names and those items found in topical lists in the Appendices-names of the days of the week and the months and the seasons of the year, (Appendix II) and the names of the Arab states. (Appendix III)

In case of English homonyms with identical spelling, nouns are listed before adjectives and adjectives before verb. Thus:

1. present (noun) = gift

2. present (adjective) = attending

3. present (verb) = offer, introduce

Expressions of more than one word are entered under the key word, usually a noun or an adjective. Thus

characterized by, be

is to be read "to be characterized by". A semicolon(;) marks the end of this expression; thus

completed, be; take place

means "to be completed, to take place". Otherwise the semicolon separate non-synonyms, as in

around, approximately; around, surrounding

The notation "E. subj. ⟶ A. obj." means that the subject of the English expression corresponds to the object of the Arabic expression, while the English object corresponds to the Arabic subject. An example is "I received it" ⟶

وَصَلَنِي (literally, "it reached me"). Otherwise, no grammatical information is given; for matters of form or usage see the Arabic-English Glossary or Subject Index for the appropriate grammatical note in the body of the book.

In the Arabic entries the semicolon (؛) separates synonyms, e.g.

newspaper   جَرِيدَةٌ ــ جَرَائِدُ ؛ صَحِيفَةٌ ــ صُحُفٌ

As in the body of the book, the ــ denotes plural and parentheses ( ) denote a feminine, e.g.

red   أَحْمَرُ (حَمْرَاءُ) ــ حُمْرٌ

The slash / precedes a variant form.

A

activity	نَشاطٌ ــ ات
aba, cloak	عَباءَةٌ ــ اتٌ
A.D.	ميلاديٌّ
able (to do s.th.), be	اِسْتَطاعَ، اِسْتِطاعَةٌ؛	add (to)	أَضافَ ، إضافَةٌ إلى
	تَمَكَّنَ ، تَمَكُّنٌ مِن	addition to, in	إلى جانِبِ
about, approximately	حَوْلَ	additional	إِضافِيٌّ
about, concerning	عَن ؛ حَوْلَ؛ بِشَأْنِ	address	عُنْوانٌ ــ عَناوينُ
about to (do s.th.), be	كادَ ــَ (يَفْعَلُ	advance, go forward, progress	تَقَدَّمَ ، تَقَدُّمٌ
	أَنْ يَفْعَلَ)	advance in rank, be promoted	تَرَقَّى ، تَرَقٍّ
above, over	فَوْقَ	advancement, progress	تَقَدُّمٌ
absent	غائِبٌ ــ ونَ	advocate	دَعا ــُ ، دُعاءٌ إلى
absolutely	مُطْلَقاً	affect	أَثَّرَ ، تَأْثيرٌ في
abundant, widespread	مُنْتَشِرٌ		وعَلى
administer, manage	أَدارَ ، إدارَةٌ	afraid (of), be	خافَ ــَ ، خَوْفٌ ،
accept	قَبِلَ ــَ ، قَبولٌ		مَخافَةٌ (مِن)
accomplish, realize	حَقَّقَ ، تَحْقيقٌ	after	بَعْدَ
accomplishment	تَحْقيقٌ	after that	بَعْدَ ذٰلِكَ
accursed	رَجيمٌ	age, era	عَهْدٌ ــ عُهودٌ
acquire	حَصَلَ ــُ ، حُصولٌ عَلى	age (of a person)	عُمْرٌ ــ أَعْمارٌ
act, deed	فِعْلٌ ــ أَفْعالٌ	Ages, Middle	الْقُرونُ الْوُسْطى
act meanly toward	أَساءَ، إساءَةٌ إلى	ago	مُنْذُ
action, activity	نَشاطٌ ــ ات	agree on	اِتَّفَقَ ، اِتِّفاقٌ عَلى
active in the service of, be	عَمِلَ ــَ ، عَمَلٌ عَلى	agreed upon that, it is	مِنَ الْمُتَّفَقِ عَلَيْهِ أَنَّ

agreement	اِتِّفاقٌ – اتٌ	anger s.o.	أَغْضَبَ ، إِغْضابٌ
aim, objective	هَدَفٌ – أَهْدافٌ	angry, become	غَضِبَ ـَ ، غَضَبٌ
airplane	طائِرَةٌ – اتٌ	announce, publish	نَشَرَ ـُ ، نَشْرٌ
airport	مَطارٌ – اتٌ	annulled, be	اِنْفَسَخَ – اِنْفِساخٌ
align o.s. with	اِنْحازَ،اِنْحِيازٌ إِلى	another	آخَرُ – ونَ
alive, living	عائِشٌ – ونَ	answer	رَدٌّ – رُدودٌ؛
all	كُلٌّ ؛ جَميعٌ		إِجابَةٌ – اتٌ
alliance	حِلْفٌ – أَحْلافٌ	answer s.o.	رَدَّ ـُ ، رَدَّ عَلى؟
almost (do s.th.)	كادَ ـَ (يَفْعَلُ		أَجابَ ، إِجابَةٌ
	أَنْ يَفْعَلَ)	answer s.th. (e.g., a letter)	أَجابَ، إِجابَةٌ عَلى
alone, by himself	وَحْدَهُ	antiquities	آثارٌ
also	أَيْضاً ؛ كَذلِكَ	any (with neg.; in a statement)	أَيٌّ
and also	كَما		
always	دائِماً	apologize (for)	اِعْتَذَرَ ، اِعْتِذارٌ(عَن)
amazement, surprise	عَجَبٌ ؛ دَهْشَةٌ	apostle; messenger	رَسولٌ – رُسُلٌ
ambassador	سَفيرٌ – سُفَراءُ	appear, come in view	ظَهَرَ ـَ ، ظُهورٌ
among	بَيْنَ ؛ مِن	appear, be published	صَدَرَ ـُ ، صُدورٌ
amount	مَبْلَغٌ – مَبالِغٌ	application (for)	طَلَبٌ – اتٌ (لِ)
ancestor	جَدٌّ – أَجْدادٌ	appoint	عَيَّنَ ، تَعْيينٌ
ancient	قَديمٌ – قُدَماءُ	appointment (to an office)	تَعْيينٌ
ancient times, in	قَديماً	appointment (time)	مَوْعِدٌ – مَواعِدُ – مَواعيدُ
and	وَ ؛ فَ	appreciate, esteem	قَدَّرَ – تَقْديرٌ
and also, and in addition	كَما	approach (to)	إِقْبالٌ (عَلى)
and so, and then	فَ	approach	أَقْبَلَ ، إِقْبالٌ عَلى
angel	مَلاكٌ – مَلائِكَةٌ	approach (time)	حانَ ـِ (الْوَقْتُ)
anger	غَضَبٌ		

369

approximately	حَوْلَ	assist s.o. (in)	سَاعَدَ ، مُسَاعَدَةٌ (عَلَى وفي) ؛
Arab (n. or adj.), Arabic, Arabian	عَرَبِيٌّ - عَرَبٌ		نَصَرَ ـُ ، نَصْرٌ
Arab League	اَلْجَامِعَةُ ٱلْعَرَبِيَّةُ	assistance	مُسَاعَدَةٌ
Aramaic (language)	اَلآرَامِيَّةُ	association	جَامِعَةٌ ـ اتٌ
area, region, zone	مِنْطَقَةٌ ـ مَنَاطِقُ	at (the place or time of)	عِنْدَ؛ لَدَى ؛ فِي؛ بِـ
arise	قَامَ ـُ ، قِيَامٌ	at first	فِي بِدَايَةِ ٱلأَمْرِ
army (pl.)	جُنُودٌ	at length	طَوِيلاً
around, approximately; around, surrounding	حَوْلَ	at that time	عِنْدَئِذٍ ؛ حِينَئِذٍ ؛ وَقْتَئِذٍ
arrival (at)	وُصُولٌ (إِلَى) ؛ بُلُوغٌ	at the time that (conj.)	لَمَّا ؛ حِينَ؛ عِنْدَمَا
arrive (at, in), reach	وَصَلَ ـِ ، وُصُولٌ (إِلَى)؛ بَلَغَ ـُ ، بُلُوغٌ	atmosphere	جَوٌّ ـ أَجْوَاءٌ، جِوَاءٌ
		attach, enclose (to, in) (e.g., a letter)	أَرْفَقَ ، إِرْفَاقٌ (بِـ)
art	فَنٌّ ـ فُنُونٌ	attain, reach	بَلَغَ ـُ ، بُلُوغٌ ؛ وَصَلَ ـِ ، وُصُولٌ إِلَى
College of the Arts	كُلِّيَّةُ ٱلآدَابِ		
article, essay	مَقَالَةٌ ؛ مَقَالٌ ـ اتٌ	attempt	حَاوَلَ ، مُحَاوَلَةٌ (أَنْ)
as (prep.)	كَ	attempt	مُحَاوَلَةٌ ـ اتٌ
as (conj.)	كَمَا ، مِثْلَمَا	attend, be present at	حَضَرَ ـُ ، حُضُورٌ
as a result of	نَتِيجَةً لِـ		
as for	أَمَّا ... فَ	attitude (towards)	مَوْقِفٌ ـ مَوَاقِفُ (مِن)
as if	كَأَنَّ	author	كَاتِبٌ ـ كُتَّابٌ ؛ أَدِيبٌ ـ أُدَبَاءُ
ashamed (of), be	خَجِلَ ـَ ، خَجَلٌ (مِن)		
ask (about)	سَأَلَ ـَ ، سُؤَالٌ (عَن)	automobile	سَيَّارَةٌ ـ اتٌ
ask for, request	طَلَبَ ـُ ، طَلَبٌ		B
assembly	مَجْلِسٌ ـ مَجَالِسُ	B.A. degree	بَكَالورْيُوس

B.C.	قَبْلَ الْمِيلادِ	begin (with)	بَدَأَ ـَ ، بَدْءٌ (بِـ)
Bachelor's Degree	بَكالورِيُوس	begin (to do s.th.)	بَدَأَ ـَ ، بَدْءٌ ؛
bad, evil	سَيِّئٌ		أَخَذَ ـُ ، أَخْذٌ ؛
basic	أَساسِيٌّ		جَعَلَ ـَ ، جَعْلٌ ؛
bazaar	سوقٌ – أَسْواقٌ		أَقْبَلَ ، إِقْبالٌ عَلى
be	كانَ ـُ ، كَوْنٌ	beginning (of)	بِدايَةٌ ؛ بَدْءٌ
be, be found	وُجِدَ ، يوجَدُ،وُجودٌ	beginning, in the	في بِدايَةِ الأَمْرِ
be...still	ما زالَ، لا يَزالُ	behave	تَصَرَّفَ ، تَصَرُّفٌ
bear, carry	حَمَلَ ـِ ، حَمْلٌ	behavior	تَصَرُّفٌ – ات
bear, give birth to	وَلَدَ ، يَلِدُ، وِلادَةٌ	behind	وَراءَ
bear on, have to do with	اِتَّصَلَ ، اِتِّصالٌ بِـ	behind, be or become; be late	تَأَخَّرَ ، تَأَخُّرٌ
beautiful	جَميلٌ – ونَ ؛	being, existence	كَوْنٌ
	حَسَنٌ – حِسانٌ	being, existing	قائِمٌ – ونَ
beauty	جَمالٌ	belief (in)	اِعْتِقادٌ (بِـ) ؛ إيمانٌ (بِـ)
because	لِأَنَّ	believe (in)	اِعْتَقَدَ، اِعْتِقادٌ (بِـ) ؛
because of	بِسَبَبِ		آمَنَ، إيمانٌ (بِـ)
become	أَصْبَحَ ؛ صارَ ـِ، صَيْرٌ ،	believe s.o. to be telling the truth, s.th. to be true	صَدَّقَ ، تَصْديقٌ
	صَيْرورَةٌ، مَصيرٌ	believe, be of the opinion that	اِعْتَقَدَ، اِعْتِقادٌ ؛
bedouin	بَدَوِيٌّ – بَدْوٌ		رَأى ، رَأْيٌ؛ ظَنَّ ـُ،
before (sequence) (prep.)	قَبْلَ		ظَنٌّ
before (place), in front of	أَمامَ	believer	مُؤْمِنٌ – ونَ
		belonging to	لِـ
		beloved	حَبيبٌ – أَحِبّاءُ
before (conj.)	قَبْلَ أَنْ	below	تَحْتَ
before (adv.), previously	مِنْ قَبْلُ	benefit (from)	اِسْتَفادَ، اِسْتِفادَةٌ (مِنْ)
befriend s.o.	صادَقَ ، مُصادَقَةٌ		

benefit s.o.	نَفَعَ ـَ ، نَفْعٌ	boundary	حَدٌّ ـ حُدُودٌ
besides	إلى جانِبِ	bounty, blessing	نِعْمَةٌ ـ نِعَمٌ ، ات
best; better	أَحْسَنُ	boy	وَلَدٌ ـ أَوْلادٌ
bet, make a bet	تَراهَنَ ، تَراهُنٌ	branch	فَرْعٌ ـ فُرُوعٌ
beverage	شَرابٌ ـ أَشْرِبَةٌ	bray	نَهَقَ ـَ ، نَهْقٌ
bewildered, be	اِرْتَبَكَ ، اِرْتِباكٌ	bride	عَرُوسٌ ـ عَرائِسُ
bewilderment	اِرْتِباكٌ	bride and groom, newlyweds	عَرُوسانِ
Bible, the	اَلْكِتابُ الْمُقَدَّسُ	bridegroom	عَرِيسٌ
big	كَبِيرٌ ـ كِبارٌ	bring	أَحْضَرَ ، إِحْضارٌ ؛
birth	وِلادَةٌ		جاءَ ـِ ، مَجِيءٌ بِ ؛
birth to, give	وَلَدَ يَلِدُ ، وِلادَةٌ		حَضَرَ ـُ ، حُضُورٌ بِ
black	أَسْوَدُ (سَوْداءُ) ـ سُودٌ		
blackboard	لَوْحٌ ـ أَلْواحٌ	bring about, cause	سَبَّبَ ، تَسْبِيبٌ
blessing	نِعْمَةٌ ـ ات ، نِعَمٌ	bring in, introduce s.th.	أَدْخَلَ ، إِدْخالٌ
bloc	كُتْلَةٌ ـ كُتَلٌ	bring s.o. back	عادَ ـُ ، عَوْدَةٌ بِ
blond	أَشْقَرُ (شَقْراءُ) ـ شُقْرٌ	bring up, rear, educate	رَبَّى ، تَرْبِيَةٌ
blue	أَزْرَقُ (زَرْقاءُ) ـ زُرْقٌ	broadcast	أَذاعَ ، إِذاعَةٌ
board	لَوْحٌ ـ أَلْواحٌ	brother	أَخٌ ؍ أَخُو ـ إِخْوَةٌ
bond, fetter	قَيْدٌ ـ قُيُودٌ	brotherly	أَخَوِيٌّ
bond, tie	رابِطَةٌ ـ رَوابِطُ	brown, coffee-colored	بُنِّيٌّ
book	كِتابٌ ـ كُتُبٌ	brown, brown-skinned (person)	أَسْمَرُ (سَمْراءُ) ـ سُمْرٌ
bookstore	مَكْتَبَةٌ ـ ات		
boom	نَهْضَةٌ ـ ات	build	بَنى ـِ ، بِناءٌ ؛
born, be	وُلِدَ يُولَدُ ، وِلادَةٌ		أَقامَ ، إِقامَةٌ
both	كِلا	building	بِناءٌ ـ أَبْنِيَةٌ

372

bus	أُوتوبيس ـ ات	carry out, perform	أَدَّى ، تَأْدِيَةٌ
but, however	لكِنَّ ؛ لكِنْ	cast, throw	أَلْقى ، إِلْقاءٌ
but, on the contrary, rather	إِنَّما	castle	قَصْرٌ ـ قُصورٌ
		catalogue	قائِمَةٌ ـ قَوائِمُ
but, indeed, more than that	بَلْ	cause, reason, motive	سَبَبٌ ـ أَسبابٌ
buy	اِشْتَرى ، شِراءٌ	cause	سَبَّبَ ، تَسْبيبٌ
by, by means of	بِـ	cedars	أَرْزٌ
by God (oath)	وَاللهِ	celebrate	اِحْتَفَلَ ، اِحْتِفالٌ بِـ
		celebration	حَفْلَةٌ ـ حَفَلاتٌ
C		center	مَرْكَزٌ ـ مَراكِزُ
cabinet	وِزارَةٌ ـ اتٌ	century	قَرْنٌ ـ قُرونٌ
café	مَقْهى ـ مَقاهٍ	ceremony	حَفْلَةٌ ـ حَفَلاتٌ
caliph	خَليفَةٌ ـ خُلَفاءٌ	certain, sure (of)	مُتَأَكِّدٌ ـ ونَ (مِن)
call, summon	دَعا ُ ، دَعْوَةٌ	certain (of), become	تَأَكَّدَ ، تَأَكُّدٌ (مِن)
call for, advocate	دَعا ُ ، دَعا إِلى		
call s.o. by the name of	سَمّى ، تَسْمِيَةٌ ؛ دَعا ُ ، دَعا بِـ	chain, fetter	قَيْدٌ ـ قُيودٌ
camel	جَمَلٌ ـ جِمالٌ	chair	كُرْسِيٌّ ـ كَراسٍ
can, be able	اِسْتَطاعَ ، اِسْتِطاعَةٌ ؛	change (s.th.)	غَيَّرَ ، تَغْييرٌ
	تَمَكَّنَ ، تَمَكُّنٌ مِن	change (intrans.)	تَغَيَّرَ ، تَغَيُّرٌ
canal	قَناةٌ ـ قَنَواتٌ	character, nature	خُلْقٌ ـ أَخْلاقٌ
cancel	أَلْغى ، إِلْغاءٌ	characterized (by), be	اِمْتازَ ، اِمْتيازٌ بِـ
candidate	مُرَشَّحٌ ـ ونَ	characteristic	صِفَةٌ ـ اتٌ
capability	تَمَكُّنٌ مِن ؛ اِسْتِطاعَةٌ	chart, table	لَوْحَةٌ ـ اتٌ
capital (city)	عاصِمَةٌ ـ عَواصِمُ	charter	ميثاقٌ ـ مَواثيقُ
car	سَيّارَةٌ ـ اتٌ	check	شيكٌ ـ اتٌ
carry	حَمَلَ ِ ، حَمْلٌ	child	وَلَدٌ ـ أَوْلادٌ

Christ	اَلْمَسِيحُ	coffeehouse	مَقْهًى ـ مَقَاهٍ ؛
Christian	مَسِيحِيٌّ ـ ونَ ؛		قَهْوَةٌ ـ قَهَوَاتٌ
	نَصْرَانِيٌّ ـ نَصارى	college	كُلِّيَّةٌ ـ اتٌ
Christianity	اَلْمَسِيحِيَّةُ	College of the Arts	كُلِّيَّةُ الآدابِ
church	كَنِيسَةٌ ـ كَنائِسُ	common, ordinary, popular; colloquial (adj.)	عامِّيٌّ
cinema	سِينَما	colloquial Arabic	اَلْعامِّيَّةُ
city	مَدِينَةٌ ـ مُدُنٌ	color	لَوْنٌ ـ أَلْوانٌ
civil, civilian	مَدَنِيٌّ	combine...and...	جَمَعَ ـَ ، جَمْعٌ بَيْنَ...
civil rights	اَلْحُقوقُ الْمَدَنِيَّةُ		(وَ...)؛ رَبَطَ ـِ
civilization	حَضارَةٌ		بَيْنَ ... وَبَيْنَ
class; classroom	صَفٌّ ـ صُفوفٌ	combination of...and	جَمْعٌ بَيْنَ ... وَ
class, type, kind	شَكْلٌ ـ أَشْكالٌ	come (to)	جاءَ ـِ ، مَجِيءٌ (إلى)؛
classical	كِلاسِيكِيٌّ		حَضَرَ ـُ ، حُضورٌ الى؛
Classical (Literary) Arabic	اَلْفُصْحى		أَقْبَلَ ، إِقْبالٌ على
clear, obvious	واضِحٌ	come!	تَعالَ
clear, be or become	وَضَحَ ـِ ، وُضوحٌ	come out, be issued	صَدَرَ ـُ ، صُدورٌ
cleared, free (of), become	بَرِىءَ ـَ ، بَراءَةٌ (مِنْ)	come to a stop	وَقَفَ ـِ ، وُقوفٌ ، وَقْفٌ
cloak, aba	عَباءَةٌ ـ اتٌ	come to an agreement (on)	اِتَّفَقَ ، اِتِّفاقٌ (عَلى)
clock	ساعَةٌ ـ اتٌ	come to realize	وَجَدَ ـِ ، وُجودٌ ؛
cloth, fabric, material	قُماشٌ ـ أَقْمِشَةٌ		عَرَفَ ـِ ، مَعْرِفَةٌ
club, league, society	رابِطَةٌ ـ رَوابِطُ	coming, next	قادِمٌ ـ ونَ ؛ مُقْبِلٌ
code, law	قانونٌ ـ قَوانينُ	command	سَيْطَرَ عَلى
coffee	قَهْوَةٌ	commander	قائِدٌ ـ قُوّادٌ ، قادَةٌ
		Commander of the Faithful	أَميرُ الْمُؤْمِنينَ

comment on	فَسَّرَ ، تَفْسِيرٌ	conduct, behavior	تَصَرُّفٌ ـ ات
commerce, trade	تِجَارَةٌ	conduct o.s., behave	تَصَرَّفَ ، تَصَرُّفٌ
common, general	عامٌّ	conference	مُؤْتَمَرٌ ـ ات
Communist	شيوعِيٌّ ـ ون	confidence	ثِقَةٌ
company	شَرِكَةٌ ـ ات	confirm	ثَبَّتَ ، تَثْبِيتٌ
complete, conclude, perfect	أَكْمَلَ ، إِكْمَالٌ	conflict, contradiction	خِلافٌ ـ ات
complete, bring to an end	أَنْهَى ، إِنْهاءٌ	confused, be	اِرْتَبَكَ ، اِرْتِباكٌ
completed, be; take place	تَمَّ ـِ	confusion	اِرْتِباكٌ
completed, be; come to an end	اِنْقَضَى ، اِنْقِضاءٌ؛ اِنْقَطَعَ ، اِنْقِطاعٌ	congratulate s.o. (on/for)	هَنَّأَ ، تَهْنِئَةٌ (عَلَى وبِـ)
completion	إِكْمالٌ؛ إِنْهاءٌ؛ اِنْتِهاءٌ مِن	Congress	كونْغِرس
		connect s.th. (with)	رَبَطَ ـِ ، رَبْطٌ (إِلَى)
compose	أَلَّفَ ، تَأْلِيفٌ؛ وَضَعَ ـَ ، وَضْعٌ	connected with, be	اِتَّصَلَ ، اِتِّصالٌ بِـ
		connection	رابِطَةٌ ـ رَوابِطُ
compute	عَدَّ ـُ ، عَدٌّ	connection, relationship (with)	عَلاقَةٌ ـ ات (بِـ)
comrade	صاحِبٌ ـ أَصْحابٌ	conquer	فَتَحَ ـَ ، فَتْحٌ
concept, idea	فِكْرَةٌ ـ فِكَرٌ	conquest	فَتْحٌ ـ فُتوحٌ
concern, interest, care	اِهْتِمامٌ ـ ات؟ هَمٌّ ـ هُمومٌ	conservative	مُحافِظٌ ـ ون
concern o.s. with	اِهْتَمَّ، اِهْتِمامٌ بِـ	consider, look into	نَظَرَ ـُ ، نَظَرٌ في
concern s.o.	هَمَّ ـُ ، هَمٌّ	consider (s.th. to be s.th.) (two acc.)	اِعْتَبَرَ ، اِعْتِبارٌ؛ عَدَّ ـُ ، عَدٌّ؛ ظَنَّ ـُ ، ظَنٌّ؛ رَأَى ـَ ، رَأْيٌ
concerning	عَن؛ حَوْلَ؛ بِشَأْنِ		
condition	حالٌ ـ أَحْوالٌ؛ وَضْعٌ ـ أَوْضاعٌ	console s.o. (over)	عَزَّى ، تَعْزِيَةٌ (عَن)

375

consolidate	ثَبَّتَ ، تَثْبِيتٌ ؛ وَطَّدَ ، تَوْطِيدٌ	conversation, spoken language	تَخاطُبٌ
consolidation	تَثْبِيتٌ ؛ تَوْطِيدٌ	convince s.o.	أَقْنَعَ ، إِقْناعٌ
constitution	دُسْتُورٌ ـ دَساتِيرُ	convinced (of), be-come	تَأَكَّدَ ، تَأَكُّدٌ (مِن)
construct, build	بَنَى ـِ ، بِناءٌ ؛ أَقامَ ، إِقامَةٌ	co-operate (with s.o.)	تَعاوَنَ ، تَعاوُنٌ
		co-operate (in)	اِشْتَرَكَ ـ اِشْتِراكٌ في
construction	بِناءٌ	co-operation	تَعاوُنٌ
consummate a marri-age	دَخَلَ عَلَيْها	copy, transcript	نُسْخَةٌ ـ نُسَخٌ
contemporary	مُعاصِرٌ ـ ون	correspond with	راسَلَ ، مُراسَلَةٌ
contemporary of, be	عاصَرَ ، مُعاصَرَةٌ	correspond with e.o.	تَراسَلَ ، تَراسُلٌ
content o.s. with s.th.	اِكْتَفَى ، اِكْتِفاءٌ بِ	correspondent, re-porter	مُراسِلٌ ـ ون
continue (doing s.th.)	اِسْتَمَرَّ ، اِسْتِمْرارٌ	cost, price	ثَمَنٌ ـ أَثْمانٌ
	ظَلَّ ـَ ، ظَلٌّ ، ظُلُولٌ ؛ بَقِيَ ـَ ، بَقاءٌ	count	عَدَّ ـُ ، عَدٌّ
		country	بَلَدٌ ـ بِلادٌ ؛ بِلادٌ ـ بُلْدانٌ ؛ دَوْلَةٌ ـ دُوَلٌ
continue (an activity)	تابَعَ ، مُتابَعَةٌ		
contrary, on the	بِالْعَكْسِ	course, of	طَبْعاً
control (of)	سَيْطَرَةٌ (عَلى)	cover (e.g., expenses)	أَدَّى ، تَأْدِيَةٌ
control	سَيْطَرَ عَلى	cradle	مَهْدٌ ـ مُهُودٌ
control o.s.	تَمالَكَ نَفْسَهُ	crash, fall	سَقَطَ ـُ ، سُقُوطٌ
convention; confer-ence	مُؤْتَمَرٌ ـ ات	create	جَعَلَ ـَ ، جَعْلٌ
converse	تَحَدَّثَ ، تَحَدُّثٌ	creation	كَوْنٌ ـ أَكْوانٌ
conversation	مُحادَثَةٌ ـ ات ؛ حَدِيثٌ ـ أَحادِيثُ ؛ حِوارٌ ؛ تَحَدُّثٌ	credentials	أَوْراقُ اعْتِمادٍ
		crime	جَرِيمَةٌ ـ جَرائِمُ

376

cry	يَبْكي ‚ بُكاءٌ بَكى	decree	قَضى ‚ قَضاءٌ ‚
culture, refinement	ثَقافَةٌ ــ ات	deep, profound	عَميقٌ
culture, civilization	حَضارَةٌ ــ ات	defend	دافَعَ ‚ مُدافَعَةٌ عَنْ؛
current, present	حاضِرٌ ــ ون؛حالِيٌّ ــ ون		حافَظَ ‚ مُحافَظَةٌ عَلى
curriculum	مَنْهَجُ التَّعْليمِ ــ	defense (of)	دِفاعٌ (عَنْ) ؛مُحافَظَةٌ
	مَناهِجُ التَّعْليمِ		عَلى
custom, habit	عادَةٌ ــ ات	define	حَدَّدَ ‚ تَحْديدٌ
cut off, be	اِنْقَطَعَ ‚ اِنْقِطاعٌ	degree, diploma	شَهادَةٌ ــ ات
D		delegate	مَنْدوبٌ ــ ون
dabka (a folk dance)	دَبْكَةٌ	delight (with)	إِعْجابٌ (بِـ)
dam	سَدٌّ ــ سُدودٌ	deliver (a speech)	أَلْقى ‚ إِلْقاءٌ (مُحاضَرَةً)
damned, accursed	رَجيمٌ	demand	مُطالَبَةٌ ــ ات
date	تاريخٌ ــ تَواريخُ	demand	طالَبَ ‚ مُطالَبَةٌ بِـ
daughter	بِنْتٌ / اِبْنَةٌ ــ بَناتٌ	demon	جِنِّيٌّ ــ جِنٌّ
day	يَوْمٌ ــ أَيّامٌ	demonstrate, show	أَظْهَرَ ‚ إِظْهارٌ
day, on that	يَوْمَئِذٍ	deny s.th. to s.o.	مَنَعَ ‚ مَنْعٌ ٠٠ عَنْ
day after, the	الْغَدُ	Department of State	وِزارَةُ الْخارِجِيَّةِ
deal with, treat	تَناوَلَ ‚ تَناوُلٌ	departure	سَفَرٌ ــ أَسْفارٌ ؛
dean	عَميدٌ ــ عُمَداءُ		اِنْصِرافٌ
dear (to)	عَزيزٌ ــ أَعِزّاءُ (عَلى)	depend on	اِعْتَمَدَ ؛اِعْتِمادٌ عَلى
dear, sweetheart	حَبيبٌ ــ أَحِبّاءُ	depict, portray	صَوَّرَ ‚ تَصْويرٌ
death	مَوْتٌ ؛وَفاةٌ ــ وَفَياتٌ	deputy	مَنْدوبٌ ــ ون
debt of, be to the	كانَ عَلى	deputation	بَعْثَةٌ ــ بَعَثاتٌ
decide	قَرَّرَ ‚ تَقْريرٌ	describe s.th. (as)	وَصَفَ بِـ، وَصْفٌ(بِأَنَّ)
decision	تَقْريرٌ ــ تَقاريرُ	desert	صَحْراءُ ــ صَحارى

377

desire (for)	رَغْبَةٌ ـ رَغَبَاتٌ (في)	direct, manage	أَدَارَ ، إِدَارَةٌ
desire, wish, want	وَدَّ / وَدِدْتُ يَوَدُّ ،	director	مُدِيرٌ ـ ونَ
	وُدٌّ ، وِدَادٌ ؛	disagree (with)	اِخْتَلَفَ، اِخْتِلَافٌ (مَعَ)
	أَرَادَ ، إِرَادَةٌ ؛	disagreement	خِلَافٌ ـ اتٌ
	رَغِبَ ـَ ، رَغْبَةٌ في؛	disciple, student	تِلْمِيذٌ ـ تَلَامِيذُ
	شَاءَ ـَ ، مَشِيئَةٌ	discipline	تَأْدِيبٌ
detail	تَفْصِيلٌ ـ تَفَاصِيلُ	discuss	بَحَثَ ـَ ، بَحْثٌ
determine	قَرَّرَ ، تَقْرِيرٌ	discussion	بَحْثٌ ـ بُحُوثٌ ؛
develop, evolve	تَطَوَّرَ ، تَطَوُّرٌ		مُحَادَثَةٌ ـ اتٌ
development	تَطَوُّرٌ ـ اتٌ	dismiss	طَرَدَ ـُ ، طَرْدٌ
devil	شَيْطَانٌ ـ شَيَاطِينُ	display, show	أَبْدَى ، إِبْدَاءٌ؛
devote (o.s.) to	اِنْصَرَفَ ،اِنْصِرَافٌ إِلَى		أَظْهَرَ ، إِظْهَارٌ
dialect	لَهْجَةٌ ـ اتٌ	dissertation	رِسَالَةٌ ـ رَسَائِلُ
dialogue, conversation	حِوَارٌ	dissolution	حَلٌّ ـ حُلُولٌ
dictionary	قَامُوسٌ ـ قَوَامِيسُ	dissolve	أَلْغَى ، إِلْغَاءٌ؛
die	مَاتَ ـُ ، مَوْتٌ		حَلَّ ـُ ، حَلٌّ
differ (from)	اِخْتَلَفَ ، اِخْتِلَافٌ (عَن)	distance	مَسَافَةٌ ـ اتٌ
difference	اِخْتِلَافٌ ـ اتٌ؛اِمْتَازَ،اِمْتِيَازٌ (بِـ)	distinguished (by), be	
difference of opinion	خِلَافٌ ـ اتٌ		فَرَّقَ ، تَفْرِيقٌ،تَفْرِقَةٌ
different (from); various	مُخْتَلِفٌ (عَن ، مِن)	divide, separate	
		divided (into), be	اِنْقَسَمَ ،اِنْقِسَامٌ (إِلَى)
difficult	صَعْبٌ ـ صِعَابٌ	division, part	قِسْمٌ ـ أَقْسَامٌ
dig	حَفَرَ ـِ ، حَفْرٌ	divorce	طَلَاقٌ
dinar	دِينَارٌ ـ دَنَانِيرُ	divorce	طَلَّقَ ، طَلَاقٌ
diploma	شَهَادَةٌ ـ اتٌ	divorced woman	طَالِقٌ

378

do	فَعَلَ ـَ ، فِعْلٌ	during	أَثْناءَ ؛ خِلالَ
do with, have to; bear on	اِتَّصَلَ ، اِتِّصالٌ بِ	duty (for)	واجِبٌ ـ اتٌ (عَلى)
doctor, M.D.	طَبيبٌ ـ أَطِبّاءُ ؛	dwell, live	سَكَنَ ـُ ، سَكَنٌ
	دُكْتورٌ ـ دَكاتِرَةٌ	dying	مائِتٌ ـ ون
doctor, Ph.D	دُكْتورٌ ـ دَكاتِرَةٌ	**E**	
		each	كُلٌّ
doctorate	دُكْتوراةٌ	eager for, longing for s.o.	مُشْتاقٌ ـ ون إلى
dollar	دولارٌ ـ اتٌ	ear	أُذُنٌ ـ آذانٌ
domestic (not foreign)	داخِليٌّ	earlier	مِنْ قَبْلُ
dominate	سَيْطَرَ ، سَيْطَرَةٌ عَلى	east	شَرْقٌ
domination	سَيْطَرَةٌ عَلى	easy	سَهْلٌ ـ سُهولٌ
donkey	حِمارٌ ـ حَميرٌ ، أَحْمِرَةٌ	eat	أَكَلَ ـُ ، أَكْلٌ
door	بابٌ ـ أَبْوابٌ	economy	اِقْتِصادٌ
double	ضاعَفَ ، مُضاعَفَةٌ	edition	طَبْعَةٌ ـ اتٌ
doubt (about)	شَكٌّ ـ ، شُكوكٌ (في)	educate	عَلَّمَ ، تَعْليمٌ ؛
doubt s.th.	شَكَّ ـُ ، شَكٌّ في		رَبّى ، تَرْبِيَةٌ ؛
dowry	مَهْرٌ		خَرَّجَ ، تَخْريجٌ
draft (a document)	وَضَعَ ـَ ، وَضْعٌ	education	تَعْليمٌ ، تَرْبِيَةٌ
drama; a play	اَلْفَنُّ التَّمْثيليُّ	educational, pedagogical	تَرْبَوِيٌّ
draw	رَسَمَ ـُ ، رَسْمٌ ؛		
	صَوَّرَ ، تَصْويرٌ	effect (on)	تَأْثيرٌ (عَلى)
draw near, approach	أَقْبَلَ ، إِقْبالٌ عَلى	effort	جَهْدٌ ـ جُهودٌ
draw near (time)	حانَ ـِ (اَلْوَقْتُ)	eight	ثَمانِيَةٌ
drink	شَرابٌ ـ أَشْرِبَةٌ	eighteen	ثَمانِيَةَ عَشَرَ
drink	شَرِبَ ـَ ، شُرْبٌ	eighth	ثامِنٌ
		eighty	ثَمانونَ

elapse (time)	اِنْقَضَى ، اِنْقِضَاءٌ ؛ مَرَّ ـُ ، مُرُورٌ	England	إِنْكِلْتَرَا
elect	اِنْتَخَبَ ، اِنْتِخَابٌ	English	إِنْكِلِيزِيٌّ ـ إِنْكِلِيز
election	اِنْتِخَابٌ ـ ات	English language	اَلْإِنْكِلِيزِيَّةُ
elegant, witty, nice	ظَرِيفٌ ، ظُرَفَاءُ ، ظِرَافٌ	engraving	حَفْرٌ
eleven	أَحَدَ عَشَرَ	enough, be	كَفَى ـِ ، كِفَايَةٌ
eleventh	حَادِيَ عَشَرَ	enough!	كَفَى
embarrassment	حَرَجٌ	enshroud	كَفَّنَ ، تَكْفِينٌ
embark on	أَقْبَلَ ، إِقْبَالٌ عَلَى	enter, go in	دَخَلَ ـُ ، دُخُولٌ (عَلَى)
embassy	سِفَارَةٌ ـ ات	enter, take in	أَدْخَلَ ، إِدْخَالٌ
emirate	إِمَارَةٌ ـ ات	entire	كُلٌّ
employ, hire	وَظَّفَ ، تَوْظِيفٌ	epistle	رِسَالَةٌ ـ رَسَائِلُ
employ, use	اِسْتَخْدَمَ ، اِسْتِخْدَامٌ	equal (to)	مُسَاوٍ (لِـ)
employee	مُوَظَّفٌ ـ ون	Equal Rights Law	قَانُونُ التَّسَاوِي فِي الْحُقُوقِ
enclose (in)	أَرْفَقَ ، إِرْفَاقٌ (بِـ)		
encounter, meet, find	وَجَدَ يَجِدُ ، وُجُودٌ ؛ لَقِيَ ـَ ، لِقَاءٌ	era	عَهْدٌ ـ عُهُودٌ ؛ عَصْرٌ ـ أَعْصُرٌ ، عُصُورٌ ، أَعْصَارٌ
encourage	شَجَّعَ ، تَشْجِيعٌ		
end	نِهَايَةٌ ؛ اِنْتِهَاءٌ ؛ اِنْقِطَاعٌ	erect, build	أَقَامَ ، إِقَامَةٌ
end of	آخِرٌ ـ أَوَاخِرُ	especially	خَاصَّةً
end, come to an end	اِنْتَهَى ، اِنْتِهَاءٌ ؛ اِنْقَطَعَ ، اِنْقِطَاعٌ	essay; article	مَقَالَةٌ ، مَقَالٌ ـ ات
		establish, found	أَنْشَأَ ، إِنْشَاءٌ ؛ أَقَامَ ، إِقَامَةٌ ؛ أَسَّسَ ، تَأْسِيسٌ
endure, last	دَامَ ـُ ، دَوَامٌ		
enemy	عَدُوٌّ ـ أَعْدَاءٌ	establish, confirm	ثَبَّتَ ، تَثْبِيتٌ
energy	نَشَاطٌ ـ ات		
engineer	مُهَنْدِسٌ ـ ون	establishment	إِنْشَاءٌ ؛ تَأْسِيسٌ ؛ تَثْبِيتٌ ؛ إِقَامَةٌ

even	حَتَّى	existence	كَوْنٌ ، وُجودٌ
even if	وَإِنْ ؛ وَلَوْ	existing	قائِمٌ ، مَوْجودٌ
evening (time of day)	مَساءٌ ؛ لَيْلٌ	expenses	تَكْليفٌ ــ تَكاليفُ
evening (one)	مَساءٌ ــ أَمْساءٌ ؛	experience	خِبْرَةٌ
	لَيْلَةٌ ــ لَيالٍ	expert	مُتَخَصِّصٌ ــ ون
every	كُلٌّ	expertise	خِبْرَةٌ
evidence, proof	دَلالَةٌ ــ دَلائِلُ ؛ ات	explain	فَسَّرَ ، تَفْسيرٌ
evil (n.)	شَرٌّ ــ شُرورٌ	explorer	رَحّالٌ ــ رَحّالَةٌ
examination	اِمْتِحانٌ ــ ات	exporting, export	إِصْدارٌ
examine closely	تَفَحَّصَ ، تَفَحُّصٌ	expound on	فَسَّرَ ، تَفْسيرٌ
example, for	مَثَلاً	express	عَبَّرَ ، تَعْبيرٌ عَن
excavation	حَفْرٌ	expression	تَعْبيرٌ ــ تَعابيرُ
exceed, be more than	زادَ ــِ ، زِيادَةٌ عَلى	extent, limit	حَدٌّ ــ حُدودٌ
excellency (term of respect)	حَضْرَةٌ ــ حَضَراتٌ	external	خارِجِيٌّ
excellent	حَسَنٌ ــ حِسانٌ ؛	extremist	مُتَطَرِّفٌ ــ ون
	مُمْتازٌ ــ ون	eye	عَيْنٌ ــ عُيونٌ ؛ طَرْفٌ
except	إِلّا ؛ سِوى	eyesight	بَصَرٌ ــ أَبْصارٌ
excerpt	مُقْتَطَفٌ ــ ات		
exchange	تَبادَلَ ، تَبادُلٌ	F	
exchange for, in	عِوَضاً عَن	face	وَجْهٌ ــ وُجوهٌ
exercise, drill	تَمْرينٌ ــ تَمارينُ	fact: the fact that	أَنَّ
exert (efforts)	بَذَلَ ــُ ، بَذْلٌ (جُهود)	factory	مَصْنَعٌ ــ مَصانِعُ
exhibit, show, present (to)	عَرَضَ ــِ ، عَرْضٌ (عَلى)	fall	سَقَطَ ــُ ، سُقوطٌ ؛ وَقَعَ ــَ ، وُقوعٌ
exist, be found	وُجِدَ يوجَدُ ، وُجودٌ	fall asleep	نامَ ــَ ، نَوْمٌ
		fall in love with	أَحَبَّ ، حُبٌّ

fall silent	سَكَتَ ـُ ، سُكوتٌ	figure, literary	أَديبٌ ـ أُدَباءُ
false; error	خَطَأٌ	film, movie	فِلْمٌ ، فيلْمٌ ـ أَفْلامٌ
family (immediate)	عائِلَةٌ ـ ات	final	أَخيرٌ ؛ آخِرٌ
family, folks	أَهْلٌ ـ أَهالٍ	find; find s.o. to be s.th.	وَجَدَ ـِ ، وُجودٌ
famous (for)	مَشْهورٌ ـ ونَ (بِـ)	find, meet	لَقِيَ ـَ ، لِقاءٌ
far, far-away (from)	بَعيدٌ ـ بُعَداءُ (عَنْ)	find out (about), learn (of)	عَرَفَ ـِ ، مَعْرِفَةٌ
farewell!	وَداعاً ؛ مَعَ السَّلامَةِ	fine, good	حَسَنٌ ـ حِسانٌ
fashion, mold, make	جَبَلَ ـِ ، جَبْلٌ	fine!	حَسَناً
father	أَبٌ / أَبو ـ آباءُ	fine, (I'm) fine, well	بِخَيْرٍ
fear (of)	خَوْفٌ (مِنْ)	finish, be finished with	فَرَغَ ـُ ، فُروغٌ مِنْ
fear, be afraid (of)	خافَ ـَ ، خَوْفٌ	finish, bring to an end	أَنْهى ، إِنْهاءٌ
	مَخافَةٌ (مِنْ)	finish, complete	أَكْمَلَ ، إِكْمالٌ
feast, feast day, holiday	عيدٌ ـ أَعيادٌ	first	أَوَّلُ (أولى)
feel, sense	شَعَرَ ـُ ، شُعورٌ بِـ	first, at	في بِدايَةِ الأَمْرِ
festive event	حَفْلَةٌ ـ حَفَلاتٌ	first class honors	مَرْتَبَةُ الشَّرَفِ الأُولى
few	قَليلٌ ـ قَلائِلُ ، قِلالٌ	five	خَمْسَةٌ
fiancé, fiancée	خَطيبٌ ـ خُطَباءُ	flag	عَلَمٌ ـ أَعْلامٌ
field	مَيْدانٌ ـ مَيادينُ	follow, pursue; observe	اِتَّبَعَ ، اِتِّباعٌ
fifteen	خَمْسَةَ عَشَرَ		
fifteenth	خامِسَ عَشَرَ	follow, succeed, come after	تَلا ـُ ، تُلُوٌّ
fifth	خامِسٌ	following, next	تالٍ ـ ونَ
fifty	خَمْسونَ	following day	غَدٌ
fight, struggle	كافَحَ ، مُكافَحَةٌ		
fight, oppose, resist	قاوَمَ ، مُقاوَمَةٌ	food	طَعامٌ ؛ أَكْلٌ

foot	قَدَمٌ ـ أَقْدَامٌ	freedom	حُرِّيَّةٌ ـ اتَ
for	لِ	French	فَرَنْسِيٌّ ـ ونَ
for example	مَثَلاً	friend	صَدِيقٌ ـ أَصْدِقَاءُ
for the purpose of	لِ ، لِكَيْ		صَاحِبٌ ـ أَصْحَابٌ
for the price of	بِ	friends with, become	صَادَقَ ، مُصَادَقَةٌ
forbear	صَبَرَ ـ ، صَبْرٌ عَلَى	friends with s.o., become	تَصَادَقَ ، تَصَادُقٌ
forbid s.th. (to s.o.)	مَنَعَ ـَ ، مَنْعٌ عَنْ	from	مِنْ
foreign	أَجْنَبِيٌّ ـ أَجَانِبُ	from, since	مُنْذُ ، مِنْ
foreign affairs	خَارِجِيَّةٌ	front of, in	أَمَامَ
foreign minister	وَزِيرُ الْخَارِجِيَّةِ	fun, pleasure	لَهْوٌ
foreigner	أَجْنَبِيٌّ ـ أَجَانِبُ	function, task	وَظِيفَةٌ ـ وَظَائِفُ
form, shape	شَكْلٌ ـ أَشْكَالٌ	funny, curious	طَرِيفٌ
formal, official	رَسْمِيٌّ ـ ونَ	furnish evidence (of)	دَلَّ ـُ دَلالَةٌ (عَلَى)
fortunately	لِحُسْنِ الْحَظِّ	future	مُسْتَقْبَلٌ
forty	أَرْبَعُونَ		
forward	إِلَى الْقُدَّامِ ، إِلَى الْأَمَامِ		G
		gain	رَبِحَ ـَ ، رِبْحٌ
		gain control of	تَمَالَكَ ، تَمَالُكٌ
found, establish	أَسَّسَ ؛ أَنْشَأَ ؛ أَقَامَ	garden	جَنَّةٌ ـ اتَ
found, be; exist	وُجِدَ ، يُوجَدُ ، وُجُودٌ	general, (military)	قَائِدٌ ـ قُوَّادٌ، قَادَةٌ
four	أَرْبَعَةٌ	general, common, universal	عَامٌّ
fourteen	أَرْبَعَةَ عَشَرَ	generally	عَامَّةً
fourteenth	رَابِعَ عَشَرَ	generosity	كَرَمٌ
fourth	رَابِعٌ	generous	كَرِيمٌ ـ كُرَمَاءُ، كِرَامٌ
fragment, selection	قِطْعَةٌ ـ قِطَعٌ	get, obtain	حَصَلَ ـُ ، حُصُولٌ عَلَى
franc (coin)	فِرَانْكٌ ، فَرَنْكٌ ـ اتَ		

383

get going	سارَ ـِ ، سَيْرٌ	go in, enter	دَخَلَ ـُ ، دُخولٌ
get in touch with	إتَّصَلَ ، إتِّصالٌ بِـ	go on doing s.th.	ظَلَّ ـَ ، ظُلولٌ
gift	هَدِيَّةٌ ـ هَدايا ؛	go out (of, from)	خَرَجَ ـُ ، خُروجٌ (مِن)
	هِبَةٌ ـ ات	go up to, approach	أقْبَلَ ، إقْبالٌ عَلى
girl	بِنْتٌ / إبْنَةٌ ـ بَناتٌ ؛	go to bed, go to sleep	نامَ ـَ ، نَوْمٌ
	فَتاةٌ ـ فَتَياتٌ	goal	هَدَفٌ ـ أهْدافٌ
give (s.o.) (s.th.)	أعْطى ، إعْطاءٌ ؛	god	إلهٌ ـ آلِهَةٌ
	وَهَبَ ـَ هِبَةً ، وَهْبٌ	God	اللهُ
give, grant s.o. s.th.	مَنَحَ ـَ ، مَنْحٌ	going	زاهِبٌ ، سائِرٌ
give birth to	وَلَدَ ـِ ، وِلادَةٌ	going to, will	سَوْفَ ؛ سَـ
give credence to	صَدَّقَ ، تَصْديقٌ	goldsmith	صائِغٌ ـ صاغَةٌ
give in marriage	زَوَّجَ ، تَزْويجٌ	good	جَيِّدٌ ـ جِيادٌ
give s.o. the nick-name of	لَقَّبَ ، تَلْقيبٌ بِـ	good, upright	صالِحٌ ـ ون
give s.o. his full share of	وَفّى ، تَوْفِيَةٌ	good morning!	صَباحُ الخَيْرِ بِصَباحِ النّورِ
		good things, prosper-ity	خَيْرٌ ـ خُيورٌ
give s.o. more of s.th.	زادَ ـِ ، زِيادَةٌ	good bye!	وَداعاً ؛ مَعَ السَّلامَةِ ؛
give success to (:God)	وَفَّقَ ، تَوْفيقٌ		إلى اللِّقاءِ
given abundantly, be	تَوَفَّرَ ، تَوَفُّرٌ	govern, rule	حَكَمَ ـُ ، حُكْمٌ
glance	طَرْفٌ	government	حُكومَةٌ ـ ات
globetrotter	رَحّالة	governmental, state-run	حُكوميٌّ
go	ذَهَبَ ـَ ، ذَهابٌ ؛	grace, blessing	نِعْمَةٌ ـ ات ، نِعَمٌ
	سارَ ـِ ، سَيْرٌ	graduate (s.o.)	خَرَّجَ ، تَخْريجٌ
go away, leave	سافَرَ ، سَفَرٌ ؛	grammar rule	قاعِدَةٌ ـ قَواعِدُ
	إنْصَرَفَ ، إنْصِرافٌ	grandfather	جَدٌّ ـ جُدودٌ، أجْدادٌ

grant (s.o.) s.th.	مَنَحَ َ، مَنْحٌ	harshness, treat with	قَهَرَ َ، قَهْرٌ
grasp, take hold of	أَمْسَكَ ، إِمْساكٌ	hasten to	أَسْرَعَ ، إِسْراعٌ إِلى
great	عَظيمٌ ـ عُظَماءُ	hatred	بُغْضٌ
	كَبيرٌ ـ كِبارٌ	have (E. subj. ☜، مَعَ ، عِنْدَ ، لِ كانَ A. obj.)
green	أَخْضَرُ (خَضْراءُ) ـ خُضْرٌ		لَدى
greet	حَيّا ، تَحِيَّةٌ	have confidence in	وَثِقَ ِ، ثِقَةٌ في، بِ
greeting(s)	سَلامٌ ؛ تَحِيَّةٌ ـ اتٌ	have mercy on	رَحِمَ َ، رَحْمَةٌ
grieve, be sad (at, over)	حَزِنَ َ، حُزْنٌ (لِ، عَلى)	have to, must	وَجَبَ ِ، يَجِبُ ، وُجوبٌ أَنْ
		have to do with	اِتَّصَلَ ، اِتِّصالٌ بِـ
groom	عَريسٌ	he	هُوَ
group, faction	طائِفَةٌ ـ طَوائِفُ	he (it) is not	لَيْسَ
guest	ضَيْفٌ ـ ضُيوفٌ	head	رَأْسٌ ـ رُؤوسٌ
guest of honor	ضَيْفُ الشَّرَفِ	head, chief	رَئيسٌ ـ رُؤَساءُ
		hear	سَمِعَ َ، سَماعٌ
H		hearken to	أَنْصَتَ ، إِنْصاتٌ لِ
habit, custom	عادَةٌ ـ اتٌ	heart	قَلْبٌ ـ قُلوبٌ ؛
<u>hadith</u>, prophetic tradition	حَديثٌ ـ أَحاديثُ		فُؤادٌ ـ أَفْئِدَةٌ
half	نِصْفٌ ـ أَنْصافٌ	held, be (meeting)	اِنْعَقَدَ ، اِنْعِقادٌ
hand	يَدٌ ـ أَيادٍ	Hellenic	هِلينِيٌّ
handsome	جَميلٌ ـ ونَ ؛	Hello!	مَرْحَباً
	حَسَنٌ ـ حِسانٌ	help s.o. (with)	ساعَدَ، مُساعَدَةٌ (عَلى) ؛
happen	جَرى ِ، جَرْيٌ ؛		نَصَرَ ُ، نَصْرٌ
	وَقَعَ َ، وُقوعٌ	hence	مِنْ ثَمَّ
happy (at, with)	سَعيدٌ ـ سُعَداءُ (بِ)		وَ
harm, hurt	أَساءَ ، إِساءَةٌ إِلى	here	هُنا
harsh, become	اِشْتَدَّ ، اِشْتِدادٌ	high	عالٍ

385

history	تَارِيخٌ	humility	ذُلٌّ
hit, strike	ضَرَبَ ــِ ، ضَرْبٌ	hundred	مِئَةٌ ، مَائَةٌ ــ اتٌ
hold (a meeting)	عَقَدَ ــِ ، عَقْدٌ	hundreds of	مِئَاتٌ مِن
holiday	عِيدٌ ــ أَعْيَادٌ	hurt, harm	أَسَاءَ ، إِسَاءَةٌ إِلَى
holy	مُقَدَّسٌ ــ ونَ	husband	زَوْجٌ ــ أَزْوَاجٌ
home	بَيْتٌ ــ بُيُوتٌ	**I**	
homeland	بِلَادٌ ، وَطَنٌ ــ أَوْطَانٌ	I	أَنَا
honor	شَرَفٌ	i.e., that is	أَيْ
honor of, in	عَلَى شَرَفِ	idea	فِكْرَةٌ ــ فِكَرٌ
honor	أَكْرَمَ ، إِكْرَامٌ	if	إِنْ ، إِذَا ، لَوْ .. لَ
honorable	كَرِيمٌ ــ كُرَمَاءُ ، كِرَامٌ	ignorance	جَهْلٌ
honors first class	مَرْتَبَةُ الشَّرَفِ الأُولَى	ignorant	جَاهِلٌ ــ ونَ
hope	أَمَلٌ ــ آمَالٌ ، رَجَاءٌ	illiterate	أُمِّيٌّ ــ ونَ
hope	رَجَا ــُ ، رَجَاءٌ	immersed in, become	اِنْغَمَسَ ، اِنْغِمَاسٌ فِي
hospitality	حُسْنُ الضِّيَافَةِ	importance	أَهَمِّيَّةٌ
hotel	فُنْدُقٌ ــ فَنَادِقُ	importance to, be of	هَمَّ ــُ ، هَمٌّ
hour	سَاعَةٌ ــ اتٌ	important	هَامٌّ
house	بَيْتٌ ــ بُيُوتٌ	impose s.th. on	فَرَضَ ــِ ، فَرْضٌ عَلَى
	دَارٌ ــ دُورٌ	improve, get better	تَحَسَّنَ ، تَحَسُّنٌ
how?	كَيْفَ ؟	improve, make better	حَسَّنَ ، تَحْسِينٌ
how are you?	كَيْفَ الحَالُ ؟	improve, mend, repair	أَصْلَحَ ، إِصْلَاحٌ
how (beautiful she is)!	مَا (أَجْمَلَهَا)	improvement, betterment	تَحْسِينٌ ، إِصْلَاحٌ
how many? how much?	كَمْ ؟	in	فِي ، بِ
human being	إِنْسَانٌ	include	شَمِلَ ــَ ، شَمْلٌ ، شُمُولٌ
		included (in a written document), come	جَاءَ ــِ فِي ، بِ

386

including	مِنْها ...	institute	مَعْهَد ـ مَعاهِد
income, revenue	دَخْل	instruction	تَعْليمٌ ـ تَعاليمُ،
increase, grow larger	اِزْدادَ ، اِزْدِياد		ـ ات
		intellectual	فِكْرِيّ
incumbent upon	واجِبٌ عَلى	intense	شَديدٌ ـ اِشِدّاء
indeed!	إِنَّ ، وَٱللَّهِ	intense, become (more) intensify	اِشْتَدَّ ، اِشْتِداد
independence	اِسْتِقْلالٌ		
independent, be or become	اِسْتَقَلَّ ، اِسْتِقْلال	interest, concern, care	اِهْتِمامٌ ـ ات
Indian	هِنْدِيّ ـ هُنود	interest, concern s.o.	هَمَّ ـُ ، هَمّ
indicate	دَلَّ ـُ ، دَلالةٌ عَلى	interest in, take	اِهْتَمَّ ، اِهْتِمامٌ بِـ
indication	دَلالةٌ ـ دَلائِل، ات	interior affairs (cabinet)	داخِلِيّةٌ
individual	فَرْدٌ ـ أَفْراد	internal	داخِلِيّ
induce	اِسْتَنْبَطَ ـ اِسْتِنْباط	international	دُوَلِيّ
industry	صِناعةٌ ـ ات	interview	مُقابَلةٌ ـ ات
influence (on)	تَأْثيرٌ (عَلى)	interview, meet	قابَلَ ، مُقابَلة
influence	أَثَّرَ ، تَأْثيرٌ عَلى/في	introduce s.o. to	قَدَّمَ ، تَقْديمٌ إِلى
influenced by, be	تَأَثَّرَ ، تَأَثُّرٌ في	introduce s.th. into	أَدْخَلَ ، إِدْخالٌ عَلى
inform (of)	أَخْبَرَ ، إِخْبارٌ (بِـ)	invite (to)	دَعا ـُ ، دُعاءٌ (إِلى)
inhabitant	ساكِنٌ ـ سُكّان	Islam	اَلْإِسْلام
inner, interior	داخِلِيّ	Islamic	إِسْلامِيّ
inquire (about) search (for)	تَفَحَّصَ ، تَفَحُّص (عَن)	island	جَزيرةٌ ـ جَزائِرُ، جُزُر
inside	داخِلَ	isn't that so?	أَلَيْسَ كَذٰلِكَ ؟
insist (on)	أَصَرَّ ، إِصْرارٌ (عَلى)	issue, number (magazine)	عَدَدٌ ـ أَعْدادٌ
insistence	إِصْرارٌ	it	هُوَ ، هِيَ
instead of	عِوَضاً عَن		

J

jest	دِعَابَةٌ ـ اتٌ	know	عَرَفَ ـِ ، مَعْرِفَةٌ ؛
Jew, be a	هَادَ ـُ ، هَوْدٌ		عَلِمَ ـَ ، عِلْمٌ ؛
jinni, genie	جِنِّيّ ـ جِنٌّ		دَرَى ـِ ، دِرَايَةٌ (بِـ)
job, position, work	وَظِيفَةٌ ـ وَظَائِفُ ؛	knowledge, science	عِلْمٌ ـ عُلُومٌ
	عَمَلٌ ـ أَعْمَالٌ	knowledge, acquaintence	مَعْرِفَةٌ ـ مَعَارِفُ
join in	شَارَكَ ، مُشَارَكَةٌ فِي	known for	مَعْرُوفٌ ـ ونَ بِـ
joke	دِعَابَةٌ ـ اتٌ	known for, be	عُرِفَ بِـ
journalistic; journalist	صَحَفِيّ ـ ونَ	known that, it is	مِنَ ٱلْمَعْرُوفِ أَنَّ
Judaism	ٱلْيَهُودِيَّةُ	Koran	ٱلْقُرْآنُ
judge	قَاضٍ ـ قُضَاةٌ	Koranic verse	آيَةٌ ـ اتٌ
judge	حَكَمَ ـُ ، حُكْمٌ عَلَى	kubba	كُبَّةٌ
just as	كَمَا أَنَّ		

K

L

kabob	كَبَابٌ	lady	سَيِّدَةٌ ـ اتٌ
keep on (doing s.th.)	اِسْتَمَرَّ ، اِسْتِمْرَارٌ	lady of the house	سَيِّدَةُ ٱلْبَيْتِ
	بَقِيَ ـَ ؛ ظَلَّ ـَ	lady, young	آنِسَةٌ ـ اتٌ
kind, type, class	شَكْلٌ ـ أَشْكَالٌ	language	لُغَةٌ ـ اتٌ
kind, sect, faction	طَائِفَةٌ ـ طَوَائِفُ	large	كَبِيرٌ ـ كِبَارٌ
kind to, be	أَحْسَنَ ، إِحْسَانٌ لِـ	last, final	آخِرٌ ـ أَخِيرٌ
king	مَلِكٌ ـ مُلُوكٌ	last, past (time)	مَاضٍ
kingdom	مَمْلَكَةٌ ـ مَمَالِكُ	last, endure	دَامَ ـُ ، دَوَامٌ ، دَيْمُومَةٌ
kiss	قَبَّلَ ، تَقْبِيلٌ / قُبْلَةٌ	last, continue	اِسْتَمَرَّ ، اِسْتِمْرَارٌ
		late	مُتَأَخِّرٌ ـ ونَ
		late, be, be delayed	تَأَخَّرَ ، تَأَخُّرٌ

later, after that	بَعْدَئِذٍ
latter part of	آخِرٌ ـ أَوَاخِرُ
laugh	ضَحِكَ ـَ ، ضِحْك
law	قَانُونٌ ـ قَوَانِينُ
lay, lay down	وَضَعَ ـَ ، وَضْعٌ
lead, conduct s.o.	سَارَ ـ ، سَيَّرَ ، مَسِيرٌ
leader	قَائِدٌ ـ قُوَّادٌ ، قَادَةٌ
league	جَامِعَةٌ ، جَمْعِيَّةٌ
learn, come to know, find out about	عَرَفَ ـِ ، مَعْرِفَةٌ
	عَلِمَ ـَ ، عِلْمٌ
learn (through study), become educated	تَعَلَّمَ ، تَعْلِيمٌ
learning, knowledge	عِلْمٌ
leave, leave behind	تَرَكَ ـُ ، تَرْكٌ
leave, go away	اِنْصَرَفَ ، اِنْصِرَافٌ
leave, set out, depart	سَافَرَ ، سَفَرٌ
lecture	مُحَاضَرَةٌ ـ اتٌ
lecture	حَاضَرَ ، مُحَاضَرَةٌ
lend	أَقْرَضَ ، إِقْرَاضٌ ، قَرْضٌ
lesson	دَرْسٌ ـ دُرُوسٌ
letter, epistle	رِسَالَةٌ ـ رَسَائِلُ
liberation	تَحْرِيرٌ
library	مَكْتَبَةٌ ـ اتٌ
lieu of, in	عِوَضاً عَنْ
life, life-blood	حَيَاةٌ ـ حَيَوَاتٌ

like, take a liking to	أَحَبَّ ، حُبٌّ
like, find pleasing (E. subj. → A. obj.)	أَعْجَبَ ، إِعْجَابٌ
like	مِثْلَ ، كَ
likes of, the	مِثْلٌ
likewise	كَذَلِكَ
limit	حَدٌّ ـ حُدُودٌ
linguistic	لُغَوِيٌّ ـ ونَ
link	رَابِطَةٌ ـ رَوَابِطُ
list, catalog	قَائِمَةٌ ـ قَوَائِمُ
listen (to)	اِسْتَمَعَ ، اِسْتِمَاعٌ (لِ) ، أَنْصَتَ ، إِنْصَاتٌ (لِ)
literary	أَدَبِيٌّ
literary figure	أَدِيبٌ ـ أُدَبَاءُ
literature	أَدَبٌ ـ آدَابٌ
little	صَغِيرٌ ـ صِغَارٌ
live, be alive	عَاشَ ـِ ، عَيْشٌ ، مَعِيشٌ
live, dwell, reside	سَكَنَ ـُ ، سَكَنٌ
loan	قَرْضٌ ـ قُرُوضٌ
local	مَحَلِّيٌّ
located, found	وَاقِعٌ
located, situated, be	وَقَعَ ـَ ، وُقُوعٌ
long	طَوِيلٌ ـ طِوَالٌ
long ago	قَدِيماً
longing for s.o.	مُشْتَاقٌ ـ ونَ إِلَى

389

look (at)	نَظَرَ ـُ ، نَظَرٌ (إلى)	make a speech	أَلْقَى ، إِلْقاءُ (مُحاضَرَةٍ)
look for, search for	بَحَثَ ـَ ، بَحْثٌ عَنْ	make s.th. into s.th.	جَعَلَ ـَ ، جَعْلٌ
	فَتَّشَ ، تَفْتيشٌ عَنْ	man	رَجُلٌ ـ رِجالٌ
look into, consider, study	نَظَرَ ـُ ، نَظَرٌ في	man, human being	إِنْسانٌ
lord	رَبٌّ ـ أَرْبابٌ	man, young	شابٌّ ـ شَبابٌ
lose (not to win)	خَسِرَ ـَ ، خَسِرَ ، خَسارَةٌ	man of letters	أَديبٌ ـ أُدَباءُ
lose, miss, be bereft of	فَقَدَ ـِ ، فِقْدانٌ	manage, run	أَدارَ ، إِدارَةٌ
		management	إِدارَةٌ
love	حُبٌّ	manifest	أَبْدى ، إِبْداءٌ ؛
love, fall in love with	أَحَبَّ ، حُبٌّ		أَظْهَرَ ، إِظْهارٌ
lower, decrease, lessen	خَفَضَ ـِ ، خَفْضٌ	manifestation	مَظْهَرٌ ـ مَظاهِرُ
lunch	غَداءٌ	manner, procedure, method	مَنْهَجٌ ـ مَناهِجُ
		mansion, palace	قَصْرٌ ـ قُصورٌ
M		manual	يَدَوِيٌّ
M.A. degree	ماجِسْتير	many, numerous	كَثيرٌ ـ كِثارٌ
magazine	مَجَلَّةٌ ـ ات	many of	كَثيرٌ مِنْ
magnificent	رائِعٌ	march, walk	سارَ ـِ ، سَيْرٌ، مَسيرٌ
mail, post	بَريدٌ	march s.o.	سارَ ـِ ، سَيْرٌ ،
main, principal	رَئيسِيٌّ		مَسيرٌ بِـ
maintain, preserve	حافَظَ ، مُحافَظَةٌ عَلى		
major, main	رَئيسِيٌّ	mark, trace	أَثَرٌ ـ آثارٌ
majority of	مُعْظَمٌ ؛ غالِبٌ	market, bazaar	سوقٌ ـ أَسْواقٌ
make, do	فَعَلَ ـَ ، فِعْلٌ	marriage	زَواجٌ
make, create	جَعَلَ ـَ ، جَعْلٌ	marriage with, consummate a	دَخَلَ عَلَيْها
make s.o. happy	أَسْعَدَ ، إِسْعادٌ ؛	marry, get married to s.o. (from)	تَزَوَّجَ ، تَزَوُّجٌ (مِنْ)
	سَرَّ ـُ ، سُرورٌ		

390

English	Arabic		English	Arabic
marry s.o. to s.o.	زَوَّجَ ، تَزْوِيجٌ / زَوَاجٌ		memoirs	مُذَكِّرَاتٌ
master, lord	رَبٌّ ـُ ، أَرْبَابٌ ؛		mention	ذَكَرَ ـُ ، ذِكْرٌ
	سَيِّدٌ ـ سَادَةٌ		mercy on, have	رَحِمَ ـَ ، رَحْمَةٌ
master, dominate	سَادَ ـُ ، سِيَادَةٌ		messenger, apostle	رَسُولٌ ـ رُسُلٌ
master's degree	مَاجِسْتِير		middle	أَوْسَطُ (وُسْطَى)
maternal uncle	خَالٌ ـ أَخْوَالٌ		Middle Ages	الْقُرُونُ الْوُسْطَى
matter	أَمْرٌ ـ أُمُورٌ ؛		middle of, in the; in the midst of	وَسْطَ
	شَأْنٌ ـ شُؤُونٌ		(military) campaign	حَمْلَةٌ ـ حَمَلَاتٌ (عَلَى)
may God make...prosper	اللّٰهُ يُوَفِّقُ		minister (cabinet)	وَزِيرٌ ـ وُزَرَاءُ
maybe	لَعَلَّ؛ قَدْ (يَفْعَلُ)		minister, prime	رَئِيسُ وِزَارَةٍ ؛
meaning	مَعْنًى ـ مَعَانٍ			رَئِيسُ وُزَرَاءُ
means, it	مَعْنَاهُ أَنَّ		ministry (cabinet)	وِزَارَةٌ ـ ات
meet, become acquainted with	تَعَرَّفَ ، تَعَرُّفٌ عَلَى		minute (of time)	دَقِيقَةٌ ـ دَقَائِقُ
meet, meet with	اِجْتَمَعَ ، اِجْتِمَاعٌ (مَعَ،		miscellaneous	مُتَفَرِّقٌ
	بِـ) ؛ قَابَلَ ، مُقَابَلَةٌ ؛		Miss	آنِسَةٌ ـ ات
	الْتَقَى ، الْتِقَاءٌ (بِـ)		mission, expedition	بَعْثَةٌ ـ بَعَثَاتٌ
meet, encounter, come across, find	لَقِيَ ـَ ، لِقَاءٌ		Mister	سَيِّدٌ ـ سَادَةٌ
			moderate	مُعْتَدِلٌ ـ ونَ
meet, receive, welcome	اِسْتَقْبَلَ ، اِسْتِقْبَالٌ		modern	حَدِيثٌ ـ حِدَاثٌ ،
meeting, get-together, gathering, assembly	اِجْتِمَاعٌ ـ ات			حُدَثَاءُ
meeting, encounter, get-together	لِقَاءٌ		mold, fashion, shape	جَبَلَ ـِ ، جَبْلٌ
			monarchy	مَمْلَكَةٌ ـ مَمَالِكُ
meeting, interview	مُقَابَلَةٌ ـ ات		money, cash	نَقْدٌ ـ نُقُودٌ
member	عُضْوٌ ـ أَعْضَاءٌ ؛		money, property	مَالٌ ـ أَمْوَالٌ
	فَرْدٌ ـ أَفْرَادٌ			

month	شَهْرٌ ــ أَشْهُرٌ
morals	خُلُقٌ ــ أَخْلاقٌ
morning	صَباحٌ
most (adverb), very	جِدّاً
most of	مُعْظَمٌ؛ غالِبٌ؛ أَكْثَرُ
mother	أُمٌّ ــ أُمَّهاتٌ؛ والِدَةٌ ــ ات
motion, movement	حَراكٌ
mountain	جَبَلٌ ــ جِبالٌ
mouth	فَمٌ ــ أَفْواهٌ
move, transfer, change residence (to)	اِنْتَقَلَ، اِنْتِقالٌ (إلى)
move, get moving, go	سارَ ــِ، سَيْرٌ، مَسيرٌ، مَسيرَةٌ
move about, roam	رَحَلَ ــَ، رَحيلٌ
movement, renaissance, rebirth, boom	نَهْضَةٌ ــ ات
movement, motion	حَراكٌ
movie	فيلْمٌ / فِلْمٌ ــ أَفْلامٌ
movies, cinema	سينَما
Mr.	سَيِّدٌ ــ سادَةٌ
Mrs.	سَيِّدَةٌ ــ ات
much	كَثيرٌ ــ ونَ، كِثارٌ
museum	مَتْحَفٌ ــ مَتاحِفُ
must	وَجَبَ يَجِبُ، وُجوبٌ (على) (أَنْ)؛ واجِبٌ (على) (أَنْ) على...أَنْ

Muslim	مُسْلِمٌ ــ ونَ
mythical	أُسْطوريٌّ

N

Nabateans	أَنْباطٌ
name	اِسْمٌ ــ أَسْماءٌ
name, call s.o. s.th.	سَمَّى، تَسْمِيَةٌ؛ دَعا ــُ، دُعاءٌ؛ قالَ ــُ، قَوْلٌ لِـ
nation, state	دَوْلَةٌ ــ دُوَلٌ؛ أُمَّةٌ ــ أُمَمٌ
nation, people	شَعْبٌ ــ شُعوبٌ
national, nationalist, nationalistic, patriotic	وَطَنِيٌّ ــ ونَ؛ قَوْمِيٌّ ــ ونَ
nationalism	قَوْمِيَّةٌ
nationalize	أَمَّمَ، تَأْميمٌ
native, indigenous	بَلَدِيٌّ ــ ونَ
naturally, of course	طَبْعاً
nature	طَبيعَةٌ
nature, character	خُلُقٌ، أَخْلاقٌ ــ ات؛ صِفَةٌ ــ ات
near (prep.), in the vicinity of	قُرْبَ
near, close by (to)	قَريبٌ (مِن)
necessary (for s.o.) (to do s.th.)	واجِبٌ (على) أَنْ
necessary (for s.o.) that, it is	يَجِبُ (على) أَنْ؛ مِنَ الواجِبِ (على) أَنْ

necessitate s.th.	تَطَلَّبَ ، تَطَلُّبٌ	no; no!	لا
need (for)	حاجَةٌ ـ اتٌ (إلى)	no doubt!	لا شَكَّ
need of, be in; to need s.th.	كانَ بِحاجَةٍ إلى ؛ اِحْتاجَ ، اِحْتِياجٌ إلى	noble	كَريمٌ ـ كِرامٌ، كُرَماءُ
		non-	غَيْرُ ، عَدَمُ
neighbor	جارٌ ـ جيرانٌ	non-alignment	عَدَمُ الاِنْحيازِ
nevertheless	عَلى الرَّغْمِ مِنْ ذلِكَ؛	nonetheless	مَعَ ذلِكَ
	مَعَ ذلِكَ	noon	ظُهْرٌ
new, another	جَديدٌ ـ جُدُدٌ	north	شَمالٌ
new, modern	حَديثٌ ـ حِداثٌ، حُدَثاءُ	not	لا ؛ ما ؛ لَمْ ؛
newlyweds	عَروسانِ		غَيْرُ ؛ عَدَمُ ؛ لَيْسَ
news, news item	خَبَرٌ ـ أَخْبارٌ	note	مُذَكِّرَةٌ ـ اتٌ
newspaper	جَريدَةٌ ـ جَرائِدُ؛	nothing	لا شَيْءَ
	صَحيفَةٌ ـ صُحُفٌ	now	الآنَ
newspaper-(adj.)	صَحَفِيٌّ	number	عَدَدٌ ـ أَعْدادٌ
newspaperman, journalist	صَحَفِيٌّ ـ ونَ	number of, a	عَدَدٌ مِنْ
		numerous	كَثيرٌ ـ ونَ ، كِثارٌ
next, following	تالٍ		
nice, witty, clever	ظَريفٌ ـ ظُرَفاءُ	**O**	
nickname s.o. s.th.	لَقَّبَ ، تَلْقيبٌ بِ	O!	يا ؛ أَيُّها (أَيَّتُها)
night, a night	لَيْلَةٌ ـ اتٌ ، لَيالٍ	oath	يَمينٌ ـ أَيْمُنٌ، أَيْمانٌ
night (as opposed to day), nighttime	لَيْلٌ	object, aim, target	هَدَفٌ ـ أَهْدافٌ
		obligation (for s.o.)	واجِبٌ ـ اتٌ (على)
nine	تِسْعَةٌ	obtain, acquire	حَصَلَ ـ ، حُصولٌ على
nineteen	تِسْعَةَ عَشَرَ	obvious, clear	واضِحٌ
ninety	تِسْعونَ	occasion, opportunity, connection	مُناسَبَةٌ ـ اتٌ
ninth	تاسِعٌ		

occur, take place	جَرَى ـِ ، جَرْيٌ ؛	one thousand	أَلْفٌ
	وَقَعَ ـَ ، وُقوعٌ	one time	مَرَّةٌ
o'clock	ساعَةٌ	only	فَقَطْ ؛ (لا) ... إِلّا
odd, strange	عَجيبٌ ـ ونَ	open	فَتَحَ ـَ ، فَتْحٌ
ode	قَصيدَةٌ ـ قَصائِدُ	opine	رَأَى ـَ ، رَأْيٌ (أَنَّ)
of, out of	مِنْ	opinion, viewpoint	رَأْيٌ ـ آراءٌ ؛ نَظَرٌ
of, concerning	عَنْ	opinion (that), be of the	رَأَى ـَ ، رَأْيٌ (أَنَّ)
of, belonging to; a friend of mine	لِ ؛ صَديقٌ لي	opinion, of one	عَلى رَأْيٍ واحِدٍ
of course	طَبْعاً	opinion of, in the	عِنْدَ ؛ في رَأْيِ
office (place)	مَكْتَبٌ ـ مَكاتِبُ	oppose, resist	قاوَمَ ، مُقاوَمَةٌ
office, position	وَظيفَةٌ ـ وَظائِفُ	or	أَوْ ؛ أَمْ
official, formal	رَسْمِيٌّ ـ ونَ	order, system	نِظامٌ ـ أَنْظِمَةٌ
official, employee	مُوَظَّفٌ ـ ونَ	order that, in	لِ ؛ لِكَيْ ؛ حَتّى
often	كَثيراً	order that...not, in	لِكَيْلا ؛ كَيْلا ؛ لِئَلّا
oil	زَيْتٌ ـ زُيوتٌ	organization	مُنَظَّمَةٌ ـ ات
old, ancient	قَديمٌ ـ قُدَماءُ	orientalist	مُسْتَشْرِقٌ ـ ونَ
old (person); older, oldest (sibling)	كَبيرٌ ـ كِبارٌ ـ كُبَراءُ	origin, source	أَصْلٌ ـ أُصولٌ ؛ مَصْدَرٌ ـ مَصادِرُ
on, on top of	عَلى	original	أَصْلِيٌّ
on, upon (doing s.th.)	عِنْدَ ؛ لَدى	orphan	يَتيمٌ ـ أَيْتامٌ ، يَتامى
on, on the subject of	في	other, another	آخَرُ ـ ونَ
once	مَرَّةٌ	other than	غَيْرُ
one	واحِدٌ	Ottoman	عُثْمانِيٌّ
one, someone	أَحَدٌ (إِحْدى)	outer, outside (adj.)	خارِجِيٌّ
one hundred	مِئَةٌ ، مائَةٌ		

outside, outside of (prep.)	خَارِجَ	participation	اِشْتِرَاكٌ ، مُشَارَكَةٌ
over, above	فَوْقَ	party, festivity	حَفْلَةٌ - ات
overtake	أَدْرَكَ ، إِدْرَاكٌ	party (political)	حِزْبٌ - أَحْزَابٌ
owner (of)	صَاحِبٌ - ون	pass (:time)	مَضَى - ، مُضِيٌّ ؛
owners (of)	أَهْلٌ		اِنْقَضَى ، اِنْقِضَاءٌ ؛
			مَرَّ - ، مُرُورٌ
P		pass by, pass through	مَرَّ - ، مُرُورٌ بِ
pact, alliance	حِلْفٌ - أَحْلَافٌ	past, last	مَاضٍ - ون
paint, depict	صَوَّرَ ، تَصْوِيرٌ	paternal	أَبَوِيٌّ
palace, castle	قَصْرٌ - قُصُورٌ	paternal uncle	عَمٌّ - أَعْمَامٌ
paper	وَرَقٌ - أَوْرَاقٌ	patient over, be	صَبَرَ - ، صَبْرٌ عَلَى
paper, piece or sheet of	وَرَقَةٌ - ات	pay a visit to	زَارَ - ، زِيَارَةٌ
paradise	جَنَّةٌ	peace	سَلَامٌ
parents	وَالِدَانِ	pedagogical	تَرْبَوِيٌّ
parliament	بَرْلَمَان	pen	قَلَمٌ - أَقْلَامٌ
part	قِسْمٌ - أَقْسَامٌ ؛	pencil	قَلَمٌ - أَقْلَامٌ
	جُزْءٌ - أَجْزَاءٌ	peninsula	جَزِيرَةٌ - جَزَائِرُ ،
partial to, be	اِنْحَازَ ، اِنْحِيَازٌ إِلَى		جُزُرٌ
part in, take	اِشْتَرَكَ ، اِشْتِرَاكٌ	people (human beings)	نَاسٌ ، أُنَاسٌ
	في	people, folk, family	أَهْلٌ - أَهَالٍ
participate in	اِشْتَرَكَ ،	people, nation	شَعْبٌ - شُعُوبٌ
	اِشْتِرَاكٌ في	people, ordinary	أَبْنَاءُ الشَّعْبِ
participate with s.o. in	شَارَكَ ،	perceive, sense	شَعَرَ - ، شُعُورٌ بِ
	مُشَارَكَةٌ في	perfect	كَامِلٌ ؛ تَامٌّ

perform, carry out	أَدَّى ، تَأْدِيَةٌ ؛ قَامَ ـُ ، قِيَامٌ بِـ	place	مَكَانٌ ـ أَمَاكِنُ ، أَمْكِنَةٌ ، مَحَلٌّ ـ ات ، مَحَالٌّ
perhaps	لَعَلَّ ؛ قَدْ (يَفْعَلُ)		
period (of time), interval	مُدَّةٌ ـ مُدَدٌ؛ زَمَانٌ	place, status, position	مَكَانَةٌ
period, era, age	عَصْرٌ ـ عُصُورٌ، أَعْصَارٌ؛ عَهْدٌ ـ عُهُودٌ	place, put	وَضَعَ يَضَعُ ، وَضْعٌ
		play, drama	تَمْثِيلِيَّةٌ
permissible	مُبَاحٌ	please, delight s.o.	أَعْجَبَ ، إِعْجَابٌ
permissible, legitimate, become	حَلَّ ـِ ، حَلَالٌ	please, gladden, make happy	سَرَّ ـُ ، سُرُورٌ
permit s.o. (to do s.th.)	سَمَحَ ـَ ، سَمَاحٌ لِـ (بِـ)	pleasure at, liking s.th.	إِعْجَابٌ بِـ ، سُرُورٌ بِـ
persist, endure	اِسْتَمَرَّ ، اِسْتِمْرَارٌ	pleasure, fun	لَهْوٌ
persist, persevere (in)	أَصَرَّ، إِصْرَارٌ (عَلَى)	pocket	جَيْبٌ ـ جُيُوبٌ
person	إِنْسَانٌ	poem	شِعْرٌ ـ أَشْعَارٌ
personal, private	خَاصٌّ	poem; ode	قَصِيدَةٌ ـ قَصَائِدُ
Ph. D.	دُكْتُورَاة	poet	شَاعِرٌ ـ شُعَرَاءُ
Pharoah	فِرْعَوْنُ	poetry	شِعْرٌ ـ أَشْعَارٌ
philosophy	فَلْسَفَةٌ	point (to)	دَلَّ ـُ ، دَلَالَةٌ (عَلَى)
photograph	صَوَّرَ ، تَصْوِيرٌ	point where, to the	حَتَّى، إِلَى أَنْ
picture, photo	صُورَةٌ ـ صُوَرٌ	policy	سِيَاسَةٌ ـ ات
picture, depict	صَوَّرَ ، تَصْوِيرٌ	political; politician	سِيَاسِيٌّ ـ ونَ
piece	قِطْعَةٌ ـ قِطَعٌ	politics	سِيَاسَةٌ
piece of paper	وَرَقَةٌ ـ ات	poor	فَقِيرٌ ـ فُقَرَاءُ
pilgrim (to Mecca)	حَاجٌّ ـ حُجَّاجٌ، حَجِيجٌ	position, status, rank	مَكَانَةٌ
pious	صَالِحٌ ـ ونَ	position, attitude (on)	مَوْقِفٌ ـ مَوَاقِفُ (مِنْ)

position, job	وَظيفَةٌ ـ وَظائِفُ	present, offer, submit, introduce	قَدَّمَ ، تَقْديمٌ ،
possessions, property	مِلْكٌ ـ أَمْلاكٌ		تَقَدَّمَ ، تَقَدُّمٌ بِـ ،
post, mail	بَريدٌ		عَرَضَ ـِ ، عَرْضٌ
poverty	فَقْرٌ	preserve, keep	حافَظَ ، مُحافَظَةٌ عَلى
power of, in the	بِيَدِ	president	رَئيسٌ ـ رُؤَساءُ
powerful, strong	قَوِيٌّ ـ أَقْوِياءُ	president (of a republic)	رَئيسُ جُمْهوريَّةٍ
praise be to God	الْحَمْدُلِلَّهِ	press, newspaper-(adj.)	صَحَفِيٌّ
praise	مَدَحَ ـَ ،مَدْحٌ	prestige, status, position	مَكانَةٌ
prefer s.th. (over)	فَضَّلَ ، تَفْضيلٌ (عَلى)	pretend	تَظاهَرَ ، تَظاهُرٌ بِـ
pre-Islamic	جاهِلِيٌّ ـ ونَ	prevail, rule	سادَ ـُ ، سِيادَةٌ
present, ready (for)	مُسْتَعِدٌّ ـ ونَ (لِ)	prevail (peace)	اِنْتَشَرَ ، اِنْتِشارٌ
preparatory	تَمْهيدِيٌّ	prevalent	سائِدٌ
-(school)	إعْدادِيٌّ	prevent	مَنَعَ ـَ ، مَنْعٌ
prepare s.th.	أَعَدَّ ، إعْدادٌ	previously, before	مِنْ قَبْلُ
prepare o.s., get ready (for)	اِسْتَعَدَّ، اِسْتِعْدادٌ (لِ)	price, cost	ثَمَنٌ ـ أَثْمانٌ
prepared, ready, willing (to, for)	مُسْتَعِدٌّ ـ ونَ (لِ)	price of, for the	بِـ
presence of, in the, with; before	لَدى ، عِنْدَ، أَمامَ	primary (school)	اِبْتِدائِيٌّ
present, gift	هَدِيَّةٌ ـ هَدايا ،	prime minister	رَئيسُ وُزَراءَ ،
	هِبَةٌ ـ اتٌ		رَئيسُ وِزارَةٍ
present, attending, existing	حاضِرٌ ـ ونَ ،	prince, emir	أَميرٌ ـ أُمَراءُ
	مَوْجودٌ ـ ونَ	principal, main	رَئيسِيٌّ
		print	طَبَعَ ـَ ، طَبْعٌ
present, current	حالِيٌّ ، حاضِرٌ	printing, edition	طَبْعَةٌ ـ اتٌ
		private, personal	خاصٌّ

problem	مُشْكِلَةٌ ـ اتٌ ، مَشاكِلُ	public school	مَدْرَسَةٌ حُكومِيَّةٌ
produce, bring forth, make	أَنْتَجَ ، إِنْتاجٌ	publication, publishing	نَشْرٌ ، إِصْدارٌ
produce, bring about, cause	سَبَّبَ ، تَسْبيبٌ	publish	نَشَرَ ـُ ، نَشْرٌ ؛ أَصْدَرَ ، إِصْدارٌ
professor	أُسْتاذٌ ـ أَساتِذَةٌ	punishment, discipline	تَأْديبٌ
profit, gain (from)	رَبِحَ ـَ ، رِبْحٌ (مِن)	pupil, student, disciple	تِلْميذٌ ـ تَلاميذُ ، تَلامِذَةٌ
profit, benefit (from)	اِسْتَفادَ ، اِسْتِفادَةٌ (مِن)	pursue, follow	تابَعَ ، مُتابَعَةٌ
profound	عَميقٌ	put, place	وَضَعَ يَضَعُ ، وَضْعٌ
program	مَنْهَجٌ ـ مَناهِجُ	put off, postpone	أَجَّلَ ، تَأْجيلٌ
program of instruction	مَنْهَجُ التَّعْليمِ	put out, produce	أَنْتَجَ ، إِنْتاجٌ
progress, advancement	تَقَدُّمٌ		
progress, advance	تَقَدَّمَ ، تَقَدُّمٌ	**Q**	
promise (s.th.)	وَعَدَ يَعِدُ ، وَعْدٌ (بـ)	qasida, ode	قَصيدَةٌ ـ قَصائِدُ
promoted, be	تَرَقَّى ، تَرَقٍّ	quarter, one-fourth	رُبْعٌ ـ أَرْباعٌ
property, possessions, wealth	مالٌ ـ أَمْوالٌ ؛	queen	مَلِكَةٌ ـ اتٌ
	مِلْكٌ ـ أَمْلاكٌ	question, query	سُؤالٌ ـ أَسْئِلَةٌ
prophet	نَبِيٌّ ـ أَنْبِياءُ	question, doubt (about)	شَكٌّ ـ شُكوكٌ (في)
prophetic tradition, hadith	حَديثٌ ـ أَحاديثُ	Qur'ān	قُرْآنٌ
protect, preserve	حافَظَ ، مُحافَظَةٌ عَلى	Qur'anic verse	آيَةٌ ـ اتٌ
provide, supply	وَفَّرَ ، تَوْفيرٌ		
provided in full measure, be	تَوَفَّرَ ، تَوَفُّرٌ	**R**	
province, state	وِلايَةٌ ـ اتٌ	raise, lift up, erect	أَقامَ ، إِقامَةٌ
		rather, on the contrary	بَلْ ، إِنَّما
		reach, arrive (at)	وَصَلَ يَصِلُ ، وُصولٌ (إلى) ؛ بَلَغَ ـُ ، بُلوغٌ

398

read	قَرَأَ ـَ ، قِرَاءَةٌ	regarding, concerning	بِشَأْنِ ؛ حَوْلَ
reading (n.)	قِرَاءَةٌ	region, area, zone	مِنْطَقَةٌ ـ مَنَاطِقُ
ready (for), prepared, willing (to)	مُسْتَعِدٌّ ـ ون (ل) ؛ حَاضِرٌ ـ ون (ل)	regret: we regret, we are sorry that (Eng. subj. ⟶ A. obj.)	يُؤْسِفُنَا أَنْ
ready, prepare s.th.	أَعَدَّ ، إِعْدَادٌ	regulation, rule, law	قَانُونٌ ـ قَوَانِينُ
real	حَقِيقِيٌّ	reign, rule	سَادَ ـُ ، سِيَادَةٌ
realization, accomplishment	تَحْقِيقٌ	relate (e.g., a tale)	حَكَى ـِ ، حِكَايَةٌ
realize, make s.th. come true	حَقَّقَ ، تَحْقِيقٌ	relationship (to), connection (with)	عَلَاقَةٌ ـ ات (بِـ)
realize, come to know	عَرَفَ ـِ ، مَعْرِفَةٌ	relative, kinsman	قَرِيبٌ ـ أَقَارِبُ ، أَقْرِبَاءُ
realm, sphere, area	مَيْدَانٌ ـ مَيَادِينُ	religion	دِينٌ ـ أَدْيَانٌ
reason, cause	سَبَبٌ ـ أَسْبَابٌ		
receive, be a recipient of (Eng. subj. ⟶ A. obj.)	جَاءَ ـِ ، مَجِيءٌ ؛ وَصَلَ يَصِلُ ، وُصُولٌ ؛ بَلَغَ ـُ ، بُلُوغٌ	remain, stay	بَقِيَ ـَ ، بَقَاءٌ
		reminder, memo	مُذَكِّرَةٌ ـ ات
		renaissance	نَهْضَةٌ ـ ات
receive, welcome s.o.	اِسْتَقْبَلَ ، اِسْتِقْبَالٌ	render (a service) (to)	قَدَّمَ ، تَقْدِيمٌ (خِدْمَةً) (ل)
recent	أَخِيرٌ ؛ حَدِيثٌ ـ حَدَثَاتٌ ، حَدَثَاءُ	render, make s.th. s.th else (two acc.)	جَعَلَ ـَ ، جَعْلٌ
recently	أَخِيرًا ؛ حَدِيثًا	renew	جَدَّدَ ، تَجْدِيدٌ
recognize, know s.o.	عَرَفَ ـِ ، مَعْرِفَةٌ	report	تَقْرِيرٌ ـ تَقَارِيرُ ؛
reconciliation, rationalization (between	تَوْفِيقٌ (بَيْنَ)		نَشْرَةٌ ـ نَشَرَاتٌ
		reporter, correspondent	مُرَاسِلٌ ـ ون
red	أَحْمَرُ (حَمْرَاءُ) ـ حُمْرٌ	represent	مَثَّلَ ، تَمْثِيلٌ
refuse, reject	رَفَضَ ـِ ، رَفْضٌ	representative	مُمَثِّلٌ ـ ون ؛ مَنْدُوبٌ ـ ون
regard, consider s.o. as (with two acc.)	رَأَى يَرَى ، رَأْيٌ		

reproach, chide	نَهَرَ ـَ ، نَهْر	restore, renew	جَدَّدَ ، تَجْدِيد
republic	جُمْهُورِيَّة ـ ات	restrain, control o.s.	تَمَالَكَ ، تَمَالُك (نَفْسَهُ)
republican	جُمْهُورِيّ	result	نَتِيجَة ـ نَتَائِج
repulse, reproach, chide	نَهَرَ ـَ ، نَهْر	resulting from, as a result of	نَتِيجَةً لـِ
request (for)	طَلَب ـ ات (لِ)	return (to)	عَوْدَة ،رُجُوع (إلى)
request	طَلَبَ ـُ ، طَلَب ؛	return, go/come back	رَجَعَ ـِ ، رُجُوع ؛ عَادَ ـُ ، عَوْدَة
	رَجَا ـُ ، رَجَاء		
require, need	اِحْتَاجَ ،اِحْتِيَاج إلى	return s.th.	رَدَّ ـُ ، رَدّ
require, necessitate	تَطَلَّبَ ، تَطَلُّب	reveal, show	أَبْدَى ، إِبْدَاء
researcher	بَاحِث ـ ون	revenue, income	دَخْل
reside, live	سَكَنَ ـُ ، سَكَن ؛	revere	بَجَّلَ ، تَبْجِيل
	أَقَامَ ، إِقَامَة	revive	جَدَّدَ ، تَجْدِيد
residence, stay	سَكَن ؛ إِقَامَة	revolution, revolt	ثَوْرَة ـ ات
resist, oppose	قَاوَمَ ، مُقَاوَمَة	reward, recompense	أَجْر ـ أُجُور
resolve, solve	حَلَّ ـُ ، حَلّ	rich (in)	غَنِيّ ـ أَغْنِيَاء (بِ)
resource	مَوْرِد ـ مَوَارِد	right (n.), right to (do s.th.)	حَقّ ـ حُقُوق
respect	اِحْتِرَام	right, to be	كَانَ عَلى حَقٍّ
respect, honor	اِحْتَرَمَ ، اِحْتِرَام	right, correct	صَحِيح
respond, answer	أَجَابَ ، إِجَابَة (عَلى) ؛	right, proper	صَالِح
	رَدَّ ـُ ، رُدُود	ring	خَاتِم ـ خَوَاتِم
response, answer	إِجَابَة ـ ات ؛	rise (to one's feet)	وَقَفَ يَقِف ، وُقُوف ؛
	رَدّ ـ رُدُود		قَامَ ـُ ، قِيَام
responsible (for)	مَسْؤُول ـ ون (عَن)	rise (in rank), be promoted	تَرَقَّى ، تَرَقٍّ
restaurant	مَطْعَم ـ مَطَاعِم		

400

river	نَهْرٌ ـ أَنْهَارٌ	saying, wise; maxim	حِكْمَةٌ ـ حِكَمٌ
road	طَرِيقٌ ـ طُرُقٌ	scant, scarce	قَلِيلٌ ـ قَلَائِلُ ،
roster, list	قَائِمَةٌ ـ قَوَائِمُ		قِلَالٌ
row	صَفٌّ ـ صُفُوفٌ	scattered	مُنْتَشِرٌ ـ ونَ
royal, royalist	مَلَكِيٌّ ـ ونَ	school	مَدْرَسَةٌ ـ مَدَارِسُ
ruins	آثَارٌ	school (of a university), college	كُلِّيَّةٌ ـ اتٌ
rule, regulation	قَانُونٌ ـ قَوَانِينُ	School of Arts	كُلِّيَّةُ الآدَابِ
rule, principle, model	قَاعِدَةٌ ـ قَوَاعِدُ	school, public	مَدْرَسَةٌ حُكُومِيَّةٌ
rule, governance	حُكْمٌ	science	عِلْمٌ ـ عُلُومٌ
rule, govern	حَكَمَ ـُ ، حُكْمٌ	scientific	عِلْمِيٌّ
rule, prevail	سَادَ ـُ ، سِيَادَةٌ	scream	صَرَخَ ـُ ، صُرَاخٌ
ruler, governor	حَاكِمٌ ـ حُكَّامٌ	scribe	كَاتِبٌ ـ كُتَّابٌ
run, manage	أَدَارَ ، إِدَارَةٌ	sea	بَحْرٌ ـ بِحَارٌ
	S	search for	بَحَثَ ـَ ، بَحْثٌ عَنْ ؛
sacred	مُقَدَّسٌ ـ ونَ		فَتَّشَ ، تَفْتِيشٌ عَنْ ؛
sad, be	حَزِنَ ـَ ، حُزْنٌ ،		تَفَحَّصَ ، تَفَحُّصٌ عَنْ
sadness	حَزَنٌ	seat s.o.	أَجْلَسَ ، إِجْلَاسٌ
same, the	نَفْسُ الـ	secede (from)	اِنْفَصَلَ ، اِنْفِصَالٌ
satan	شَيْطَانٌ ـ شَيَاطِينُ		(عَنْ)
say	قَالَ ـُ ، قَوْلٌ	second	ثَانٍ
say nothing, remain silent	سَكَتَ ـُ ، سُكُوتٌ	secondary	ثَانَوِيٌّ
		secretary	سِكْرِتِيرٌ ـ ونَ
say, that is to; that is, i.e.	أَيْ	Secretary of State	وَزِيرُ الخَارِجِيَّةِ
saying, proverb	مَثَلٌ ـ أَمْثَالٌ	section, part	قِسْمٌ ـ أَقْسَامٌ

see	رَأَى يَرَى ، رُؤْيَةٌ ؛	seventh	سابِعٌ
	شاهَدَ ، مُشاهَدَةٌ ؛	seventy	سَبْعونَ
	لَمَحَ ـَ ، لَمْحٌ	several	عَدَدٌ مِن
selection, excerpt	مُقْتَطَفٌ ـ ات	severe, intense	شَديدٌ ـ أَشِدّاءُ ،شِدادٌ
self	نَفْسٌ ـ نُفوسٌ ،أَنْفُسٌ	severe, become, in-tensify	اِشْتَدَّ ، اِشْتِدادٌ
self-control, regain	تَمالَكَ ، تَمالُكَ		
	نَفْسَهُ	shame, disgrace, em-barrassment	خَجَلٌ
sell	باعَ ـِ ، بَيْعٌ	shape, form	شَكْلٌ ـ أَشْكالٌ ؛
send	أَرْسَلَ ، إِرْسالٌ		صورَةٌ ـ صُوَرٌ
send back	رَدَّ ـُ ، رَدٌّ	shape, form, create	جَبَلَ ـِ ، جَبْلٌ
sense, meaning	مَعْنًى ـ مَعانٍ	share in	اِشْتَرَكَ،اِشْتِراكٌ في
sense, feel	شَعَرَ ـُ ، شُعورٌ	she	هِيَ
sentence; clause	جُمْلَةٌ ـ جُمَلٌ	sheet of paper	وَرَقَةٌ ـ ات
sentence, pass sen-tence on	حَكَمَ ـُ ، حَكَمَ عَلى	ship	سَفينَةٌ ـ سُفُنٌ
separate, divide	فَرَّقَ ، تَفْريقٌ ،	short	قَصيرٌ ـ قِصارٌ
	تَفْرِقَةٌ	shorten	أَقْصَرَ ، إِقْصارٌ
serious, important	هامٌّ	show, evidence	دَلَّ ـُ ، دَلالَةٌ (عَلى)
serve	خَدَمَ ـِ ، خِدْمَةٌ	show, reveal	أَبْدى ، إِبْداءٌ ؛
service	خِدْمَةٌ ـ خَدَماتٌ		أَظْهَرَ ، إِظْهارٌ
service of, be active in the	عَمِلَ ـَ ، عَمِلَ عَلى	show concern for	اِهْتَمَّ ، اِهْتِمامٌ بِـ
		shroud	كَفَّنَ ، تَكْفينٌ
set, appoint (a date)	حَدَّدَ ، تَحْديدٌ	shut up, fall silent	سَكَتَ ـُ ، سُكوتٌ
set up, establish	أَقامَ ، إِقامَةٌ	side with	اِنْحازَ ، اِنْحِيازٌ إِلى
seven	سَبْعَةٌ	sight, eyesight	بَصَرٌ ـ أَبْصارٌ
seventeen	سَبْعَةَ عَشَرَ	sign, trace	أَثَرٌ ـ آثارٌ

402

silent, remain	سَكَتَ ـُ ، سُكوتٌ	social, societal	اِجْتِماعِيٌّ
similar to, like	مِثْلَ	socialist	اِشْتِراكِيٌّ
since, ever since	مُنْذُ	society, community	مُجْتَمَعٌ ـ ات
sincere (to)	مُخْلِصٌ ـ ونَ (لِ)	society, association	جَمْعِيَّةٌ ـ ات ؛
sincere (to), be	أَخْلَصَ ، إِخْلاصٌ		رابِطَةٌ ـ رَوابِطُ
	(لِ)		جامِعَةٌ ـ ات
sing	غَنَّى ، غِناءٌ	sociological	اِجْتِماعِيٌّ
singer	مُغَنٍّ ـ مُغَنّونَ	soldier	جُنْدِيٌّ ـ جُنودٌ
singing	غِناءٌ	solution	حَلٌّ ـ حُلولٌ
sister	أُخْتٌ ـ أَخَواتٌ	solve	حَلَّ ـُ ، حَلٌّ
sit down, sit up	جَلَسَ ـِ ، جُلوسٌ	some	بَعْضٌ
situated, be	وَقَعَ يَقَعُ ، وُقوعٌ	someone	أَحَدٌ (إِحْدى)
situation, condition, state	وَضْعٌ ـ أَوْضاعٌ ؛	something	شَيْءٌ ـ أَشْياءُ
	حالٌ ـ أَحْوالٌ ؛	something which	مِمّا ، ما
	مَوْقِفٌ ؛ شَأْنٌ	sometimes	أَحْياناً ؛ قَدْ (يَفْعَلُ)
six	سِتَّةٌ	son	اِبْنٌ ـ أَبْناءُ
sixteen	سِتَّةَ عَشَرَ	son (dimunitive)	بُنَيٌّ
sixteenth	سادِسَ عَشَرَ	song	أُغْنِيَةٌ ـ أَغانٍ
sixth	سادِسٌ	sons and daughters	الْبَنونُ وَالْبَناتُ
sixty	سِتّونَ	soon	قَريباً
slave girl, servant	جارِيَةٌ ـ جَوارٍ	soul	نَفْسٌ ـ نُفوسٌ ، أَنْفُسٌ
sleep	نامَ ـَ ، نَوْمٌ	source, origin	مَصْدَرٌ ـ مَصادِرُ
small, little	صَغيرٌ ـ صِغارٌ	south	جَنوبٌ
small (in number), few	قَليلٌ ـ قَلائِلُ ، قِلالٌ	spacious	واسِعٌ

speak (to) (about)	تَحَدَّثَ ، تَحَدُّثٌ ، حَديثٌ (إلى) (عَن) ، تَكَلَّمَ ، تَكَلُّمٌ ، كَلامٌ	start, found, establish	أَنْشَأَ ، إِنْشاءٌ
		state, nation, country	أَقامَ ، إِقامَةٌ دَوْلَةٌ ـ دُوَلٌ ، أُمَّةٌ ، أُمَمٌ ،
special	خاصٌّ		بَلَدٌ ، بُلْدانٌ ، بَلَدٌ ـ بِلادٌ
specialist	مُتَخَصِّصٌ ـ ونَ		
speech, talk	كَلامٌ ؛ حَديثٌ		
speech, oration	خِطابٌ ـ اتٌ ، أَخْطِبَةٌ	state, province	وِلايَةٌ ـ اتٌ ،
		status, position, rank	مَكانَةٌ
spite of, in	عَلى الرَّغْمِ مِن ٠٠ فَ	stay, remain, be left	بَقِيَ ـَ ، بَقاءٌ
spread out, widespread	مُنْتَشِرٌ ـ ونَ	stay, reside, dwell	أَقامَ ، إِقامَةٌ
spread out, become	اِنْتَشَرَ ، اِنْتِشارٌ	stick, rod (f.)	عَصاً ـ عُصِيٌّ
stage, phase	مَرْحَلَةٌ ـ مَراحِلُ	still, is still	ما زالَ ، لا يَزالُ
stage, theatre	مَسْرَحٌ ـ مَسارِحُ	stop, come to a standstill, take a stand (on)	وَقَفَ يَقِفُ ، وُقوفٌ
stand, attitude, position (on)	مَوْقِفٌ ـ مَواقِفُ		(في)
stand, stand up	قامَ ـُ ، قِيامَةٌ ،	stop, come to an end	اِنْقَطَعَ ، اِنْقِطاعٌ
stand, come to a stop	وَقَفَ يَقِفُ ، وُقوفٌ	stop (doing s.th.)	كَفَّ ، كَفَّ عَن
standing, on foot; stopped	قائِمٌ ـ ونَ ،	stop talking, fall silent	سَكَتَ ـُ ، سُكوتٌ
	واقِفٌ ـ ونَ	story, tale	قِصَّةٌ ـ قِصَصٌ ،
star	كَوْكَبٌ ـ كَواكِبُ		حِكايَةٌ ـ اتٌ
start, begin s.th.	بَدَأَ ـَ ، بَدْءٌ	story is, the whole	كُلُّ ما في الأَمْرِ
start, begin (to do s.th.)	بَدَأَ ـَ ، بَدْءٌ ، أَخَذَ ، جَعَلَ ، أَقْبَلَ عَلى	strange, odd, amazing	عَجيبٌ ـ ونَ
		strange, odd, foreign, peculiar, astonishing	غَريبٌ ـ غُرَباءُ

404

stranger, foreigner	أَجْنَبِيٌّ – أَجَانِبُ ؛ غَرِيبٌ – غُرَبَاءُ	successful, render s.o. (God)	وَفَّقَ تَوْفِيقٌ
street	شَارِعٌ – شَوَارِعُ ؛ طَرِيقٌ – طُرُقٌ	such a...as	مِثْلُ
		such and such	كَذَا وَكَذَا
strike, hit	ضَرَبَ – ، ضَرْبٌ	sufficient, be	كَفَى – ، كِفَايَةٌ
strong, powerful	قَوِيٌّ – أَقْوِيَاءُ	sultanate	سَلْطَنَةٌ
strong, intense, become	اِشْتَدَّ ، اِشْتِدَادٌ	summary, resumé	مُوجَزٌ
		summer	صَيْفٌ – أَصْيَافٌ
struggle, fight	مُكَافَحَةٌ ؛ عِرَاكٌ	supervise	أَشْرَفَ ، إِشْرَافٌ عَلَى
struggle	كَافَحَ ، مُكَافَحَةٌ	supervisor	مُشْرِفٌ – ون
student	طَالِبٌ – طُلَّابٌ ؛ تِلْمِيذٌ – تَلَامِذَةٌ ، تَلَامِيذُ	supervision over	إِشْرَافٌ عَلَى
		supper	عَشَاءٌ
study, studies	دِرَاسَةٌ – ات	suppose, think (two acc.)	ظَنَّ – ، ظَنٌّ
study	دَرَسَ – ، دَرْسٌ ، دِرَاسَةٌ	surprise, amazement	دَهْشَةٌ ؛ عَجَبٌ
study, look into, consider	نَظَرَ – ، نَظَرٌ فِي	surprise s.o.	أَدْهَشَ ، إِدْهَاشٌ
		surprised, be	تَعَجَّبَ ، تَعَجُّبٌ
study mission	بَعْثَةٌ دِرَاسِيَّةٌ	surround	أَحَاطَ ، إِحَاطَةٌ بِـ
style	أُسْلُوبٌ – أَسَالِيبُ	suspect, doubt	شَكَّ – ، شَكٌّ (فِي)
subject, topic	مَوْضُوعٌ – مَوَاضِيعُ	suspicion (about)	شَكٌّ – شُكُوكٌ (فِي)
subject of, on the	فِي	sweetheart	حَبِيبٌ – أَحِبَّاءُ
submit (e.g., an application)	تَقَدَّمَ ، تَقَدُّمٌ بِـ ؛ قَدَّمَ ، تَقْدِيمٌ	system, order	نِظَامٌ – أَنْظِمَةٌ
			T
subsequent, following	تَالٍ	table	طَاوِلَةٌ – ات
succeed (in)	نَجَحَ – ، نَجَاحٌ (فِي)	table, chart, tablet	لَوْحَةٌ – ات
success (in)	نَجَاحٌ (فِي)	take	أَخَذَ – ، أَخْذٌ

take, conduct s.o. (to)	سارَ ـِ ، سَيْرٌ بِـ	text, passage	نَصٌّ ـ نُصوصٌ
	(إلى) ؛ ذَهَبَ ـَ ،	thank (for)	شَكَرَ ـُ ، شُكْرٌ (عَلى)
	ذَهابٌ بِـ (إلى)	thank you! thanks!	شُكْراً
take s.o. back	عادَ ـُ ، عَوْدَةٌ بِـ	thanks (for)	شُكْرٌ (عَلى)
take a liking to	أَحَبَّ ، حُبٌّ	that (demonstrative)	هٰذا (هٰذِهِ)؛ ذٰلِكَ
take an interest in	اِهْتَمَّ ، اِهْتِمامٌ بِـ		(تِلْكَ)
take out, remove	أَخْرَجَ ، إِخْراجٌ	that, who (relative)	اَلَّذي (اَلَّتي)
take place, happen	جَرى ـِ ، جَرْيٌ	that (conjunction)	أَنَّ ؛ إِنَّ ؛ أَنْ
take up residence (in)	سَكَنَ ـُ ، سَكَنٌ (في)	that, the fact that	أَنَّ
tall	طَويلٌ ـ طِوالٌ	that which, what (indefinite relative)	ما
target	هَدَفٌ ـ أَهْدافٌ	that which...by way of	ما ٠٠ مِنْ
tea	شايٌ	that is (to say), i.e.	أَيْ
teach	عَلَّمَ ، تَعْليمٌ ؛	theater	مَسْرَحٌ ـ مَسارِحُ
	دَرَّسَ ، تَدْريسٌ	then, at that time	عِنْدَئِذٍ ؛ حينَئِذٍ؛
teacher	مُعَلِّمٌ ـ ونَ ؛		وَقْتَئِذٍ ؛ ساعَتَئِذٍ
	مُدَرِّسٌ ـ ونَ	then, after that, thereupon	ثُمَّ ، وَمِنْ ثَمَّ
technical	فَنِّيٌّ		
tell, inform	أَخْبَرَ ، إِخْبارٌ	then, in that case, therefor	إِذاً ، إِذَنْ
tell, say to	قالَ ـُ ، قَوْلٌ لِـ	theory	نَظَرٌ
tell, relate	حَكى ـِ ، حِكايَةٌ	there	هُناكَ
temple	هَيْكَلٌ ـ هَياكِلُ	there is, there are	هُناكَ
ten	عَشَرَةٌ	there is no doubt	لا شَكَّ
tent	خَيْمَةٌ ـ خِيامٌ	therefore, then	لِذٰلِكَ ؛ عَلى ذٰلِكَ ؛
tenth	عاشِرٌ		إِذا ، إِذَنْ
termination, end	نِهايَةٌ ـ اتٌ		

these	هَؤُلاءِ	time, one	مَرَّةٌ ــ اتٌ
thesis, dissertation	رِسَالَةٌ ــ رَسَائِلُ	time, period of	مُدَّةٌ ــ مُدَدٌ
they	هُم ؛ هُنَّ ؛ هُما	time has come	حانَ (الْوَقْتُ)
thing	شَيْءٌ ــ أَشْياءُ	time (of appointment)	مَوْعِدٌ ــ مَواعِدُ ؛
think	فَكَّرَ ، تَفْكِيرٌ		مِيعادٌ ــ مَواعِيدُ
think, consider s.o. as s.th. (two acc.)	اِعْتَبَرَ ، اِعْتِبارٌ ؛	title, caption	عُنْوانٌ ــ عَناوِينُ
	رَأَى ، يَرَى ، رَأْيٌ ؛	title, nickname	لَقَبٌ ، تَلْقِيبٌ بِـ
	ظَنَّ ــ ، ظَنٌّ	to, toward	إلَى
thinker, intellectual	مُفَكِّرٌ ــ ونَ	to, for	لِ
third (ordinal)	ثالِثٌ	today	الْيَوْمَ
third (fraction)	ثُلُثٌ ــ أَثْلاثٌ	together	مَعاً
thirteen	ثَلاثَةَ عَشَرَ	tomorrow	غَداً
thirteenth	ثالِثَ عَشَرَ	tonight	اللَّيْلَةَ
thirty	ثَلاثُونَ	too, also	أَيْضاً ؛ كَذلِكَ
this	هذا (هَذِهِ)	touch with, be in	اِتَّصَلَ ، اِتِّصالٌ بِـ
those	أُولائِكَ	trace, sign	أَثَرٌ ــ آثارٌ
thought, idea	فِكْرَةٌ ــ فِكَرٌ	trade, commerce	تِجارَةٌ
thousand	أَلْفٌ ــ آلافٌ	transfer, move to, change one's resi-dence, school, etc. to	اِنْتَقَلَ ، اِنْتِقالٌ إلَى
thousands of	أُلوفٌ مِنْ		
three	ثَلاثَةٌ	transfer, transport s.th.	نَقَلَ ــ ، نَقْلٌ
ticket	تَذْكِرَةٌ ــ تَذاكِرُ	translate	تَرْجَمَ ، تَرْجَمَةٌ
time	وَقْتٌ ــ أَوْقاتٌ ؛	transmit, pass on	نَقَلَ ــ ، نَقْلٌ
	زَمَنٌ ــ أَزْمانٌ ؛	transmit, broadcast	أَذاعَ ، إذاعَةٌ
	حِينٌ ــ أَحْيانٌ	transport	نَقَلَ ــ ، نَقْلٌ
time, era, age	عَهْدٌ ــ عُهودٌ		

407

travel, trip	سَفَرٌ ، أَسْفارٌ	two	إِثْنانِ (إِثْنَتانِ)
travel (to)	سافَرَ ، سَفَرٌ (إِلى) ؛	type, model, pattern	نَموذَجٌ ـ نَماذِجُ
	رَحَلَ ـَ ، رَحيلٌ	type, kind, class	شَكْلٌ ـ أَشْكالٌ
	(إِلى)	U	
traveler, great	رَحّالٌ ـ رَحّالَةٌ	ugly	قَبيحٌ ـ قِباحٌ
treat with respect	بَجَّلَ ، تَبْجيلٌ	un-	غَيْرُ ؛ عَدَمُ
treatise, disserta-tion	رِسالَةٌ ـ رَسائِلُ	uncle	عَمٌّ ـ عُمومٌ ، أَعْمامٌ ؛
			خالٌ ، أَخْوالٌ
trip	سَفَرٌ ـ أَسْفارٌ ؛	under, underneath	تَحْتَ
	رِحْلَةٌ ـ رَحَلاتٌ	understand	فَهِمَ ـَ ، فَهْمٌ
triumph (over)	اِنْتَصَرَ ، اِنْتِصارٌ (عَلى)	undertake	قامَ ـُ ، قِيامَةٌ بِـ
triumph (over), let s.o.	نَصَرَ ـُ ، نَصْرٌ (عَلى)	unemployment	بِطالَةٌ
true, correct	صَحيحٌ	unify	وَحَّدَ ، تَوْحيدٌ
true or false	صَوابٌ أَمْ خَطَأٌ	union	وَحْدَةٌ
truly	حَقّاً ؛ إِنَّ	unit	وَحْدَةٌ ـ ات
trust, have confi-dence in	وَثِقَ يَثِقُ ،	unite (intrans.)	اِتَّحَدَ ، اِتِّحادٌ
	ثِقَةٌ ، وُثوقٌ بِـ	unite (trans.)	وَحَّدَ ، تَوْحيدٌ
truth	حَقٌّ ـ حُقوقٌ	unity	وَحْدَةٌ
try, attempt	حاوَلَ ، مُحاوَلَةٌ	university	جامِعَةٌ ـ ات
turn (one's) atten-tion	اِنْصَرَفَ ، اِنْصِرافٌ	unless	إِلّا إِذا
	إِلى	until	حَتّى ؛ إِلى أَنْ
twelfth	ثانِيَ عَشَرَ	untrue	غَيْرُ صَحيحٍ
twelve	إِثْنا عَشَرَ	upon (doing s.th.)	عِنْدَ ؛ لَدى
twenty	عِشْرونَ	upside down	مَقْلوبٌ ـ ونَ
twice	مَرَّتَيْنِ	use to, be of; to benefit	نَفَعَ ـَ ، نَفْعٌ

use, benefit (from)	اِسْتَفادَ ، اِسْتِفادَةٌ
use, employ, utilize	اِسْتَخْدَمَ ، اِسْتِخْدامٌ
usually	عادَةٌ

V

vacant	خالٍ - ونَ
various	مُخْتَلِفٌ - ون
verily	إنَّ
very	جِدّاً
victorious (over), be	اِنْتَصَرَ ، اِنْتِصارٌ (عَلى)
view, opinion (on)	رَأْيٌ (في) ، نَظَرٌ (في)
view of, in the, in the opinion of	عِنْدَ ، في رَأْيِ ، في نَظَرِ
village	قَرْيَةٌ - قُرًى
visit	زِيارَةٌ - ات
visit; (with cognate accusative) pay a visit to	زارَ - ُ ، زِيارَةٌ
visiting	زائِرٌ - ونَ
visitor	زائِرٌ - زُوّارٌ
vocabulary items	مُفْرَداتٌ
voice, noise	صَوْتٌ - أَصْواتٌ
volume, tome	جُزْءٌ - أَجْزاءٌ

W

wait (for)	اِنْتَظَرَ ، اِنْتِظارٌ
waiting (for), be	كانَ في الاِنْتِظارِ
walk	سارَ - ِ ، سَيْرٌ
walk around (من)	تَجَوَّلَ ، تَجَوُّلٌ
wall	حائِطٌ - حيطانٌ
want, wish, desire	وَدَّ / وَدِدْتُ يَوَدُّ ، وُدٌّ ، وِدادٌ ، أرادَ ، إرادَةٌ ، شاءَ -َ ، مَشيئَةٌ
war (f.)	حَرْبٌ - حُروبٌ
watch; clock	ساعَةٌ - ات
watch, look at	شاهَدَ ، مُشاهَدَةٌ
water	ماءٌ - مياهٌ
way, road	طَريقٌ - طُرُقٌ
we	نَحْنُ
wealth, property	مالٌ - أَمْوالٌ
wealth, riches	ثَرْوَةٌ - ات
wealthy, rich (in)	غَنِيٌّ - أَغْنِياءُ (بِ)
wedding	عُرْسٌ - أَعْراسٌ
week	أُسْبوعٌ - أَسابيعُ
weep, cry	بَكى - ِ ، بُكاءٌ
welcome!	أَهْلاً وَسَهْلاً
welcome s.o.	رَحَّبَ - تَرْحيبٌ (بِ)
well-known (for)	مَعْروفٌ - ونَ (بِ) ، مَشْهورٌ - ونَ (بِ)
west	غَرْبٌ
what? (interrogative pronoun)	ماذا ، ما

what? (interrogative adjective), which?	أَيُّ (أَيَّةُ)
what (relative pronoun), that which	ما ؛ اَلَّذِي
what a...he is!	يا لَهُ .. مِن
when? (interrogative)	مَتى
when (relative), whenever	لَمَّا ؛ حِينَ؛ عِنْدَما
where? (interrogative)	أَيْنَ
where (relative)	حَيْثُ
which? (interrogative adjective)	أَيُّ (أَيَّةُ)
which, that (relative)	اَلَّذِي (اَلَّتِي)
while	وَ (اَلْحال)
white	أَبْيَضُ (بَيْضاءُ) بِيضُ
who? (interrogative)	مَنْ
who (relative)	اَلَّذِي (اَلَّتِي)ـ اَلَّذِينَ
who, the one who, whoever (indefinite relative)	مَنْ
whole	كُلُّ
whose?	لِمَنْ
why?	لِماذا
wide	واسِعٌ
widespread	مُنْتَشِرُ ـ ونَ
wife	زَوْجَةٌ ـ اتٌ
will, wish, desire	إِرادَةٌ ؛ مَشِيئَةٌ ؛ رَغْبَةٌ
will, going to (do s.th.)	سَ / سَوْفَ (يَفْعَلُ)
will not (do s.th.)	لَنْ (يَفْعَلَ)
will, wish	شاءَ ، مَشِيئَةٌ
willing, ready (to)	مُسْتَعِدُّ ـ ونَ (لِ)
win, gain	رَبِحَ ـَ ، رِبْحٌ
window	شُبَّاكٌ ـ شَبابِيكُ
wing	جَناحٌ ـ أَجْنِحَةٌ
wisdom, word of wisdom	حِكْمَةٌ ـ حِكَمٌ
wise; wise person	حَكِيمٌ ـ حُكَماءُ
wish, desire (for)	رَغْبَةٌ ـ اتٌ (فِي)
wish, want	أَرادَ ، إِرادَةٌ ؛ وَدَّ / وَدِدْتُ يَوَدُّ ، وُدُّ ، وُدادٌ ؛ شاءَـَ، مَشِيئَةٌ ؛ رَغِبَ ـَ ، رَغْبَةٌ (فِي)
wish, hope	رَجا ـُ ، رَجاءٌ
with, accompanied by	مَعَ
with, by means of	بِ
with, at the place of	عِنْدَ ؛ لَدى
without (prep.)	بِدُونِ؛ دُونَ
without (conj.)	دُونَ أَنْ
without exception, absolutely	مُطْلَقاً
witness	شَهِدَ ـَ ، شَهادَةٌ

woman	امْرَأَةٌ/الْمَرْأَةُ ـ نِساءٌ، نِسْوَةٌ	you (honorific)	حَضْرَتُكَ ـ حَضَراتُكُمْ
		you're welcome!	عَفْواً
woman, young	فَتاةٌ ـ فَتَياتٌ	young (person)	صَغيرٌ ـ صِغارٌ
womanly, female	نِسائِيٌّ	youth, young man	شابٌّ ـ شَبابٌ
word	كَلِمَةٌ ـ اتٌ		

Z

work	عَمَلٌ ـ أَعْمالٌ	zone, region, area	مِنْطَقَةٌ ـ مَناطِقُ
work	عَمِلَ ـَ، عَمَلٌ		
work for	عَمِلَ ـَ، عَمَلٌ عَلى		
worker, laborer	عامِلٌ ـ عُمّالٌ		
world	عالَمٌ ـ عَوالِمُ؛ دُنْيا		
worse, worst	أَسْوَأُ		
worship	عَبَدَ ـُ، عِبادَةٌ		
write	كَتَبَ ـُ، كِتابَةٌ		
write, compose	أَلَّفَ، تَأْليفٌ		
writer, author	كاتِبٌ ـ كُتّابٌ		

Y

year	سَنَةٌ ـ سَنَواتٌ،سِنونَ؛ عامٌ ـ أَعْوامٌ
yellow	أَصْفَرُ (صَفْراءُ)ـ صُفْرٌ
yes	نَعَمْ
yesterday	أَمْسِ
you	أَنْتَ ـ أَنْتُمْ، (أَنْتِ ـ أَنْتُنَّ) أَنْتُما ـ أَنْتُمْ

ARABIC-ENGLISH GLOSSARY

This glossary contains all the active vocabulary--words the student is ss responsible for--in this book. It also contains all the passive vocabulary found in the drills and exercises, as well as many words appearing in grammatical notes to illustrate a particular rule. These words are all bracketed [ ].

The order of entries in the list parallels that of <u>A Dictionary of Modern Written Arabic</u> by Hans Wehr, edited by J Milton Cowan, Cornell University Press, Ithaca, in order to acquaint the student as soon as possible with Arabic dictionary usage. There are also some dictionary drills in the book to introduce the student to the arrangement of lexical items. In brief, words are listed by <u>root</u>; verbs, if any, are given first, by verb Form number. Next come short nouns and adjectives, followed by longer ones, and finally nouns that have prefixed <u>m-</u>, verbal nouns, and participles. The following are conventions peculiar to this book:

The symbol # indicates a new root; in case of two homophonous roots, both such roots are identified by ##.

Feminine nouns and adjectives are not entered if they are automatically derivable from the masculine by the feminine suffix ــة -a(t)un. Thus, مُعَلِّمٌ 'teacher' (male) implies مُعَلِّمَةٌ 'teacher' (female).

Nisba adjectives are identified by the notation (nisba) before the English translation; they follow immediately the nouns from which they are derived, unless otherwise noted.

Place names and personal names are also included. Compound names are entered under the first name only; thus, the following are all found under the letter أ : أَبُو نُوَاس   ،   أَحْمَد شَوْقِي ، أَنْوَر السَّادَات

For topical groupings of vocabulary items--names of the days and months and of the Arab states--and for particular parts of speech see the various Appendices.

For abbreviations see the Introduction to this volume.

ا

أَ # (interrogative particle)

آبُ # August (Syria, Lebanon, Jordan, Iraq)

أَبُ # see أبو

إِبْنٌ # see بنو

أَبٌ / أَبُو ‒ آبَاءٌ # father

أَبَوِيٌّ (nisba) paternal, fatherly

يَا أَبَتِ O my father!

أَلأَبَوَانِ (d. of أَبٌ) the parents, father and mother

أَبُو العَلاءِ المَعَرِّي Abū al-'Alā' al-Ma'arrī (late Abbasid poet and author)

أَبُو الفَرَجِ الأَصْبَهَانِيّ. Abū al-Faraj al-Iṣbahānī (Medieval literary figure)

أَبُو نُوَاسٍ Abū Nuwās (Abbasid poet)

أَثَّرَ ، تَأْثِيرٌ (فِي ، عَلَى) # II to affect, influence, make an impression on

تَأَثَّرَ ، تَأَثُّرٌ (بِ ، فِي) V to be influenced, affected, impressed (by)

أَثَرٌ ‒ آثَارٌ # track, trace, sign; ancient monument, ruin; (p.) antiquities

أَثَرِيٌّ (nisba) ancient, historical; archeological

أَجْرٌ ‒ أُجُورٌ # wages, pay, recompense, reward

أَجَّلَ ، تَأْجِيلٌ # II to put off, delay, postpone

أَحَدٌ (إِحْدَى) # one; somebody, someone, anybody, anyone (esp. in negative sentences and questions); (with neg.) no one

أَخَذَ ‒ُ ، أَخْذٌ # to take; (with foll. indic.) to begin, start (doing s.th.) (imperative = خُذ)

تَأَخَّرَ ، تَأَخُّرٌ (عَن) # V to be, become late, delayed; to linger, hesitate; to fall behind (s.th.)

أَخِيرٌ ‒ ون ، أَوَاخِرُ last, final, ultimate; latter; (foll. by noun of time) the last part of, the end of

اليَوْمُ الآخِرُ Judgment Day, The Last Day

إِلَى آخِرِهِ et cetera, and so on

آخَرُ ‒ ون ، (أُخْرَى ‒ أُخْرَيَاتٌ) . other, another, one more

أَخِيرٌ last; latest, final; recent; the second of two, latter

أَخِيراً finally; recently, lately

أَخٌ / أَخُو ‒ إِخْوَةٌ # brother

أَخَوِيٌّ brotherly, fraternal

أُخْتٌ ـ أَخَوَاتٌ اخو   sister

[أَدَّبَ ، تَأْدِيبٌ] # II to educate, re-
fine; to discipline,
punish

أَدَبٌ ـ آدَابٌ   literature, belles-
lettres; (p.) let-
ters, culture

كُلِّيَّةُ الآدَابِ   College of Arts and
Humanities

أَدِيبٌ ـ أُدَبَاءُ   man of letters,
writer, author

[أَدَّى ، ـ تَأْدِيَةٌ] # II to carry out, perform; to cover (ex-
penses)

إِذَا # if; when; whenever

إِلاَّ إِذَا   unless

[إِذَاً ، إِذَنْ] # then, therefore, in
that case

أُذُنٌ ـ آذَانٌ # (f.) ear

تَارِيخٌ ـ تَوَارِيخٌ # history; date

أَرَامْكُو # ARAMCO (The Arabian
American Oil Co.)

آرَامِيَّةٌ # Aramaic (language)

الأُرْدُنُّ # Jordan

أَرْزٌ # (collective) cedar,
cedars

أَسَّسَ ، تَأْسِيسٌ # II to establish,
found, set up

أَسَاسِيٌّ   fundamental, basic

أُسْتَاذٌ ـ أَسَاتِذَةٌ # professor; teacher;
(form of address to
intellectuals)

إِسْرَائِيلُ # Israel

بَنُو إِسْرَائِيلَ   the children of
Israel (Qur'anic
verse); the Israe-
lites

[آسِفَ ، إِسَافٌ] IV to be distressing
regrettable to;
(A. obj. = E. subj.)
to regret

الأَسْكَنْدَرِيَّةُ # Alexandria

أَسْوَانُ # Aswan

إِصْبَهَانُ # Isfahān (city in Iran)

[أَصْلٌ ـ أُصُولٌ] # origin, source; root
cause

[أَصْلِيٌّ] (nisba) original;
genuine

أَغُسْطُس # August (Egypt and N.
Africa)

أُفٍّ # (interjection espres-
sing anger or dis-
pleasure)

أَفْرِيقِيَا ، أَفْرِيقِيَةٌ # (f.) Africa

أَفْلاطُونُ # Plato

الأُقْصُرُ # Luxor (root is QSR)

أُكْتُوبَرُ # October (Egypt and N.
Africa)

تَأَكَّدَ ، تَأَكَّدَ (مِن) # V to become certain,
convinced (of)

أَكَلَ ـ ، أَكْلٌ # to eat (imperative: كُلْ)

أَكْلٌ   eating; food

أَلاَّ (= أَنْ لا) # that...not, lest

إِلاَّ # except; (with negative) only

إِلاَّ إِذَا   unless

أَلَخ # (abbreviation of
إِلَى آخِرِهِ)

أَلَّذِي ، أَللَّذَانِ، # (relative pronoun)
أَلَّتِي، ـ أَللَّذَيْنِ، who, that, which
أَللَّتَانِ
(أَللَّتِي ـ أَللَّتَيْنِ، أَللَّوَاتِي)

414

أُمُورٌ – أَمْرٌ #	matter, affair, concern (أَمْرٌ) plus pronoun suffix is often used as a paraphrase for an independent pronoun, e.g. أَمْرُهُ (= هو)
[كُلُّ ما في الأَمْرِ]	the whole story is...
في بِدايَةِ الأَمْرِ	in the beginning, at first
[إِمارَةٌ – ات]	emirate, principality
الإِماراتُ العَرَبِيَّةُ المُتَّحِدَةُ	United Arab Emirates
[أُمَراءُ – أَميرٌ]	prince, emir, commander
[أَميرُ المُؤْمِنينَ]	Commander of the Faithful (title of a Caliph
مُؤْتَمَرٌ – ات	conference; convention
أَمْريكا #	America
أَمْريكِيٌّ، أَمْريكانِيٌّ – ون، أَمْريكانٌ	American
أَمْسِ	(adv.) yesterday
[آمَنَ، إيمانٌ (بِ)] #	IV to believe (in)
[مُؤْمِنٌ – ون]	believer
[أَميرُ المُؤْمِنينَ]	Commander of the Faithful (title of a Caliph)
أَنْ #	(foll. by subjunctive or perfect tense) that (conj.)
إلى أَنْ	until; to the point where
إِنْ #	if, if it should be that
وَإِنْ	even if
أَنَّ #	the fact that, that (conj.)

أَلْفٌ – آلافٌ #	thousand
أُلُوفٌ مِنْ	thousands of
أَلَّفَ، تَأْليفٌ #	II to compose, write (a book)
[إِلَهٌ – آلِهَةٌ] #	god, deity
أَللهُ	God
[وَاللهِ]	By God!, indeed!
[أَللهُ يُوَفِّقُ]	God will make you prosper, give you success
إلى #	to; up to; as far as, until
إلى أَنْ	until; to the point where
إلامَ = إلى ما)	'to what?' up to where? how far?
إلى اللِّقاءِ	'goodbye'
أَمْ #	or
[أَمَّمَ، تَأْميمٌ] #	II to nationalize
أُمٌّ – أُمَّهاتٌ	mother
أُمّ كُلْثوم	Umm Kulthum (a great modern Egyptian singer)
[أُمِّيٌّ – ون]	illiterate
أُمَّةٌ – أُمَمٌ	nation, people
الأُمَمُ المُتَّحِدَةُ	The United Nations
أَمامَ	in front of
أَمّا ... فَ #	as for...
أَمّا بَعْدُ، وَبَعْدُ	(phrase linking introduction and body of book, letter) now then, now to our topic...
الأَمازون #	The Amazon

إِنَّ (قَالَ after a form of) that (conj.)

إِنَّ # (intensifying particle) verily, indeed

إِنَّما but, rather, but rather; only

أَنا # I

أَنْتَ ـ أَنْتُما ـ أَنْتُم you

أَلْأَنْدَلُسُ # Andalusia, Spain

ناسٌ # (coll.) people (indefinite also أُناسٌ)

إِنْسانٌ man, human being, person

آنِسَةٌ ـ ات، أَوانِسُ young lady, miss

إِنْكِلْتْرا # England

إِنْكِليزِيٌّ، إِنْجِليزِيٌّ English (n. or adj.)

ـ إِنْكِليزٌ، إِنْجِليزٌ

أَلْإِنْكِليزِيُّ، الْإِنْجِليزِيُّ the English language, English

أَهْلٌ ـ أَهالٍ # people; family; owners; deserving

[حَرْبٌ أَهْلِيَّةٌ] civil war

أَهْلاً وَسَهْلاً welcome! hello!

أَوْ # or

أُوتوبيسٌ ـ ات # bus

أُورُبّا، أُورُوبّا، أُروبّا # (f.) Europe

[آلٌ] # family; clan; people

آلُ عِمْران the Family of 'Imrān (Qur'anic verse)

أَوَّلُ (أُولى) أَوائِلُ first

أَوَّلاً first, firstly

أَلآنَ # now

آيَةٌ ـ ات # Qur'anic, Koranic verse

أَيْ # that is to say, that is, i.e.

أَيْ # (vocative particle) O!

أَيّ # (interrogative noun) what?, which?; (in a statement) any, any... at all; (with a negative) not any, no

إِيّا # with pronominal suffix to express the accusative; إِيّاكَ أَنْ take care not to..., be careful not to...

إِيرانُ # Iran

إِيرانِيٌّ ـ ون (nisba) Iranian

أَيْضاً # also

أَيْلُولُ # September (in Syria, Leb. Jordan, Iraq)

أَيْنَ # where?

أَيُّها # (f. also أَيَّتُها) (vocative particle) O!

بِ # in, at, on; by, by means of, with; for (the price of); (makes verb of moving causative e.g. ذَهَبَ بِ 'to take')

بِدونِ without

بِغَيْرِ without

بِذَلِكَ thereby

ألبَتْراءُ #	Petra (city in Jordan; ancient Nabatean capitol)
بَجَّلَ ، تَبْجِيلٌ #	II to treat with respect, reverence
بَحَثَ ـَ ، بَحْثٌ #	to discuss
بَحَثَ ، بَحَثَ عَنْ	to look for, search for
[بَحْثٌ ـ بُحوثٌ، أبْحاثٌ]	discussion; research; study
باحِثٌ ـ ون	researcher
بَحْرٌ ـ بِحارٌ، [بُحورٌ، أبْحارٌ] #	sea
البَحْرُ الأبْيَضُ المُتَوَسِّطُ	the Mediterranean Sea
البَحْرُ الأحْمَرُ	the Red Sea
البَحْرَيْنُ	Bahrain
بَدَأَ ـَ ، بَدْءٌ (بِ) #	to begin, start (with)
بِدايَةٌ	beginning
في بِدايَةِ الأمْرِ	in the beginning, at first
[اِبْتِدائِيٌّ]	initial, primary, elementary
تَبادَلَ ، تَبادُلٌ #	VI to exchange
أبْدى ، إبْداءٌ #	IV to reveal, manifest, show, display
بَدَوِيٌّ ـ بَدْوٌ	bedouin
بَذَلَ ـُ ، بَذْلٌ #	to exert
بَذَلَ جُهوداً	to exert great effort, take great pains
بُرْتُقالٌ #	orange (fruit)
بُرْتُقالِيٌّ	orange-colored, orange

[بَرِىءَ مِنْ يَمِينِهِ] #	to become cleared of one's oath
[اِسْتِبْراءٌ]	probation (Islamic law)
[بَرِيدٌ] #	mail, post
بَرْلَمانٌ #	parliament
إبْراهيمُ طوقان #	Ibrāhīm Tūqān (modern Palestinian poet)
إبْراهيمُ بْنُ عَبّاسٍ الصّولِيُّ	Ibrāhīm b. 'Abbās al-Ṣūlī
بَريطانِيا (العُظْمى) #	(Great) Britain
بَسْكِنْتا #	Baskinta (town in Lebanon)
بَشّارُ بْنُ بُرْدٍ #	Bashshār b. Burd (Abbasid poet)
[بَصَرَ ـ أبْصارٌ] #	eyesight, vision; glance
البَصْرَةُ #	Basra (city in Iraq)
[بِطالَةٌ] #	unemployment
ألبَعْثُ #	the Baath Party
بَعْثَةٌ ـ ات	mission; deputation; foreign study mission
بَعْثَةٌ دِراسِيَّةٌ	study mission (group of students or fellowships)
بَعْدُ #	(adv.) then, thereupon; afterwards, after that, later
لَمْ ... بَعْدُ	not yet, still...not
[فيما بَعْدُ]	afterwards, later
[أمّا بَعْدُ؛ وبَعْدُ]	(phrase linking introduction and body of letter, book) now then, now to our topic...

بَعْدَ	(prep.) after; (with time expression) in, e.g. بَعْدَ أيّامٍ 'in a few days'		بَلَدِيّ	(nisba) native, local, domestic (not foreign)
مِنْ بَعْدِ	after		بَلَغَ ـُ ، بُلوغٌ #	to reach, attain; to come to the ears of
بَعْدَئِذٍ	then, after that, afterwards		[مَبْلَغٌ ـ مَبالِغٌ]	amount, sum of money
بَعيدٌ ـ بُعَداءُ، بِعادٌ (عَنْ)	distant, far (away) (from)		بولاقٌ #	Bulaq (a district of Cairo)
بَعْضٌ #	part, portion; some, some of		اِبْنٌ ـ أَبْناءُ #	son; (p.) children
بَعْضُ الشَّيْءِ	somewhat		بَنونٌ / بَنَوِيّ (nisba of اِبْنٌ)	filial
بَعْلَبَكّ #	Baalbek (Roman monument in Lebanon)		اِبْنُ بَطّوطة	Ibn Battuta (medieval traveler)
بَغْدادُ #	Baghdad		اِبْنُ خَلْدونَ	Ibn Khaldoun (medieval historian and sociologist)
[بُغْضٌ] #	hatred		بَنو إسْرائيلَ	the children of Israel (Qur'anic verse); the Israelites
[بَقَرٌ] #	(coll.) cows, heifers		اِبْنةٌ ـ بَناتٌ	daughter
[بَقَرةٌ ـ ات]	(unit noun) cow		بِنْتٌ ـ بَناتٌ	girl; daughter
بَقِيَ ـَ ، بَقاءٌ #	to remain, stay; (with foll. imperfect) to go on, continue (doing s.th.)		[البَنونُ وَالبَناتُ]	sons and daughters
			[أَبْناءُ الشَّعْبِ]	ordinary people
بَكالوريوس #	B.A., bachelor's degree		[بُنَيَّ]	my little son, my dear son (diminutive of اِبْني)
[بَكى ـِ ، بُكاءٌ] #	to weep, cry		[بُنٌّ] #	(coll.) coffee beans, coffee
حائِطُ المَبْكى	the Wailing Wall (Jerusalem)		بُنّيّ	(nisba) coffee-colored, brown
بَلْ #	but, rather		بَنْكٌ ـ بُنوكٌ #	bank
بَلْ وَ	and even, but also		بَناما #	Panama
بَلَدٌ ـ بِلادٌ، بُلْدانٌ #	(m. and f.) country		بَنى ـِ ، بِناءٌ #	to build, construct
بِلادٌ	(f.) country; homeland		بِناءٌ ـ أَبْنِيةٌ	a building; structure
بِلادُ الشّامِ	Syria			

تَرَكَ ـُ ، تَرْك # to leave, leave, behind

تُرْكِيّ - أَتْراك # Turkish; Turk

تِسْعَة # nine

تِسْعون (nom.) ninety; (foll. by definite n.) nintieth

تاسِع ninth

تِشرين الأَوَّل # October

تَعِزّ Ta'izz (city in Yemen)

[تِلميذ ـ تَلاميذ] # disciple, student

تَلا ـُ ، تُلُوّ # to follow

تالٍ following, subsequent, next

تَمَّ ـِ # to be completed; to take place

تونِس # Tunis; Tunisia

[ثَبَّتَ ، تَثْبيت] # II to consolidate, strengthen; to prove, establish

[ثَرْوَة ـ ات] # wealth

ثَقافَة ـ ات # culture, refinement

ثُلْث ـ أَثْلات # one-third

ثَلاثَة three

ثالِث third

ثالِثاً thirdly

ثَلاثون (nom.) thirty; (foll. by definite noun) thirtieth

مِن ثَمَّ # hence, therefore

باب ـ أَبْواب # door

[مُباح] # permissible

بور سَعيد # Port Said

بَيْت ـ بُيوت # house, home

بَيت لَحم Bethlehem

بَيروت # Beirut

أَبْيَض (بَيْضاء) - بيض # white

البَحْر الأَبْيَض المُتَوَسِّط the Mediterranean Sea

[بَياض] whiteness

باعَ ـِ ، بَيْع # to sell (s.th. to s.o.)

بَيْن # between

تابَعَ ، مُتابَعَة # III to continue, pursue

اِتَّبَعَ ، اِتِّباع VIII to follow, adhere to, observe (rule, etc.)

تِجارَة # commerce

تَحْت # under, underneath; below, beneath

يُحَدّ ، مُتَّحِدة # see under وحد

مُتْحَف ـ مَتاحِف # museum

تَدْمُر # Palmyra (ancient in N. Syria)

تَرْجَمَ ، تَرْجَمَة # (quad.) to translate

تَرْجَمَة ـ ات translation, interpretation

تاريخ # see ارخ

ثُمَّ

ثُمَّ	then
# ثَمَنٌ ـ أَثْمَانٌ	price, cost
# ثَمَانِيَةٌ	eight
ثَمَانُونَ	(nom.) eighty; (foll. by definite n.) eightieth
ثَامِنٌ	eighth
# أَثْنَاءَ	during
إِثْنَانِ	(d. nom) two
ثَانٍ	second
ثَانِياً	secondly
ثَانَوِيٌّ	(nisba) secondary
# ثَوْرَةٌ ـ ات	revolution, rebellion, revolt (against)
ثَوْرِيٌّ	revolutionary (n. or adj.), rebel

ج

# جُبْرَانُ خَلِيلُ جُبْرَانُ	Kahlil Gibran (Lebanese-American writer)
# [جَبَلَ ـُ ، جَبْلٌ]	to mold, fashion, shape
جَبَلٌ ـ جِبَالٌ	mountain
# جُحَا	Juha (The central character of countless amusing anecdotes depicting life and customs in Near Eastern countries)
# اَلجَاحِظُ	Al-Jahiz (medieval writer)
### [جَدٌّ ـ أَجْدَادٌ]	ancestor; grandfather

## جَدَّدَ ـ تَجْدِيدٌ	II to renew, restore, revive
جِدّاً	very
جَدِيدٌ ـ جُدُدٌ	new
# جَرِيرٌ	Jarir (Umayyid poet)
# جَرِيدَةٌ ـ جَرَائِدُ	newspaper
# جَرَشُ	Jerash (city in Jordan)
# [جَرِيمَةٌ ـ جَرَائِمُ]	crime
# جَرَى ـ ، جَرْيٌ	to take place, occur, happen
[جَارِيَةٌ ـ ات، جَوَارٍ]	girl; slave girl, servant
# [جُزْءٌ ـ أَجْزَاءٌ]	part, portion, section; volume, tome
# جَزِيرَةٌ ـ جَزَائِرُ ، جُزُرٌ	island; peninsula
اَلجَزِيرَةُ العَرَبِيَّةُ	Arabian Peninsula
اَلجَزَائِرُ	Algeria; Algiers
# جَعْفَرُ البَرْمَكِيُّ	Ja'far the Barmakide
# جَعَلَ ـَ ، جَعْلٌ	to make, create, make (s.th. into s.th.), render; (with foll. indicative) to begin to (do s.th.)
# مَجَلَّةٌ ـ ات	magazine, periodical
# جَلَسَ ـِ ، جُلُوسٌ	to sit, sit down
أَجْلَسَ ، إِجْلاسٌ	IV to ask or make s.o. sit down, seat s.o.
[مَجْلِسٌ ـ مَجَالِسُ]	assembly, council, board

جَمَعَ ـَ ، جَمْع #	to gather, collect, combine
جَمَعَ بَيْنَ ... وَ	to combine...and...
اِجْتَمَعَ ، اِجْتِماع (مَعَ ، بِـ)	VIII to meet (with)
جَمْعِيَّة	association, society, league, club, assembly
الجَمْعِيَّةُ العامَّة	the General Assembly
جَميع	all
الجَميع	everyone, everybody
جَميعاً	all together, one and all; entirely, wholly
اِجْتِماع ـ ات (بِـ)	meeting (with)
اِجْتِماعِيّ	social; sociological; societal; group (adj.)
[جامِع ـ جَوامِع]	mosque
جامِعَة ـ ات	university; league, association
الجامِعَةُ العَرَبِيَّة	the Arab League
مُجْتَمَع ـ ات	society; community
##جُمْلة ـ جُمَل	sentence, clause
جَمال	beauty
جَمالُ عَبْدُ النّاصِر	Jamal 'Abd al-Nasser
جَميل ـ ون	beautiful, handsome
##[جَمَل ـ جِمال]	camel
جُمْهورِيَّة ـ ات #	republic
الجُمْهورِيَّةُ العَرَبِيَّةُ المُتَّحِدَة.	the United Arab Republic
رَئيسُ جُمْهورِيَّة	president (of a republic)

[جِنِّيّ ـ جِنّ] #	(coll.) jinn; (p. = jinn), genie, demon
[جَنَّة ـ ات،جِنان]	garden; paradise
جَنوب #	south
إلى جانِب	in addition to; besides; apart from
أَجْنَبِيّ ـ أَجانِب	foreign; foreigner
[جَناح ـ أَجْنِحة] #	wing
[جُنود] #	(p.) army; soldiers
[جُنْدِيّ ـ جُنود]	soldier
جُهْد ـ جُهود #	exertion; effort, attempt, endeavor
[جَهْل] #	ignorance
[جاهِل ـ ون]	ignorant
[جاهِلِيّ]	(nisba) Pre-Islamic
[جَوّ ـ أَجْواء،جِواء] #	atmosphere; air
أَجابَ ، إجابة #	IV to answer, respond to s.o.; to comply with (a request)
[أَجابَ إلى]	IV to answer, respond to s.o.
أَجابَ عَن ، عَلى	IV to answer, respond (to s.o.) concerning (a question, etc.)
إجابة ـ ات	answer, response
جَيِّد ـ جِياد #	good, excellent
جَيِّداً	well
أَجْوَد	better
جار ـ جيران #	neighbor
جورجي زَيْدان #	Jurji Zaydan (modern journalist and writer

[تَجَوّلَ ، تَجَوّلٌ] # V to walk, roam, wander around

جاءَ ـِ ، مَجيءٌ to come (imperative = تَعالَ)

[جاءَ في] to be included, mentioned, said (in a written document)

جاءَ بـ to bring

[جَيْبٌ ـ جُيوبٌ] # pocket

ح

IV أَحَبّ ، حُبّ ، مَحَبّةٌ to love, like; to take a liking to, fall in love with; to wish, want, like to do s.th.

حُبّ love

حَبيبٌ ـ أَحِبّاءُ beloved, sweetheart; dear

حَتّى (prep.) until, up to, as far as; (conj.: foll. by perfect) until, to the point that; (foll. by subjunctive) in order that, so that; until; (adverb) even

لَم ... حَتّى scarcely had...when

[حاجّ ـ حُجّاجٌ ، حَجيجٌ] # pilgrim, hadji (honorific title of one who has performed the pilgrimage to Mecca)

الحِجازُ # the Hejaz

[حَدّ ـُ ، حَدّ] # to delineate; to set bounds to, limit, restrict

حَدّدَ ، تَحْديدٌ II to define; to limit, set bounds (to)

حَدّ ـ حُدودٌ extent, limit; boundary

تَحْديدٌ definition

حَدّثَ ، حَديثٌ (بـ) II to tell, relate to s.o. (about s.th.)

تَحَدّثَ، تَحَدّثَ (إلى وَعَنْ) V to speak (to)(about), converse (with)(about)

حَديثٌ ـ حِداثٌ new, modern

حَديثاً recently, lately

[حَديثٌ ـ أَحاديثُ] hadith, prophetic tradition; conversation

[مُحادَثةٌ ـ ات] talk, conversation, discussion

[مُتَحَدّثٌ ـ ون] spokesman

حُرّيّةٌ ـ ات freedom, liberty

[تَحْريرٌ] liberation, freeing

حَرْبٌ ـ حُروبٌ (f.) war

[حَرْبٌ أَهْليّةٌ] civil war

الحَرْبُ العالَميّةُ the World War

[حَرَجٌ] # embarrassment, anguish

[حَراكٌ] # motion, movement

VIII احْتَرَمَ ، احْتِرامٌ to respect, honor, revere

حِزْبٌ ـ أَحْزابٌ (political) party

حَزِنَ ـ حُزْنٌ (لـ، عَلى) to be sad, grieve (over, because of)

[حُزْنٌ (عَلى)] sadness (over)

[مُحْزِنٌ] saddening, sad (news, etc.)

حَسّنَ ، تَحْسينٌ II to improve (s.th.)

Arabic (left column)	English	Arabic (right column)	English
[أَحْسَنَ ، إِحْسانٌ (بـ)]	IV to be kind, do good (to)	حَفَرَ ـِ ، حَفْرٌ #	to dig, excavate; to engrave
تَحَسَّنَ ، تَحَسُّنٌ	V to improve, get better	حافَظَ ، مُحافَظةٌ على #	III to preserve, maintain; to protect, defend
حُسْنٌ	beauty, handsomeness; goodness	[مُحافِظٌ ــ ون]	conservative
[لِحُسْنِ الحَظِّ]	fortunately	حافِظ إبْراهيم	Hāfiẓ Ibrāhīm (modern Egyptian poet)
[حُسْنُ الضِّيافَةِ]	hospitality	احْتَفَلَ ، احْتِفالٌ (بـ) #	VIII to celebrate (s.th.); to honor, welcome (s.o.)
حَسَنٌ ــ حِسانٌ	fine, good, excellent; beautiful, handsome	حَفْلةٌ ــ ات	party, festive event; celebration; ceremony
حَسَنًا	(that will be) fine!	حَقَّقَ ، تَحْقيقٌ #	II to realize, accomplish, achieve
أَحْسَنُ	better, best; nicer, nicest	حَقٌّ ــ حُقوقٌ	truth; correctness; right; one's due
حُسَيْنٌ	Hussein	[أَعْرِفُ... حَقَّ المَعْرِفَةِ]	I know...very well
حَسّانُ بْنُ ثابِتٍ	Ḥassān b. Thābit (poet of the Prophet Muhammad)	[الحُقوقُ المَدَنِيَّةُ]	Civil Rights
حَصَلَ ـُ ، حُصولٌ على #	to obtain, get	[التَّساوى في الحُقوقِ]	Equal Rights
حَضَرَ ـُ ، حُضورٌ #	to attend, be present (at)	[حَقًّا]	truly, actually, in fact, really
حَضَرَ إلى	to come to	كانَ على حَقٍّ	to be right
حاضَرَ ، مُحاضَرةٌ	III to lecture, give a lecture	حَكَمَ ـُ ، حُكْمٌ #	to govern, rule
أَحْضَرَ ، إِحْضارٌ	IV to bring, take	حَكَمَ ـُ ، حُكْمٌ على (بـ)	to pass judgment on; to judge; to sentence s.o. (to s.th.)
حَضْرةٌ ــ حَضَراتٌ	(title of respect) excellency	حِكْمةٌ ــ حِكَمٌ	wisdom; saying, word of wisdom
حَضْرتُك	your excellency, you	[حَكيمٌ ــ حُكَماءُ]	wise (n. and adj.)
[حَضارةٌ ــ ات]	civilization; culture	حُكومةٌ ــ ات	government
مُحاضَرةٌ ــ ات	lecture	[حاكِمٌ ــ ون، حُكّامٌ]	governor, ruler
حاضِرٌ ــ ون	present, attending; current (time)	حَكى ـِ ، حِكايةٌ #	to tell, relate
[حَظٌّ : لِحُسْنِ الْحَظِّ]#	fortunately	حِكايةٌ ــ ات	story, tale

Arabic (right)	English (right)
[حَمَلَ لِـ ، إِلى]	to bring (s.th.) to (s.o.)
[حَمْلَة ـ ات (على)]	military campaign (against), attack (on)
# VIII اِحْتاجَ ، اِحْتِياجٌ إِلى ، لِـ	VIII to need, require, be in need of
حاجَة ـ ات	need
بِحاجَةٍ إِلى	in need of
[حِوارٌ]	dialogue, conversation
# VII اِنْحازَ ، اِنْحِيازٌ إِلى	VII to side with; be partial to, aligned with
اِنْحِيازٌ (إِلى)	alignment (with)
عَدَمُ الاِنْحِياز	non-alignment
# IV أَحاطَ ، إِحاطَةٌ بِـ	IV to surround
حائِطُ المَبْكى	the Wailing Wall
# III حاوَلَ ، مُحاوَلَةٌ (أَن)	III to attempt, try (s.th.), (to do s.th.)
مُحاوَلَةٌ ـ ات	attempt, effort
[حالٌ ـ أَحْوالٌ]	(m. and f.) condition, state, circumstance
كَيْفَ الْحالُ؟	how are you?
حالِيٌّ ـ ون	present, current
أَلْجُمْلَةُ الْحالِيَّةُ	the ḥāl sentence, circumstantial clause (Arabic grammar)
حَوْلَ	about; around, surrounding; approximately; over, concerning
# II حَيّا ، تَحِيَّةٌ	II to greet s.o.
حَياةٌ ـ حَيَواتٌ	life

Arabic (left)	English (left)
# حَلَّ ـ ُ ، حَلٌّ	to solve, resolve; to dissolve, disband, break up
[حَلَّ ـ ، حِلٌّ]	to be, become permissible
[اِحْتَلَّ ، اِحْتِلالٌ]	VIII to occupy, take over
حَلٌّ ـ حُلولٌ	solution, resolution; dissolution, breaking-up
مَحَلٌّ ـ ات ، مَحالٌّ	place, location
مَحَلِّيٌّ ـ ون	(nisba) local
حَلَبُ	Aleppo
[حِلْفٌ ـ أَحْلافٌ]	pact, alliance
# [حَمْدٌ]	praise
أَلْحَمْدُ لِلّهِ	praise be to God
أَحْمَدُ	Ahmed
أَحْمَدُ أَمين	Ahmad Amin (modern Egyptian essayist)
أَحْمَدُ شَوْقي	Ahmad Shawqi (modern Egyptian poet)
مُحَمَّدٌ بَغدادِيّ	Muhammad Baghdādī
مُحَمَّدٌ عَبْدُ الْوَهّاب	Muhammad Abd al-Wahhab (contemporary Egyptian musician)
#[اِحْمَرَّ ، اِحْمِرارٌ]	IX to turn red
[حُمْرَةٌ]	redness
[حِمارٌ ـ حَمير ، أَحْمِرَةٌ]	donkey
أَحْمَرُ (حَمْراءُ) ـ حُمْرٌ	red
أَلْبَحْرُ الْأَحْمَرُ	the Red Sea
أَلْقَصْرُ الْحَمْراءُ	the Alhambra
# حَمَلَ ـ ، حَمْلٌ	to carry, bear; to lift, load on

حَياوِيّ	(nisba) lively, full of life, vital	خارِج	outside of
تَحِيّة ـ ات	greeting(s)	خارِجِيّ	(nisba) outer, external
حَيْثُ #	(relative adverb) where, wherever	أَلْخارِجِيّةُ	foreign affairs
[حانَ ـ] #	to be time; to draw near, come, approach (time)	أَلْخَرْطُومُ #	Khartoum
		خَسِرَ ـ ، خَسارة #	to lose, suffer a loss of
حِينٌ ـ أَحْيانٌ	time; occasion	خاصّ #	special; private
حِينَ	when, at the time that	خاصّةً	especially
		[مُتَخَصِّص ـ ون]	specialist, expert
أَحْيانًا	sometimes	أَخْضَرُ ـ (خَضْراءُ) خُضْرة #	green
حِينَئِذٍ	at that time	[خُضْرة]	greenness
خ		خَطَأ #	error
أَخْبَرَ ، إِخْبارٌ (بِـ) #	IV to inform s.o. (of s.th.), tell s.o. (s.th.)	[خِطاب ـ ات] #	speech
		[خَطيب ـ خُطَباءُ]	fiancé
خَبَرٌ ـ أَخْبارٌ	news item	[تَخاطُب]	conversation
[خِبْرة]	experience; expertise	[خَفَضَ ـ ، خَفْض] #	to lower, drop
[خاتَم ـ خَواتِمُ] #	ring	خِلالَ #	during
[خَجِلَ ـ ، خَجَلٌ] #	to be ashamed	أَلْخَليلُ بْنُ أَحْمَدَ	al-Khalil b. Aḥmad
خَدَمَ ـ ، خِدْمة #	to serve, render a service	خالِدُ بْنُ الوَليدِ #	Khālid b. Al-Walīd
اِسْتَخْدَمَ ، اِسْتِخْدامٌ	X to use, employ	أَخْلَصَ ، إِخْلاصٌ (لِـ) #	IV to be sincere, loyal, devoted, faithful (to)
خِدْمة ـ ات	service	مُخْلِص ـ ون	sincere
خَرَجَ ـ ، خُروجٌ (مِن) #	to go our (of)	اِخْتَلَفَ ، اِخْتِلافٌ (عَن) #	VIII to differ, vary (from);
خَرَّجَ ، تَخْريجٌ	II to graduate (transitive); to educate	اِخْتَلَفَ (مَع) (في)	VIII to differ, disagree (with) (over)
أَخْرَجَ ، إِخْراجٌ	IV to take out, remove, expel	اِخْتَلَفَ بِاخْتِلافِ	VIII to vary according to the various...
خارِجٌ	exterior		
في الخارِجِ	abroad		

425

دعو

[خَلِيفَة - خُلَفَاءُ] (m.) caliph

خِلاف - ات difference; differ-ence of opinion, disagreement, con-flict

مُخْتَلِف - ون various, differing, different

مُخْتَلِف (with foll. gen., in m.s. only) various

[خُلُق - أَخْلاق] # character, morals, morality

[خال] # empty, vacant

خَمْسَة # five

خَمْسُون (nom.) fifty; (fol-lowing a definite n.) fiftieth

خامِس fifth

[خاف َ ، خَوْف ، مَخافَة] to be afraid, fear

[خال - أَخْوال] # maternal uncle

خَيْر - خُيُور # good (things); bles-sing, benefit; wel-fare

بِخَيْر fine, (I'm) fine

[خَيْمَة - خِيام] # tent

د

داغ هَمَرْشولد # Dag Hammarskjold

[دَبْكَة] # dabka (a folk dance)

دَخَلَ ُ ، دُخُول # to enter, go in, come in

[دَخَلَ على] to enter s.o.'s room or house, drop in on s.o.; to consummate marriage with (a woman

أَدْخَلَ ، إِدْخَال (على) IV to introduce; bring in(to)

[دَخْل] income, revenue

[داخِل] interior, inside

داخِل inside of, within

داخِلِيّ (nisba) inner, in-ternal; domestic

داخِلِيّة internal affairs

دَرَسَ ُ ، دِراسَة ، دُرُوس # to study

دَرَسَ على to study under s.o.

دَرَّسَ ، تَدْرِيس II to teach, instruct

دَرْس - دُرُوس lesson

دِراسَة - ات study, studying

مَدْرَسَة - مَدارِس school

مَدْرَسَة حُكُومِيّة public school

[مَدْرَسَة لُغَوِيّة] linguistic school

مُدَرِّس - ون instructor, teacher

[أَدْرَكَ ، إِدْراك] # IV to overtake

[دَرى - ، دِرايَة (بِـ)] # to know, be aware (of)

[دُسْتُور - دَساتِيرُ] # constitution

[دُعابَة - ات] # joke, jest

دَعا ُ ، دُعاء # to call (to), call up-on; to invite (to) (لِ ، إلى)

دَعا بِـ to call, name (s.o.) s.th.

دَعا إلى to call for, advocate, urge

دَعْوة invitation

[دِفاعٌ (عَن)] # defense (of)		[دينارٌ – دَنانيرُ] # dinar

ن

ذا # this one

كَذا   thus

كَذا وكَذا   such-and-such

ذلِكَ (تِلْكَ) –   (pron.) that (more remote in space or time)
أولائِكَ

بِذلِكَ   thereby

لِذلِكَ   therefore

مَعَ ذلِكَ   in spite of that, nevertheless

على ذلِكَ   therefore

كَذلِكَ   likewise; also

ألَيْسَ كَذلِكَ   isn't that so? n'est-ce pas?

[ذاكَ (تاكَ) –]   that one
أولائِكَ

هذا (تِلْكَ)   see under   ها

ذَكَرَ ُ ، ذِكْرٌ # to mention, relate, tell of

تَذْكِرَةٌ – تَذاكِرُ   ticket

مُذَكِّرَةٌ – ات   note, reminder; (p.) memoirs

[ذُلٌّ] # humility

ذَهَبَ َ ، ذَهابٌ # to go (to)

ذَهَبَ بِـ   to take

ذاهِبٌ – ون (إلى)   going (to)

أذاعَ، إذاعَةٌ (على) # IV to broadcast, transmit (to)

دَقيقَةٌ – دَقائِقُ # minute (of time)

دُكْتورٌ – دَكاتِرَةٌ # doctor

دُكْتوراه   doctorate

دَلَّ ُ ، دَلالَةٌ (على) # to show, point (to), indicate, give evidence (of)

دِمَشْقُ # Damascus

دُنْيا # (f.) world; this world (as opposed to الآخِرَةُ 'the hereafter'), worldly existence

دُنْيَويٌّ ، دُنْياويٌّ   (nisba) wordly, secular, temporal

أَدْهَشَ ، إدْهاشٌ # IV to surprise, astonish, amaze

[دَهْشَةٌ]   surprise, amazement

أَدارَ ، إدارَةٌ # IV to direct, manage, administer

دارٌ – دورٌ ، دِيارٌ   (f.) house

مُديرٌ – ون   director

دَوْلَةٌ – دُوَلٌ # state, country, power

دُوَليٌّ   (nisba) international

دولارٌ – ات # dollar

دامَ ُ ، دَوامٌ # to last, endure

دائِماً   always

دونَ # without

بِدونِ   without

ديسَمْبَر # December (Egypt and N. Africa)

دينٌ – أدْيانٌ # religion

ر	
رَأْسٌ - رُؤُوسٌ #	(m. and f.) head
رَئِيسٌ - رُؤَسَاءُ	president, head, chief
رَئِيسُ الوُزَرَاءِ	prime minister
رَئِيسُ الوِزَارَةِ	prime minister
رَئِيسِيٌّ - ون	(nisba) main, principal
[رَأَى يَرَى، رُؤْيَةٌ] #	to see
رَأَى يَرَى، رَأْيٌ (أَنَّ)	to opine, be of the opinion (that)
رَأْيٌ - آرَاءٌ (في)	opinion, view (on)
[عَلَى رَأْيٍ وَاحِدٍ]	of one opinion, in complete agreement
[رَبٌّ - أَرْبَابٌ] #	lord; master
[الرَّبُّ]	the Lord
رَبِحَ - ، رِبْحٌ (مِن) #	to gain, profit (from); to win s.th.
رَبَطَ - ، رَبْطٌ (إلى ،بَيْنَ، وَبَيْنَ) #	to bind, tie (to); to connect (with); to combine (s.th. with)
الرِّبَاطُ	Rabat
رَابِطَةٌ - رَوَابِطُ	bond, tie; connection, link
[الرَّابِطَةُ القَلَمِيَّةُ] #	The Literary Club
رُبْعٌ - أَرْبَاعٌ #	(one)-quarter, one-fourth
أَرْبَعَةٌ	four
أَرْبَعُونَ	(nom.) forty; (following def. noun) fortieth
رَابِعٌ	fourth
رَابِعًا	fourthly

[اِرْتَبَكَ ، اِرْتِبَاكٌ] #	VIII to be confused, bewildered
[رَبَّى ، تَرْبِيَةٌ] #	II to bring up, rear, raise; to educate, teach, instruct (a child)
تَرْبِيَةٌ - ات	education; upbringing
تَرْبَوِيٌّ	(nisba) educational, pedagogical
[مَرْتَبَةُ الشَّرَفِ الأُولَى] • #	first class honors
رَجَعَ - ، رُجُوعٌ #	to return, go, come back
رَجَعَ -	to take, bring back
رَجُلٌ - رِجَالٌ #	man
[رَجِيمٌ] #	cursed, damned
رَجَا - ، رَجَاءٌ (أَنْ) #	to hope; to wish; to request (that)
رَحَّبَ ، تَرْحِيبٌ - #	II to welcome
مَرْحَبًا	hello!
رَحَلَ - ، رَحِيلٌ (عَن) #	to move about; to depart; leave (from)
[رِحْلَةٌ - رَحَلَاتٌ]	travel, journey, trip
[رَحَّالٌ، رَحَّالَةٌ - رَحَّالَةٌ]	great traveler, explorer, globetrotter
[مَرْحَلَةٌ - مَرَاحِلُ]	stage, phase
[رَحِمَ - ، رَحْمَةٌ] #	to have mercy on, compassion on, sympathy for
رَدَّ - ، رَدٌّ (عَلَى) #	to return, send back; to answer, reply, respond (to s.o.)
رَدٌّ - رُدُودٌ (عَلَى)	answer, reply, response (to)

رَاسَلَ ، مُراسَلَة # III to correspond with	اِزْرَقَّ ، اِزْرِقاق # IX to turn blue
أَرْسَلَ ، إِرْسال IV to send	زُرْقَة ، زُرَق blueness
تَراسَلَ ، تَراسُل VI to correspond with one another	أَزْرَقُ (زَرْقاءُ) – زُرْق blue
[رَسول – رُسُل] messenger; apostle	زَمَنَ – أَزْمان # time; period, stretch of time
رِسالَة – رَسائِل letter; thesis, dissertation	زَنُّوبِيَة ، زَنُّوبِيا # Zenobia (queen of Palmyra)
مُراسِل – ون reporter; correspondent	زَيْنَب Zaynab (f. name)
رَسَمَ – ُ ، رَسْم # to draw	أَلْأَزْهَر # Al-Azhar (university)
رَسْمِيّ official, formal, ceremonial	[زَوَّج ، تَزْويج] # II to give in marriage
مُرَشَّح – ون # candidate, nominee	تَزَوَّج ، تَزَوُّج ، زَواج (مِن) V to get married to, to marry
رَغِبَ – َ ، رَغْبَة في # to desire, wish for	زَوْج – أَزْواج husband
عَلى الرَّغْمِ مِنْ..فَ # in spite of...	زَواج marriage, getting married
رَفَضَ – ُ ، رَفْض # to refuse, reject	زارَ – ُ ، زِيارَة # to visit
[أَرْفَقَ ، إِرْفاق] # IV to attach, enclose	زائِر – ون visiting
تَرَقَّى ، تَرَقٍّ # to advance (in rank), be promoted, rise	زائِر – زُوَّار visitor, guest
مَرْكَز – مَراكِزُ # center, headquarters, main office	زالَ – ُ ، زَوال # to cease
مَرْكَزِيّ (nisba) central	ما زالَ / لا يَزالُ to be still, yet
[تَراهَنَ ، تَراهُن] # VI to bet	زَيْت – زُيوت # (coll.) oil; petroleum
أَرادَ ، إِرادَة # IV to want, wish, desire	[زادَ – ِ ، زِيادَة] # to give s.o. more of s.th.
روسيا # Russia	[زادَ – ِ ، زِيادَة عَلى] to exceed, be more than
أَلرِّياض # Riyadh	اِزْدادَ – اِزْدِياد VIII to increase, grow larger, multiply
[رائِع] # magnificient	
أَلرّومان # the Romans	

سَرَّ ـُ ، سُرُورٌ #	to please, gladden, make happy
[سُرَّ ، سُرُورٌ (بِ) ، مِنْ ، لِ)]	(passive) to be pleased (at, by), be happy (to)
سُرُورٌ (بِ)	pleasure (at), delight (at)
أَسْرَعَ ، إِسْرَاعٌ (إِلَى) #	IV to hasten (to)
[أُسْطُورِيّ] #	mythical
سَاعَدَ ، مُسَاعَدَةٌ (عَلَى ، فِي) #	III to help, assist (in)
أَسْعَدَ ، إِسْعَادٌ	IV to make s.o. happy
سَعِيدٌ ـَ سُعَدَا(بِ)	happy (at, about)
السَّعُودِيَّةُ	Saudi Arabia
سُعَادُ	Su'ad (f. name)
أَسْعَدُ	As'ad (m. name)
سَافَرَ ، سَفَرٌ #	III to travel; go on a trip, leave
سَفَرٌ ـ أَسْفَارٌ	departure; travel, trip
[سَفِيرٌ ـ سُفَرَاءُ]	ambassador
[سَفَارَةٌ ـ ات]	embassy
سَفِينَةٌ ـ سُفُنٌ #	ship
[سَقَطَ ـُ ، سُقُوطٌ]	to fall; to crash (:airplane)
سَكَتَ ـُ ، سُكُوتٌ (عَنْ) #	to fall silent, say nothing (about)
سِكْرِتِيرٌ ـ ون #	secretary
سَكَنَ ـُ ، سَكَنٌ (فِي، بِ) #	to live, dwell, reside; to take up residence (in)
سَاكِنٌ ـ سُكَّانٌ	inhabitant, resident, occupant, (p.) occupation
سَ #	(future particle) will, going to
سَأَلَ ـَ ، سُؤَالٌ #	to ask
سُؤَالٌ ـ أَسْئِلَةٌ	question
مَسْؤُولٌ ـ ون (عَنْ)	responsible (for); an official
سَبَأُ #	Sheba
سَبَّبَ ، تَسْبِيبٌ #	II to cause, bring about, produce
سَبَبٌ ـ أَسْبَابٌ	cause; reason
بِسَبَبِ	by reason of, because of
سِبْتَمْبِر #	September (Egypt and N. Africa)
سَبْعَةٌ #	seven
سَبْعُونَ	(nom.) seventy; (following definite n.) seventieth
أُسْبُوعٌ ـ أَسَابِيعُ	week
سَابِعٌ	seventh
سِتَّةٌ #	six
سِتُّونَ	(nom.) sixty; (following definite n.) sixtieth
[مَسْجِدٌ ـ مَسَاجِدُ] #	mosque
المَسْجِدُ الأَقْصَى	Al-'Aqsa Mosque
سَدٌّ ـ سُدُودٌ #	dam
السَّدُّ العَالِي	the High Dam
سَادِسٌ #	sixth
مَسْرَحٌ ـ مَسَارِحُ #	theater

أُسْلُوبٌ ــ أَسَالِيبُ # style, method

[سَلْطَنَةٌ ــ ات] # sultanate

سَلامٌ # peace; greeting

ٱلسَّلامُ عَلَيْكُمْ greetings! lit., 'peace be upon you'

وَعَلَيْكُمُ السَّلامُ greetings! lit., 'and with you be peace' (reply to السَّلامُ) (عَلَيْكُمْ)

[سَلامَةٌ] well-being, safety

مَعَ السَّلامَةِ goodbye

سَلِيمٌ Salim (m. name)

الأِسْلامُ Islam

إِسْلامِيٌّ (nisba) Islamic

مُسْلِمٌ ــ ون muslim

سُلَيْمانُ الحَكِيمُ Solomon the Wise

سُلَيْمانُ بْنُ داوُدَ Sulayman b. Dāwūd

سَمَحَ ـَ ، سَماحٌ (لـ) (بـ) # to permit (s.o.) (s.th.)

سُمْرَةٌ # brownness (of skin)

سَمِيرٌ Samir (m. name)

أَسْمَرُ ــ سُمْرٌ (سَمْراءُ ـ سَمْراواتٌ) dark-complexioned, brown-skinned = (person)

سَمِعَ ـَ ، سَماعٌ # to hear

إِسْتَمَعَ ، إِسْتِماعٌ (لـ ، إلى) VIII to listen (to)

سامي # Sami (m. name)

سَمَّى ، تَسْمِيَةٌ # II to name, call s.o. s.th.

إِسْمٌ ــ أَسْماءُ name

سَنَةٌ ــ سَنَواتٌ # year

سَنَوِيٌّ (nisba) annual, yearly

سَهْلٌ (على) # easy (for)

أَساءَ ، إِساءَةٌ إلى IV to hurt, harm, act meanly toward

[سَيِّئٌ ــ ون] bad, evil

[أَسْوَأُ] worse, worst

[إِسْوَدَّ ، إِسْوِدادٌ] ## IX to turn black

[سَوادٌ] blackness

أَسْوَدُ (سَوْداءُ) ــ سُودٌ black

ٱلسُّودانُ the Sudan

سادَ ـُ ، سِيادَةٌ ## to prevail, reign, master, rule

سَيِّدٌ ــ سادَةٌ mister, Mr.; gentleman

ٱلسَّيِّدُ المَسِيحُ Christ

سَيِّدَةٌ ــ ات lady; Mrs.

سَيِّدَةُ البَيْتِ the lady of the house

[سُورَةٌ ــ سُوَرٌ] # sura, chapter of the Koran

سوريا ، سورية # Syria

سِياسَةٌ ــ ات policy; politics

سِياسِيٌّ ــ ون politician; political; diplomatic

ٱلسُّوَيْسُ # Suez

ساعَةٌ ــ ات # hour; time; watch; clock

ساعَتَئِذٍ in that hour

سَوْفَ ، سَـ # (future particle) will, going to

شَأْنٌ – شُؤُونٌ # matter; situation

بِشَأْنِ in regards to, regarding, concerning s.th.

شايٌ # tea

[شابٌّ – شُبّانٌ، شبابٌ] # young man, youth

شُبّاكٌ – شَبابيكُ # window

[شَجَّعَ، تشجيعٌ] # II to encourage

اِشتَدَّ، اِشتِدادٌ # VIII to become harsh, severe; strong, more violent, more intense; to intensify

[شَديدٌ – أَشِدّاءُ] intense; strong

[أَشَدُّ (مِن)] more intense (than); most intense (also used with acc. indefinite noun; أَشَدُّ سَواداً 'more black, blacker')

شَرٌّ – شُرورٌ # evil; harm

شَرِبَ –، شُرْبٌ # to drink

[شَرابٌ، أَشرِبَةٌ] drink, beverage

شارِعٌ – شَوارِعُ # street

أَشرَفَ، إِشرافٌ عَلى # IV to supervise

ضَيفٌ – ضُيوفٌ guest

[ضَيفُ الشَرَف] guest of honor

شَريفٌ Sharif (m. name)

شَرقٌ # east

أَلشَرقُ الأَوسَطُ the Middle East

مُستَشرِقٌ – ون orientalist

شارَكَ، مُشارَكةٌ في # III to participate, join in

مَسافَةٌ – ات distance

[سوقٌ – أَسواقٌ] # (f.) bazaar, market

ساوى، مُساواةٌ # III to be equivalent, equal to

[تَساوى، تَساوٍ] VI to be equal, similar

سِوى (prep.) other than, except, besides

[التَساوي في الحُقوقِ] Equal Rights

مُساوٍ لِ equivalent, equal to

السُوَيدُ # Sweden

سيبَوَيْهِ # Sibawayhi (medieval Arab grammarian)

سارَ –، سَيْرٌ، [سَيْرورَةٌ، مَسيرٌ، مَسيرَةٌ، تِسْيارٌ] # to move, get going; to march, walk, go; to progress, function, run

سارَ بِ to take, lead, conduct, march s.o.

سارَ عَلى مَنهَجٍ to behave according to, like

سَيّارَةٌ – ات car, automobile

سَيطَرَ، سَيطَرةٌ عَلى # (quad.) to control, dominate

سَيفُ الدَولةِ الحَمْدانيّ. # Sayf al-Dawla al-Hamdani

سيناءُ Sinai

سينَما cinema, movies

ش

الشّامُ # Syria; Damascus

بِلادُ الشّام Syria

اِشْتَرَكَ ، اِشْتِرَاكّ فِي	VIII to participate; cooperate in
شَرِكَةّ ـ ات	company
[اِشْتِرَاكِيّ ـ ون]	socialist
مُشْتَرَكّ	common, joint
# اِشْتَرَى ، شِرَاءّ	VIII to buy (Form I VN)
# شَعْبّ ـ شُعُوبّ	a people; nation
شَعْبِيّ	(nisba) popular, folk-, national
أَبْنَاءُ الشَّعْب	the ordinary people
# شَعَرَ ـُ ، شُعُورّ (بـ)	to feel, perceive, sense (s.th.)
شِعْرّ ـ أَشْعَارّ	poetry; poem
شَاعِرّ ـ شُعَرَاءُ	poet
# أَشْقَرُ ـ شُقْرّ (شَقْرَاءُ ـ شَقْرَاوَاتّ)	blond, fair
[شُقْرَةّ ، شُقْرّ]	blondness
# شَكَّ ـُ ، شَكّ (فِي، بـ)	to doubt, suspect, question
شَكّ ـ شُكُوكّ (فِي، بـ)	doubt; suspicion, uncertainty (about)
لا شَكَّ (فِي، بـ)	there is no doubt (about); no doubt (about)
# شَكَرَ ـُ ، شُكْرّ (عَلَى)	to thank s.o., be grateful to s.o. (for)
شُكْرّ ـ شُكُورّ	thanks; gratefulness, gratitude
شُكْرًا	thanks! thank you!

# [شَكْلّ ـ أَشْكَالّ]	type, kind, class, form
مُشْكِلَةّ ـ ات، مَشَاكِلُ	problem
## شَمِلَ ـَ ، شَمْلّ ؛ شَمَلَ ـُ ، شَمْلّ ، شُمُولّ	to include, comprise, contain
## شَمَالّ	north
# [شَهِدَ ـَ ، شَهَادَةّ]	to witness, testify
شَاهَدَ ، مُشَاهَدَةّ	III to see; to watch
شَهَادَةّ ـ ات	degree, diploma
# شَهْرّ ـ أَشْهُرّ، شُهُورّ	month
مَشْهُورّ ـ ون (بـ)	famous (for)
# شَهْرَزَادّ	Shahrazad (of the Arabian Nights)
# شَهْرَيَارّ	Shahriyar (of the Arabian Nights)
# [مُشْتَاقّ ـ ون إِلَى]	eager for; longing to, looking forward to
# شَاءَ ـَ ، مَشِيئَةّ	to wish, want; to will
شَيْءّ ـ أَشْيَاءُ	thing, something
لا شَيْءَ	nothing
[بَعْض الشَّيْء]	somewhat
# [مَشِيخَةّ ـ ات ، مَشَايِخُ]	Sheikdom
# [شَيْطَانّ ـ شَيَاطِينُ]	Satan, devil
# [شُيُوعِيّ ـ ون]	communist
# شِيكّ ـ ات	check

صَدَّقَ ، تَصْدِيقٌ	# II to give credence to, believe (s.o. to be telling the truth, s.th. to be true)	صابِىءٌ ـ ون، الصّابِئَةُ	# Sabian
صَادَقَ ، مُصَادَقَةٌ	III to be, become friends with, to befriend (s.o.)	أَصْبَحَ	# IV to become, come to (be)
[تَصَادَقَ ، تَصَادُقٌ]	VI to become friendly	صَبَاحٌ	morning
صَدِيقٌ ـ أَصْدِقاءُ	friend	صَبَاحَ الخَيْرِ	good morning!
[أَصَرَّ ، إِصْرَارٌ] (عَلَى)	# IV to persist (in)	صَبَاحَ النُّورِ	good morning! (reply to صَبَاحَ الخَيْرِ)
[صَرَخَ ـُ ، صُرَاخٌ]	# to scream, yell	صَبَرَ ـ ، صَبْرٌ (عَلَى)	# to be patient, forbearing (over s.th.); to endure (s.th.)
تَصَرَّفَ ، تَصَرُّفٌ	# V to behave, conduct oneself	صَحِيحٌ ـ صِحَاحٌ	# right, true, correct
انْصَرَفَ ، انْصِرَافٌ (عَنْ)	VII to go away, leave (s.th.); to give up, abandon, relinquish (s.th., s.o.)	صاحِبٌ ـ أَصْحابٌ ، صَحْبٌ ، صَحَابَةٌ	# friend, comrade
انْصَرَفَ إِلَى	VII to turn one's attention to, devote o.s. to	صَحْرَاءُ ـ صَحَارَى ، صَحَارٍ ، صَحْرَاوَاتٌ	# desert
صَعْبٌ ـ صِعَابٌ (عَلَى)	# hard, difficult (for)	صَحْرَاوِيٌّ	(nisba) desert, desolate, waste
صَغِيرٌ ـ صِغَارٌ	# little, small; young (person)	صَحِيفَةٌ ـ صُحُفٌ ، صُحُفِيٌّ	# newspaper (nisba) journalistic, newspaper (adj.), press-, news-; journalist, newspaperman
صَفٌّ ـ صُفُوفٌ	# class, course; classroom; row, line		
صَفْحَةٌ ـ صَفَحَاتٌ	# page, leaf, sheet	قُبَّةُ الصَّخْرَةِ	# Dome of the Rock (the Mosque of Omar in Jerusalem)
[اصْفَرَّ ، اصْفِرَارٌ]	## IX to turn yellow		
[صُفْرَةٌ]	yellowness, yellow (n.)	صَدَرَ ـُ ، صُدُورٌ	# to come out, appear, be published
أَصْفَرُ (صَفْرَاءُ) ـ صُفْرٌ	yellow	أَصْدَرَ ، إِصْدَارٌ	IV to export; to publish
صِفْرٌ	## zero	مَصْدَرٌ ـ مَصَادِرُ	origin, source; verbal noun (Arabic grammar)
[أَصْلَحَ ، إِصْلاحٌ]	# IV to improve		
[إِصْلاحٌ]	improvement, betterment, mending, correction		

[صَالِحٌ]	good, right; pious
#صِنَاعَةٌ ـ ات	industry
مَصْنَعٌ ـ مَصَانِعُ	factory
صَنْعَاءُ	San'ā' (capital of Yemen)
#صَوَابٌ	correct, true
[صَوْتٌ ـ أَصْوَاتٌ]#	voice; sound
#صَوَّرَ ، تَصْوِيرٌ	II to paint, draw; to picture, depict, portray
صُورَةٌ ـ صُوَرٌ	image, picture; form, shape
[صَائِغٌ ـ صَاغَةٌ]#	goldsmith; jeweler
#الصُّومَالُ	Somalia
#صَارَ ـِ ، صَيْرُورَةٌ ، صَيْرُورَةٌ ، مَصِيرٌ	to become, come to be; (with foll. indicative) to come to, get to the point of
#صَيْفٌ ـ أَصْيَافٌ	summer
#الصِّينُ	(f.) China

ض

#ضَحِكَ ـَ ، ضَحِكَ ، ضَحْكَةٌ	to laugh
[ضُحًى]#	(m. and f.) forenoon, late morning
[ضَرَبَ ـِ ، ضَرْبٌ]#	to strike, hit
[ضَاعَفَ ، مُضَاعَفَةٌ]#	III to double; to multiply, compound
[ضِلِّيلٌ]#	wandering; errant

[أَلْمَلِكُ الضِّلِّيلُ]	the Wandering King (أمرُؤُ القَيْسِ pre-Islamic poet)
[أَضَافَ ، إِضَافَةٌ (إلى)]#	IV to add (to)
ضَيْفٌ ـ ضُيُوفٌ	guest
[ضَيْفُ الشَّرَفِ]	guest of honor
[ضِيَافَةٌ]	hospitality
[حُسْنُ الضِّيَافَةِ]	hospitality
الإضافةُ	the iḍāfa construction

ط

#طَاوِلَةٌ ـ ات	table
#طَبِيبٌ ـ أَطِبَّاءُ	doctor, M.D.
#طَبَعَ ـَ ، طَبْعٌ	to print
[طَبْعًا]	of course, naturally
طَبْعَةٌ ـ ات	printing; edition
[طَبِيعَةٌ ـ طَبَائِعُ]	nature; character
[طَرَدَ ـُ ، طَرْدٌ (من)]#	to reject, dismiss, expel (from)
[طَرْفٌ]#	eye; glance, look
[بِلَمْحِ الطَّرْفِ]	in the twinkling of an eye; instantly
[طَرِيفٌ]	funny, odd
[مُتَطَرِّفٌ ـ ون]	extremist, radical
#طَرِيقٌ ـ طُرُقٌ	(m. and f.) way; road, street
طَارِقُ بْنُ زِيَادٍ	Tariq b. Ziyād (Muslim military commander)
#طَعَامٌ ـ أَطْعِمَةٌ	food
مَطْعَمٌ ـ مَطَاعِمُ	restaurant

طَلَبَ ـُ ، طَلَب #	to request
طالَبَ ، مُطالَبَة بِـ	III to demand (of s.o.) s.th.
تَطَلَّبَ ، تَطَلُّب	V to require, necessitate
طَلَب ـ ات	request; application; demand
طالِب ـ طُلّاب	student
طَلَّقَ ، طَلاق #	II to divorce
طَلاق	divorce
[طَلاق بالثَلاثَة]	definite (irrevocable) divorce
[طالِق]	(f.) divorced
طَنجة #	Tangiers
طه حُسَين #	Tāhā Hussein (contemporary Egyptian writer)
تَطَوَّرَ ، تَطَوُّر #	V to develop, evolve (intran.)
[أَطاعَ ، إطاعة] #	IV to obey s.o.
اِستَطاعَ ، اِستِطاعَة	X (with acc. object or foll. by أَنْ) to be able to, can
[طائِفَة ـ طَوائِفُ] #	group; sect, party, faction
طَويل ـ طِوال #	long; tall
طَويلاً	at length, a long time
مَطار ـ ات #	airport
طائِرَة ـ ات	airplane

ظ

[ظَريف] #	elegant, witty
ظَلَّ ـَ ، ظَلَّ ، ظُلول #	(with foll. indicative or participle) to continue, go on, remain, persist in (doing s.th.)
[ظَنَّ ـُ ، ظَنّ] #	to suppose, think (s.o. or s.th. to be s.th.)
ظَهَرَ ـَ ، ظُهور #	to emerge, come to light; to appear, seem
أَظهَرَ ، إظهار	IV to show, demonstrate
[تَظاهَرَ ، تَظاهُر (بِـ)]	VI to pretend, simulate (s.th.)
ظُهر ـ أَظهار	noon
الظَّهران	Dhahran (city in Saudi Arabia)
[مَظهَر ـ مَظاهِرُ]	appearance; manifestation

ع

[عَباءَة ـ ات] #	cloak, 'aba
[عَبَدَ ـُ ، عِبادة] #	to worship
عَبدُ اللهِ السَّلّال	Abdulla al-Sallāl
[عَبَّرَ ، تَعبير عَنْ] #	II to express
اِعتَبَرَ ، اِعتِبار	VIII to consider s.o. as s.th.
عَبّاس مَحمود العَقّاد #	'Abbās Mahmūd al-'Aqqād (modern Egyptian essayist, critic
عُثمانيّ #	Ottoman

[عَدُوّ - أَعْداءٌ] # enemy	عُثمان ... أَلدَّوْلةُ العُثْمانِيَّةُ the Ottoman Empire
[اِعْتَذَرَ ، اِعْتِذارٌ] # VIII to apologize (for) (عَن)	أَعْجَبَ ، إعْجابٌ # IV to please, delight s.o.
عَرَبِيّ - عَرَبٌ # Arab, Arabic, Arabian	[أُعْجِبَ ، إعْجابٌ بـ] IV (passive) to admire, be proud of
أَلْعَرَبِيَّةُ the Arabic language, Arabic	تَعَجَّبَ ، تَعَجُّب V to be surprised, amazed (at) (مِن)
أَلْجامعةُ العَرَبِيَّةُ the Arab League	[عَجَبٌ - أَعْجابٌ] surprise, amazement
[تَعْرِيبٌ] translating into Arabic	عَجِيبٌ - ون strange, odd
[عُرْسٌ - أَعْراسٌ] # wedding	إعْجاباً بـ out of admiration for
[عَروسٌ - عَرائِسُ] (f.) bride	عَدَّ - عَدٌّ ، عِدّ # to count, compute; (with two acc.) to consider (s.th.) to be (s.th.)
[عَروسان] bridal couple, newly-weds	أَعَدَّ ، إعْدادٌ IV to prepare, make s.th. ready
[عَرِيسٌ] bridegroom	اِسْتَعَدَّ ، اِسْتِعْدادٌ (لِ) X to be ready, willing (to), prepared (for)
عَرَضَ - عَرْضٌ # to exhibit, show, submit s.th. (to) (عَلى)	عَدَدٌ - أَعْدادٌ number; issue (of a magazine)
عَرَفَ - مَعْرِفة # (perfect) to find out (about), learn, know; (imperfect) to know	عَدَدٌ مِن a number of, several
[أَعْرِفُ...حَقَّ الْمَعْرِفة] I know...very well	[إعْدادِيّ] preparatory; elemtary (school)
عُرِفَ بـ (pass.) to be well-known, famous for	مُسْتَعِدّ - ون (لِ) ready, prepared (for), willing (to)
تَعَرَّفَ ، تَعَرُّف عَلى V to become acquainted with s.o.	[مُعْتَدِلٌ - ون] # moderate
[عُرْفٌ - أَعْرافٌ] heights, elevated place	عَدَمٌ # non-being, nonexistence; (with foll. gen. verbal noun) non-, un-, in-, dis-
مَعْرِفةٌ - مَعارِفُ knowledge; acquaintance	عَدَمُ الانْحِياز non-alignment
[عَلى غَيْرِ مَعْرِفةٍ] in spite of not being acquainted with s.o.	

اِعْتَقَد ، اِعْتِقاد (بـ)	VIII to believe (in)
بالعَكْس	# on the contrary
على العَكْسِ مِنْ	in contrast with, contrary to
عَلَّ ، لَعَلَّ	# (with foll.acc.) perhaps, maybe, might (with implied expectation)
عَلاقة - ات (بـ)	# relationship (to), connection (with)
عَلِمَ - َ ، عِلْم (بـ)	# to know, have knowledge of, be familiar with
عَلَّم ، تَعْليم	II to teach s.o. or s.th.; to educate s.o.
أعْلَم ، إعْلام (بـ)	IV to inform, notify, tell s.o. (about s.th.)
تَعَلَّم ، تَعَلُّم	V to learn; to become educated
عِلْم (بـ)	knowledge (of)
عِلْم - عُلوم	learning; knowledge; science
عِلْميّ	(nisba) scientific; learned, scholarly
عَلَم - أعْلام	flag, banner
عالَم - عَوالِم	world
تَعْليم	education
مُعَلِّم - ون	teacher
تَعال (تَعالَيْ) -	# (imperative) come!
تَعالَوْا	
على	on, over; to the debit of, against; on the basis of

وزارةُ المَعارِف	ministry of education
مَعْروف (بـ)	known, well-known (for)
المَعْروف أنَّ	it is known that...
العِراق	# Iraq
[عِراك]	# struggle
عَزيز - أعِزّاء (على)	# dear, beloved (to)
[عَزّى ، تَعْزِية]	# II to console, offer condolances to
عَشَرة	# ten
عِشْرون	(nom.) twenty; (foll. definite n.) twentieth
عاشِر	tenth
عاصَر ، مُعاصَرة	# III to be contemporary to
[عَصْر - أعْصُر	period, age, era
عُصور ، أعْصار]	
العَصْر الجاهِليّ	the pre-Islamic era
مُعاصِر - ون	contemporary
عاصِمة - عَواصِم	# capital, capital city
عُضْو - أعْضاء	# member
أعْطى ، إعْطاء	# IV to give (s.o.) (s.th.)
عَظيم - عُظَماء ، عِظام ، عِظائِم ،	# great, big, grand, vast, enormous
مُعْظَم	(w. foll. gen.) most of
عَفْواً	# you're welcome!
عَقَد - ِ ، عَقْد	# to hold (a meeting)
اِنْعَقَد ، اِنْعِقاد	VII to be held (meeting)

عَلَى ذٰلِكَ	and so, therefore	آلُ عِمْرَان	the Family of 'Imrān (Qur'anic verse)
[عَلَى غَيْرِ مَعْرِفَةٍ]	in spite of not being acquainted with s.o.	عَمِيقٌ #	deep, profound
كَانَ عَلَى حَقٍّ	to be right	عَمِلَ َ، عَمَلٌ #	to do, act, be active, work (also: فِي in a field)
دَرَسَ عَلَى	see دَرَسَ		
عَلامَ	on what? what for? why?	يَعْمَلُ مُعَلِّمًا	'he works as a teacher, his job is teaching'
(= عَلَى مَا ؟)			
عَلِيٌّ	Ali (m. name)	عَمِلَ عَلَى	to work for, be active in the service of
عَالٍ - عَالُونَ	high		
[عَمٌّ - أَعْمَامٌ، أَعْمُومٌ] #	paternal uncle	عَمَلٌ - أَعْمَالٌ	work, labor, job
		[مُنَظَّمَةُ الْعَمَلِ الدُّوَلِيَّةُ]	International Labor Organization
[اِبْنُ الْعَمِّ]	paternal cousin (m.)	عَامِلٌ - عُمَّالٌ	worker, laborer
عَامٌّ	general	عُمَانُ ###	Oman (sultanate)
[عَامَّةً]	generally, in general	عَمَّانُ ###	Amman
اَلْجَمْعِيَّةُ الْعَامَّةُ	the General Assembly	عَنْ #	about, concerning, of; away from
عَامِّيٌّ	(nisba) colloquial		
اَلْعَامِّيَّةُ	colloquial Arabic	عَمَّ = عَنْ + مَا	about, concerning what?
عَنْ + مَا = عَمَّا #		عِنْدَ #	at, with, on (time or place); among; (with verbal noun) on, upon; in the view, opinion of; to have (A. subj. = E. obj.)
اِعْتَمَدَ ، اِعْتِمَادٌ عَلَى #	VIII to depend, rely on		
[عَمِيدٌ - عُمَدَاءُ]	dean	مِنْ عِنْدِ	from the place (house, office, etc.) of
[أَوْرَاقُ اِعْتِمَادٍ]	credentials (diplomatic)	مِنْ عِنْدِهِ	of his own, which he makes up, impromptu
عُمْرٌ - أَعْمَارٌ #	age (of a person)	عِنْدَمَا	when, whenever
فِي الْخَمْسِينَ مِنْ عُمْرِهِ	at the age of fifty	عِنْدَئِذٍ	then, at that time, at that point
كَمْ عُمْرُهُ ؟	how old is he?		
عُمْرُهُ عِشْرُونَ سَنَةً	he is twenty years old.	عُنْوَانٌ - عَنَاوِينُ #	title; address

بِعُنْوانٍ by the title of	غَرْبٌ # west
مَعْنىً ـ مَعانٍ # meaning, sense	غَرِيبٌ ـ غُرَباءُ stranger (n.); strange (adj.)
عَهْدٌ ـ عُهودٌ # age, era, time	ألمَغْرِبُ Morocco; North Africa
[مَعْهَدٌ ـ مَعاهِدُ] institute	غَضِبَ ـَ، غَضَبٌ # to become angry (at, with s.o.)
عادَ ـُ، عَوْدَةٌ # to return, go back, come back	(مِنْ، عَلى)
عادَ بِـ to take, bring s.o. back	أغْضَبَ، إغْضابٌ IV to anger (s.o.)
أعادَ، إعادَةٌ IV to repeat, reiterate	غَضَبٌ anger
عادَةٌ ـ ات custom, habit	غالِبٌ #[winner, victor, conquerer;](with foll. genitive) most, majority of
عادَةً usually	
عِوَضاً عَنْ # instead of, in lieu of; in exchange for	[إنْغَمَسَ، إنْغِماسٌ] # VII to become immersed (in)
عائِلَةٌ ـاتٌ، عَوائِلُ # family	(في)
عامٌ ـ أعْوامٌ # year	غَنّى، غِناءٌ # II to sing
تَعاوَنَ، تَعاوُنٌ # VI to cooperate (with e.o.)	أُغْنِيَةٌ ـاتٌ، أغانٍ song
[عيدٌ ـ أعْيادٌ] # feast day, holiday	غَنِيٌّ ـ أغْنِياءُ (بِـ) rich, wealthy (in)
عاشَ ـِ، عيشَةٌ، مَعيشٌ # to live, be alive	مُغَنٍّ ـ ون singer, vocalist
عَيَّنَ، تَعْيينٌ # II to appoint s.o. as s.th.	(مُغَنِّيَةٌ ـ ات)
عَيْنٌ، عُيونٌ (f.) eye	[غائِبٌ ـ ون] # absent
ع	[أغَيَّرَ، تَغْييرٌ] # II to change (s.th.)
[تَغابُنٌ] # mutual fraud	تَغَيَّرَ، تَغَيُّرٌ V to be changed, change
غَدٌ # the morrow, the following day	غَيْرُ other than; non-, un-, in-, dis-
غَداً tomorrow	غَيْرَ except, save, but
[غَداءٌ] lunch	بِغَيْرِ without
	تَغْييرٌ change

[فَرَنْكٌ ، فَرَنْكٌ ـات] # franc (coin)

ف

فَ # and; and then; and so	[انْفَسَخَ ، انْفِساخٌ] # VII to be annulled
[فُؤادٌ ـ أَفْئِدَةٌ] # heart	فَسَّرَ ، تَفْسيرٌ # II to explain, expound, interpret, comment on
فَتَحَ ـَ ، فَتْحٌ # to open; to conquer	
[فَتَّشَ ، تَفْتيشٌ عَنْ] # II to search, look for	أَلْفُصْحى # Classical (Literary) Arabic
[مُفَتِّشٌ ـ ون] inspector	[فَصَّلَ ، تَفْصيلٌ] # II to distinguish, classify
فَتاةٌ ـ فَتَياتٌ # girl, young woman	[انْفَصَلَ ، انْفِصالٌ] VII to secede; to separate o.s.; to be separated
[تَفَحَّصَ ، تَفَحُّصٌ # V to search (for), inquire (about), examine (عَنْ)]	فَصْلٌ ـ فُصولٌ season (of year)
فَدْوى طوقانُ # Fadwā Tūqān (contemporary Palestinian woman poet)	[تَفْصيلٌ ـ تَفاصيلُ] detail
	فَضَّلَ ، تَفْضيلٌ # II to prefer (s.o. or s.th.) to على
[فَرْدٌ ـ أَفْرادٌ] # individual; member	فَعَلَ ـَ ، فِعْلٌ # to do, act; to make
فَريدٌ Farid (m. name)	فِعْلٌ ـ أَفْعالٌ doing, action, deed
فَريدٌ الأَطْرَشُ Farīd al-Atrash (contemporary singer)	فَقَدَ ـِ ، فَقْدٌ ، # to lose, miss, be deprived of
مُفْرَداتٌ (p.) vocabulary items	فُقْدانٌ
أَلْفَرَزْدَقُ # Al-Farazdaq (Umayyad poet)	فَقْرٌ # poverty
[فَرَضَ ـِ ، فَرْضٌ عَلى] # to impose s.th. upon	فَقيرٌ ـ فُقَراءُ (في) poor (in)
[فَرْعٌ ـ فُروعٌ] # branch	فَقَطْ # only
فِرْعَوْنِيٌّ # pharaonic	فَكَّرَ ، تَفْكيرٌ # II to think (of, about)
[فَرَغَ ـَ ، فُروغٌ مِنْ] # to finish doing s.th.	(بِـ)
فَرَّقَ ، تَفْريقٌ ، # II to separate, divide, disperse تَفْرِقَةٌ	فِكْرَةٌ ـ فِكَرٌ idea, thought, concept
[مُتَفَرِّقٌ] scattered, dispersed; miscellaneous	فِكْرِيٌّ intellectual
فَرَنْسا # France	مُفَكِّرٌ ـ ون thinker

441

فَلَسْطِينُ # Palestine	قَامُوسٌ - قَوَامِيسُ # dictionary
فَلْسَفَةٌ # philosophy	قُبَّةُ الصَّخْرَة # the Dome of the Rock (the Mosque of Omar in Jerusalem)
فِلْمٌ ، فيلمٌ - أَفْلَامٌ # film, movie	قَبِيحٌ - قِبَاحٌ # ugly
فَمٌّ - أَفْوَاهٌ # mouth	قُبْرُصُ # Cyprus
فَنٌّ - فُنونٌ # art	قَبِلَ ـَ ، قُبُولٌ # to accept; to approve of
فَنِّيٌّ (nisba) technical, artistic, professional	[قَبَّلَ ، تَقْبِيلٌ] II to kiss
[أَلْفَنُّ التَّمْثِيلِيُّ] dramatic arts, theater	قَابَلَ ، مُقَابَلَةٌ III to meet (with)
[فِنْجانٌ - فَنَاجِينُ] # cup	أَقْبَلَ ، إِقْبَالٌ (عَلَى) IV to approach, come, go (to s.o.); to devote o.s. to (s.th.); to begin to (do s.th.)
فُنْدُقٌ - فَنادِقُ # hotel	
فَهِمَ ـَ ، فَهْمٌ # to understand, comprehend	اسْتَقْبَلَ ، اسْتِقْبَالٌ X to receive, welcome, meet
فَوْقَ # over, above, over and above	اسْتِقْبالٌ - ات reception, welcome
فَوْقَ ذٰلِكَ moreover, futhermore	قَبْلَ before
	قَبْلَ الْمِيلاد B.C.
في # in; at; on, on the subject of	مِنْ قَبْلُ from before, prior to
فيمَ (في + ما =) in what?	مِنْ قَبْلُ ، قَبْلُ before, earlier, previously, formerly
فيما بَعْدُ afterwards, later	مُقابَلَةٌ - ات an interview
	مُسْتَقْبَلٌ future (n.)
اسْتَفادَ ، اسْتِفادَةٌ # X to benefit (from); to utilize, use (مِنْ ، بِـ)	قَدْ # (with perfect: denotes completion of act) has, had, already; (with indicative) perhaps, maybe; may; sometimes
فَيْروزُ # Fayruz (contemporary Lebanese woman singer)	قَدَّرَ ، تَقْدِيرٌ # II to appreciate, esteem; to assess, evaluate
ق	أَلْقُدْسُ # Jerusalem

مُقَدَّس – ون	holy, sacred	قَرْنٌ – قُرُونٌ	# century
[ألكِتابُ المُقَدَّس]	The Bible	[ألقُرُونُ الوُسْطى]	the Middle Ages
# قَدَّمَ ، تَقْدِيمٌ	II to present, offer; to render (services) introduce s.o. (to) (إلى)	قَرْيَةٌ – قُرًى	# village
تَقَدَّمَ ، تَقَدُّمٌ	V to advance, progress	# اِنْقَسَمَ ، اِنْقِسامٌ (إلى)	VII to be divided, separated (into)
تَقَدَّمَ بـ	V to submit, present, come forward with	قِسْمٌ – أَقْسامٌ	division, part, section; department
قَدَمٌ – أَقْدامٌ	(f. or m.) foot	قاسِمٌ أَمِين	Qasim Amin (modern Egyptian essayist)
قَدِيمٌ – قُدَماءُ	old, ancient	# قِصّةٌ – قِصَصٌ	story
قَدِيمًا	in ancient times, long ago	# قَصِيدَةٌ – قَصائِدُ	ode, qaṣīda
[إلى قُدّامِ]	forward	اِقْتِصادٌ	economy
قادِمٌ – ون	coming; next (month, etc.)	# [أَقْصَرَ ، إقْصارٌ]	IV to shorten s.th.
[تَقْدِمَةٌ – ات،	gift, present	قَصْرٌ – قُصُورٌ	castle, palace
تَقادِمُ]		قَصِيرٌ – قِصارٌ	short
# قَرَّرَ ، تَقْرِيرٌ	to decide	ألأَقْصُرُ	Luxor
[تَقْرِيرٌ – تَقارِيرُ]	a report	# ألمَسْجِدُ الأَقْصى	Al-Aqsa Mosque
# قَرَأَ – ، قِراءَةٌ	to read	# [قَضى ـِ ، قَضاءٌ]	to decree, judge
ألقُرْآنُ	the Qur'an, Koran	اِنْقَضى ، اِنْقِضاءٌ	VII to elapse, go by, pass (with على : 'over, by')
قُرْبَ	# near, in the vicinity of	قاضٍ – قُضاةٌ	judge
قَرِيبٌ – ون (مِنْ)	near (to), close (by)	قَطَرُ	# Qatar
قَرِيبٌ – أَقارِبُ ،	relative, relation	# اِنْقَطَعَ ، اِنْقِطاعٌ	VII to be cut off; to stop, come to an end
أَقْرِباءُ		[قِطْعَةٌ – قِطَعٌ]	piece, fragment
[قَرِيبًا]	soon, before long	# [مُقْتَطَفٌ – ات]	excerpt, selection
# أَقْرَضَ ، قَرْضٌ	IV to lend, loan	# قاعِدَةٌ – قَواعِدُ	grammar rule

(left column)		(right column)	

قام ُ ، قِيام # to rise up, arise

قام بـ to undertake, concern o.s. with, practice s.th.

قاوَمَ ، مُقاوَمَة III to oppose, resist, fight

أقامَ ، إقامَة IV to reside, dwell, stay; to construct, build, set up

قَوْمِيّ national, nationalist-(ic)

قَوْمِيَّة nationalism

قائِم - ون standing; existing

قائِمَة - قَوائِم list, roster, catalogue

كَنيسَةُ القِيامَة church of the Holy Sepulchre

قَوِيّ - أقوِياءُ # strong, powerful

[قَيْد - قُيودٌ] # bond, chain

ك

كَ # like, as

كَذا thus, so

[كَذا وَكَذا] such-and-such

كَذلِكَ likewise; also (see also under ذا)

كَما (foll. by a verb) as, just as, and also, and in addition

كَما أنَّ (not foll. by a verb) as, just as, and also

[كُبَّة] # kubba

[كَبابٌ] kabob

كَبير - كِبار # large, big; old (person); senior; eminent

إستَقَلَّ ، إستِقلال # X to be, become independent

قَليلٌ - قَلائِل، قِلال few, small (in number), scant

أقَلُّ (مِن) less (than); least (also used with acc. indefinite noun: أقَلّ سَواداً 'less black')

قَلْبٌ - قُلوبٌ # heart

[مَقْلوبٌ] upside down

قَلَمٌ - أقْلامٌ # pen; pencil

[قُماشٌ - أقمِشَةٌ] # cloth, material

قانونٌ - قَوانينُ # law; code; regulation

[قانونُ التَّساوي في الحُقوقِ] equal rights law

[قانونُ الحُقوقِ المَدَنِيَّةِ] civil rights law

[أقْنَعَ ، إقناعٌ (بـ)] # IV to convince s.o. (of)

قَناةٌ - قَنَواتٌ # canal

[قَهَرَ - ، قَهْرٌ] # to treat with harshness

ألقاهِرَةُ Cairo

قَهْوَةٌ - قَهَواتٌ # coffee; café, coffeehouse

مَقْهىً - مَقاهٍ café, coffeehouse

قائِدٌ - قُوّادٌ، قادَةٌ # leader, commander, general

قالَ ُ، قَوْلٌ (لَ) # to say (to), tell

[قالَ لِ] to call s.o. (s.th.)

مَقالَةٌ ، مَقالاتٌ article, essay

444

مُكَافِح ــ ون   fighter, combatant

[كَفَّنَ ، تَكْفِين] # II to shroud

[كَفَى ــِ كِفَايَة ،] # to be sufficient, enough

[كَفَى !]   that's enough!

[اِكْتَفَى ، اِكْتِفَا بِـ] VIII to content o.s. with s.th.

كُلّ # all; each, every; any; everything

أَلْكُلّ   everything

كُلّ مَا فِي الأَمْرِ   the whole story is

كُلّ مَنْ   everyone who

كُلّ مَا   everything that

كُلِّيَّة ــ ات   college, school (of a university)

كُلِّيَّة الآدَاب   College of Arts and Humanities

كِلا ،كِلَيْ (كِلْتَا ،كِلْتَيْ) # both

[كلاسِيكِيّ] # classical

[تَكْلِيف ــ تَكَالِيف] # expenses

تَكَلَّم ،تَتَكَلَّم ، كَلام # V to speak, talk

كَلِمَة ــ ات   word

كَلام   speech, speaking, conversation

كَمْ # how much? (foll. by acc. s. indef. noun) how many? (in statements) how much!

كَمْ وَلَدَاً   how many children?

كَمْ عُمْرُهُ ؟   how old is he?

كَمْ سُرِرْنَا بِهِ   how pleased we were with it!

كِبَارُ الْمُوَظَّفِينَ   senior employees

كَتَبَ ــُ ، كِتَابَة # to write

كِتَاب ــ كُتُب   book

أَلْكِتَابُ الْمُقَدَّس   the Bible

كَاتِب ــ كُتَّاب   writer, author; scribe

مَكْتَب ــ مَكَاتِب   office

مَكْتَبَة ــ ات   library; bookstore

[كُتْلَة ــ كُتَل] # bloc

كَثِير ــ كِثَار # much; many

كَثِير مِنْ   many of, many

كَثِيراً   very, very much; often

أَكْثَرُ (مِنْ)   more (than); most (also used with acc. indefinite noun: أَكْثَرُ سَوَاداً 'blacker')

كَذا ، لِذٰلِكَ # see كذا

كَرَّرَ ، تَكْرَار # to repeat

كُرْسِيّ ــ كَرَاس ،كَرَاسِيّ # chair

أَكْرَمَ ، إِكْرَام # IV to honor, do honor to; to treat hospitably

[كَرَم]   generosity

[كَرِيم ــ كُرَمَاءُ]   generous, noble, honorable

كَرِيم   Karīm (m. name)

كَعْب بْن زُهَيْرٍ # Ka'b b. Zuhayr (early Muslim poet)

[كَفَّ ــِ ، كَفَّ عَنْ] # to stop (doing s.th.)

كَافَحَ ، مُكَافَحَة، كِفَاح # III to struggle, fight, combat

أَكْمَلَ ، إِكْمَالٌ # IV to finish, complete, perfect

كانونُ ٱلأَوَّلُ # December (Syr., Leb., Jord., Iraq)

[كَنِيسَةٌ ـ كَنائِسُ] # church

[كَنِيسَةُ ٱلقِيامَةِ] Church of the Holy Sepulchre

أَلْكُوَيْتُ # Kuwait

كادَ ـَ # (foll. by indic. or by أَنْ and subjunctive) to be on the point of (doing s.th.), be about to (do s.th.), almost (do s.th.)

أَلْكوفَةُ # Kufa (town in Iraq)

كَوْكَبٌ ـ كَواكِبُ # star

كانَ ـُ ، كَوْنٌ # to be

[كَوْنٌ ـ أَكْوانٌ] being, creation, existence; the universe, cosmos; the world

مَكانٌ ـ أَماكِنُ ، أَمْكِنَةٌ place, location

مَكانَ in place of, instead of

لَوْ كُنْتُ مَكانَكَ if I were you

مَكانَةٌ ـ ات position, status, rank; prestige

كَيْ ، لِكَيْ # see لِ

كَيْلا ، لِكَيْلا # see لِ

كَيْفَ # how?

كَيْفَ ٱلحالُ how are you?

ل

لَـ # (intensifying particle) indeed! (see also لَوْ)

لِ # (prep.) to, to the credit, favor of; belonging to, of; (conj.) in order that, so that; (with jussive) let, have (indirect command); to have (A. obj. ⟶ E. subj.)

صَديقٌ لي a friend of mine

لِذلِكَ therefore, for that reason

يا لَهُ مِنْ ... what a...he is!

لِأَنَّ (conj.) because

لِكَيْ ، كَيْ ، لِأَنْ (with subjunctive) in order that, so that

لِكَيْلا ، كَيْلا، لِئَلّا (with subjunctive) in order that..not

لِماذا why?

لا # no; not

لا شَكَّ no doubt

لكِنْ ، لكِنَّ # but, however

لُبْنانُ # (m.) Lebanon

لَدى # at, by (place and time); in the presence of, before, with; (w. verbal n.) on, upon (doing s.th.); to have (A. obj. ⟶ E. subj.)

أَلَّذي # see under الذي

لَعَلَّ # see عَلَّ

446

لُغَة ‒ ات # — language

لُغَوِيٌّ – ون — (nisba) language-related, linguistic; linguist, grammarian

أَلْعُلومُ اللُّغَوِيَّةُ — linguistics

[أَلْغَى ، إِلْغاءٌ] # — IV to nullify, annul; to cancel

لَقَّبَ ، تَلْقيبٌ بِـ # — II to give s.o. the title, nickname of

لَقِيَ ‒ ، لِقاءٌ # — to encounter, meet; to find

أَلْقَى ، إِلْقاءٌ # — IV to cast, throw (off); to make, deliver (a speech)

[إِلْتَقَى ، إِلْتِقاءٌ (بِـ)] — VIII to meet, encounter

لِقاءٌ — meeting, encounter

إِلى اللِّقاءِ — goodbye

لَمْ # — (with jussive) did not, has not

لَمْ ... بَعْدُ — not yet, still...not

لَمْ ... حَتَّى — scarcely had...when

لَمّا # — when, at the time that

[لَمَحَ ‒ ، لَمْحٌ] # — to see, behold

[بِلَمْحِ الطَّرْفِ] — in the twinkling of an eye, instantly

لَنْ # — (with subjunctive) will not, will never

لَنْدَن # — London

لَهْجَة ‒ لَهَجات # — dialect

[لَهْوٌ] # — pleasure, fun

لَوْ ... لَـ # — if, if it were that; (foll. by indicative)

would that, if only...!

لَوْ أَنَّ ... لَـ — if; if only, would that...

وَلَوْ — even if

لَوْحٌ – أَلْواحٌ # — blackboard

[لَوْحَة ‒ ات] — board; tablet, chart

لَوْنٌ – أَلْوانٌ # — color

لِيبِيا # — Libya

لَيْسَ # — not to be, he (it) is not

لَيْلٌ # — (coll.) nighttime, night (as opposed to daytime)

لَيْلَة ‒ ات ، # — (unit noun) a night; evening

لَيالٍ ، [اللَّيالِ]

ما # — (interrog. pron.) what? (spelled مَ as obj. of invariable prep., e.g. عَلامَ)

كُلُّ ما — everything that

ماذا — (object or subject of verb) what?

لِماذا ، لِمَ — why?

ما (أَعْجَبَ) — how (strange) is...!

ما — (relative pron.) that which, what, whatever

ما ... مِنْ — that which...in the way of, the...that

مِمّا (=مِنْ + ما) — a thing which, something which

ما — (neg.) not

ماجِستير # — master's degree, M.A.

مِئَةٌ / مِائَةٌ #	(one) hundred
مِئاتٌ مِنْ	hundreds of
مَتى #	when? (in indirect questions) when, whenever
[مَثَّلَ ، تَمْثيلٌ] #	II represent
مِثْلٌ	(with following genitive) the likes of, something like, such a...as
مِثْلَ	(prep.) like, similar to
مَثَلاً	for example
[مُمَثِّلٌ - ون]	representative
[أَلْفَنُّ التَّمْثيليُّ]	dramatic arts, theater
تَمْثيليَّةٌ	a play, drama
إمْتِحانٌ - ات #	examination
ميخائيل نُعَيْمَة #	Mikhā'īl Nu'aymī (contemporary Lebanese writer)
مُدَّةٌ - مُدَدٌ #	period (of time)
[مَدَحَ ـَ ، مَدْحٌ] #	to praise
مَدينَةٌ - مُدُنٌ ، مَدائِنُ #	city
أَلْمَدينَةُ	Medina (city of the Prophet
مَدَنيٌّ	(nisba) urban; civilized; civilian; civil
[أَلْحُقوقُ المَدَنيَّةُ]	Civil Rights
مَرَّ ـُ ، مُرورٌ #	to pass
مَرَّ بـ ، عَلى	to pass by, go by, go through

إسْتَمَرَّ ، إسْتِمْرارٌ (في)	X to last; to persist (in s.th.); (w. foll. indic.) to continue, keep on (doing s.th.)
مَرَّةٌ - ات	one time; once
إمْرُؤُ القَيْسِ #	Imru' al-Qays (pre-Islamic poet)
إمْرَأَةٌ - نِساءٌ ، نِسْوَةٌ	(with definite article (الْمَرْأَةُ) woman
نِسائيٌّ	(nisba of نِساءٌ) womanly, female, feminine
مَرْيَمُ #	Maryam, Miriam, Mary (f. name)
(أَلسَّيِّدُ) أَلْمَسيحُ #	Christ
أَلْمَسيحيَّةُ	Christianity
مَسيحيٌّ - ون	(nisba) Christian
[أَمْسَكَ ، إمْساكٌ] #	IV to grasp, take hold of
مَساءٌ ـ أَمْسِيَةٌ ، أُمْسياتٌ #	evening
مَساءَ الخَيْرِ	good evening!
مَساءً	in the evening
مِصْرُ #	Egypt
مَضى ـ ، مُضيٌّ #	to leave, pass (time)
[ماضٍ ـ ماضونَ]	past, bygone; last (time)
مَعَ #	with, together with; in spite of
مَعَ ذلِكَ	in spite of that, nevertheless
مَعَ أَنَّ	in spite of the fact that
مَعاً	together; at one and the same time; both

يا لَهُ مِنْ   what a...he is

مَنَحَ ـَ ، مَنْحٌ # to grant (s.o.) (s.th.)

مُنْذُ # (prep.) since, for; ago; (conj.) since, since the time that

مَنَعَ ـَ ، مَنْعٌ (مِنْ، عَنْ) # deny, prevent, forbid (s.th.) (to s.o.)

[مَهْدٌ ـ مُهودٌ] # cradle, bed

[تَمْهيديّ] introductory, preliminary, preparatory

[مَهْرٌ ـ مُهورٌ] # dowry

ماتَ ـُ ، مَوْتٌ # to die

موريتانيا # Mauritania

مالٌ ـ أَمْوالٌ # money, property, wealth

ماءٌ ـ مِياهٌ # water

مَيّ زِيادَةُ # Mayy Ziyada (contemporary Lebanese-Egyptian woman writer)

مَيْدانٌ ـ مَيادينُ # realm, field; arena; sphere of activity; city square

امْتازَ ، امْتيازٌ بِ # VIII to be distinguished, characterized by

تَمْييزٌ discrimination; tamyīz accusative of specification (Arabic grammar)

امْتيازٌ distinction, honor

ميمٌ # (f.) mīm (name of the letter م)

ن

ناسٌ ، أُناسٌ # see under أنس

مَكّةُ # Mecca

أَلْمَكْسيكُ # (m.) Mexico

تَمَكَّنَ ، تَمَكَّنَ مِنْ # V to be able to, capable of

مَكانٌ See كون

[تَمالَكَ نَفْسَهُ ، تَمالَكَ] # VI to control, restrain o.s.

مِلْكٌ ـ أَمْلاكٌ property, possessions

مَلِكٌ ـ مُلوكٌ king

[أَلْمَلِكُ الضَّليلُ] the Wandering King (أَمْرُؤُ القَيْسِ pre-Islamic poet)

مَلَكيّ (nisba) kingly, royal; royalist

مَلِكَةٌ ـ ات queen

[مَلَكٌ ـ مَلائِكَةٌ] angel

مَمْلَكَةٌ ـ مَمالِكُ kingdom, monarchy

[مَمْلوكٌ ـ مَماليكُ] mamluke

مَنْ # (interrog. pron.) who? (indef. pron.) whoever, the one who

مَنْ ... مِنْ the...who...
كُلُّ مَنْ everyone who

مِنْ # from, (from) among, of; out of, because of; namely, such as; (with indef. elative) than

مِمّا ، مِمَّ (مِنْ ـ ما) see ما

ما ... مِنْ see ما

مِنْ عِنْدِهِ of his own, which he makes up, impromptu

مِنْ عِنْدِ from the place of

مِنْ قَبْلُ previously, earlier, before, formerly

نَشَرَ ُ ، نَشْر # to publish; to announce	[اِسْتَنْبَطَ ، اِسْتِنْباط] # X to derive, extract. deduce, induce
اِنْتَشَرَ ، اِنْتِشار VIII to be scattered, spread out, widespread; to prevail (peace)	أَنْباط Nabateans
نَشْر publication	[نَبِيّ ــ أَنْبِياء] # prophet
نَشْرَة ــ نَشَرات report; bulletin	[نَبَوِيّ] (nisba) prophetic; of or pertaining to the Prophet Muhammad
نَشاط ــ ات # energy, activity, action	أَنْتَجَ ، إِنْتاج # IV to produce, put out
[أَنْصَتَ ، إِنْصات (إلى)] # IV to listen, hearken (to)	[نَتيجة ــ نَتائِج] result, consequence
[نَصَرَ ُ ، نَصْر (على)] # to help, assist, let triumph (s.o.) (against, over)	نَتيجةً لـ as a result of
اِنْتَصَرَ ، اِنْتِصار (على) VIII to be victorious, triumph (over)	إِنْتاج production, output; literary output
[نَصْرانِيّ ــ نَصارى] Christian	[ناتِجاً عَن] resulting from
نِصْف ــ أَنْصاف # half	نَجيب مَحفوظ # Nagīb Mahfouz (contemporary Egyptian novelist)
مِنْطَقة ــ مَناطِق # region, area, zone	نَجَحَ ُ ، نَجاح (في) # to succeed (in)
نَظَرَ ُ ، نَظَر (إلى) # to look (at), consider, view	أَلْمُنْجِد # al-Munjid (name of a dictionary)
نَظَرَ في to look into, study, examine	نَحْن # we
اِنْتَظَرَ ، اِنْتِظار VIII to wait (for), await	اِنْتَخَبَ ، اِنْتِخاب # VIII to elect
نَظَر ــ أَنْظار gaze, look; view, opinion; theory	اِنْتِخاب ــ ات election
كان في الاِنْتِظار to be waiting	مَنْدوب ــ ون # delegate, representative, deputy (parliament)
النَّظّام # al-Nazzām (m. name)	نازِك المَلائِكة # Nazik al-Mala'ika (modern Iraqi woman poet and critic)
نِظام ــ أَنْظِمة ، نُظُم # system, order	[مُناسَبة ــ ات] # occasion; opportunity
مُنَظّمة ــ ات organization	[نُسْخة ــ نُسَخ] # copy (of a book, etc.)
نَعَم # yes	(إِمْرَأة) نِساء # women (pl. of
[نِعْمة ــ ات ، نِعَم] grace, bounty, blessing	أَنْشَأَ ، إِنْشاء # IV to establish, found, start

نَفْسٌ ــ أَنْفُسٌ # (f.) soul; self;

نَفَعَ ــَ ، نَفْعٌ # to be of use to, benefit

نَقْدٌ ــ نُقُودٌ # cash, coins, money

نُقْطَةٌ ــ نُقَطٌ # a drop

نَقَلَ ــُ ، نَقْلٌ # to transmit, transport, transfer s.th.

إِنْتَقَلَ ، إِنْتِقالٌ (إلى) VIII to move, transfer (to) (intrans.)

أُنْمُوذَجٌ ــ نَماذِجُ (مِنْ) # type, model, pattern; example (of)

مَنْهَجٌ ــ مَناهِجُ # program; manner, procedure, way

مَنْهَجُ التَّعْلِيمِ program of instruction, curriculum

سارَ عَلَى مَنْهَجٍ to behave like (s.o.)

نَهَرَ ــَ ، نَهْرٌ # to repulse, reproach, repel

نَهْرٌ ــ أَنْهارٌ، أَنْهُرٌ river

نَهْضَةٌ ــ ات # rebirth, renaissance; movement; boom

[نَهَقَ ــَ ، نَهْقٌ] # to bray

أَنْهَى ، إِنْهاءٌ # IV to complete, finish s.th.

[إِنْتَهَى ، إِنْتِهاءٌ (مِنْ)] VIII to end, come to an end, be finished (with) (s.th.)

نِهايَةٌ ــ ات end, termination

[الإِنْتِهاءُ مِنْ] finishing with, completing s.th.

أَنْوَرُ السّاداتُ # Anwar al-Sadat (Egyptian president)

تَناوَلَ ، تَناوُلٌ # to deal with, take up, treat; to eat, drink, have

نَوالُ السَّعْداوِي Nawāl al-Saʿdawī (modern Egyptian woman essayist)

نامَ ــَ ، نَوْمٌ # to sleep, fall asleep, go to sleep; to go to bed

نِيسانُ # April (Syr., Leb., Jord., Iraq)

النِّيلُ # the Nile

هـ

هَدَفٌ ــ أَهْدافٌ # target; goal; aim, object, objective; intention

هَدِيَّةٌ ــ هَدايا # gift, present

هَذا ــ هَذانِ ، # this, that
هَذَيْنِ ــ هَؤُلاءِ
(هَذِهِ ــ هاتانِ ،
هاتَيْنِ ــ هَؤُلاءِ)

الأَهْرامُ # al-Ahram (Egyptian newspaper; lit., 'The Pyramids')

هارونُ الرَّشِيدُ # Haroun al-Rashīd (Abbasid caliph)

هَلْ # (interrogative particle)

الهِلالُ # al-Hilal (Egyptian literary periodical; lit., 'The Crescent')

[هِلِينِيٌّ] # Hellenic

هُمْ # they (m.p.)

هَمَّ ــُ ، هَمٌّ # to interest, concern, be of importance or concern to

إِهْتَمَّ ، إِهْتِمامٌ VIII to take an interest (in), show concern (over)

451

أَهَمِّيَّة	importance	# وَثِقَ يَثِقُ ، ثِقَة (بِـ)	to trust, have confidence (in)
اِهْتِمام ـ ات	interest, concern, care	[مِيثاقٌ ـ مَواثيقُ]	charter
هامّ	important, momentous, grave, serious; interesting	# وَجَبَ يَجِبُ ، وُجوب (عَلى) (أَنْ)	be necessary, incumbent (on s.o.) (that he do...)
# هُنَّ	they (f.p.)	[واجِبٌ ـ ات (عَلى)]	duty (for s.o.)
# هُنا	here	# وَجَدَ يَجِدُ ، وُجود	to find; to come to realize; (pass.) to exist, be
هُناكَ	there; there is, there are		
# [هَنَّأَ ، تَهْنِئَة (عَلى ، بِـ)]	II to congratulate s.o. (on or on the occasion of)	مَوْجود	found; present, existing
		# [مُوجَزٌ]	summary
# الهِنْد	India	# وَجْه ـ وُجوه	face
[هِنْدِيّ ـ هُنود]	Indian (n. or adj.)	[وِجْهَة ـ ات]	object, aim
هِنْد	Hind (f. name)	# وَحَّدَ ، تَوْحيد	II to unify, unite
# مُهَنْدِس ـ ون	engineer	اِتَّحَدَ ، اِتِّحاد	VIII to unite, be united; to federate (with)
# هُوَ	he		
## هود	Hūd (Qur'anic verse)	[وَحْدَهُ]	alone, he by himself
## [هادَ ـِ ، هَوْد]	to follow the Jewish scriptures, to be a Jew	وَحْدَة ـ ات	unity, union; unit
		واحِد	one
# هِيَ	she	اِتِّحاد	federation
# [هَيْكَل ـ هَياكِلُ]	temple	الأُمَمُ المُتَّحِدَة	the United Nations
و		الوِلاياتُ المُتَّحِدَة (الأَمْريكِيَّة)	the United States (of America)
# وَ	and; (in ḥāl construction) while, as with (foll. by genitive) by! (in oaths)	# وَدَّ وَدِدْتُ ، يَوَدُّ ، وُدّ	to wish, want, desire
		وِداد	Widad (f. name)
والله	By God! indeed!	# [وَداعاً]	good-by, farewell!
وَإِنْ	even if	# مَوْرِد ـ مَوارِدُ	resource
وَلَوْ	even if	# وَرَق ـ أَوْراق	(coll.) paper
وَ بَلْ	and even, but also	[أَوْراقُ اعْتِمادٍ]	credentials (diplomatic)

452

وَرَقَةٌ ــ ات	(unit noun) sheet, piece of paper
# وَراءَ	behind
مِنْ وَراءِ	from behind
# وَزيرٌ ــ وُزَراءُ	minister (cabinet)
وَزيرُ الخارِجيَّةِ	foreign minister, secretary of state
رَئيسُ الوُزَراءِ ، رَئيسُ الوِزارَةِ	prime minister
وِزارَةٌ ــ ات	ministry (cabinet)
وِزارَةُ الخارِجيَّةِ	Ministry of Foreign Affairs; Department of State (U.S.)
# وَسْطَ	middle, midst, in the middle of
أَوْسَطُ (وُسْطى)	middle, central
الشَّرْقُ الأَوْسَطُ	the Middle East
[القُرونُ الوُسْطى]	the Middle Ages
البَحْرُ الأَبْيَضُ المُتَوَسِّطُ	the Mediterranean Sea
# [أَوْسَعَ يَسَعُ ، سَعَةٌ]	to be wide, roomy, spacious (enough for)
واسِعٌ	wide, spacious; extensive
# وَصَفَ يَصِفُ ، وَصْفٌ ، وَصَفَهُ (بِأَنَّهُ)	to describe, depict s.th. (as being)
[صِفَةٌ ــ ات]	characteristic
# وَصَلَ يَصِلُ ، وُصولٌ	to arrive; (with object pronoun) to reach; (A. obj.→ E. subj.) to receive
اِتَّصَلَ ، اِتِّصالٌ (بِ)	VIII to be connected with, bear on, have

	to do with; to get in touch with, contact (s.o.)
وَصْلَةٌ	juncture, connection; the sign ٱ indicating that its ا has no vowel (Arabic grammar)
واصِلُ بْنُ عَطاءٍ	Wasil b. 'Ataa'
# [أَوْصى ، إيصاءٌ ، تَوْصِيَةٌ]	IV to advise, enjoin counsel, advice
# وَضَحَ يَضِحُ ، وُضوحٌ	to be, become clear; to come to light
واضِحٌ	clear, distinct; obvious
# وَضَعَ يَضَعُ ، وَضْعٌ	to put, place, lay; to compose, draft (a document)
وَضْعٌ ــ أَوْضاعٌ	situation, condition
مَوْضوعٌ ــ مَواضيعُ	subject, topic
# [تَوْطيدٌ]	consolidation
# وَطَنِيٌّ	national; nationalist(ic)
# وَظيفَةٌ ــ وَظائِفُ	office, position, job; function, task
مُوَظَّفٌ ــ ون	employee; official; functionary
# وَعَدَ يَعِدُ ، وَعْدٌ (بِ)	to promise s.o. (s.th.)
مَوْعِدٌ ــ مَواعِدُ ، مَواعيدُ	time, appointment (ميعادٌ pl. مَواعيدُ) 'appointment' is commonly used as p. of (مَوْعِدٌ)
# [وَفَّرَ ، تَوْفيرٌ (لِ)]	II to provide s.th. abundantly (to s.o.)

وفر

تَوَفَّرَ ، تَوَفُّر	V to be given abundantly, provided in full measure
# وَفَّقَ	II to render s.o. successful (:God)
أَللَّهُ يُوَفِّقُكَ	'God will make you prosper, grant you success.'
اِتَّفَقَ ، اِتِّفاقٌ (عَلَى)	VIII to agree, come to an agreement (upon)
[تَوْفِيقٌ (بَيْنَ)]	reconciliation (between)
تَوْفِيقُ الحَكِيم	Tawfīq al-Hakīm (contemporary Egyptian dramatist)
مِنَ المُتَّفَقِ عَلَيْهِ (أَنْ)	it is agreed upon (that)
# وَفَّى ، تَوْفِيَة	II to give s.o. his full share of
[وَفاةٌ]	death
# وَقْتَئِذٍ	then, at that time
وَقْتٌ ـ أَوْقاتٌ	time
# وَقَعَ يَقَعُ ، وُقوعٌ	to lie, be located, situated; to fall down, drop; to come to pass, take place, happen, occur
واقِعٌ	located, situated
# وَقَفَ يَقِفُ ، وُقوفٌ	to come to a stop, stop; to stand up, rise to one's feet;
[مَوْقِفٌ ـ مَواقِفُ (مِنْ)]	attitude, stand (on)
# وَلَدَ يَلِدُ ، وِلادَةٌ	to give birth to
وُلِدَ، يُولَدُ، وِلادَةٌ	(passive) to be born
وَلَدٌ ـ أَوْلادٌ	child; boy
وِلادَةٌ	birth, childbirth
[مِيلادٌ]	birth, time of birth, birthday

[قَبْلَ المِيلاد]	before the birth (of Christ), B.C.
[مِيلادِيّ]	(nisba) A.D.
والِدٌ	father
والِدان	(nominative) parents
# وِلايَةٌ ـ ات	state, province
الوِلاياتُ المُتَّحِدَةُ الأَمْرِيكِيَّةُ	The United States (of America)
# وَهَبَ يَهَبُ ، هِبَةً وَهْبٌ	to grant, present, give (s.o.) (s.th.), endow (s.o.) (with s.th.)
هِبَةٌ ـ ات	gift

ي

# يا	(vocative particle) o
يا لَهُ مِنْ	what a...he is!
# يَتِيمٌ ـ أَيْتامٌ	orphan
# يَدٌ ـ أَيْدٍ، أَيادٍ	(f.) hand
[بِيَدِ]	in the power of (s.o.)
يَدَوِيّ	(nisba) manual
# الجُمْهورِيَّةُ العَرَبِيَّةُ اليَمَنِيَّةُ	Arab Republic of Yemen
[يَمينٌ ـ أَيْمُنٌ، أَيْمانٌ]	oath
[بَرِىءَ مِنْ يَمينِهِ]	to become cleared of one's oath
# يَهودِيّ ـ يَهودٌ	Jew, Jewish
اليَهودِيَّةُ	Judaism
# يَوْمٌ ـ أَيّامٌ	day
اليَوْمَ	today
[اليَوْمُ الآخِرُ]	Judgment Day, The Last Day

454

يوم

بَعْدَ أَيَّامٍ   in a few days

يَوْمِيّ   (nisba) daily

يَوْمَئِذٍ   on that day

*References following ii. are to Part Two; other references are to Part One.

456

ACTION (in verbs)

  future 502

  habitual 502

  progressive 502

ACTOR (in iḍāfas) 310-12

ADJECTIVAL IḌĀFAS 560-1; ii. 98

ADJECTIVAL VERBS ii. 272

ADJECTIVES

  adjective iḍāfas 560-1; ii. 98

  broken plurals of 267-72

  case 111-13

  of color 468; ii. 53, 144-6

  comparative 340-2; ii. 53, 146

  of defect 468; ii. 88-92

  definite 149

  diptotes 273-6

  dual 405

  elative 340-5; ii. 20

    tamyīz ii. 53

  gender 113, 115; ii. 20

  indeclinable ii. 14-17

  invariable ii. 19-20

  modified by adverb or prepositional phrase 141-2

  modifying first term of iḍāfa 253-5

  modifying non-human nouns 256-7

  modifying nouns 140-2, 256-7; ii. 98

  negation ii. 198

  nisba 144-6, 198

  noun-adjective phrases 140-2

  numerals 294-5

  ordinal = elative 345

  positive 344

  predicate adjective 128

  sound plural 198

  strings 142; ii. 97-8

superlative 340-4

verbal (= active participle) 515

the adjectives أَشَدُّ and أَكْثَرُ in comparative and superlative degree ii. 146

ADVERBS 457-9

  opposed to prepositions ii. 242

  as predicate of equational sentence 215

  relative adverb حَيْثُ ii. 255

  أَمْسِ 328

  الآنَ 'now' 328

  بَعْدُ 'afterwards' ii. 242

  بَعْدَ ذٍ 'after that' ii. 291

  جِدًّا 'very' 136

  جَمِيعًا 'all' 540

  قَبْلُ ، مِنْ قَبْلُ 'previously' ii. 242-3

  هُنَاكَ 'there' 324

ADVERBIAL 327-9, 457-9

  adverbial accusative ii. 291

  adverbial expression of time ii. 216, 291

  حِينَ 'when' ii. 216

  suffix ذٍ ii. 291

  function 327-9, 457

  modifier 158, 327-9

    cognate accusative 347-8

    word order 158

  phrase 158, 563

  of time 327-9

  use of the accusative 327-9, 457-8

AFFIRMATIVE

  equational sentences 132-4

AFFIX -t- 398

459

PRESENT PERFECT MEANING

    active participles 517, 533

PROCLAMATIONS ii. 289

PROGRESSIVE ACTION 502

    past progressive 503

    progressive meaning

        active participles 516, 532

        imperfect tense 263

PRONOUNS: See also PRONOUN SUFFIXES

    after إِيَّا ii. 290-1

    demonstrative 104

    dual 405

    gender 103-4

    helping vowel ـُ u 188

    indefinite relatives مَنْ and
        ما 586-8

    independent 103-4, 148, 184-5, 499

        emphasis and contrast 206, 499

        helping vowel u 183

        plural 182-3

        as subject of equational sentence 133

    interrogative 105, 170-1

    pause form (2s) 104

    preceding verb for emphasis ii. 306

    relative 449, 451; ii. 215

    of separation ضَمِيرُ الْفَصْلِ 143-4

    substitute pronoun 574-5

    word order 107

PRONOUN SUFFIXES

    changing of vowel u to i 149, 185, 220

    dual 405-6

    helping vowel u 188

    in iḍāfas 161

    making nouns definite 140

    with nouns 148-9

    plural 184-5

    with prepositions 216-8

    singular 148-9

        1 s 217-8

    -tumuu- 220

    with verbs 219-20

    with كُلّ 299-300

PRONUNCIATION

    assimilation of n to m 171

    assimilation of u to i in 3 person suffixes 149, 185, 220

    initial CC 485

    loss of u in وَهُوَ and وَهْيَ 147

PROPER NOUNS 140, 161

PURPOSE

    accusative of ii. 229-30

    particles 385

QUADRILITERALS

    active participle

        Form QI muFaSTiL 551

        Form QII mutaFaSTiL 551

    passive voice ii. 11

    verbal noun

        Form QI FaSTaLa(t) 551

        Form QII taFaSTuL 551

    verbs 549-52

QUESTIONS

    yes--no 105, 135

RADICALS 227-30

    definition 228

    doubled last radical (Form IX) 468

    doubled middle (Form II) 330 473

    identical 267, 272, 342

    symbols (FML) 228, (FSTL) 550

STEM VOWEL ·233, 265

   imperfect tense 236-7

   I-X 473-5

STRESS ON وَ 'AND' 147

SUBJECT 160

   after إِنَّ and its sisters 363-5

   of clause 363-5

   demonstrative pronouns 173

   equational sentences 103

    in accusative 363-5

    following predicate 213-4, 215-6, 324

   grammatical subject 324

    interrogative pronoun 170

   logical subject 324

   marker 231

    imperfect tense 234-6, 264, 284, 420

    perfect tense 132, 154-5, 167, 235

   of passive verb 552

SUBJUNCTIVE 235, 263-4, 383-5

   after أَنْ ii. 214

   assimilated verbs

    Form I ii. 66

   defective

    derived verbs ii. 160-72

    Form I ii. 131-40

   doubled verbs

    derived verbs ii. 109

    Form I ii. 82

   dual 408

   hollow verbs

    derived Forms ii. 39-45

    Form I ii. 6-10

   passive 579

   uses 384-5

SUBORDINATE CLAUSE 505-6

SUBORDINATING CONJUNCTION وَ 535

SUBSTITUTE PRONOUN (IN TOPIC-COMMENT 575

SUFFIXES: See also PRONOUN SUFFIXES, SUBJECT MARKERS

   diptote 275

   dual 408

   feminine 114-5, 145, 168

   nisba 145

   هُنَّ ii. 291

   of verbal nouns ii. 24-9

"SUN LETTERS" 124

SUPERLATIVE DEGREE 340, 343-4

  TAA' MARBUUṬA 114

    on broken plurals 271

  tamyīz ii. 53

TELLING TIME 301-2

TENSES 154, 263

   imperfect 502-6, 154, 263

   meaning 504

   past imperfect 502-6

   perfect 154, 167-8, 203, 263, 504

    negative 234-8

     performative function ii. 288-9

   present perfect 517-8, 532-3

   uses of 441-2

"THERE IS/THERE ARE" هُنَاكَ 324

TIME

   adverbials of 327-9

   noun ii. 216

   past 502-5

   present 505

   telling time 301-2

477